10,000
DREAMS
INTERPRETED

10,000 DREAMS

INTERPRETED

Pamela Ball

ARCTURUS

ARCTURUS

This edition published in 2010 by Arcturus Publishing Limited
26/27 Bickels Yard, 151–153 Bermondsey Street,
London SE1 3HA

ISBN: 978-1-84837-621-2
AD000002EN

Printed in England

With acknowledgements
and many, many thanks to my daughter Fiona
without whom the book would not have been written,
and to James Eden who offered support and a shoulder
many, many times. Thanks also to my family for
putting up with my bad temper.

Pamela Ball

CONTENTS

10,000 DREAMS EXPLAINED

The Penguin Dictionary of Psychology defines a dream in the following way: 'A train of hallucinatory experiences with a certain degree of coherence, but often confused and bizarre, taking place in the condition of sleep and similar conditions.'

Sleeping and Dreaming

Dreams are said to be the mind's way of making sense of the various types of input with which it has had to cope. It has certainly been proved that the human being needs sleep in order to function successfully. Indeed sleep deprivation has a profound effect on efficiency and ability, and the function of dreams seems to be to balance the psychological and physiological activity within us. Mental and physical breakdown occurs very quickly without the relief of the dreaming process.

During waking hours the focus of our activity is generally geared towards the external and conscious. We are continually taking in information which must be either used immediately or stored until we can categorise it and fit it into some kind of pattern. We have the ability to 'read' our fellow humans and situations. We are capable of assessing what is going on, making decisions and producing realisations and insights in the light of fresh information. Both the information and the insights are stored for later use, and can appear in dreams in an apparently random fashion.

There are those people who do not believe that dreams have any particular function in our lives other than being some kind of repository for information received. It has been suggested that dreams are a kind of white noise or background hum similar to that which emanates from any piece of electrical equipment.

On some levels this may well be true. They are a sort of self-cleaning, self-clearing process which makes room each night for the next day's information. The question then arises, however, as to where the cleared material goes. It is a little like the housewife who spring-cleans, throws some of her rubbish away and stores the rest in the attic. What is left is then put to good use in the home. In the case of dreams, the rubbish, or what is not perceived as being needed is returned to the general tip or the collective unconscious. The material which may be useful in the future is then put away to be drawn on at random, and the remainder is left available for easy access.

Another way of looking at this process is to think of the mind as being a huge computer. In the waking state we are continually feeding in information, which is not filed in any particularly efficient way. Dreams perform two functions. One is the correct sorting and filing of inform-ation. The second is the presentation of information necessary for the dreamer to function successfully within the world in which he lives. As this internal computer becomes more powerful it needs to spend less time and effort sorting the incoming information, and more time searching for relevant information to enable it and its manager to function more effectively.

Dreams tap into this information database of memory, experience, perception and cultural belief, and form new ideas and concepts. They also present us with a way of solving problems which may seem impossible on a conscious level. When the limitations that the conscious mind places on the thought processes are removed, the mind is free to roam wherever it pleases. Free from inhibition, it will create scenarios and situations which defy explanation by the logical side of the person-ality. In looking for explanations we have to become more creative and open in the pursuit of knowledge. We can thereby tap into not only our own storehouse of images, but also into an even more subtle level of information available to everyone. This is the level that Jung labelled the Collective Unconscious.

The term 'unconscious' is taken to delineate many functions and aspects of Self. It is that aspect of our being that scans our life experience, knowledge of which is retained in a level of memory to which we seldom have access. Information processing then becomes the development of a concept of reality in the understanding of what is probable and what would be severely out of the ordinary. Much of that which we call the unconscious forms a set of basic physiological and psychological functions – our way of surviving. It is also a collection of inherited norms of conduct, beliefs and ideals.

As the collective unconscious becomes more accessible to us, it becomes obvious that there are certain patterns which continually emerge. These basic patterns often have been adjusted to fit the dreamer's experience and sometimes need to be readjusted so that they can be made to fit better. Many dreams take place which enable us to have access to the basic patterns and many more to enable us to make the very subtle adjustments necessary.

The Exploration of Dreams

The more we explore this information database, the more subtle the explanations become, but oddly enough the simpler, easier and more pertinent we will find them. Thus, dreams will often have to be interpreted from more than one perspective in order to be fully understood. Because the human being is naturally holistic (that is, a whole person), dream interpretation cannot be an exact science and must take into account the dreamer's understanding of himself. He may not be looking for psychological or spiritual interpretation, but simply an easy explanation of the dream. The aim is to recognise that:

1 We are attempting to achieve a particular goal or target, or actively pursuing an objective which may be, as yet unattainable. We are able to take account of all information available in order to achieve success.

2 We need to focus directly on emotions such as anger, jealousy, fear and pain.

3 We directly use aspects of sexuality and spirituality.

This book attempts to address that aim by giving the reader choices. The first interpretation shown is the more conventional one. It may be that such a simple explanation of one or more of the dream images is ample for the dreamer's needs. The second has a slightly more psychological slant, and often goes more fully into the likely significance for the dreamer, sometimes highlighting a particular course of action which may be appropriate. The third is a simple short explanation of the accepted spiritual meaning, which gives the dreamer the opportunity to work interpretations through more fully using his own techniques. He may choose to use meditation or guided imagery, since these share much of the symbolism of dream imagery.

By assessing which of the interpretations is the most likely – or perhaps if more than one is applicable – the dreamer is able fully to understand the emotional content, the symbolism, the process and the reason for each particular dream.

If we so wish, we can record our dreams and build up a library of our own. We can monitor our own progress as we learn more and more about ourselves and the private world from which we create. The more accessible that world becomes, the more control we have over external circumstances. As we gain more control on a conscious level, the richer our life becomes. We are more able to control our own destiny, and to use the energy which becomes available to us to create a sustainable future.

The Language of Dreams

It has been suggested that dream interpretation is like learning a new language; this is very true except that the language is actually already known to us and it is simply a matter of re-learning it. The baby sees before it speaks, and interprets what it sees on a very simplistic level. To all intents and purposes it has no reason to believe anything other than that it is the centre of its own universe. A jumble of impressions gradually gains meaning and order, and a meaningless medley of sound achieves some kind of significance. The feelings associated with the impressions and the sounds become recognisable. If what is occurring is acceptable, the process of sorting becomes automatic. As the baby becomes better able to receive and quantify information, the sense of wonder becomes less, and the process of discovery also becomes more automatic. Re-learning dream language is simply remembering the process of sorting and the recognition of the symbolism.

Initially the situation, or the environment in which the dreamer found themselves, needs interpreting. This gives an indication of the context of the dream. For instance, to dream of being in a school would indicate a learning environment, and the dreamer could then relate this to their present circumstances. The dreamer then focuses on how they felt, or on which emotions they experienced, so that there is an understanding of the dream scenario. (Just as a playwright will set the scene so that his audience understands his play, so the mind will set the scene for what needs to be realised.)

After this, the symbolism of the various images then needs deciphering and recognising as suggestions, parable, innuendo or perhaps even word play. For instance, a fire grate was interpreted as 'great' passion in one particular dream. The people in the dream are then seen as significant within the drama which has been created, and finally the entire assortment is put together through the actions of the various participants.

The drama played out in dreams is often non-sequential; the scenes shifting apparently without rhyme or reason. If it is accepted that the mind gives emphasis in a subjective way to what must be revealed, then there is a type of order. Once the theme of the dream is revealed, then the various aspects can be given definition and the symbols interpreted.

The language of dreams does have common themes, and commonly accepted meanings, but just as every language has its dialects, so also does this one. We each have our own dialect which arises from our own experience, family stories, perceptions and emotions. The only interpretation which is truly valid is our own, though we can ask for help from others who speak the same language, or we can take the time to learn a new terminology. So the interpretations of being in a boat and catching a huge fish would differ depending on whether the dreamer was a fisherman or not. The first may be focusing on his emotions within the work situation, while the second is trying to deal with his ability to achieve success and the emotions associated with that.

How to Use This Book

It is best to record dreams as soon as you can after they happen. This can be done by using a tape recorder or writing down everything you can remember about the dream: that is, what happened, who or what was in the dream, what was said or done, what you as the dreamer felt about it, what emotions were present, and how everything hung together. It is recommended, for ease of interpretation, that you write down alphabetically each symbol, object, feeling or emotion remembered. It is also suggested that you get into the habit of keeping a dream diary – that is, recording every dream which occurs over a specified period.

The entries in '10,000 DREAMS EXPLAINED' are, on the whole, divided into three categories under each heading. The first interpretation is a purely conventional one. Perhaps this is the one that is most easily understood – the most obvious. The second classification goes slightly more fully into the meaning of the object or feeling, and looks at it from a psychological point of view – what it does to us or for us. The third explanation is a simple sentence which gives the more Spiritual or esoteric meaning. Because that interpretation needs slightly more intuition, it can be used as a trigger for the reader to explore the meaning more fully for himself.

1 Read the whole of each explanation and try to decide which of the three interpretations seems more real. Many explanations are in **bold** type to help interpretation and many are cross-referenced. Some which have many different aspects to them, such as Animals, Family and Journey, have their own section within the alphabetical listing.

2 Make a brief note of the most important aspects of the dream.

3 Do this for each entry into your notebook, then reconstruct the dream as it happened.

EXAMPLE

I was looking at a picture which was quite dark and dingy, and probably old. Whoever was with me, I think a man, was rubbing at the picture to clean it and put his finger through the bottom left corner. Next I was running down a path with a close female friend to warn a couple who had bought the picture that it was damaged. The woman seemed unconcerned.

Alphabetical list
Bottom, buy
Clean, concern, corner, couple
Dark, dingy, damaged
Female, finger, friend
Looking, left
Man
Old
Picture, path
Running
Woman

The dreamer, after some thought, worked out the explanation that although her recent past experiences had been somewhat dark and dismal, she could now make moves, with the help of a man, possibly a therapist, to explore them, even though it could make her feel vulnerable. With the support of her friend, who was a particularly strong character, she could develop similar strengths, and face the issues involved in being part of a couple again. She could also accept that as a woman she was no longer hurt or troubled by the experience.

If she had wished to go even deeper into an explanation, she could have worked, as suggested below, on each image individually to gain more insight into her own understanding and possible courses of action.

Gaining Insight into Dreams

There will be immediate insights and clarifications, and this may well be enough to allow you to interpret the dream successfully (some meanings will fit your scenario more conventionally, some psychologically and some esoterically). Once you are used to interpreting your dreams, it is likely to be a mixture of all three. Of course, there may be many interpretations of the same dream which are equally valid. The dream vocabulary is so multi-faceted, and the personality so complex, that several simultaneous explanations are possible.

One of the most effective ways of gaining insight into dreams, particularly if the dream is difficult to interpret, is to work with a friend, or friends, who support us as we explore our own dreams. We can often gain tremendous resources by taking the time to explore all facets of the dream. Those supporting the dreamer listen carefully while the dream is described and ask questions so they can understand for themselves the imagery and feelings experienced. At this point the idea is for the friends to gain a clear image of, but not explore, the dream.

Often by talking about the dream in this way, the dreamer remembers certain aspects which had not brought to conscious memory. Perhaps a character or image is seen in a different light, which enables the interpretation to be enhanced. Additionally, some interaction between dream characters may become obvious which offers new insights. It is important that the supporting friends ask only questions which clarify the position, and do not ask leading questions.

Firstly the dream is explored from the dreamer's personal point of view. and can be described subjectively, e.g. 'I was...', 'We were...', 'I seemed...' Then it is possible to work more objectively with the images (e.g. 'The room was in a large house', 'The tree was very odd'). This process is quite important, since it shifts the dreamer's perspective, and moves him into more of an observer's role.

The next step is for the dreamer to choose one of the characters or images in the dream, to 'become' that character, and experience the dream from that particular viewpoint. Since all the parts of our dreams are aspects of ourselves (even objects such as cars, trees or houses), by experiencing the scenario from a different perspective, we gain additional insight into ourselves. This process can be continued with each image within the dream until the dreamer considers that he understands. With practice, the dreamer becomes more proficient at interpreting his own symbols. The process of sorting the images and making more sense of the context of the dream can then be considerably speeded up.

History and Belief

Dream interpretation has a long and chequered history. Probably some of the best known are those recorded in the Bible, such as the feast and famine one which was interpreted by Joseph (incidentally, Joseph must have had a great deal of insight available to him through dreams, since he was a prolific dreamer himself). Ancient peoples had great faith in prophetic or clairvoyant dreams which they called visions. They believed that they were sent by the gods as warnings and guidance. In the light of the modern day belief that many dreams come from the Higher Self, or more spiritual side of ourselves, we have come almost full circle.

By the fourth century AD, dreams were considered important enough for a seer called Artemidorus to have put on record 'The Five Books of Dream Interpretation'. Until the nineteenth century, when Freud began to look at dreams, many of the interpretations which Artemidorus gave were accepted as accurate. Indeed, many books on dream interpretation still hold traces of his interpretations.

The early psychoanalysts, particularly Freud, believed that a number of dreams could be explained according to our attitude to our own sex and sexuality. It is more likely that this explanation pertained because less was understood about the mechanisms of the mind. The dreamer therefore linked in to his basic knowledge of himself. As more information became available to therapists and dream workers through research, it became apparent that this was not the only basis for explanation. In order to protect themselves, therapists often claimed that it was only possible to decode dreams with professional help. This is patently untrue, unless the dreamer is receiving medication for depression or some such difficulty. The language of dreams is universal, as already suggested. A basic primer, such as this book, enables the dreamer to begin his journey of exploration. By training himself to record dreams of whatever type, the dreamer becomes his own therapist.

Freud's work on dreams arose from his own work as a psychoanalyst, and was based on the belief that they were disguised expressions of what went on below the surface of the mind. The dreamer, therefore, would need someone else to interpret his dreams for him, preferably someone skilled in the art of untangling the various images. Since the mind used a whole plethora of mechanisms to hide information from the dreamer, there also had to be someone available who understood the working of the mind. Who better than a psychoanalyst?

Freud did believe that the analyst had to tune into the patient in a very particular way. He had to be aware of how the patient's mind worked, and had to cultivate 'listening with the third ear' (this could be better described as hearing what the patient had to say, rather than listening). It is worthwhile noting that he perhaps did not take into account that the interpretations would be coloured by the unconscious inhibitions and awarenesses of the analyst himself. By finding out what associations the dream image had for the dreamer, additional information could be gleaned. This could be done by word association, which works both on the sound of the word, and on what further thoughts this generates. By being able to take these dream images back to their starting point, much knowledge could be gained as to the clients' unconscious motivations. Past incidents and traumas can be remembered through association which can help to clarify how the dreamer should act in everyday life. Remembered perceptions are, however, very subjective, and what is perceived as abuse – whether sexual or otherwise – need not necessarily be so.

Freud also believed that, in dreams, two thoughts could be condensed into one image. This is undoubtedly so, but he saw this process as disguising unconscious wishes. The unconscious wish would therefore have to be disentangled in order to be interpreted. It is possible that – rather than disguising the wish – the mind is trying to make it known. Presenting the image in a dream in a way that forces us to think about it creates an environment which allows us to bring things through to full consciousness in a positive way. It again is perhaps worthwhile noting that, as a psychoanalyst, Freud was dealing with people who, at that time, had a vested interest in keeping things hidden. Culturally the climate was one of inhibition and repression.

Freud's dream displacement theory suggests that anything that happens in dreams is actually something else, that nothing is what it seems. Any emotion felt is a symbol for another feeling or emotion which we are afraid to face. We can only handle it by making it into something with which we can deal. Sometimes this is undoubtedly so, since this happens in waking life. We will laugh when we feel like crying, get angry when we really want to be hugged. Freud saw this displacement as an attempt to confuse the dreamer and prevent interpretation, rather than seeing it as alerting the dreamer to the appropriateness of the original feeling.

Freud also perceived a phenomenon which he called secondary revision. This occurs when the dream appears to rerun itself and throw up a different and more ordered way of looking at the original dream. It is as though the first thoughts the dreamer has on waking need to be ordered and made sense of by the rational mind. Freud again thought that this was a disguise mechanism, whereas it may now be thought of more as reinforcement. The waking mind will remember more successfully the creation of whatever new order is presented, and will understand that new order in a suitably logical way to allow a rational interpretation. There is no reason why this should be a disguise mechanism – as Freud believed – except that the logical mind belongs more to the waking dreamer than the sleeping self.

Many of Freud's theories do have relevance, particularly insofar as symbolism is concerned. The mind will substitute other objects and alternatives as being symbolic of, or standing for, something else. There are common interpretations for many of those basic patterns shared by all human beings. What is not certain however is that all of this symbolism arises from an infantile sexuality, buried or otherwise. He did recognise that the kind of sexual symbolism he encountered was apparently universal. He assumed that this would create incredulity in his clients but again, since many of his patients were sexually repressed, this would hardly be surprising. He simply asked his clients to recognise the sex symbolism apparent in folklore myths and fairy tales. An analyst was simply more practised than most in interpreting the relevance of the symbols. Through a knowledge of the universality of such symbols, the analyst could make intelligent assumptions as to what was a possible course of action. It would also be possible to widen the patient's under-standing of his own symbolism.

As Freud's pupils became aware that it was highly dangerous to give the analyst the power to be right all the time, and to be directive in his interpretation – 'If it doesn't mean this, then it must mean that' – a movement arose to widen the interpretation of dreams. Jung, having been a pupil of Freud, wrote: '. . . It is true that there are dreams which embody suppressed wishes and fears, but what is there which the dream cannot on occasion embody? Dreams may give expression to ineluctable truths, to philosophical pronouncements, illusions, wild fantasies . . . anticipations, irrational experiences, even telepathic visions and heaven knows what besides.'

He suggested that one way to interpret dreams was to recognise that dream elements and characters are part of the dreamer's own personality and could be interpreted as such. This kind of subjective approach could give insight into the dreamer's personality and fears and doubts in a way that was totally liberating. There could then be no violence done to the integrity of the dreamer, since the interpretation would be subjective rather than objective. The analyst was there only to assist in the interpretation.

It was from this suggestion that his work on the Archetypes arose. He recognised the validity of the sexual impulse arising from the duality of the masculine and feminine. In doing so he accepted that there were certain parts of ourselves which we hid, but that what was principally important was the overt content of the dream. It was what was revealed which was of note, not what it concealed. He believed that there were times when dreams exposed a hidden conflict or difficulty, but at other times it would reveal an unrecognised potential or possibility – either in everyday life or on a psychological level. He insisted that every dream was concerned with the present situation of the dreamer, and not primarily with the past. He accepted the validity of certain common symbols and indeed then went on to use the word 'universal' in the understanding of a collective unconscious – or a store of information to which we all have access. Because he believed that the dream could be interpreted in whatever way was most useful to the dreamer, he also recognised that dreams could be interpreted in many ways.

Jung saw man as being aware of this rich drive towards integration, which he called the 'archetype of the self'. The drive to wholeness was influenced by certain themes within this great unconscious. These themes tended largely to deal in opposites or with duality. He felt that there was in existence a negative double, a personal demon formed from all the dark repressed sides of our personality, which was there to trip the individual up and destroy him if that were possible. This shadow could be confronted, and the most efficient way of being able to do this was through the rich strata of myths and legends. Not only could the positive/negative aspects be recognised, so also could the basic male/female dichotomy, those aspects which he called the animus/anima. By being able to gain communication with those parts of the personality which were hidden, and to set up a kind of interior conversation, we should be able to progress forward with a great deal of ease. When an alien part of the personality was accessed – often through a series of dreams – it could be integrated back in to the whole.

Later work, done by principally Calvin Hall on dream content and by Fritz Perls, suggested that dreaming was a very personalised activity. Hall felt that dreams were a kind of personal document which gave clues as to the particular state of affairs within the psyche of the individual, and were a kind of read-out to enable us to discover what we are thinking about and dealing with when we are asleep. Most of the images were symbols for this process. Who better to read the document than the writer himself? There were four things to bear in mind: 1) The dreamer creates his own dream, and therefore it is a subjective reality. 2) The dreamer is responsible for the content of the dream. 3) The dreamer has multiple concepts at any one time, and all of these may be valid. We may simply see ourselves in a particular way at any one time. 4) Dreams can be read in series in order to enhance the interpretation. This interpretation can answer four main questions 1) How I see myself. 2) How I see others. 3) How I see my impulses and 4) How I see my conflicts.

In the late 1960s Fritz Perls developed his own philosophy of Gestalt which means wholeness, and believed that it was possible to reclaim those parts of our personalities which had become lost. He called dreams 'the royal road to integration'. If each image in the dream is an alienated part of ourselves, then it is wise to look at the necessity of giving each part of the dream its own voice and the opportunity to express itself, and therefore to become whole. Those wholenesses can then be integrated to become a greater whole.

Historically, while all this therapy and 'making better' was going on, dream interpretation was much more of a parlour game, and many of the early books of meanings reflected this. Whatever we play at in a dream might just be fun or suggest great seriousness. We might be able to explore new feelings, concepts and ideas in a safe way before trying them out in everyday life. Quite why dreaming of a donkey suggests, for instance, a lovers' quarrel or overcoming some type of affliction is not immediately obvious. One can only assume that people were less able to apply good judgement, and accepted what they were told. Perhaps this is why dream interpretation was given such a bad reputation.

When dreams entered the laboratory, as it were, scientific methods were applied to research. It was discovered that the brain generates weak electrical impulses, known as brain waves. These have been recorded in the unborn foetus and prove that there is a great deal of dreaming before birth.

The electrical activity of the brain is greatest when there is mental effort, concentration or watchfulness. This is known as Beta wave activity, which can be evoked by anxiety and is recorded at frequencies of thirteen cycles per second and above, up to about twenty-six per second. These waves are associated with poltergeists.

In a state of relaxation, electrical activity falls; Alpha brain waves range from eight or nine to eleven or twelve cycles per second. A feature of the state of deep meditation practised by Yoga, Zen and Sufism is sustained Alpha rhythms in the front and centre of the brain.

Theta brain waves, slower than the waves associated with relaxation, are in the range of four to seven cycles per second. They register during feelings of embarrassment and frustration. Interestingly, however, Theta waves are also connected with creativity and inspiration. Perhaps they are the interface between the physical and the spiritual realms.

Delta brain waves range from 0.5 to three cycles per second and are connected with deep sleep and, apparently, the release of the growth hormone. Irregular Delta rhythms are very common in the months before and after birth. This ties in with the more esoteric belief that a baby 'dreams' himself into existence.

Gamma brain waves range from twenty-seven cycles plus per second, and as yet are not fully investigated, nor generally accepted as being distinct from Beta.

Brain activity research continues. It has been discovered that a signal of 18,000 hertz fed into the brain induces mystical feelings. Some researchers suggest that the brain is a filter whose purpose it is to reduce the amount of data which would otherwise invade our consciousness and to eliminate what is superfluous. This filter or reducing valve is bypassed in certain states when information is 'paranormally' perceived.

Rapid Eye Movement (REM) was discovered to occur during periods of sleep and it was accepted that the dreamer was apparently scanning some kind of information 'database'. If the dreamer was woken during these periods he was more likely to remember his dreams. Thus an external record of images could be collected. It became apparent that there were many common themes within the dream process – for instance, many people dream of falling. A common occurrence in dreams is the appearance of people known to us – such as family – and many dreams deal with the issues of failure or success. Also, the chaotic aspect in dreams was accepted as the norm, rather than being unusual. Sleep research laboratories, while giving an environment in which dreams can be explored, are not necessarily as valid as those dreams which occur under normal conditions. However, some of the techniques used – such as being woken at regular intervals, the conscientious recording of dreams and the use of statistical analysis – can be of great help in dream interpretation. Work that is at present going on becomes a synthesis of all these methods.

Personal Research

If so minded the dreamer should be able to set up his or her own mini laboratory and consulting room at home. For the dedicated follower of dreams the 'laboratory' consists of an alarm clock, paper and pens or a tape machine and copious amounts of common sense. By waking up at set times during the night, not necessarily the same time each night, and recording what is going on, the dreamer can compile and store a great deal of information.

This information can be used and quantified in many different ways. Statistical information about one's own dreams can then be stored, which will enhance the understanding. For instance it might be discovered that a certain set of circumstances triggers off a particular type of dream. We might dream of being pursued by animals each time we have dinner with our boyfriend at a particular restaurant. We need to set out the variables to discover the real meaning. Is it our boyfriend who is 'pursuing' us or is it the waiter who looks so knowingly at us when we walk in? We may not consciously have registered the fact, but something has certainly made us uncomfortable. Perhaps it may be that that particular set of circumstances – eating out, two men and nice food – was the first time we thought about the principles of vegetarianism. The dream interpretation belongs to us.

A deliberately slightly bizarre image was been chosen to illustrate the process which can be gone through. It may suffice just to record that we dream more vividly after having seen our boyfriend.

The laboratory turns into a consulting room the moment the dreamer asks: 'But what did that mean?' Strictly the question should be, 'But what did that mean to me?' We are our own best interpreters and therapists. We decide what the dream means and also what we are going to do about it. We decide whether we are going to interpret the dream in terms of Freud's theory of displacement or Jung's theory of Archetypes, Hall's theory of Dream Content or Perls' Gestalt Therapy. We may choose any or all of these interpretations. We decide what action we are going to take over these insights, and above all we decide to what degree we will allow our dreams to affect our everyday lives and vice versa.

This particular book attempts to draw all the strands of dream interpretation together so that the dreamer can develop to their highest potential. The premise is that if he understands himself, he can understand the world he lives in. If he understands the world he lives in and the influence it can have on him, then he can accept responsibility for that world. If he acknowledges responsibility for the effect he has on his waking world, he must explore his own hidden world. If he is prepared to explore the hidden world he can gain access to universal wisdom. If he uses universal wisdom, he creates a better future. If he creates a better future, he can live in the world and also be of it. He lives both a successful interior and exterior life.

ARCHETYPES

Three facets of an individual's personality show themselves separately in dreams. Sometimes they appear as people the dreamer knows, sometimes as fictitious or mythical characters or beings and sometimes as other images.

The most difficult side of the individual has been called the Shadow and is the personification of one's worst faults and weaknesses. It is the part of ourselves that is the same sex as ourselves, but has been suppressed because it is frightening and unmanageable. Then there is the Anima, or in a woman, the Animus – that part that is of the opposite sex within the dreamer. In a man it is all that is instinctive, feminine and sensitive. In a woman, it is her masculine attributes of logic and objectivity. Finally, there is the ideal or True Self, which holds the highest possible creative potential that is attainable within the individual and is most likely initially to communicate through dreams. Although the Self first appears as potential belonging to the future, as the other aspects become properly integrated the individual may then become the whole real many-sided Self.

If the dreamer is prepared to work with the archetypal images and to understand them, the dream figures can help to create a sustainable reality that exists beyond any of them. They will then have fulfilled their function and so will be unlikely to reappear in dreams, except in times of stress. Because the most important quality of the inner being is energy, which can then become power, each of these dream images represents a different aspect of those vital forces the individual has at his disposal, and each in its own way can stimulate this energy into action.

For an understanding of the archetypal figures and their functions, it is important to keep the correct aim in focus. Personal growth takes place as we learn to understand and integrate each of these facets of our character. Each aspect of the personality must grow in its own sphere without disturbing the function of the others. As each aspect matures, we are able to understand more and more about ourselves. When conflict does arise between them, while the process may be painful it should not be destructive. The interaction between them should both enhance and hone the character; those parts, having first been seen as separate entities and then understood, should become familiar and properly integrated into the whole personality. Then it really is a case of the 'whole being greater than the sum of the parts'.

The Ego

When in the dream state we are observing what is going on, the part that observes is the Ego. Because it is the most conscious aspect of us, we tend to be more aware in dreams of the conflicts it has with other aspects.

When the Ego has become split off or separate from other parts of the personality, we do not experience the world correctly. We become selfish and untrusting, have difficulty in relating to others – and sometimes our surroundings – and often cannot accept anything except our own viewpoint. When this process goes too far, other aspects 'kick back' as it were, and try to redress the balance through dreams.

The Ego is the part of us that assesses our external reality, but if we are not careful, the need for an inner rightness – an exaggerated need for fantasy – can overtake this reality. Developing objective self-criticism, observation of our fantasies and patience can create a balance.

The proper balance necessary between the inner and the outer, between logic and intuition or reason and imagination means that the Ego must be brought under control, although it can never be given up altogether.

The Shadow
(A FIGURE OF THE SAME SEX AS THE DREAMER)

This appears in a dream as the person whom the dreamer fails to recognise; a vague instinctual figure, sometimes standing behind the dreamer. Often initially this figure appears to be the opposite sex to the dreamer and can therefore be confused with the animus and anima. It is only later that it is accepted as the same sex. It is the part of his potential that the dreamer never developed; this is the neglected side of the individual. It contains those aspects of his character that have already been thwarted and frustrated; but above all, parts which have never been recognised.

Everyone has his or her individual Shadow, and it is nearly always the worst side of himself that he or she has failed to recognise. The sensitive altruist may well have a brutal egotistic Shadow; the courageous individual will have a cowardly Shadow; the artist may be sadistic. Meeting the Shadow is painful: it is the shock of seeing ourselves as we really are at our worst. When we are able to face this dreadful entity with humility we can accept ourselves, and from that acceptance learn to see the rest of reality honestly. This is the way to greater understanding of others, and of new insights into the unconscious. When we have the courage to face the Shadow, to admit its very existence and to recognise it for what it is, we are able to create a true reality rather than some distorted fantasy. We can then often resurrect those normal instincts, appropriate reactions and creative abilities that we have consciously suppressed and buried along with the malicious and destructive sides of the personality. This vital energy when harnessed and understood becomes a force for forward movement rather than a dangerous enemy.

One way to consciously meet the Shadow is to think of all the things we dislike most about people, add to that everything we find hard to deal with in man's treatment of his fellow man and try to imagine what sort of person this would be . This will be a fairly accurate picture of our own particular Shadow. Our first reaction is to be thankful that we are not like that, but if we ask our family and loved ones if they can perceive those qualities within us, the answer will probably be yes. When we can honestly sit down and pinpoint the behaviour patterns within ourselves, we are moving towards wholeness. Often we will have an obsessive dislike of one particular set of characteristics, which if we are honest, frighten us because they are only just below the surface within ourselves. Homophobic behaviour is a case in point, since many people are terrified of their own sensitivity and creativity. The Shadow will often appear in dreams as someone we heartily dislike, are afraid of, or envy, but whom we cannot ignore. We begin to grow when we realise that some change in circumstance has given us an opportunity to bring it to the surface rather than ignore it in the hope that it will go away. When we work with these frightening dream images, we can often stop projecting the negative aspects outward and use the energy formerly spent protecting or suppressing them in growth and creativity. We can begin to mature and be real.

The child has a need to be right within his or her own little world, and will begin very early on to create a type of reality where this can happen. This means suppressing parts of the personality which don't fit, because this is the only way they can be dealt with. It also often means accepting the projections of other people's personalities because he or she does not have enough information to do anything else. The conflict between the inner shadow personality and the outer information then becomes highly destructive either on an inner or outer level. Dreaming can enable us to integrate the Shadow into the personality in such a way that we are able to live more fully both on an inner level and on an outer level. Dreams can both alert us to the need for integration and assist in the process.

When we concentrate totally on either the inner realm or the outer reality, we limit the scope and richness of our lives. We also run the risk of yet again creating fantasies and illusions. The introvert needs to begin to experience the outer reality, and the extrovert to experience the inner self. This is a fresh experience that allows us to experience life in a new and, for us, innovative way.

When we are not prepared to explore both sides of our personality, we lose a great deal because the way in which we have experienced life most comfortably becomes more difficult. The extrovert discovers that he is unable to cope with his relationship with the outside world, and the introvert loses his sense of inner peace.

Anima/Animus
(A FIGURE OF THE OPPOSITE SEX TO THE DREAMER)

When young people begin relationships outside the family circle, they usually project their own ideal of the opposite sex onto their partner. They then have difficulty when that person in no way matches that ideal. This confusion of the inner ideal with the outer reality can cause a problem throughout life in any male/female relationship. No-one can quite approximate to the feminine within the man or the masculine within the woman.

These figures have been called the Anima and the Animus. If we can come to terms with them and accept them for what they are, they become the origin of our understanding of the opposite sex as well as helping us to open up to the inner realms. If this potential for androgyny (inner union) is neglected or abused, in later life the individual is likely to be cut off from contact with the important aspects of the opposite sex. It is possible that the suppressed inner function may come to the fore making a man behave in an unstable fashion whereas a woman may, for instance, become quarrelsome.

Anima

This is the emotional and intuitive side of the male's nature. Principally his mother, but additionally all the women the individual has known, will help to form his image of the feminine and give focus to all the feminine forces within him. In dreams this female figure may show herself as a completely unknown woman, aspects of women the dreamer has known, or as feminine deities.

Dreams make an attempt to offset unbalanced conscious attitudes. The Anima will often appear when a man is neglecting the feminine side of himself, for instance by forcing everything he is into the masculine which puts the qualities of tenderness, obedience and sensitivity beyond his grasp. As he becomes more aware of the feminine principle, the dreamer is more able to develop warmth and genuine feeling and to accept the feminine qualities of spontaneity, receptivity and other such sensitive and adaptable characteristics. If he fails to integrate these feminine attributes properly he will be perceived as rigid, world-weary or irresponsible. The suppressed feminine may also erupt into moodiness and temper tantrums.

When he does not understand his Anima, he will constantly project his own negative image of the feminine onto each woman he meets and will not understand when all women appear to have the same faults.

Often, instead of accepting the Anima as an inner aspect of his own personality intended to be an ally, a man will project it onto an unobtainable 'object' avoiding proper contact with the opposite sex. When she is thwarted, the Anima turns into the completely negative feminine illusion who destroys all around her. The Anima becomes the guide to inner wisdom only when man confronts his destructive side and learns how to handle the energy he has available.

Animus

This part of the personality is the masculine part within a woman's character. When a woman learns how to integrate this properly she is able to develop the logical deliberating side of herself, along with the ability to develop self-awareness. This inner masculine is affected by her early contact with the masculine. Interestingly, if the men around her have not particularly developed in their own understanding of themselves, a woman's animus can reflect that lack of understanding. While the Animus is completely different for each woman, it is only when she is prepared to develop this side of herself into an almost completely separate personality that she will be able to use it as a natural guide to the deeper layers of her own personality.

The Animus usually manifests itself in dreams to highlight the woman's need to develop the masculine traits in her personality. Often a woman can become confused because her judgement has been distorted by the conventional assumptions that she has not questioned and made her own. They have been handed down as truths, and the woman has not been prepared to look at her own inner convictions. Only when she is able to develop her own judgement can she then use the masculine within to good effect without over-developing the need to compete with men, or equally to be destructive to other women.

If the negative side of the Animus dominates her ability to think and plan, she may become obstinate and self-seeking, feeling that life, and particularly men, owes her success. When in dreams the Animus surfaces over and over again in one form or another she must develop that side of herself that can judge without being judgmental, create strategy without being rigid, and can deliberately rather than instinctively maintain a hold on her inner reality.

The Animus, like the Anima, can be projected by a woman onto the men around her. Continuously she will be disappointed and disillusioned by the man if she does not realise that she is trying to mirror her own masculine side. Relationships will continually fail for the same reasons each time until she understands that this has nothing to do with her partner, and everything to do with her. When she takes responsibility for her own immaturity she can progress and grow and so can the relationships she has.

Dreams allow us access to the peculiar characteristics which make each of us unique. When we have accessed the Animus or Anima we can allow ourselves to manage them in waking life and to take advantage of the energy released. There may be conflict between the masculine attributes and the feminine ones, but once some kind of a balance is established the integration of the whole character can take place. This leads to a much greater awareness, and ease of life.

The Self

The Self is the Archetype of potential. It has in fact always been present, but has been hidden behind the necessary development of the personality. While the Shadow and Animus/Anima have almost deliberately been neglected, the Self holds the secret of the integrated Self. Because the true potential beckons from the future the first experience in dream form may be a figure encouraging us to move forward. Later it can become a symbol of wholeness which we are able to work with in the here and now to create a sustainable future.

As man begins to reach out further and further to understand the world he inhabits there becomes available to him a whole area of material which, if he dares, he is able to access and make use of. This is the unknown, unknowable higher spiritual quality held within everyone. His own experience of it is unique, but its knowledge is truly universal. It is the inner guidance which we need to understand and trust. By learning to access this information we learn once again that we are part of a greater whole with all its glory.

When we first meet this aspect we are often aware of it as a holy figure or some aspect of the particular god we have worshipped – Christ, Buddha, Krishna and so on. As we become more familiar with the information we receive, we begin to appreciate that we do not need the form and personalised attributes we have invested it with, but can have direct awareness of our own existence. We exist through time and space as an entity but also involved in all things. It is often perceived as a knowledge we have already had without being fully conscious of it. We interact not just with other people but also with everything. We cannot exist without the interaction which goes on at every level in our lives, and must appreciate that we are ultimately all part of one greater whole. It is, as it were, a two-way traffic between the uniqueness and the glory of our being.

When images of this archetype – such as a guru, a god, a saintly animal, a cross, a mandala or other geometric shape – begin to appear in dreams we are ready to face the process of becoming whole. We are capable of moving beyond an egocentric awareness to a wider appreciation of a greater reality. This reality becomes so much part of our personal experience that we stand in danger of confusion. We belong to the human race, and must live within our created world. We also belong to the spiritual world and have a personal responsibility within that realm. Only by achieving a balance between the two, and a full interaction, can we hope to be whole. By being prepared to inter-weave the two and pay attention to the demands and benefits of both do we live our lives successfully.

When negative or destructive images occur connected with this part, we are aware that we are neglecting the power of the Self. It is often at this point that we make a decision to advance and to change for the better. If we do not, often change will be forced upon us.

The Great Mother / Mother Earth.

This archetype is the embodiment of all the aspects of femininity, both positive and negative, suggests total wholeness in a woman, and is the ability to make use of all areas of her personality. In reaching for this perfection, woman must use and clarify all the separate functions of her being. She must learn to use sensation, feeling, thinking and intuition as her tools rather than as weapons. This archetype is not the exclusively mothering side of woman, but is a much more spiritual inner sense of Self. All life, and the instinctual awareness of its processes, is her domain, and can be cultivated in many different ways.

A Woman's Self

Every woman is the embodiment of feminine energy. Her focus is on the intangible side of life, on instinct and on feeling. Her abilities express themselves through the functions of sensation, feeling, intellect and intuition. She knows and understands the processes of life and death and of rebirth. Her images tend to be of fullness and nurturing, but also of the erotic and earthly.

She seeks to procreate, but at the same time knows she holds within the ability to destroy. She can be ruthless within that destruction, seeing no point in maintaining that which she considers imperfect. In each individual woman there is a striving to express each function as fully and completely as possible, and she will tend to compensate for what she feels to be her own inadequacies, by seeking balance through her man. Thus, the mothering type of woman seeking union with a man who needs mothering is often perceived, as is the virago with the hen-pecked husband. The interesting thing is that these relationships work until such times as either partner recognises that they can develop other sides of their personality.

The Wise Old Man

This is the prime archetype for the man's whole Self, in all its aspects. Like the Great Mother for the feminine, he is the composite figure of all the masculine attributes, properly understood and integrated. When a person recognises that the only appropriate guidance is that which comes from within, the Wise Old Man often appears in dreams. It is as though his appearance is triggered by desperation on the part of the dreamer. By pulling on the deep reserves of the unconscious, a guardian and friend appears to be a source of inspiration and under-standing, to give advice and to support necessary decisions. Within the

Wise Old Man are combined the functions of sensation, feeling, thinking and intuition.

A Man's Self

A man's Self will express itself much more through intellect, logic and conscious spirit. The civilised world and a technological society can mean that men are forced into the position of having to make discriminations and judgements, which completely deny the intuitive function. Primitive tribes had a much greater affinity with the earth and therefore less need to use intellect, but there is a tendency to have the pendulum swing totally the other way. Each individual again grows into maturity by developing the functions of thinking or intellect, sensation, emotion and intuition. In this day and age as man understands more of the process of separation from the mother, as a process of individuation and growth, so also he appreciates his need to be separate from, and yet connected with, his unconscious self. Provided he does not try to over-compensate by developing the macho side of himself at the expense of everything else, he will eventually reach a state of balance which allows him to relate to the rest of the world on his own terms. He will achieve an integration which allows him to function properly as a human being. If he loses himself too much on an intellectual level, his dreams will begin to depict the danger he is in.

The unconscious mind appears to sort information by comparing and contrasting. When we are aware of conflict within ourselves – whether this is between the inner and the outer selves, the masculine and feminine or whatever – we may dream in pairs (e.g. masculine/feminine, old/young, clever/stupid, rich/poor). It is as though there is some kind of internal pendulum which eventually sorts out the opposites into a totally unified whole.

The juggling that goes on in this way can take place over a period of time. A dream clarifying the masculine side of ourselves may be followed by a dream clarifying the feminine. Often in dream interpretation, looking at the opposite meaning to the obvious can give us greater insight into our mental processes.

The Dreamer's 'Dictionary'

It is almost as though one's own dream dictionary is stored in an accessible form. The ability to access the information becomes almost like that of a computer. With experience the dreamer can very quickly recognise the themes and tendencies within his dreams. These become a rich source of material for growth. To use another image, the material which is personally available to the dreamer is 'composted' with other available knowledge, and becomes accessible in a different form, to provide new images.

The belief that dreams are a way of sorting out the information which is absorbed in waking life has already been mentioned. Once one has begun to process one's dreams, the insights gained can enable us to solve many problems. While initially dreams do not serve this purpose, if the waking self is prepared to make the effort to understand, dreams can become a very effective source of information. As the dreamer learns more about his own process of dreaming he is more able to consolidate the link between his inner Self and his waking personality. The Self, which Jung described as a centre, is then able to co-operate more fully with the waking personality. There is a finer and more accessible mature character which develops and becomes available to others. Once this synthesis has taken place the person is able to achieve changes in his ordinary everyday life which appear to be quite phenomenal. New opportunities become part of the norm for the dreamer, new relationships which fulfil his needs present themselves, and there is a great sense of belonging to a greater whole.

This ability of the mind to produce information from increasingly deeper levels of awareness can be harnessed. Many dreams have been recorded in which an apparently unsolvable puzzle has been interpreted. For example, Albert Einstein claimed to have dreamt during adolescence of a sledge which travelled at the speed of light. Working with this image over a long period led to the Theory of Relativity. Frederich Kekule was totally unable to characterise and define the structure of benzene. He dreamt of one of the oldest spiritual symbols of all, the snake that eats his own tail – or ouroborus – and was thus able to describe the molecular formula of the benzene ring.

When one has a problem, by thinking about it and mulling it over just prior to sleep, the answer will often be 'dreamt out'. This can happen spontaneously, or over a period of time. Firstly the problem needs to be defined. Record everything you know or have learnt about the subject. Make a decision as to what further information is needed, or what insight you require. Keep the issues simple, and choose just one on which to work. If you are capable of spending time gathering information during the day, or cogitating on the subject, this both helps to focus your own mind and produces data for the dream process.

Before sleep, use some technique or creative visualisation which allows you to store the information you have. This could be seeing yourself putting it in a box, loading up the internal computer, passing it to your higher self, or whatever. Use an image which gives you satisfaction. In the morning, if there has been a dream, write it down. It is wise to keep a record of all dreams happening during this period, since the answer may take some time to appear, and the resolution may not necessarily occur in one dream. We instinctively know when we have resolved a problem. This process can then be further enhanced if necessary by working further but in a similar way with other insights gained. In the main, when there are personality or life problems to adjust it is better for the changes to happen over a longer period since attitudes and beliefs take a long time to consolidate.

Types of Dreams

It is generally recognised that dreams tend to be of two types, those that Jung called 'big' and 'little' dreams. Often it is easier to record these in different ways; for example if the dreamer chooses to write down his dreams by using two different books. Important dreams are usually easily remembered and the relevance recognised fairly quickly by the dreamer, whereas the significance of lesser dreams may not become apparent until all the themes and dimensions have been explored. Frequently, important and less important dreams can be compared and contrasted by the dreamer. The themes which are first presented in 'big' dreams are often enhanced and better understood by subsequent 'little' dreams. The more proficient the dreamer becomes at recording his dreams, the more easily they are remembered.

A further way of categorising dreams is of dividing them into 'good' or 'bad' dreams. With a greater degree of knowledge, the dreamer can often change the outcome of a bad dream into a good one. This is called RISC technique and was developed in America as a therapeutic tool.

The four steps are: 1) Recognise a bad dream while it is occurring. 2) Identify the bad feeling. 3) Stop the dream. 4) Change negative into positive. Initially it may be necessary to wake up in order to undertake any of these steps. Gradually, with a greater proficiency, the dreamer is able to do this while remaining asleep.

Because change takes approximately six weeks to occur on a psychological level, the dreamer needs to be patient while learning these new techniques. Often, changes in attitude are noticed fairly quickly, but do not become habitual until six to eight weeks have passed. Occasionally it is the dreamer who is most surprised by the changes which occur. He may become more able to deal with issues which have previously proved difficult, or find that inner conflict is more easily and efficiently handled. By beginning to work with opposites – however they may present themselves – those opposites become more easily appreciated and handled in waking life.

Sometimes in dreams there is an intensity of emotion which can be extremely frightening, We may be incapable of feeling such an emotion in everyday life, but for some reason can allow ourselves to be terrified in nightmares. It is almost as though we know we can escape from the situation simply by waking up. One of the features of nightmares is feeling stuck in impossible situations or of trying to escape. Often there appears to be no explanation for this until we explore past experiences and anxieties. Being able to disentangle such disturbing images, and treat them in isolation, brings a greater understanding of our doubts and fears.

One of the most frequent dream themes is that of some form of anxiety. Anxiety dreams – while less intense than nightmares – often allow us to replay, and thus capture, those aspects of our lives which cause us difficulty. Many dreams seem to be about things we are afraid of, but only because they have more impact than others. Disturbing elements in our dreams arise from our memories, stray thoughts or impressions and our own emotions which we deliberately suppress during waking hours. Subliminal worries and problems can be allowed to surface with safety in anxiety dreams. While the images may appear to be the important part of such a dream, it is actually the emotion experienced which needs to be faced and recognised. By doing this, we become able to handle ordinary, everyday anxieties.

When we are capable of recognising what power our imagination has on our emotions and body, we can start the process of handling anxiety. If we cannot meet our feelings of fear or emotional pain we allow ourselves to be controlled by them. Dreaming can allow us deliberately to access and explore our anxieties. Often by deliberately facing our hidden anxieties, dreams will give us information on what action needs to be taken to enable us to avoid making mistakes. Knowledge of the future may be revealed through hidden anxieties.

Precognitive dreams are an interesting phenomenon. Opinions vary as to whether there are really such things. Suffice to say that when anxieties are dealt with and further insights gained, the dream function will often access the best course of action available and give the information through images. That course of action is then usually chosen by the dreamer, though it may be that the conscious mind does not readily accept the situation.

Magical dreams are also part of the framework of awareness, though there are those who will deny their existence. Dreams have often been proved to give information in more esoteric ways. Number and colour, and all of the symbolism contained therein, are a valid part of dream interpretation and with a little knowledge can create a structure which allows access to what would otherwise be hidden information. Tradition which is based on wisdom, and rituals and ceremonies built around a knowledge of symbolism, are thus accessed. Personal management of the creative side of oneself becomes possible both through dreams and the directed use of power in the waking state and dreams can act as a monitor for correct behaviour.

Modern Day Use of Dreams

As everyday life becomes more stressful and traumatic, the human being needs to be able to use dreams as a safety valve or curative tool. We need to be able to pacify an Inner Self which constantly battles with an external reality and vice versa. Dreaming is one way of doing this. Dream workshops or groups can be a valuable adjunct in stress management. Often business difficulties and problems can be resolved using dream images, without actually needing to outline the actual problem itself.

As meditation becomes a more effective tool in self-management, many dream images are recognisable within the framework of meditation. There is often a crossover between the two techniques and there can be greater understanding within both disciplines. In the future, techniques which enable us to alter consciousness, and to be more in touch with our creative selves, will be usable both during sleep and waking hours. Dealing with dream images is one such technique.

The lucid dream has already been mentioned, as a way of making adjustments in one's everyday life. In lucid dreaming we know we are dreaming and we know we can change the outcome of the dream, so there is no reason why we cannot change the outcome of our lives. By learning how to manage our dreams we can enhance our lifestyles. We are capable of developing the relationship between the logical, rational side and the instinctive, intuitive side (the left- and right-hand sides of the brain). This should enable us to achieve personal success. Creative visualisation coupled with lucid dreaming would then become a very potent tool for the advancement of the whole human race.

When we become aware of our ability to be creative within the external world, there begins a two way traffic. It is as though there is a dialogue which goes on between the internal and external self. The two parts of us, rather than being in conflict, begin to co-operate with one another. When this co-operation is consolidated, it should be possible to make things happen in an almost magical way.

The inner self which knows what is needed to enhance our lives will be directive, but will also respond more positively to feedback. The outer self will have more confidence in itself and its ability to create the right environment and scenarios. The dream function will then, as well as being capable of balancing what is right for the individual, become able to envisage what is the right action on a more global level.

There is already enough evidence to perceive that, through telepathic dreams, information can be exchanged between two people. If this telepathic faculty were developed in dreams to include numbers of people, there could be a tremendous force for change within the world. There is much work which is already being done through group meditation and, by using group dreaming, work would be done on both an inner and outer level. There are small groups of people who are already practising such techniques – were it to be developed further, much energy could be created.

Each person has the ability to use his or her psychic skills in specific ways. Here 'psychic' means 'in touch with self'. There are those who have the ability to 'read' the past and those who can appreciate the future. Others have more of a concern for the present. when all talents are able to be used in conjunction, there there is the ability to create harmony within the world. With that ability, the human race will be able to take responsibility for its place in the Universe. It will truly be a world where our spiritual selves are glorified by matter.

So, whether you wish to use this book simply to find out what one particular symbol means, or whether you wish to enhance your everyday lives, or even – like me – wish to have a better world to live in, please enjoy it and share it with your friends.

SLEEP AND SPIRITUALITY

Activity in sleeping and dreaming

Sleep itself – in relation to the ordinary everyday world – is passive, yet there is considerable activity going on the whole time. If we define activity as movement, then there are, in fact, several types of movement going on at any one time. Physical movement of the body takes place many times during the night (on average about once every fifteen minutes) and seems to take place at random. This is not a restless tossing and turning, but a recognisable, almost deliberate turning over, moving of the limbs and so on. Initially once one has found a comfortable position, the physical body begins to relax. At a stage when the muscles begin to relax more deeply there is something called the 'myoclonic jerk'. This is a physical muscular reaction, when the muscles themselves involuntarily let go. In sleep it is sometimes accompanied by a feeling of falling, and can be quite frightening. It can waken the sleeper again, when the whole process of relaxation must begin all over again. It is a good idea therefore to learn to relax physically before one goes to sleep, since then this particular process is considerably shortened.

Many people have suggested that dreams are caused by certain physical stimuli from our sleeping environment, such as the classic of dreaming that one's hand has been cut off, and then waking to find that one is actually lying on the hand. While it is true that such discomfort will have an effect on our level of sleep, it does not appear that it has any effect on our level of dreaming. Opinions also vary as to whether eating certain foods and other physiological stimuli have an effect on dreaming. It is for the reader, if he or she is interested, to experiment and find out whether in their own particular case there seems to be any such effect. One lady claimed that if she wishes to dream in colour then she had to eat a particular confectionary bar in order to do so. Digestion seems to have some part to play, but it is more from the point of view of physical relaxation, and the effect that digestion has on one's solar plexus. Remembering that the baby in the womb receives its nourishment through the umbilical cord, it is hardly surprising if there is not some effect on the nerve centre closest to the area. 'Solar plexus' actually means 'the gathering of the sun', and thus is a centre for physical energy. What is true is that if sleep is disturbed from a physical level, and because of this the pattern of dreaming is upset, there is a profound effect on health and temper. As the noise levels rise in urban living there is less tolerance to certain noisy activities. We only have to think of the consequences on our efficiency if sleep is upset on a regular basis by noisy neighbours for several nights running. It may not be us who suffers, it may be the person who gets knocked over by our car through our lack of attention to detail. Physical relaxation does enable us to get the best use out of sleep, and therefore to use dreaming as a tool for complete health.

One way in which a greater understanding has been gained of the links between sleeping and dreaming is the work done in sleep laboratories. In 1937 it was discovered through the invention of the electro-encephalograph that the tiny electromagnetic surges in the brain were quantifiable. It was then discovered that the form of the brain wave changed as sleep occured. Then in 1953, Aserinsky and Kleitman identified stages in sleep where rapid eye movement (REM) occured. In 1957 Rapid Eye Movement was tied in with dreaming. It appeared that REM was some sort of scanning activity. Certain common patterns have been identified in the brain activity during sleep. EEG patterns identify a kind of progression. In the waking state the wave is low, but the frequency is fast. As we relax the brain produces Alpha waves, which is in stage one of sleep, then sinks into Theta waves.

During this stage we are approaching sleep proper, and experience random images and thoughts. It is at this stage that the sorting of the day's activities occurs. That particular stage lasts for approximately ten minutes and then moves into another stage where the brainwaves change again. We spend approximately half our sleeping time in this state. Deep sleep occurs when the wave pattern changes yet again to Delta waves. After about an hour to an hour-and-a-half, another change occurs.

This is where there is a change back to what we have called stage two. At this point the sleeper is very difficult to rouse, though the brain itself is alert and active. It is almost as though the two parts of ourselves have 'unlocked' themselves. This stage is sometimes called paradoxical sleep. The body is virtually paralysed, since all voluntary muscle activity has ceased. The brain is still transmitting the messages, but there is an inhibitor in action, whereby they are suppressed. During this time, short bursts of activity occur in various parts of the body where there are numerous nerve endings (such as the ear, the eyeballs, the penis and so on). It is a little like an MOT check on a car. We check the starting motor, the brakes and so on but separately from the car itself. In sleep, changes occur in the autonomic nervous system – that part of ourselves which functions automatically, which controls breathing, blood pressure and heart rate. All dreaming occurs in this second-level period. We start off with short stages of dreaming, but in the longest period – about four hours after we have fallen asleep – these periods of dreaming activity become longer. According to research, dreaming occurs when the cortical areas of the brain are stimulated randomly, causing the higher cortical brain to attempt to make sense of the input.

There are several levels of awareness. Within the sleep state, there are three to note in particular. The first is dreaming sleep, when we are aware of the symbolism and rich imagery of dreams and are capable of accepting them as real. There is then the lucid state when we are aware that we are dreaming, and that the symbols are our creation and do not have an external reality of their own, and the third is dreamless sleep which goes beyond the concepts of thought and emotions. Each one of these states has a validity of its own, and any disturbance on any level can have a profound effect on the health of the individual.

There are a number of sleep disorders that are worthy of note, particularly since any sleep disorder affects the quality and quantity of our dreaming. The first of these is insomnia. It is probably the best known and one from which many people suffer. The causes range from depression through stress to physical problems. To understand our own insomnia it would be necessary to recognise the underlying causes and to decide what we are going to be able to do about them. In the case of physical problems there is much that can be done during preparation for sleep which will be useful. Ensuring regular habits such as regular bed times can be helpful, as can all the well-known ways of handling the problem such as hot baths and massage.

It is worth noting that Chinese medicine holds the theory that certain energy lines within the body are soothed or stimulated at certain times of the day and night, and that certain conditions, when identfied and treated, will aid the management of insomnia. The organs of the body each govern certain psychological and physiological processes. For instance, we lie awake at three o'clock in the morning worrying, and frustrated, because we cannot sleep. It might be worthwhile turning things on their head and taking a look at what is frustrating us within our everyday lives – what can we do to prevent that frustration? Once we have been able to do that, then we are able to look at the worries in a different light and keep control of our lives. Insomnia is a very difficult thing to deal with, not least because it can affect not only the individual's life, but also the lives of others round about. Sleep deprivation leads to all sorts of problems, so learning to handle it can be of prime importance. One way is to use creative visualisation or meditation. It has been said that ten minutes of meditation is worth four hours' sleep at night, so being able to make adjustments to one's lifestyle could be of help.

Another sleep disorder is sleep apnoea. This occurs when the individual stops breathing for anything up to a minute. This then brings arousal from sleep, and the individual thus is continually in a near-waking state. This condition does need medical attention.

The study of narcolepsy, which is a condition where people can fall asleep in the middle of conscious activity, has yielded inormation on muscular movement in sleep. Under normal circumstances there is an area in the brain which suppresses muscular movement. This is called the pons. If this part is damaged or is itself suppressed, then full muscular movements in connection with the dream occur. Such movements do not seem to be survival techniques or socially motivated, but are a form of release mechanism to enable the dreamer to deal with emotions and trauma. As part of that process, spontaneous movement and speech can occur. This is akin to automatism which can occur in changes of consciousness connected with many religious practices.

Nightmares and anxiety dreams have an intensity of emotion about them which we seldom feel at any other time. The commonest characteristic is the need for flight, i.e. to run away from the situation. The physiological reaction to fear of fright, fight, flight (then in the waking state, submission) seems to be involved here, except that the dreamer usually wakes up before submission. It is almost as though it would be too painful to get into that submission state. Almost inevitably, there is huge relief that one has escaped on waking. Nightmares do appear to arise from six main causes. These are:

a　　　　Childhood memories of intense emotions. These are often centred around loss, and it has been suggested that such dreams are to do with the birth process and the attendant trauma.

b　　　　Childhood fears, perhaps also centred around the same situation, though the fears at this stage also include the fear of being attacked, and also anxiety about one's internal drives. This may be to do with the child's need for survival and the satisfaction of basic needs for food, warmth and shelter. (It has been noted that, if those needs are not satisfied, the child withdraws into a world of its own. If, therefore, the rage it experiences is suppressed, this could surface later in nightmares.)

c　　　　Post-Traumatic Stress Syndrome, where again the basic need for survival is threatened. It has been found that the anxiety experienced can still surface a long time afterwards. Some people are still experiencing such nightmares many years after the event. It would appear that the brain has not been able to discharge the trauma sufficiently for the sufferer to be at peace.

d　　　　The ordinary everyday drive to survive can surface in adults as fear of the future, and seems to arise as a result of fears connected with aggression, sexuality and fear of change and growth. Essentially, it is fear of the unknown.

e　　　　Some nightmares are centred around an apparent sense of foreboding. Whether these come under the title of precognitive dreams is not decided. What does seem true is that the human being is capable of picking up information on a subliminal level, without being able to understand that information.

f Serious illness with all its fear surrounding death can obviously cause nightmares. Some help could be gained from therapy and counselling.

Recurring dreams can have an element of anxiety about them. Indeed, it may be that they are triggered off by anxiety. The element of recurrence can be of various types. The setting of the dream may always be the same. The characters in the dream may not vary, or the theme may always be the same. It is often not until the dreamer begins to explore his dreams that the anxieties and attitudes begin to change, and there is no longer a habitual response.

Sleep talking and sleep walking both seem to occur as part of a response to stimuli. There is rationality about them in the fact that they actually make sense at the time, within the context of the dreamer's life. Sleep talking seems to play a part in clearing the mind of worries and concerns. Cases have been known where intelligent conversations have been held with the dreamer, although he or she is later unaware of the fact. Sleepwalking is also apparently purposeful, in that if left alone the sleepwalker will attempt to complete whatever action was started.

Spirituality

We could define spirituality as the knowledge that there is more to life than just the ordinary everyday existence that most of us experience. Dreams help us to become accustomed to that dimension in an easy and safe way and we then have some idea of the relevance of dreaming as a learning process. Just as a child grows physically, so also must we grow spiritually through a process which is not dissimilar to the child's process of growth.

We must first become conscious of ourselves in our surroundings. We form an image of ourselves as to how we would like to be. We then learn to relate to others around us, and begin to understand ourselves and others in a feeling, connected sort of way. We learn how to handle, and above all to understand, our own emotions and to perceive that if we want a quality existence then we must be able to appreciate that we belong to a wider world and can take responsibility for ourselves, but not the blame when things go wrong. We learn to accept what happens with a degree of equanimity.

Once we have been able to do this, we are in a position to be aware of just exactly what our potential is. The world becomes exciting to be in and we can begin to adjust the original concept of how we saw ourselves into a finer and better vision. The way we express ourselves then begins to improve, and we can be more open and honest. With the realisation that we are very much part of a greater whole, we can begin to take responsibility for the creation of a better, fuller existence for ourselves and finally to accept that out of that creation we can build a finer and more stable future.

Now for an explanation, and an exploration. If we think of the physical, ordinary everyday life as being on one side of a bridge and our spiritual, aware, extraordinary life on the other side, then we have an image with which to work. The bridge is the mind, and in the middle of the bridge is a border guard with a whole file of information both on us and for us. That border guard is the dreaming self.

This is the kind of action and imaginary dialogue which might occur:

Firstly, the file is scanned to discover if you need to leave anything at the checkpoint. A bad experience which needs understanding? This is the information needed to sort it out. You wish to explore this part of your life? Here is the information you need. There is a map enclosed; some of it is in code to protect you, but it will be understandable soon. The difficulties you are likely to come across? You will have the correct information you need at the right time.

Make your stay a short one to begin with, because you have duties back home, but you are welcome any time. You may eventually wish to stay longer when you realise that you have more fun and more energy here, but you are free to come and go as you please. If it's not frightening any more, you can start integrating the two sides – because they are, after all, one – and we need to share the information. Take the information away with you and let other people know. It helps to have that information – it makes life easier somehow. Soon there will be the opportunity to make changes in the way you live and the information necessary will be available to you. Now that you can see where you have come from, you will be shown what potential there is and you can move on. Enjoy your future, you deserve it. Oh, by the way, here is your guide book; you can take responsibility for your own file now.

This book is your own coded map to enable you to read, and understand, your own 'life file'.

from

Abandoned *to* Axe

ABANDONED

1 Similar to the sense of being rejected, this represents a sense of how we experienced not being wanted when we were young. This may not actually be how it was but our feelings give us that perception. For instance, a child having had to go into hospital may have recurring dreams in adulthood of **being abandoned**, and may have problems in forming plans for future success.

2 To be abandoned, i.e. **without restraint**, within a dream may mean that we are looking for freedom. This could be emotional freedom, or the freedom to be ourselves.

3 This links with the Dionysian concept of abandoning the serious for fun.

ABNORMAL

1 Abnormality in a dream usually represents something which we instinctively feel is wrong or not balanced properly. If it is abnormal in the sense of extraordinary, such as an **abnormal feeling or sound**, it is the strangeness of it which needs to be explored. We may, for instance, dream of **someone laughing at a funeral** which would indicate that we would need to pay particular attention to the way we feel about that person.

2 An awareness of abnormality alerts us to the fact that we should be paying particular attention to areas in life which are not in line with the way we feel they should be. To dream of **a dwarf or a giant** can indicate that our attention is being drawn to particular issues to do with size or deformity. There is something in our life that may be too big to handle.

3 The abnormal or strange usually possesses magical powers, possibilities or opportunities.

ABORIGINAL

1 In dreams, the aboriginal represents that which is basically different to ourselves – perhaps elements of the unsophisticated. By being more in touch with the natural we are able to make use of different types of energy. There is within everybody a basic sense of clarity which has become covered over by experience and we often need to access this simplicity in order to cope with difficulty.

2 Psychologically, we need to use a knowledge of basic life forces which is possibly not consciously available to us. By allowing ourselves to be in touch with natural forces we can make use of them rather than fighting them.

3 Attention is drawn to the rhythm of the life processes within.

ABORTION

1 There may be a need to reject a feeling, emotion, belief or concept which could be troublesome in some way. A risk has been taken which has not worked, and we now need to put ourselves back to the way we were. We have internalised a new way of thinking or of being which, on further consideration, needs to be rejected.

2 The ability to look clearly at what we have undertaken to do or to be in our lives should be utilised. Decisions should be made which will get rid of what is no longer needed.

3 A spiritual set-back means we must abort a previously held concept.

ABROAD

1 To dream about **being or going abroad** gives us an understanding of our feelings towards the widening of our horizons, or making changes in our lives. Such dreams may also be connected with beliefs about the country in the dream *(See Places)*. We are dreaming about personal freedom or the ability to move freely around our universe.

2 There is a psychological need to get away from (escape), or leave, a situation. We are perhaps travelling towards something new. Our minds are more than capable of accepting new input and experience and will often do so on a subliminal level. We then become aware through dreams of what we have learnt, or what we have to do.

3 In a spiritual sense **going or being abroad** is all about new spiritual experiences.

ABSENCE

1 A dream about someone being absent, or of the absence of something one would expect to find, indicates that the unexpected may happen. We may be looking for something which we have already lost. Our feelings about the absence (e.g. fear or anger) may also be important. A child experiences a strong sense of loss when mother is first absent from his perceived environment, and this can cause extreme distress.

2 We are in a situation where we may suffer loss or where we may reject something we need. The type of dream where we are **in a familiar environment, but a much-loved article or person is missing**, suggests we may have a feeling of impermanence .

3 To experience an absence, or sense of nothingness suggests the Void.

ABSORB

1 To be **absorbed in what we are doing** in dreams indicates our ability to be totally focused on our action. We are capable of taking in ideas, concepts or beliefs which then become part of us and the way we function. To **absorb something into ourselves** is to consume it, in the sense of making it our own. A great deal of the process of understanding takes place through absorption of information.

2 As we mature and grow we perceive the necessity to belong to social groups. To be **absorbed into something** represents the need to belong to a greater whole, or to make efforts to integrate various parts of our lives.

3 We have the ability to integrate the various parts of our lives. Spiritually our yearning is to go back to Source.

ABYSS

1 To dream of an abyss indicates the dreamer recognises within themselves the so-called bottomless pit or void. This is an aspect of the unknown which all of us must face at some time or another in our lives. It is a risky action which must be taken without knowledge of what the outcome is going to be.

2 There is a fear of losing control, of a loss of identity, or of some type of failure. More positively, it is possible to go beyond our own boundaries or present experience. Also the abyss indicates our coming to terms with opposites such as right or wrong, good and bad.

3 The Underworld, and inferior matters, appears in dreams as the abyss.

ACCIDENT

1 Dreams of being injured, murdered or killed occur relatively frequently, and attention needs to be paid to the specific circumstances of the dream. We are usually receiving a warning to be careful or to be aware of hidden aggression, either our own or others.

2 Such dreams may highlight anxieties to do with safety or carelessness, or fear of taking responsibility.

3 Since there is no such thing as an accident in spiritual terms, it signifies Divine intervention, or interference from an authoritative source.

ACID

1 There is a corrosive influence in the dreamer's life which is usually bad but may be cleansing. There could be the feeling that the dreamer is being eaten away by some action or concept. The necessity is to become aware of something which must be used with caution, depending how, and on whom, it is being used.

2 Psychologically, there is an awareness that self-confidence and the dreamer's usual sense of well-being is being eroded by outside influences.

3 An act of corruption and evil eats away at our integrity.

ACORN

1 To dream of acorns indicates that there is a huge growth process beginning to emerge from small beginnings. There is a new potential for strength. Since acorns appear in autumn, there may be the need to harvest or gather up the ideas before they can be stored in order to give them time to work.

2 The germ of an idea is present. There is also a need for patience in dealings either with ourselves or others.

3 Life, fertility and immortality are symbolised by the acorn, as is the androgynous.

ACTION

1 The action within a dream often informs the dreamer of hidden agendas and motivations, since each of us is the producer of our own lives. What we – or others –

are doing in a dream often needs to be interpreted, as much as the articles in the dream.

2 The dreamer should be aware that action needs to be translated from dreams into waking life to enable them to move forward.

3 An action in dreams can give an indication of the dreamer's Spiritual ability.

ACTOR

1 To dream of an actor, particularly **a famous one**, is to become aware of the ego in oneself. Very often we become conscious of the roles we play in life and recognise that we are perhaps not playing the part we really want to in life.

2 We each are actors in our own play, so to see ourselves as actors suggests we may be using an artificial personality or not taking charge of our own destiny. We are being given the opportunity to create a new personality.

3 We each need to take responsibility for our actions and the act of living.

ADDER
– also see Snake and Serpent in Animals

1 A 'slippery' person or situation is present in one form or another. There may be a situation where another person cannot be trusted, or one which the dreamer knows they cannot control.

2 Because any snake is taken to represent matters to do with sex (while more properly being more to do with male sexuality), there are unresolved issues to do with sexuality or fear of sexual activity. **3** Where there is an act of depravity or deceit there is evil.

ADDICTION

1 To dream of **being addicted** indicates we have to recognise that there is a need and desire to acknowledge obsessive behaviour in ourselves or others. There is anxiety that someone or something is taking us over. To **be addicted to someone** is to have abdicated responsibility for ourselves. To **be addicted to a substance** such as tobacco or alcohol in a dream suggests an inability to relate properly to the world we live in.

2 The fear of addiction is an identification of the hold our own passions may have over us. We fear loss of control (that is, control over ourselves), but also our control of other people. To be with a **group of addicts** suggests we do not understand our own behaviour in social situations. We may be conscious of the fact that we tend to become the victim in everyday life.

3 This is connected with the pleasure seeking, hedonistic aspect of the Self.

ADDRESS
– also see Letter and Parcel

1 There is a situation in the present which needs consideration, perhaps one's current lifestyle. To **address something**, such as a letter or a parcel, can represent the need to explore possible courses of action. To be **addressing a group of people** is to be aware of the need to share our knowledge with others.

2 A known address may represent a place of safety, while a **previous address** indicates the dreamer needs to look back to old behaviour or attitudes. To dream of a **new address** suggests the need for change and challenge.

3 One's spiritual Home has been given an identity.

ADOLESCENT
– see People

ADVERTISEMENT

1 Depending on the content of the dream, this indicates those areas in our lives which need to be acknowledged or recognised. For instance, **an advertisement on a hoarding** might mean a way of working in the world, whereas a

television advert would represent a way of thinking.

2 There is a need to put ourselves on the line and to be acknowledged for who we are. If we **ourselves** are the subject of the advertisement, we should expect to be more upfront and open about our activities. If **someone we know** is advertising themselves in our dream, we may have become aware that they have the ability to help us in our activities. Conversely, our subconscious may be alerting us to their need for help.

3 Information received psychically needs acknowledgement so we can move forwards.

ADVICE

1 Receiving advice in a dream means we should consider guidance from within, possibly from a part of ourselves which is unrecognised.

2 In dreams **accepting advice** is acknowledging the need to be doing something one doesn't necessarily want to do. **Giving advice** is recognising that one is aware of information which can be helpful to others.

3 We have an inner awareness. The Higher Self will often manifest itself as a figure which is giving advice.

AEROPLANE
– also see Journey

1 Dreams of aeroplanes can represent sudden or dramatic life changes. **An aeroplane taking off** represents a leap into the unknown and taking risks. **An aeroplane landing** indicates the success of a new venture or the outcome of a calculated risk.

2 An aeroplane denotes a search for psychological freedom; a move towards independent being.

3 By association with the winged chariot, the aeroplane represents a spiritual journey.

AFFAIR

1 We need to come to terms with our own sexual needs and desires for excitement and stimulation. Dreaming of an affair allows us to release such feelings. We may feel the need to do something naughty or something which means we have to take emotional risks.

2 We could be actively seeking emotional satisfaction in a way that is unacceptable in our waking lives.

3 We are seeking an integration of opposite polarities – male/female, drive/receptivity, good/bad.

AIRPORT

1 In dreaming of an airport we are entering a stage of transition, making decisions to move into new areas of life. It may also indicate we are, or should be, making a fresh assessment of our own identity.

2 We are being put in a position where our values may need to be reassessed in the light of our own – or someone else's – authority.

3 An airport, because of its transitory nature is a place for new experiences. We are ready to consider our spiritual progression.

ALCOHOL
– also see Drunk and Intoxication and Wine

1 When alcohol appears in a dream we may need or require a largely pleasurable experience or influence. We have available means of changing perception. We can afford to let go and go 'with the flow' of what is happening to us.

2 There is the recognition of the potential for emotional confusion out of which can come clarity. When the normal constraints we put on ourselves in waking life are removed, we can often reach our own truth. The symbol of alcohol can give us permission to do this.

3 Alcohol as 'spirit' is the conjunction of opposites, and a means of changing consciousness.

ALIEN

1 There is something unknown and frightening, which needs to be faced. We have never encountered the strangeness of the being which appears in our dream, and we must handle what happens.

2 There is the potential for experiencing oneself – or a part of oneself – as not belonging. In dreams there is the realisation of being different from others in the way we live our lives.

3 Something alien suggests Evil or, as something different, the Occult.

ALONE

1 Dreaming of **being alone** highlights being single, isolated or lonely. More positively, it represents the need for independence. Loneliness can be experienced as a negative state, whereas being alone can be very positive. Often in dreams a feeling is highlighted in order for us to recognise whether it is positive or negative.

2 There is the ability to recognise the necessity to deal with one's own emotional make-up without the help of others.

3 There is a completeness, a wholeness.

ALTAR
– also see Table

1 An altar in a dream represents

the means or need to give oneself up to something that is more important than the immediate situation. Usually an altar represents religious belief of some sort. It is the table of communion – togetherness – but also it often suggests the division between the physical and the spiritual.

2 Psychologically, this depicts being sacrificed either willingly or unwillingly. The act of sacrifice, or of making sacred, needs to be made in public so that it can be properly acknowledged *(See Sacrifice)*.

3 In the presence of the Divine, we can give thanks, and be at one.

AMNESIA

1 To suffer from amnesia in a dream indicates our attempts to blot out the disliked. It also indicates a fear of change. Losing one's memory in real life can be traumatic, but in dreams it can be even more of a problem since we do not know how much we actually should remember. We do not know how much is viable, and how much is presented for the purposes of that dream only.

2 Psychologically we fear losing access to knowledge, of knowing how to behave. Often we wake up feeling we have dreamt, but cannot remember the dream. This

can be because it is too painful to deal with the trauma that lies behind the images created. We are consciously able to forget until such times as we are courageous enough to deal with those images.

3 Amnesia in dreams can suggest death, either past or present. This may not be a physical death, but a time of great change in the dreamer's life.

AMPUTATION

1 When we dream of **amputation of one of our own limbs** we risk or fear losing or cutting off, by repressing, a part of ourselves. There is loss of a facility or something we value. To dream of **amputating someone else's** limb indicates our ability to deny others their right to self-expression.

2 We have cut short an experience in some way. We are suffering from a loss of power or ability.

3 Spiritually we may be disfiguring the perfect.

ANAESTHETIC

1 To be anaesthetised in a dream highlights the fact that we are trying to avoid painful emotions, and feeling overpowered by external circumstances. It also indicates that we are trying, or being forced, to avoid something.

2 We are numbing – or avoiding – something we don't want to face. We may be creating a situation which requires external management. We perhaps need to be quiescent and let events unfold around us.

3 As with amnesia, an anaesthetic can be a possible indication of death, but usually of part of ourselves.

ANALYST

1 Whatever kind of analyst we dream about, we have within ourselves a monitor which alerts us to the need to analyse our actions and reactions. We should exercise self-awareness and analyse our lives, breaking it down into manageable parts.

2 The presence of an analyst can represent the knowledge that we are not acting appropriately in a situation in waking life.

3 We are in contact with the transformative power within.

ANCHOR

1 When an anchor appears in a dream it can generally be taken to mean the necessity to remain stable in emotional situations. We need to catch hold of a concept or idea which will give us a point of reference in difficult situations.

2 Psychologically, we need encour-

agement to develop the ability to 'hold fast' during a period of instability. If we can ride out the storm we shall survive. When **an anchor is being dragged** during a dream, the external forces are too great for us.

3 We are in the process of achieving hope of a future tranquillity.

ANDROGEN

1 If we dream of someone and cannot decide if they are male or female, we are making an attempt to reconcile the opposite sides of ourselves. We are searching for completion and wholeness.

2 We need the understanding of how our emotional selves can balance our personalities. We often need to reconcile opposing thoughts and feelings within ourselves to achieve a balanced progression.

3 The androgen can indicate a perfect spiritual balance, a state of autonomy and primordial perfection.

ANGEL
– also see Religious Imagery

1 Dreaming of angels indicates we are searching for a parental figure which gives unconditional love and support, or that we need to develop these qualities ourselves. We may be trying to introduce religious concepts into our lives.

2 The relationship with the mother or mother figure needs to be looked at as a separate entity to both her and the dreamer. The angel is the personification of that relationship.

3 Nowadays with a greater acceptance of the appearance of angelic figures they are once again accepted as messengers of the Gods – heavenly powers and enlightenment.

ANGER

1 Anger in a dream can often represent other passionate emotions. We are struggling with the right to express that which is distressing us. We probably are unable to express emotion appropriately in waking life, but can do so in dreams.

2 We can give ourselves permission to feel passion, which could be sexual or otherwise. Often the way we express emotion in dreams can give us information as to appropriate behaviour in everyday life.

3 We are suffering divine displeasure.

ANIMA/ANIMUS
– also see Introduction

1 When we dream of a figure of the opposite sex we are attempting to give meaning and validity to the attributes and qualities of that particular sex. Thus a man may be trying to access his more sensitive side, while a woman may be attempting to become more logical.

2 We are attempting to balance our psychological being through an ability to be objective about ourselves. Only through understanding that we hold within us elements of the opposite sex, can we become whole and properly integrated.

3 The polarity of the way we express our own gender is an equally valid part of our personality.

ANIMALS

1 When animals appear in a dream they usually represent an aspect of the personality which cannot be properly understood except on an instinctive level.

Animal with a cub This will represent motherly qualities and therefore the mother.

Baby animals The dreamer will be dealing with the child-like side of his or her personality, or possibly children known to him.

The hurt young animal The dreamer may perceive a difficulty in becoming mature or facing life.

Eating the animal The dream could be about the 'demons' one creates which can only be over-come by assimilating them in a constructive way. Pagan belief thought that one took up certain aspects of the animal that were superior – in certain respects – to ordinary human attitudes.

Godlike, talking awe-inspiring or wise animals, or those with human characteristics Animals have not yet become conscious of, or pitted themselves against, the power from which they came so the wisdom they show is innocent and simple. It is always important to pay attention to this aspect of animal life in fairy tales and dreams, since we need to be in touch with that part of ourselves.

Helpful animals The subconscious is producing helpful images from its depths. The figures of animals are an easy way for the dreamer to accept that help.

Killing the animal may destroy the energy derived from the instincts. Taming or harnessing the animal shows the efforts made to control the dreamer's instincts and, if possible, make them productive and useful.

To dream of trying to find some refuge from animals whether by building defences – or perhaps by running away – is indicative of the dreamer's struggle with his animal instincts, and whether the action being taken is adequate. Such instincts may be threatening or damaging to aspects of the dreamer's life.

2 When we need some sort of understanding of our own psychological urges, animals will appear which symbolise those qualities. These are:

Bear The mother *(see Family)* appears in dreams in many forms, the bear being one of them. The image may be of the possessive, devouring mother or of the all-caring mother. If it is recognised in the dream that the **bear is masculine** the image may then be of an overbearing person, or possibly the father.

Bull Usually the bull in a dream denotes the negative side of behaviour, such as destructiveness, fear or anger (for example a bull in a china shop). However, more positively, the bull is recognised as sexual passion or creative power. **Slaying the bull** indicates initiation into the world of the mature adult who succeeds in mastering his instincts and can also represent the sign of Taurus in the Zodiac.

Cat To dream of cats is to link with the feline, sensuous side in human beings, usually in women. Goddesses such as Bast the Egyptian cat goddess are usually represented as having two sides to their natures, one devious and one helpful, so the cat often denotes the capricious side of the feminine. The elegant but also the powerful, yet overly self-sufficient aspect of woman, may also be perceived as the cat.

Chameleon The dreamer is recognising either in himself or others the ability to adapt and to change according to surrounding circumstances.

Cold-blooded animals or reptiles The unfeeling, inhuman aspect of the instincts is often portrayed by reptiles and other cold-blooded animals. They are usually recognised as being destructive and alien.

Composite animals To dream of composite animals could indicate some confusion in sorting out what qualities are needed. The various qualities of the different animals of which they are made up need to be assimilated and integrated. There are two potentials of development in one figure.

Half-animal, half-man The dreamer's animal instincts are beginning to be recognised and humanised.

Cow The eternal feminine, especially the mother *(see Family)* or mother figure *(see Archetypes)* is often depicted by the cow. This is partly

because it provides milk and nourishment.

Deer/Reindeer The deer and the reindeer herd have a strict hierarchical structure. The dreamer recognises his place in the world. The deer symbolises pride/nobility.

Deformed animals The dreamer realises that some of his impulses are offensive, or revolting.

Dog – *also see individual entry* The dreamer may recognise a faithful and constant companion, a protector or more negatively, somebody the dreamer can't shake off and who might make trouble. **A dog that the dreamer owned or knew at some period of his life** There may be memories associated with that period of his life, which hold clues to present behaviour. **A huntress with dogs** The dreamer is making a connection with one of the feminine archetypes, that of the Amazon *(see Archetypes)*. **A dog guarding gates, being near a cemetery** In dreams this indicates the guardian of the threshold, and creatures which must be put to sleep or tamed before there can be an initiation into the underworld

Domesticated (tame) animals When we dream of domesticated animals we are aware of those parts of ourselves with which we have come to terms. There are passions which are being used in a controlled way although there is the suggestion that those passions were never very formidable.

Elephant To see an elephant in a dream is to recognise the qualities of patience, long memory, strength and fidelity. In the more esoteric sense it signifies radiant and glowing wisdom.

Fox A fox in a dream tells of hypocrisy, cunning and slyness.

Frog A period or act of transformation (a frog transforms from a tadpole and moves on to the land). There is something repugnant which is turning into something of value (i.e. a frog into a prince). *Also see Snake* as all reptiles have the same significance.

Goat To dream of a goat is to recognise creative energy and masculine vitality. It may also represent the dark side of human nature, promiscuousness and sexuality. **To be riding a goat** is to be trying to come to terms with the dreamer's relationship with the dark side of his nature. The goat may also represent the Devil or Satan. It is also the symbol for Capricorn.

Hare The hare highlights intuition, spiritual insight and intuitive 'leaps'. Intuition may be debased into madness by fear or ignorance. Because of its association with the moon, the hare can, in its negative aspect, signify the Priestess/Witch aspect of femininity or the Priest/Sorcerer of the masculine *(see Archetypes)*. In its positive imagery however it is the radiant hare (often holding its baby in a cave) and thus the Mother of God.

Hedgehog The hedgehog can represent evil and bad manners, or literally our inability to handle a 'prickly' situation.

Horse The horse in a dream represents the energy at the dreamer's disposal. **A white horse** depicts the spiritual awareness of the dreamer; **a brown one** the more pragmatic and down-to-earth side, while **a black horse** is the passionate side of the dreamer's nature. **A pale horse** is taken to indicate death, and **a winged horse** depicts the soul's ability to transcend the earthly plane. If the horse is **under strain or dying** there is a severe weakening of the dynamic power that carries the dreamer forward. Too much pressure may be being experienced in our lives. If the horse is **being harnessed to a cart** the dreamer may be concentrating too hard on thoroughly utilitarian objectives. **In a man's dream, a mare** will denote the Anima, a woman; or the realm of the feminine *(see Archetypes)*. **In a**

woman's dream, being kicked by a horse may indicate the Animus or her relationship with a man. **A horse that can get through any door and batter down all obstacles** is the collective Shadow *(see Introduction)* – those aspects of the personality which most people attempt to suppress. **The horse as a beast of burden** is often the Great Mother *(See Introduction)*, or mother archetype *(see Archetypes)*. In modern dreams the car has largely taken over from the horse as a symbol with many of the same associations *(see Car and Journey Sections)*.

Hyena The hyena is generally taken in dreams to signify impurity, instability and deviousness.

Jackal The jackal is associated with the graveyard, and therefore with Death. As a scavenger it is also a cleanser. Esoterically, it is the servant of the transformer, guiding souls from the earth plane into the light.

Jaguar The jaguar's main qualities are its speed and balance. It stands for the balance of power between the dark and light forces.

Kangaroo This somewhat exotic animal often stands for motherhood, and also strength.

Lamb The lamb is the innocent side of man's nature. It is said that evil cannot withstand such innocence.

Leopard The leopard represents cruelty and aggression, and traditionally the deviousness of wrongly used power.

Lion The lion stands for majesty, strength and courage. It can also represent the ego and the passions associated with it. If the dreamer is **struggling with the lion** there should be a successful development as long as the dreamer is not overpowered, or the lion killed. **A man-eating lion** shows that an aspect of the personality has slipped out of alignment, putting both the dreamer and his surroundings at risk. **A lion lying with a lamb** There is a union, or compatibility of opposites; instinct and spirit going hand in hand.

Lizard – *also see Reptiles* The lizard appearing in a dream represents instinctive action or 'one-track' thinking.

Lynx The main quality associated with the lynx is its keen eyesight, thus in a dream it can often portray objectivity.

Monkey The monkey characterises the infantile, childish and arrested side of the dreamer's character. The qualities of mischief, impudence and inquisitiveness all belong to the monkey. While these are often seen as regressive tendencies, that of lively curiosity maintains a necessary lightness of spirit.

Mare – *see Horse*

Mole The mole is often taken to represent the powers of darkness, but can often signify the blind persistence and determination which enables the dreamer to succeed.

Monster/Dragon – *also see Dragon in D Section* A fear which is beyond understanding, usually welling up from within rather than from the outside world, is often represented in dreams by monsters and dragons. **The devouring monster** The dream may deal with a recognition that ultimately we are all absorbed back into a greater whole. If the **dreamer gets the better of the monster** he will have mastery over his own fear of death, and may be able to harness this force for his own use. **Cutting out the monster's heart or other vital organ, or lighting a fire inside it,** depicts the struggle against the dark forces of the underworld.

Mouse – *also see Vermin* The mouse's quality of timidity can often be addressed in the dreamer, if it is recognised that this can arise from turbulence and lack of understanding.

Otter The otter is uniquely equipped to exist within its chosen element of water and to be able to gain subsistence from its environment, all things the dreamer may need to develop.

Ox The ox depicts the ability to be patient, and to make sacrifices for others.

Parts of animals (the limbs, eyes, mouth, etc.) These have the same significance as parts of the human body *(see Body)*. **If the four legs are particularly emphasised** – possibly in contrast with a three-legged animal – the whole rounded personality with all four functions of the mind fully developed is being highlighted.

Pig or Wild Boar The **pig** is taken in Western belief to indicate ignorance, stupidity, selfishness, and gluttony. The dreamer's better self may be beginning to recognise these unattractive qualities in himself. Without such recognition there can be no transformation or mastery of them. **Pigs and jewels** There is a conflict between the lower urges and spiritual values. Perhaps there is a failure to appreciate spiritual values. **Big litters of piglets** can represent fruitfulness, although sometimes without result, since the sow can depict the Destructive Mother *(see Archetypes)*. **Wild Boar** The wild boar depicts the archetypal masculine principal, and therefore the negative Animus in a woman's dream. *(See Introduction)*. The dreamer may be evading an issue that should be challenged and dealt with more daringly.

Prehistoric animals A trauma from the past, or from childhood, may be causing difficulty.

Rabbit Rabbits appearing in a dream can mean one of two things. The obvious connection with fertility could be important or it could be that the trickster aspect of the personality could be coming to the fore *(see Hare)*. **A white rabbit** may show the dreamer the way to the inner spiritual world and, as such, act as a guide.

Ram The ram is a symbol of masculine virility and power, and by association has those qualities of the sign of Aries in the Zodiac.

Rat – *also see Vermin* The rat signifies the diseased and devious part of the dreamer or of his situation. It can also represent something which is repulsive in some way. The dreamer may be experiencing disloyalty from a friend or colleague.

Reptiles To dream of reptiles indicates that we are looking at the more frightening lower aspects of the personality. We may have no control over these, and could

therefore be easily devoured by them. We are afraid of Death or the death process, but must go through a process of change in order to be reborn.

Seal Dreaming of a seal suggests that we are at one with the element in which we live.

Serpent – *also see Snake* The serpent is a universal symbol which can be male or female or it can be self-created. It can signify death or destruction or conversely life and also rejuvenation. It is the instinctive nature and is also potential energy. When the power of the instinctive nature is understood and harnessed, the dreamer comes to terms with his or her own sexuality and sensuality and is able to make use of the higher and more spiritual energies which become available. **In a man's dream** a snake may appear if he has not understood the feminine or intuitive part of himself, or when he doubts his own masculinity. **In a woman's dream** the snake may manifest if she is afraid of sex, or sometimes of her own ability to seduce others. Because of its connection with the Garden of Eden, the serpent is the symbol of duplicity and trickery, and also of temptation.

Sheep The sheep is renowned for its flock instinct, and it is this interpretation which is most usually accepted in dreams. The helplessness of the sheep when off balance is also another aspect which is recognisable, as is the apparent lack of intelligence. The god-fearing, 'good sheep' and also the passive and 'sheepish' may have relevance within the context of the dream. **To dream of sheep and wolves or of sheep and goats** is to register the conflict between good and evil.

Sinister Animals Any threat from animals indicates the fears and doubts the dreamer has over his ability to cope with the stirrings of the unconscious.

Snake – *also see Serpent*. Snake dreams occur – like serpent dreams – when the dreamer is attempting to come to terms with his or her more instinctive self. Inevitably, this has to do with the recognition and harnessing of energies which have been suppressed and thwarted. Since the most primeval urge is sexuality, the image of the snake is the most primitive one available. **A snake twined around the body or limb** This indicates some form of bondage, possibly being enslaved to the passions. **A snake, or worm, leaving a corpse by its mouth** This can sometimes represent the sexual act (the little death), but can also signify the

dreamer's control of his or her libido. **A snake in the grass** This image denotes disloyalty, trickery and evil. **With its tail in its mouth** This image is one of the oldest available to man and signifies completion and the union of the spiritual and physical *(see Shapes, Circle)*. **Being swallowed by a snake** This shows the need and ability to return to the ultimate, and lose our sense of space and time *(see Eating)*.

Because snakes are such a low form of life, while also being in some cases poisonous, they have become associated with death, and all that man fears. **Snake twined around a staff or similar** *(see Caduceus)* The unconscious forces that are released once the dreamer reconciles the opposing sides of himself create healing, rebirth and renewal, and this is universally represented as two snakes entwined round a central staff. It is a symbolic representation of the basic form of DNA, the 'building blocks' of life. The colours of the snake may give additional insight into the meaning of the dream *(see Colours)*.

Squirrel The squirrel represents the hoarding aspect of our personalities.

Tiger The tiger signifies royalty, dignity and power and is both a creator and a destroyer

Toad To dream of toads is to connect with whatever the dreamer may consider ugly in life, or in his behaviour. However, implicit in that ugliness is the power of transformation and growth into something beautiful. For **a toad and an eagle to appear** is to note the difference between earthly and spiritual values.

Transformation of animals In dreams, the metamorphosis of the dreamer or other people into animals and vice versa shows the potential for change within any situation.

Unicorn The unicorn is a symbol of purity and traditionally could only be owned and perceived by virgins. It is a return to, and a resurgence of, an innocence necessary in self-understanding, and it often suggests the control of the ego and selfishness.

Vermin In dreams vermin may represent the enforced contemplation of something that is unnecessary or that has invaded one's space.

Vertebrates Animals with backbones often give an understanding of the qualities associated with that animal. The smaller and lower orders of animal signify the unconscious, the higher orders the emotions.

Whale The whale, because it is a mammal which lives within water, indicates the power of resurrection and rebirth – man's ability to come back from the dead.

Weasel The weasel traditionally highlights the devious, more criminally oriented side of ourselves.

Werewolf – *see Sinister Animals*

Wild animals Usually wild animals stand for danger, dangerous passions, or dangerous people. There is a destructive force arising from the unconscious, threatening the safety of the individual. Such a dream may be a way of understanding anxiety. **Domesticating wild animals** The dreamer may have come to terms with his or her wilder side.

Wolf Dreaming of wolves may indicate that we are being threatened by others, whether singly or by the pack. The dreamer may have cruel sadistic fantasies without taking responsibility for them. **The She-wolf** The hussy, but also the carer for orphans and rejected young.

Wounded animals The dreamer may be suffering either emotional or spiritual wounds.

Zebra This animal has the same significance as the horse, but with the additional meaning of balancing the negative and the positive in a very dynamic way.

3 By understanding animals and their symbolism we approach life in a more simplistic and natural way.

ANKH

1 The symbolism is similar to that of a cross. It represents the dreamer's concept of the universe, or his religious beliefs.

2 The symbolism of the ankh is that of all encircling power and protection throughout the trials and tribulations of physical life. It is the link between the human and Divine.

3 The ankh is a key to the way to knowledge of hidden wisdom.

ANTLERS
– also see Horns

1 The deer is a noble animal, so the interpretation differs if the antlers are **mounted, as in a trophy,** or are seen **on the animal**. If the latter then the interpretation is that of something which is supernormal, and may represent intellectual powers. If the former, then antlers may be interpreted as attempting to achieve high status.

2 Psychologically these represent awareness of the potential for conflict between one's nobler self and the baser instincts.

3 Supernatural powers, fertility and nobleness of spirit are represented by antlers.

ANVIL

1 Depending on the dream circumstances, the anvil can represent the basic force of nature, brute force or a way of creating an initial spark. By creating a situation in our lives where we are going to be tried and tested, we are pitting ourselves against natural forces.

2 As an image of the spark of life and of initiation, the anvil was once a very strong symbol. That spark is now more often represented by the spark plugs in a car.

3 The anvil ties in with the Norse forge Gods. The symbolism is that of forging new life, creating new beginnings and so on.

APE
– also see Monkey in Animals

1 To dream of apes or monkeys links with the mischievous side of ourselves.

2 We all have within us the ability to mimic or to copy, and to dream of apes may alert us to this ability.

3 The ape suggests the Trickster, the mischievous side of evil.

APPLE
– also see Food and Fruit

1 In dreams this can represent

fruitfulness, love and temptation.
2 Eating an apple indicates the wish to be trying to take in information or knowledge. The apple obviously has connections with Eve's temptation of Adam.
3 Apple blossom is a Chinese symbol of peace and beauty. Spiritually an apple suggests a new beginning and a freshness of approach.

APPETITE

1 When an appetite is particularly noticeable in a dream it usually represents a desire which is unfulfilled. This will not necessarily be a physical desire, but could be emotional or spiritual.
2 To be hungry or thirsty in a dream can indicate lust and sexual desire.
3 This signifies a lust for life and a spiritual yearning.

APRON

1 This can represent a badge of office or family ties. It depends on the gender of the dreamer and the content of the dream whether this image is negative or positive.
2 If worn by the dreamer this may indicate the need for skill. If **worn by someone else** that part of the dreamer which is represented by the other person may need protecting.

3 As in Freemasonry, this suggests craftsmanship and sacrificial regalia.

APPOINTMENT

1 Dreaming of **going to an appointment** indicates we need to have an aim or a goal. The dream is bringing to our notice something our inner self feels we need to deal with. **Missing an appointment** suggests we are not paying enough attention to detail.
2 We can perhaps give ourselves a gift or a reward for good work. There is something which has to be accomplished within a certain time limit.
3 We need to keep, or make use of, time in the most spiritually effective way.

ARC

1 We need to concentrate on a particular part of our lives.
2 Psychologically, we are paying attention only to a segment or portion of what we are trying to deal with at the present time.
3 There is a dynamism available which will enhance the growth of the dreamer.

ARCH

1 When we dream of arches or doorways, we are often moving into a different environment or way of life. We have to go through some form of initiation, or acceptance ritual in order to succeed.

2 We are in the process of passing a test. We may be being protected by authority.

3 We are experiencing some form of spiritual initiation. We are being born again, given a fresh start.

ARCHETYPES

1 Archetypes are basic pictures that each of us hold deep within our subconscious. They are in a sense 'psychic' blueprints. These blueprints – while potentially perfect – can become distorted by childhood experiences, socialisation and even parental experience.

C G Jung began studying archetypes and dividing function into thinking, feeling, sensation and intuition. Following various work by his pupils, it became possible to build up a type of 'map' of the interaction between all of these functions and to discover where one's own distortions occur. Each function has a 'positive' and 'negative' quality which is perhaps better described as 'greater' and 'lesser'. Each of the masculine and feminine sides of the personality has these four functions, thus there are 64 (8 x 8) interactions possible. Where a distortion has occurred, we tend to project onto those around us the archetype with which we have most difficulty (often the Shadow). Consequently there will be a tendency to repeat situations over and over (e.g. the woman who continually finds herself in close relationships with a father-figure type, or the man who continually finds

MALE	FEMALE	POSITIVE/ NEGATIVE	FUNCTION
KINDLY FATHER OGRE	KINDLY MOTHER DESTRUCTIVE MOTHER	+ -	SENSATION
YOUTH TRAMP	PRINCESS SIREN	+ -	FEELING
HERO VILLAIN	AMAZON COMPETITOR	+ -	THINKING
PRIEST SORCERER	PRIESTESS WITCH	+ -	INTUITION

himself at odds with women executives) until we learn how to cope with – and understand – our distortion. The obverse of this is that, with awareness, one is able to accept other's projections onto oneself without being affected by them.

Perfect balance would be achieved by using all aspects of the personality as shown below.

Kindly Father and Mother are self explanatory. Ogre represents masculine anger used negatively and Destructive Mother may be wilfully destructive, or simply the smothering type – that is the mother who prevents the adequate growth of her children. Youth and Princess are the more gentle, fun-loving aspects of the personality while Tramp is the eternal wanderer and Siren is the seductress or sexually active part of femininity. Hero is the self-sufficient Messianic part of the personality, while Amazon is the 'self-sufficient' female – the efficient business woman type. Villain is the masculine part of the self who uses power for his own ends, while Competitor is the typical 'women's libber' who feels that she has no need for men. Priest and Priestess are the powers of intuition used for the 'greater good', while Sorcerer uses inner power totally dispassionately and Witch uses that same power rather more emotionally and perhaps negatively.

2 More specifically the feminine archetypes are:

Kindly Mother – This is the conventional picture of the caring mother figure, forgiving transgression and always understanding. Because much has been made of this side of femininity, until recently it was very easy to overdevelop this aspect at the expense of other sides of the personality.

Destructive Mother – This woman may be the 'smother-mother' type or the frankly destructive, prohibitive mother. Often it is this aspect who either actively prevents or – because of her effect on the dreamer – causes difficulty in other relationships.

Princess – The fun-loving, innocent childlike aspect of femininity. She is totally spontaneous, but at the same time has a subjective approach to other people.

Siren – This type is the seductress, the sexually and sensually aware woman who still has a sense of her own importance. In dreams she often appears in historic, flowing garments as though to highlight the erotic image.

Amazon – The self-sufficient

woman who feels she does not need the male; often becomes the career woman. She enjoys the cut and thrust of intellectual sparring.

Competitor – She is the woman who competes with all and sundry – both men and women – in an effort to prove that she is able to control her own life.

Priestess – This is the highly intuitive woman who has learnt to control the flow of information and use it for the common good. She is totally at home within the inner world.

Witch – The intuitive woman using her energy to attain her own perceived ends. She is subjective in her judgement and therefore loses her discernment.

The masculine archetypes are:

Kindly Father – This side of the masculine is the conventional kindly father figure who is capable of looking after the child in us, but equally of being firm and fair.

Ogre – This represents the angry, overbearing, aggressive and frightening masculine figure. Often this image has arisen because of the original relationship the dreamer had with their father or father figure.

Youth – The fun-loving, curious aspect of the masculine is both sensitive and creative. This is the

'Peter Pan' figure who has never grown up.

Tramp – This is the real freedom lover, the wanderer, the gypsy. He owes no allegiance to anyone and is interested only in what lies around the next corner.

Hero – The hero is the man who has elected to undertake his own journey of exploration. He is able to consider options and decide his next move. Often he appears as the Messianic figure in dreams. He will rescue the damsel in distress, but only as part of his growth process.

Villain – The villain is completely selfishly involved, not caring who he tramples on in his own search. He is often the aspect of masculinity women first meet in everyday relationships, so can remain in dream images as a threatening figure if she has not come to terms with his selfishness.

Priest – The intuitive man is the one who recognises and understands the power of his own intuition, but who usually uses it in the services of his god or gods. He may appear in dreams as the Shaman or Pagan priest.

Sorcerer – This is the man who uses discernment in a totally dispassionate way for neither good nor evil, but simply because he enjoys the use of power. In his more negative aspect he is the Trickster or Master of unexpected change.

3 Spiritually, when we have access to all the archetypes, we are ready to become integrated and whole.

ARENA

1 Dreaming of being **in an arena either as a player or as a spectator** highlights the fact that we may need to make the decision to move into a specifically created environment, one which gives more room for self-expression and creativity or theatricality.

2 We are developing a new focus of attention, or an area of conflict. This conflict may need to be brought out into the open, into open forum.

3 Today sport is often used as an energy release. Spiritually, an arena suggests a ritualised conflict.

ARMS

– also see Body and Weapons

1 We use our arms in all sorts of different ways, and in dreams it is often significant to note what is actually taking place. We may be defending ourselves, fighting, being held or acknowledging.

2 Arms – in the sense of **weapons** – are used to protect and defend. In olden times, there were quite a series of rituals to do

with the Page becoming the Knight and making the transit from the arms-bearer to the user.

3 The arm signifies surrender, wisdom, or action.

ARMOUR

1 We need to be aware of e motional and intellectual rigidity in either ourselves or others around us. If **we are in armour** we may be overprotecting o urselves, whereas if **others are in armour** we may be overly aware of their defence mechanisms.

2 We may be protecting ourselves from something we feel is threatening us. Our way of protecting ourselves may, however, be outdated and inappropriate in the present circumstances.

3 Armour signifies chivalry, protection and the need to protect or be protected.

ARRESTED

– also see Authority Figures in People

1 To dream of **being arrested** suggests the restraint of one's natural self-expression by moral judgements or questions of right or wrong from other people. To dream of **arresting someone else** would indicate our instinctive disapproval of that part of ourselves which is represented by that person in the dream.

2 Psychologically, we are unsure of our motives in an action we are contemplating. We should stop and carefully consider our behaviour before we act.

3 There is a need for authority.

ARROW

1 If we dream of **shooting arrows** we are aware of the consequences of actions, either our own or other people's, which cannot be recalled or revoked. Interestingly enough, arrows can also symbolise words in dreams.

2 Communications which we make could be damaging to other people. We could either hurt or be hurt by directness.

3 Arrows as weapons suggest power, energy and expertise.

ARTIST

1 The artist in a dream makes us recognise the artist in us. We are aware of the aspect of ourselves which is in contact with the irrational, creative side of the unconscious.

2 We need to make use of our desire or ability to be creative. We may also be linking with that part of ourselves which records events for posterity.

3 The Creator, the Guiding Principle often manifests as the artist in dreams.

ASCENDING

1 We are becoming conscious of being able to exercise control over passion or sexual pleasure.

2 The transition from expressing our energy through sex to expressing it in self-awareness is often shown as ascending. If we are **climbing stairs, going up in an elevator or lift** we are making a movement towards waking or becoming more aware; we are making an escape from anxiety or being down to earth and are freeing ourselves from physical constraints.

3 We are searching for spiritual awareness.

ASCENSION

1 The act of Ascension is a breakthrough to a new spiritual plane which transcends the state of being human. It is an awareness of different levels of concentration, which give a different perspective to being human.

2 Ascension is an altered state of consciousness which can occur as a result of meditation and spiritual practices. In dreams it is seen as acceptable and real, and is often accompanied by symbols of paradise.

3 Ascension frequently follows the experience of a descent into the underworld.

ASCETIC

1 There is some conflict with natural drives. There may be an avoidance of sex or contact through fear or the need for restraint. In a dream **to meet an ascetic or holy man** is to meet our higher self, and to recognise the part of ourselves which is continually seeking unity with the divine. We may be looking for simplicity.

2 Psychologically, we are searching for purity in ourselves or in others. Equally, we may be afraid of that purity within ourselves and need to come to terms with it.

3 There is an attempt to find the spiritual in our lives and also a development of will.

ASHES

1 Ashes in a dream often indicate penitence and sorrow. We are aware that we have been over-anxious and stupid within a situation, and that there is little left to be done. That situation has outlived its usefulness. After an event or person has gone we may dream of a fire that has burnt out, leaving ashes. These are what remains of our experience which will enable us to make the best of a situation.

2 A memory or a learnt wisdom needs to be retained in order for us to use information.

3 These represent purification and death, the perishable human body and mortality.

ATOM BOMB
– also see Nuclear Explosion

1 Where anxiety regarding the external world is experienced, the dreamer may need to be aware that the end of a particular way of life is imminent in an especially dramatic fashion. Often there is a sense of an explosion of destructive energy before everything must be rebuilt.

2 There is a fear of irrationality and of power which could be used wrongly. An atom bomb is a deliberately engineered explosion designed to be destructive. The dreamer may feel that someone else may destroy and nullify his carefully constructed life.

3 We have become aware of the uncontrollable forces of life and the unconscious.

ATTACK

1 Being attacked in a dream indicates a fear of being under threat from external events or internal emotions. Unknown impulses or ideas force the dreamer into taking a defensive attitude. If we are **being attacked by animals** we are turning our own aggression and/or sexuality inwards; we have fear of our own natural urges.

2 If the dreamer is the attacker he needs to defend himself by positive self-expression – he is making attempts to destroy some urge or feeling in himself or others.

3 There is a Spiritual or psychic threat.

AUDIENCE

1 If we are standing **in front of an audience** in a dream we are probably having to deal with an important issue in our lives. If we are **in the audience** we are witnessing an emotion or process of change in ourselves.

2 We need to be carefully considering some aspect of our lives, particularly one which takes place in public. We are the creators of our own play and an audience may also represent the various parts of our own personality we have created.

3 The audience tends to be the multiple parts of our personality.

AURA
– also see Nimbus and Religious Imagery

1 To perceive an aura in a dream indicates how powerful we consider ourselves – or others – to be.

2 The aura is a representation of

the power we hold within, the force field with which we repel and attract people.

3 The aura is an energy field which surrounds the physical body. It is an expression of the Self.

AUTHORITY FIGURES
(Such as teachers etc.) – see Individual Entries and also see Authority Figures in People Section

AUTUMN

1 We are being made conscious of the sense of something coming to an end. We recognise that the good in a situation can be brought in and made use of, but the rest must be given up.

2 Psychologically, we need to consider the cycles that occur in our own lives and whether some of these can be brought to an end.

3 The autumn of one's life – with the mellow feelings and all that old age brings – is symbolised by Autumn appearing in a dream.

AVALANCHE

1 If we **witness an avalanche** in our dreams we are experiencing a destructive force. If we are **in the middle of an avalanche** we are being overwhelmed by circumstances.

2 Psychologically, we need to

regain control of forces outside ourselves. We are in a position which puts us in some kind of danger.

3 The power of frozen emotions could overwhelm us.

AXE
– also see Weapons

1 When we dream of an axe we need to differentiate between whether it is being **used against us** or if **we are using** it. If it is used against us we feel we are being threatened by someone's greater power. To dream of **using an axe** indicates that we need to become aware of the destructive forces within us.

2 There is that in us which can only be dealt with in a destructive fashion. It must be cut out completely.

3 The axe represents power, thunder, conquest of error and sacrifice.

B

from

Bachelor *to* Butterfly

BACHELOR

1 To dream of **meeting a bachelor** indicates that we are searching for freedom either within our emotions or in our love life. **If the dreamer is male**, he may be wishing for the freedom to achieve something he might find difficult in partnership.

2 We need to open up the masculine side of ourselves in order to accomplish our destiny.

3 A bachelor in a dream can highlight the side of us which does not require emotional ties at this particular time.

BACK

– also see Body

1 Dreaming of **seeing someone's back** suggests we should identify the more private elements in our character. We may also find that we are vulnerable to the unexpected. If we dream of **turning our backs** we are rejecting the particular feeling being experienced in the dream.

2 There is a possibility that we are repressing our own urges or do not want to look at our inner feelings. We are in touch with the past and with memories.

3 Spiritually, we have to turn our back on the past and reject the known. It will be up to the dreamer to decide which elements of the past need rejecting.

BACKBONE

– also see Body

1 If the backbone is particularly noticeable in the dream we need to consider our main support structure.

2 Intellectually we need to consider our firmness of character.

3 In certain dreams the backbone – because it is the most stable part of our structure – signifies the Self.

BACKWARDS

1 To dream of going backwards indicates that we may be withdrawing from a situation or slow to learn from it. We may need to recognise that to continue in a particular situation will stop our progress.

2 Mentally we are not using our best faculties. When she looked backwards, Lot's wife was turned into a pillar of salt. To look back into the past can be detrimental.

3 Regressive tendencies can cause us to move backwards into previous behaviour patterns. The dreamer should take note of what is happening in his life at this time, and determine the reasons for this.

BAD

1 When we dream of something

being bad we are being made aware that the dream object is now worthless or defective. **Feeling bad** can have two meanings; one in the sense of **being naughty** and the other **not feeling right**. We are off balance in some way.

2 Our thought processes are corrupt. **If we dream of food being bad,** we are not taking sufficient care of our inner needs. A bad smell in dreams could mean that our environment is not supporting us.

3 Acknowledgement of Evil through a 'bad thing'.

BADGE

1 To have our attention drawn in a dream to a badge makes us aware of our right to belong to a group.

2 We have been singled out for particular recognition, possibly because we have certain qualities. A badge can also have the same meaning as a talisman.

3 A badge signifies an emblem of office. Dreaming of one shows our need to be accepted not just as ourselves, but also as part of a greater whole.

BAG

1 The dreamer may be having problems with the feminine elements in his or her identity.

There is an ability to use the social graces to achieve, and to cope with whatever occurs.

2 Depending on the actual bag (e.g. **a handbag a shopping bag**), we may be hiding certain aspects of ourselves from public consideration.

3 A bag spiritually signifies the Secret, the Hidden and the Occult. It will be the dreamer's decision as to whether he 'opens the bag' and makes use of its contents.

BAGGAGE

1 To be carrying extra baggage in a dream we may be carrying an extra load, either emotional or practical. We may be expecting too much of ourselves or of others. We are carrying past hurt or trauma.

2 The dreamer is under some psychological stress, and may have to decide projects or feelings can be left behind in waking life.

3 An indication of the dreamer's feelings of sorrow can manifest in dreams as baggage. However, sorrow, like baggage, may be lost as easily as it is taken on board – it is well worth the dreamer remembering this.

BAILIFF
– also see Authority Figures in People

1 When a bailiff appears in our

dream, we doubt our own ability to manage our resources. We are aware that we have overstepped the mark in a particular way and must be accountable to some type of authority.

2 We have put ourselves at risk and have not fulfilled our obligations. Unless we take responsibility for what we have done we could be 'punished' by material loss and loss of status.

3 The bailiff in dreams signifies retribution or Karma of some kind.

BAIT

1 In a woman's dream putting down bait can be an indication of her doubts about her own ability to attract a partner. She may feel that she has to entrap or ensnare a partner.

2 There is an aspect of our lives which needs bringing out into the open. We have to fool that part of ourselves which is failing to co-operate in making progress. There is some kind of enticement which has to take place.

3 Spiritually, we must 'tempt' evil in some way in order to trap it, and ultimately control it.

BAKER
– also see Oven

1 We all have within us the ability to alter our approach or attitude to situations in our lives Dreaming of a baker alerts us to this ability.

2 Our creative ability may need to be enhanced or lightened in order for us to achieve success. **If a woman dreams of baking** she will recognise this as her need to nurture.

3 The Creative Urge, which may need to be pacified, can be seen as the baker.

BALANCE

1 When we dream of trying to **maintain our balance** or of being **balanced in a difficult position** we are searching for equilibrium. To dream of searching for the **balance in a financial account** means we are looking for something which, at present, remains unrecognised and unknown.

2 To have the feeling that we are looking for the **balance of a quantity of goods** indicates we have more mental assets that we had first realised and need to start using them.

3 The Zodiac sign of Libra. Justice – and therefore balance – is symbolised by the scales. The dreamer may need to look at what his own sense of justice is, and whether or not it is being served.

BALCONY
– also see Buildings

1 To dream of being **on a balcony** indicates that we are searching for a higher status than we have at present. To dream of being **underneath a balcony** indicates that we are aware of other people's need for status.

2 Psychologically we are searching for power within a situation in which we feel powerless.

3 When we dream of being elevated in some way, we are just recognising our spiritual competence or progression.

BALD

1 To dream of **someone who is bald** indicates we are being made aware of a degree of dullness in our lives.

2 To dream of **ourselves being bald** can be somewhat ambiguous. It usually suggests a loss of intellectual prowess, but can also symbolise intelligence.

3 Baldness in a dream is recognition of the attainment of Spirituality with its attendant humility. Priests used to shave their heads to show they had nothing to hide.

BALL

1 A ball connects with the playful, childlike side of ourselves and our need to express ourselves with freedom. **Attending a ball** also suggests a need for freedom, but links with the more flamboyant side of ourselves.

2 If we are taking part in **games with a ball** *(see Games)* we are conscious of our need for both structure and freedom. Psychologically, the human being needs to celebrate special occasions. A ball – as in a **formal party** – allows him to do just this. In dreams this image may alert us to this requirement in ourselves.

3 Solar and Lunar festivals are often symbolised by the ball, as well as a feeling of impenetrable completeness.

BALLERINA
– also see Dance

1 The fairy-like appearance of the ballerina within a dream shows we are making a connection with that side of our being. Also we are searching for balance and poise.

2 We are aware of the creative side of ourselves, and the need for controlled movement. We are in touch with the expressiveness of our own inner being.

3 The ballerina symbolises music and the inner aspect of Feeling.

BALLOON

1 Very often it is the colour of balloons in our dreams which are important *(see Colour)*. However, they can also indicate a party mood or a desire for sex.

2 Balloons were once made of pig's bladders and were used by the court jester to lighten up the atmosphere around the king and to remind him that he was human. In dreams they may introduce a note of fun amid seriousness.

3 A balloon is a symbol for joy, often a feeling of 'light spirited' joy, or indeed the spirit rising.

BAMBOO

1 The pliability of bamboo indicates yielding but enduring strength. Being one of the most graceful but hardy plants, it also represents these qualities in the dreamer.

2 Intellectually, bamboo represents good breeding, long life and a fulfilling old age. It also represents the ability to yield when under pressure.

3 Perfect, but pliant, man is symbolised by the bamboo. If the dreamer recognises these two aspects within himself, he can if necessary begin to deal with flaws within his character.

BANANA
– also see Food and Fruit

1 Most dreams about fruit are to do with sexuality or sensuality.

Conventionally the banana, because of its shape, signifies the penis. However, it is also considered, because of its yielding nature, to represent the handling of masculine sexuality.

2 In conjunction with other fruit, it can be taken to mean fertility or sustenance.

3 The banana symbolises fertility.

BAND

1 If the image of a band is that of a **stripe,** there is some limitation within the dreamer's circumstances which needs to be recognised. If however the image is that of a **group of musicians**, this would indicate the need for teamwork.

2 There is an appreciation of harmony on a psychological level which needs to be made use of.

3 A band suggests harmony within the Self.

BANDAGE

1 If a **bandage is being applied** in a dream this shows the beginning of a healing process. There may be hurt feelings or emotional injuries which need attention.

2 We may have been made sick by some difficulty within our lives and need to pay attention to our ability to be healed. If **the bandage is**

coming off we may have overcome the difficulty, or we may have been careless.

3 Bandages signify preservation – as in the bandages of a mummy. So, in this instance the dreamer can analyse what he wants to preserve in his life and act accordingly.

BANK

1 The financial, mental or spiritual resources of the dreamer may need careful management. The sense of security, without which we cannot venture into the world, needs to be properly managed and monitored.

2 Our emotional resources, such as self-confidence, social ability and wisdom are held in reserve. There may be fear over the actual management of our resources.

3 A bank indicates a secure spiritual space.

BANKER

1 Money and personal resources tend to be the things with which most people have difficulty. Our need for an authority figure to help us deal with problems that arise are usually symbolised by the banker or bank manager in dreams.

2 Our internal resources need to be available to us in such a way that we have energy in reserve.

The banker represents the controlling part of ourselves.

3 A banker in a dream can suggest our right to have management of our Spiritual assets.

BANNER
– also see Flag

1 If the banner in the dream is a **commercial one**, it represents the need to have something which we may previously have ignored or rejected brought to our attention. If the banner is an old-fashioned one – as used in **medieval battles** – it indicates a need to consolidate thoughts and actions.

2 Psychologically we may adopt – or need to adopt – some kind of crusade. We need to know we have a common cause to fight for which is organised and specific.

3 A certain standard of spiritual behaviour is required of everybody. Therefore, to dream of a banner alerts us to this.

BANQUET

1 To dream of a banquet could have two meanings. If we are **serving** at one, we should be careful not to deny ourselves the good things in life by being too giving. If we are **attending** one, we should recognise our need to be nurtured.

2 We are not using our mental

faculties as well as we might. Intellectually, we are able to put ourselves in touch with a higher quality of mental nourishment than we have at present.

3 The banquet is a symbol of our need for spiritual nourishment and the need to feast on spirituality.

BAPTISM

1 To dream of **being baptised** indicates a new influence entering the dreamer's life, cleansing away old attitudes and opening up to one's inner possibilities. To dream of **baptising someone** means the dreamer is ready to pass on knowledge to other people.

2 There is the possibility that the dreamer may be having religious beliefs forced on him in some way, often for the greater good.

3 Baptism is symbolic of many things – initiation, death and rebirth, regeneration, renewal. The basic link of all these is the feeling of optimism that it brings.

BAR
– also see Public House

1 When we dream of a bar, such as an **iron bar**, we should look at how rigid or aggressive we are being in our behaviour. We need to handle ourselves with strength of purpose.

2 To **stand at a bar** may represent a barrier to our sexual enjoyment particularly in the male.

3 The bar is a symbol of our spiritual power, and power in everyday life.

BARB

1 To be surrounded by **barbed wire** in a dream indicates that we are being prevented from moving forward by either our own, or others, hurtful remarks.

2 Intellectually, we are trying to be too smart. Equally we may be trying to force other people to do something they do not want to do. **A barbed comment** is one which is specifically designed to hurt the recipient.

3 The barb is traditionally the fork that the Devil carried with him, with which to goad us into action.

BARBER

1 When we dream of **visiting a barber** we are considering a change of attitude, thought or opinion about ourselves.

2 An influence is becoming apparent in our lives which indicates a need for change. That change needs to be dictated by the way we perceive ourselves to be.

3 The old idea that one's spiritual power was held in the head gives rise to the idea that a barber signifies control of spiritual strength.

BARE

1 If the **dreamer is bare,** he or she is becoming aware of his or her vulnerability. If the **landscape is bare** there is a lack of happiness or perhaps of fertility.

2 Psychologically, we are in a situation which will not be capable of coming to fruition.

3 We are spiritually vulnerable when stripped of material things and living with the 'bare' necessities of life.

BAREFOOT

1 Depending on the circumstances of the dream, to be barefoot can indicate either poverty or the recognition of sensual freedom.

2 To be barefoot and not able to find one's shoes shows a lack of suitability, an awareness of inappropriate behaviour.

3 Being barefoot at one time indicated great humility. When Christ wished to show that he was no different to other men he washed his disciples' feet.

BASE

1 If our attention is drawn to the **base of an object** we may need to go back to the starting point of a project in which we are involved

in waking life. We should consider how stable we are in any situation.

2 To dream of **base metal** indicates that we are dealing with something which is somehow inferior and needs refining in some way.

3 Crudeness, unformed material. Our 'basic instincts' may be brought into question.

BASKET

1 To dream of a basket, particularly a full one, is to dream of full fruition and abundance. It can also represent the feminine closing principle.

2 To be **attempting to fill a basket** can mean that we are trying to increase our talents and abilities.

3 If the basket is **full of bread** it can represent sharing – as in a sacramental meal.

BAT

– also see Vampire

1 Because popular belief has it that bats are frightening, to dream of bats indicates that there are thoughts and ideas within the unconscious that may reveal themselves with frightening potential. Dreaming of a **cricket bat** or other such implement will give an indication of our attitude to controlled aggression, or to how we deal with external forces.

2 To dream of **bats attacking** us shows the need to confront fears of madness. We are not able to use implements such as cricket or baseball bats without some kind of training. To dream of using such a bat indicates a learnt degree of competence.

3 A flying bat can represent discernment or obscurity of a spiritual kind. The obscurity may also suggest some idiosyncrasy within ourselves.

BATH, BATHING

1 When we dream of **being in the bath**, it may indicate the need for cleansing of some old feelings, the need to relax, to let go. We have an opportunity to contemplate what has occurred in the past and to adopt new attitudes.

2 To dream of **bathing someone** shows the need to nurture or to have an intimate connection with that person.

3 Communal bathing depicts innocence and sensuality combined.

BATON

1 If the dream is of a **police baton**, then it can represent authority or male sexuality.

2 If however the dream is of a **drum baton** or stick, the dream may represent the need for self-expression in a more forceful way than normal.

3 Spiritual authority can be symbolised by the baton helping us to find the way we need to progress.

BAY

1 To dream of a seashore and be conscious of a bay or inlet shows we are aware of a woman's sexuality and receptiveness.

2 To be **keeping something at bay** indicates a need to be on our guard.

3 The **wolf baying at the moon** shows the overcoming of basic animal instincts.

BEACH

1 To be on a beach shows our awareness of the boundary between emotion and reality, our ability to be in touch with the elements.

2 Depending on our actions and state of mind in the dream, dreaming of a beach usually means relaxation and creativity.

3 The potential for emotional clarity is available, particularly if the **beach is deserted**.

BEACON

1 This can show, variously, a warning, the need for communication or a strongly held principle by which one lives.

2 Our emotions may be 'flaring up' and need directness of communication.

3 Beacons may light the way to spiritual enlightenment and on to spiritual sanctuary.

BEADS
– also see Necklace

1 When we dream of beads – for instance **a rosary** – we are making a connection with continuity. **To dream of beads breaking** indicates the failure of a favourite project.

2 Psychologically we are looking for perfection. In many religions prayers are counted by using beads. Repeated prayers are marked in order to ensure that the right number are said.

3 Beads made from semi-precious stones are used as spiritual reminders – as in rosaries or votive beads.

BEAN

1 To be **storing beans** in a dream may show a fear of failure, or a lack of confidence in our ability to carry through an objective, and the need to create something in the future. **To be planting beans** would suggest faith in the future, and a wish to create something

useful. Traditionally the bean was supposed to be capable of feeding, clothing and providing an object of exchange for barter.

2 Psychologically the bean can represent stored potential. We have the ability to use the stored power to achieve whatever we want.

3 The bean can signify immortality and magic power.

BEAR
– also see Animals

1 To have a **bear appear alive** in a dream indicates aggression, or if it is **dead,** the handling of one's deeper negative instincts. To dream of a **toy bear** – i.e. a teddy bear – shows a childlike need for security.

2 Psychologically, we have recognised the need to meet the force of our own creativity.

3 The bear symbolises spiritual strength and power, both latent – for example, when a bear hibernates – and also apparent.

BEARD

1 To dream of a man with a beard means we must guard against cover-up and deceit.

2 We perhaps need to consider more masculine attributes in ourselves or others.

3 Spiritually there is an ambivalence in the symbol of the beard and the meaning will depend on the dreamer's own culture. It may mean wisdom and dignity, or alternatively it may mean deceit and deviousness

BEATING

1 In dreams the act of **beating something or someone** represents our need for 'power over' by our aggression and brute force.

2 To be beaten either **physically or in a game** indicates submission on our part to a greater force.

3 Particularly if one is taking a beating, humility, anguish and grief are symbolised.

BED

– also see Furniture

1 To be **going to bed alone** in a dream can indicate a desire for a return to the safety and security of the womb. To dream of a **bed made up with fresh linen** indicates the need for a fresh approach to those thoughts and ideas that really matter to us.

2 To be **going to bed with someone else** can variously represent either our sexual attraction to that person or indicate that we need have no fear of them – depending on other circumstances within the dream.

3 A bed can represent a form of spiritual sanctuary and a sense of purity.

BED WETTING

1 In dreams, we often regress to a former state, and to dream of wetting the bed indicates anxieties over lack of control. In some cases it may also indicate a problem with sex or sexuality.

2 We may have worries about correct behaviour in society or of being condemned for improper behaviour.

3 Bed wetting can in dreams suggest a need for freedom of personal expression.

BEE

1 As a symbol of something to be feared, as well as tamed and used, the meaning of bees in dreams can be ambivalent. To be **stung by a bee** is a warning of the possibility of hurt. **Being attacked by a swarm** indicates we are creating a situation which may become uncontrollable.

2 To dream of a **queen bee** registers our need to feel, or be, superior in some way. We may possibly feel the need to be served in our chosen purpose by others. We are also aware of the need for hard work and industry.

3 The bee symbolises immortality, rebirth and order.

BEEHIVE

1 Folk-tales, such as the one about

telling one's troubles to the bees, can surface in dreams without us necessarily recognising what they mean. The beehive is said to represent an ordered community and therefore the ability to absorb chaos.

2 To dream of **tending a beehive** alerts us to the need for good management of our resources.
3 Eloquence and direct speech. Possibly a connection with the Great Mother *(See Introduction)*.

BEETLE

1 Considered by many to be dirty, in a dream the beetle carries the same symbolism as all insects – that is, something which is unclean or not properly attended to.
2 The industriousness of the beetle is often taken to represent hard work which needs to be done.
3 By its connection with the scarab beetle, it represents protection from evil. The dreamer should look at what, or who, he feels needs to be protected.

BEGGAR

1 To dream of **being a beggar** represents our own feeling of failure and lack of self-esteem. To dream of **someone else as a beggar** indicates we need to become aware of our ability to help others less fortunate than ourselves.

2 Emotions, drives and thoughts which have been 'starved' in our waking lives can often appear in dreams personalised as a beggar.
3 A beggar can be a hermit and therefore a spiritual petitioner.

BEHAVIOUR

1 Our (or others') behaviour in a dream can differ markedly from normal, since the dream state gives us the freedom to highlight aspects of ourselves of which we would not normally be aware.
2 Bizarre behaviour in ourselves or others can give us clues to our psychological state.
3 The dreamer should be aware of what is appropriate regarding his own behaviour.

BEHIND

1 To be behind someone in a dream indicates that on a subconscious level we may consider ourselves to be inferior in some way.
2 We may find we have a fear of being left behind.
3 We should look at our spiritual standing as we may, quite literally, be behind in our search for wholeness.

BELL

1 Traditionally, to **hear a bell tolling** in a dream was to be warned of disaster or of a death.

While that meaning is less prevalent now as there are more efficient ways of communication, a bell in a dream (such as a **door bell**) does warn us to be on the alert. It may also indicate that we have a desire to communicate with someone who is distanced or estranged from us.

2 Bells can indicate the conscience and our need to seek approval from others.

3 Because it can charm against the powers of destruction, a bell may be lucky for us in the sense that it can forewarn us of approaching danger.

BELLY
– also see Stomach in Body

1 To be aware of **someone else's belly** in a dream draws our attention to their emotions.

2 If our own **belly is distended** in our dream, we may be psychologically at a point where some release is necessary either through anger or frank speech.

3 Because it is the seat of the solar plexus the belly is a spiritual centre which carries vitality. It can therefore also be a focus for appetite.

BELT

1 To dream of a belt which attracts our attention represents the fact that we are perhaps being bound by old attitudes, duty and so on. An **ornate belt** can represent a symbol of power or office (as in regimental or nurses' belts).

2 Intellectually we may be 'hidebound' through outdated material.

3 A belt may be an insignia of power, and can represent either the power we have, or the power we can obtain.

BET
– see Gambling

BIBLE
– also see Religious Imagery

1 If we dream of a Bible or other religious book it usually means that we are aware of traditional moral standards. We need a code of conduct which helps us to survive.

2 We need to look very carefully at our religious beliefs, myths and legends.

3 The Bible in dreams usually indicates some kind of spiritual realisation.

BICYCLE
– also see Journey

1 To dream of **riding a bicycle** shows the need to pay attention to personal effort or motivation.

2 Psychologically we could be looking for freedom without responsibility.

3 Spiritually the bicycle signifies duality.

BIGAMY

1 To dream of **being a bigamist** indicates not being able to decide either between two loves or two courses of action. We are being presented with two alternatives both of which have equal validity.

2 When we dream we are **married to a bigamist** we need to be aware that we are being two-timed or deceived by someone very close to us.

3 Spiritually, bigamy can represent the choices one has to make, possibly between right and wrong. By association it may represent the astrological sign of Gemini.

BIRDS

1 Birds in dreams usually represent freedom, imagination, thoughts and ideas which, by nature, need freedom to be able to become evident. As far back as Pagan times, man has been fascinated by birds and by flight. Birds were believed to be vehicles for the soul and to have the ability to carry the soul to heaven. As a result, birds were very often invested with magical and mystical powers.

2 Psychologically, man often needs to project human qualities onto objects outside himself, and because birds' conduct is entirely instinctive, they can be used in dreams to understand man's behaviour.

3 Birds have come to represent the Soul – both its dark and its enlightened side.

A caged bird can indicate restraint or entrapment. **A bird flying freely** represents aspirations and desires and possibly the spirit soaring towards the Divine.

A display of plumage indicates the dreamer's facade – the way the individual sees him- or herself. **A flock of birds containing both winged and plucked birds** indicates confusion over bodily or material considerations as opposed to Spiritual aspirations. Birds can sometimes denote the feminine, free side of the being.

The golden-winged bird has the same significance as fire and therefore indicates spiritual aspirations. **A high-flying bird** Spiritual awareness or that part in us which seeks knowledge.

In a man's dream, a bird can represent the Anima *(see Introduction)*. **In a woman's dream,** it suggests the Self, in the sense of the Spiritual Self *(see Introduction)*.

White/Black birds The two aspects of the Anima or Self *(see Introduction)* may be represented as two opposites. The black bird signifies the dark, neglected or shadowy side, the white the open, clear, free side.

A pet bird Personal circumstances and emotions can have a profound effect on our self-management, and remembered happiness can be experienced in dreams about pet birds.

Chicken The imagination is being used to serve a practical function. There is potential for growth, though this may also come about through belonging to a group. The chicken can also represent stupidity and cowardice.

Cock The cock is the symbol of a new day and of vigilance or watchfulness. It represents the masculine principle and thus the need to be more upfront and courageous.

Crow Dreaming of a crow can have two meanings. Traditionally the crow warns of death but may also represent wisdom and deviousness.

Cuckoo The meaning of the cuckoo is ambivalent, since it can represent deviousness or unrequited love. As the herald of spring it indicates a change from old, stale energy to newness and freshness.

Dove The Anima *(see Introduction)*. The bringer of calm after the storm, the Soul, the peaceful side of man's nature appears in dreams as the dove.

Duck In a dream this can often denote some kind of superficiality or childishness.

Eagle Because the eagle is known to be a bird of prey, in dreams it signifies domination and supremacy. It can equally also mean perceptiveness and awareness as well as farsightedness and objectivity. **If the dreamer identifies with the eagle,** his own wish to dominate is becoming apparent though there may be some difficulty in reconciling other parts of the dreamer's nature. **If the dreamer feels threatened,** somebody else may be threatening the status quo.

Falcon The falcon shares the symbolism of the eagle. As a bird of prey, it typifies freedom and hope for those who are being restricted in any way. It can represent victory over lust.

Goose/Geese The goose is said to represent watchfulness and love. Like the swan it can represent the dawn or new life. **A flock of geese** is often taken to represent the powers of intuition and to give warning of disaster. **Wild goose** The wild goose can represent the soul and often depicts the Pagan side of our nature. Geese, in common with cats, are considered to be witches' familiars.

Hen The hen denotes providence, maternal care and procreation. When a hen crows in a dream it is taken to represent feminine domination.

Ibis The ibis, sometimes taken to be the stork, is the symbol of perseverance and of aspiration.

Jackdaw – *see Magpie.*

Kingfisher To dream of a kingfisher is to dream of dignity and calmness.

Lark A lark is traditionally supposed to represent the transcendence of the mundane.

Magpie/Jackdaw Because of the belief that magpies and jackdaws are thieves, to dream of one may indicate that an associate is attempting to take away something that the dreamer values. Also the magpie can signify good news.

Ostrich The ostrich denotes that one is attempting to run away from responsibility.

Owl The owl is sacred to Athena, goddess of strategy and wisdom, therefore in a dream the owl can describe those qualities. Because it is also associated with the night-time, it can sometimes represent death.

Peacock To see a peacock in a dream indicates a growth of understanding from the plain and unadorned to the beauty of the fully plumed bird. Like the phoenix, it represents rebirth and resurrection.

Pelican There are two meanings to the symbolism of the pelican. One is sacrifice and devotion and the other is careful and maternal love.

Penguin The penguin is thought to represent adaptability but also possibly stupidity.

Pheasant To dream of pheasants generally foretells prosperity and good fortune to come.

Phoenix The phoenix is a universal symbol of rebirth, resurrection and immortality (dying in order to live).

Quail The quail represents amorousness, sometimes courage and often good luck. In its negative form it can also represent witchcraft and sorcery.

Raven The raven can be a symbol of sin, but if it is seen to be talking it often represents prophecy. Its meaning can be ambivalent since it can represent evil, but also wisdom.

Seagull The seagull is a symbol of freedom and power.

Sparrow The sparrow represents business and industry.

Stork The stork is a symbol of new life and new beginnings.

Swallow The swallow seen in a dream represents hope and the coming of Spring.

Swan The swan is the soul of man and is often taken to be the divine bird. It can sometimes denote a peaceful death.

Turkey The turkey is traditionally a food for celebrations and festivals. To dream of it can therefore denote that there may be good times ahead.

Vulture/Buzzard The vulture is a scavenger and therefore has an association with the feminine aspect in its destructive persona.

Woodpecker The woodpecker is a guardian of both kings and trees in mythology. It is also reputed to have magical powers.

BIRTH

1 We tend to dream of birth at the beginning of a new way of life, a new attitude, new ability, or a new project – also when we become aware of the death of the old.

2 Psychologically we are coming to terms with our existence.

3 The urge to care, to love and to give birth are all suggested by dreams of birth. It may be both a spiritual and a physical need.

BITE

1 Being bitten in a dream may show that we are experiencing aggression from someone else, or conversely that our own aggressive instincts are not under control.

2 To be **biting someone or something** such as fruit within a dream indicates that there is literally an idea or a concept which we need to get our teeth into.

3 The dreamer should be aware not only of his capacity for venom, but also his capacity to be on the receiving end of a 'venomous' attack.

BIZARRE

1 Dream images are often bizarre in that someone may be doing something that is very odd, or something may have an odd or grotesque appearance. This is usually because it is important that we remember the image in order to understand.

2 The mind is capable, within dreams, of creating what may apparently be completly nonsensical. It is only after careful consideration that the dreamer recognises the relevance of the image in his everyday or working life.

3 In spiritual terms the bizarre is most likely to be the product of misunderstood information.

BLACKBIRD
– see *Birds*

BLINDFOLDING

1 If we have **been blindfolded** in a dream, it shows a deliberate attempt is being made to deceive us. If we are **blindfolding someone** else we are not being honest in our dealings with other people. This may be through ignorance on our part.

2 Psychologically we may need to spend time 'in retreat' – that is cut off from visual contact with the external world.

3 In spiritual terms, blindfolding is a rite of Passage. It is a transition between two states.

BLINDNESS

1 If we ourselves are suffering from blindness in a dream there is an unwillingness to 'see' something. We have lost sight of something or we are not seeing qualities in ourselves that we don't like.

2 Intellectually we may be aware of certain facts, but choose not to use that knowledge in the most appropriate way.

3 Spiritually, blindness is a form of ignorance. It can suggest the irrational. It is also a form of initiation.

BLOCK

1 In dreams, a block may present itself in many forms. We can experience it as a physical block – that is, something that needs to be climbed over or got round, a mental block – for instance not being able to speak or hear, or a spiritual block such as the figure of an angel or a demon appearing in our dreams.

2 Blocks appear in dreams when we need to make a special effort to overcome an obstacle to progress.

3 A preventative measure or a warning are the spiritual meanings of a block.

BLOOD
– also see Body

1 From time immemorial blood has represented the life-carrier or the life force. To dream of a **violent scene where blood appears** indicates that we are being self-destructive in some way. If we are having to **deal with blood,** we need to be aware of our own strength. If we have been injured and **someone else is dealing with the blood,** we need to look at what help is necessary to overcome hurt.

2 Emotional abuse can translate itself in dreams into **bloody wounds** either self-inflicted or being inflicted.

3 Spiritually, being aware of blood circulating through the body can symbolise the rejuvenating force.

BOAR

– also see Animals and Pig

1 One of the ways in which the dream mind can bring matters to our attention is by a play on words, and since not many people have contact with the animal boar, for this to appear in a dream usually indicates 'a bore'.

2 By its association with feasting and festivals, the boar can represent lust and gluttony.

3 Abundance and vitality. By association with mythology and children's fables it can also represent evil.

BOAT, SHIP

– also see Journeys

1 To dream about a boat or a ship very often indicates how we cope with our own emotions and those of others. It may well represent how we navigate our way through life and whether we are in control of our lives.

2 To dream of **being alone in a small boat** means we need to consider how we handle isolation and the ability to be alone. To dream of **being on a large ship** alerts us to how we handle group relationships. To dream of **missing a boat** is often the dream of a perfectionist who fears missing chances or opportunities.

3 Boats represent our attitude to death and 'The Final Journey'. They can also represent fertility and adventure.

BODY

1 The body represents the individual and is his outward physical manifestation of all that he is. In dreams, the body often represents the Ego *(see Introduction)*. Since being 'physical' is the baby's first experience of itself, the body forms the prime source of information.

2 Psychologically, most experience is translated into bodily feeling, and therefore becomes a rich source of symbolism in dreams. When emotions cannot be faced in ordinary everyday life, they very often become distorted dream symbols.

3 Physical manifestation of an inner spirituality.

Different aspects of the body can have various meanings in dreams. For example:

To dream of the **upper part of the body** is to link with the mind and the spiritual aspects of the character, while the **lower part of the body** represents the instincts and emotional aspects of a character. **An adult's head on an immature body, or a child's head on an adult body** is an indication that the dreamer needs to recognise the difference between mature thought and emotion. If there is **conflict between the upper and lower part,** it indicates that there is disharmony between the mental faculties and instinctive behaviour. **The right side or hand** being especially noticeable in dreams signifies we should take note of the logical side of our personality, whereas **the left side or left hand** indicates we need to be aware of our intuitive, creative side.

Body parts can have relevance as follows:

Abdomen, stomach, belly When the dream appears to concentrate on the abdomen, there is a need to focus on emotions and repressed feelings.

Anus – *also see Excrement.* The young child's first experience of control is as he or she gains control over bodily functions. In dreams, the mind returns to that experience as a symbol of self-realisation and self-reliance and, more negatively, of suppression and defence. Such a dream therefore is indicating an aspect of childish behaviour or egotism.

Arms We use our arms in all sorts of different ways. In dreams we may be defending ourselves, fight-ing or being held. We may also be showing passionate commitment.

Back Dreaming of seeing **some-one else's back** suggests we should identify the more private elements in our characters. We should also be aware that other people may not – at this present time – wish to share their thoughts with us. We may also find that we are vulnerable to the unexpected. If we dream of **turning our backs,** we are rejecting the particular feeling being experienced in the dream.

Backbone If the backbone is particularly noticeable in a dream, we should consider the main support structure in our lives. Intellectually, we need to consider our firmness of character.

Blood – *also see individual entry and Menstruation in M* Dreaming of blood can have one of two mean-ings. It can signify that the dreamer feels on some level that a sacrifice is being made. This links into the ancient belief that the blood somehow contained the life of the spirit, and therefore spilt blood was sacred. It can also represent renewal of life through its connec-tion with menstruation. Many people fear blood, and thus a dream about blood can highlight the need to come to terms with these fears. On a more spiritual level it represents the blood of Christ.

Breasts – *also see individual entry* Usually, to be conscious of breasts in dreams, indicates our connection with the mother figure and our need for nurturing. Such a dream can also indicate a wish to return to being an infant without responsibilities.

Constipation (in life as well as in dreams) Retention signifies an inability to let go of the past or of previous patterns of behaviour, literally to be uptight.

Excrement The dreamer may not have progressed on a subconscious level beyond a feeling that anything to do with bodily functions is dirty and self-centred. There may be an element of rebellion in the dreamer's waking life. **Playing with excrement** can represent money and value, so playing with it in a dream can highlight anxiety about money, as well as fear of responsibility. **If the excrement is transformed into living animals,** maybe rats, the dreamer is coming to terms with the fact that he is responsible for managing his own impulses. Excrement in its more spiritual meaning belongs to the realm of feelings and we may simply be trying to get rid of bad feelings. Those bad feelings can be turned into something worthwhile.

Evacuation of the bowel usually highlights our need to be free of worry and responsibility, or possibly the need to learn how to be uninhibited. It can also signify the sexual act.

Eye Any dream to do with the eye is to do with observation and discrimination. It is indicative of enlightenment and wisdom, protection and stability. It has a connection with the power of light and, in ancient times, of the sun-gods. Through its connection with Egyptian symbolism, the eye is also a talisman. **Loss of eyesight** signifies the loss of clarity and, depending on which eye, can be either the loss of logic (right eye) or the loss of intuition (left eye). **Regaining the eyesight** can indicate a return to the innocence and clear-sightedness of the child.

Fat To dream of becoming fat is to recognise the need to widen the scope of our activities in some way. If the dreamer is uncomfortable with his or her size it would indicate fear possibly of taking on too much responsibility or of not being adequate for a task.

Hair The hair represents strength and virility. In dreams **to be combing the hair** is to be attempting to untangle a particular attitude we may have. **To be**

having our hair cut is to be trying to create order in our lives. **To be cutting someone else's hair** may be to be curtailing an activity (it is possible that there may be some fear or doubt connected with sexuality). **To be bald in a dream** is to perhaps recognise one's own intelligence.

Hand The hands are one of the most expressive parts of the body and signify power and creativity. **The two hands contrasted with each other, a different object in each hand** There may be some conflict in the dreamer between his belief and his feelings. **A hand on the breast** signifies submission. **Clasped hands** indicate union or friendship, while **clenched hands** suggest a threat. **Folded hands** suggest deep repose, or a state of rest. **The hands covering the eyes** generally represent shame or horror, while **hands crossed at the wrists** suggest that one is being bound. **The open hand** represents justice and the **laying on of hands** signifies healing and blessing particularly if the hand is placed on the neck. The **hands placed together** is an indication of defencelessness, while **placed in someone else's** is an indication of a pledge of service. When the **hands are raised** this can indicate either adoration, prayer or surrender; if the **palms are turned outwards** a blessing is being given, while when they are **raised to the head** the dreamer should give a great deal of thought and care to his situation. **Washing the hands** suggests innocence or rejection of guilt, while **wringing the hands** signifies grief. **A huge hand, particularly from the sky** suggests that one has been 'specially chosen'. The **right hand** is the 'power' hand, while the left is passive and receptive. Sometimes in dreams the **left hand** can represent cheating.

Head The head is considered to be the principle part of the body. Because it is the seat of the life force, it denotes power and wisdom. Dreaming of the head suggests that we should look very carefully at the way we deal with both intelligence and folly. To dream of the **head being bowed** suggests supplication. When the **head is covered** we may be covering up our own intelligence or acknowledging somebody else's superiority. **A blow to the head** in a dream can indicate that we should reconsider our actions in a particular situation.

Heart The heart is the centre of the being and represents 'feeling' wisdom rather than intellectual wisdom. It is also representative of compassion and understanding.

Heel This suggests the part of ourselves which is strong but, at the same time, vulnerable.

Jaw The jaw often is representative of our self-expression. It also, on a more esoteric level, suggests the opening to the underworld.

Kidneys The kidneys are organs of elimination, therefore to dream of them is to be aware of the need for cleansing.

Knees The knees are symbolic of prayer and supplication, and of emotional commitment.

Limbs Whether it is partly to do with some kind of cellular memory and the growth process that takes place is uncertain, but in dreams any limb can be taken to mean sexuality and fears associated with gender issues. **Being dismembered** can be taken in its literal sense – we are being torn apart. Sometimes this can suggest the need to restructure our lives and begin again. At other times it can indicate that there is a way in which we are being threatened to the very core of our existence.

Liver The liver is representative of irritability and suppressed anger.

Lungs In Chinese medicine the lungs represent grief. They are also involved in decision-making. Spiritually, the lungs are the seat of righteousness, and the source of thoughts concerning the Self.

Mouth The mouth represents the devouring, demanding part of ourselves. It can also stand for the receptive side. The circumstances of the dream may give a clue to the correct interpretation. Sometimes the mouth can symbolise the feminine side of our nature.

Nose The nose in dreams can stand for curiosity, and also for intuition.

Penis Dreaming of a penis – either one's own or someone else's – usually highlights the attitude to penetrative sex.

Skin Skin in a dream stands for our persona or the facade we create for others. **Hard, tough skin** shows we have created a tough exterior, and are trying to protect ourselves.

Stomach *–see Abdomen in this section*

Teeth Popularly, teeth are supposed to stand for aggressive sexuality – although more properly they signify the growth process towards sexual maturity. **Teeth falling or coming out easily** indicates we are aware of going through some form of transition, similar to that from childhood to maturity, or from maturity to old age and helplessness. **If one is**

anxious about teeth dropping out it suggests there is a fear of getting old and undesirable, or an anxiety about maturing. **In a woman's dream**, if the teeth are swallowed this can signify pregnancy.

Throat Dreaming of the throat denotes awareness of our vulnerability and also of the need for self-expression.

Thumb Dreaming of a thumb suggests awareness of how powerful we are. The thumb pointing upwards represents beneficial energy, poiting downwards is negative. This latter was used as the death signal for Roman gladiators.

Tongue The tongue in dreams often signifies our ability to know when to speak and when to remain silent. It may also be to do with our own understanding of information that we wish to pass on to other people. We may have deeply felt beliefs we wish to share. Another explanation that is much more basic is that of the symbolism of the serpent and the phallus, and hence sexuality.

Urine Urine in a dream often indicates our feelings about emotional control. We may either yield to emotion or bottle it up. How we deal with urine often also tells us a great deal about our own sexuality.

Vagina Most often, dreams of the vagina are to do with one's self image. **In a woman's dream**, it highlights her receptivity. **In a man's dream** it suggests his need to be penetrative, both mentally and physically.

Womb The womb represents a return to the beginning. We all have need of basic security and shelter, and perhaps to do away with responsibility. Dreams of the womb can signify our need to satisfy those requirements. On a slightly more esoteric level the womb represents our connection with the Great Mother or Mother Earth *(see Introduction)*. Dreams of **returning to the womb** suggest our need to reconnect with the passive, more yielding side of our nature. We may need a period of self-healing and recuperation.

BONDS

There are two meanings for bonds in dreams. One is as in **savings bonds** (promissory notes) and the second as in **bindings and cords**. **1** To dream of **the former** indicates that we have a sense of commitment to a person or a principle, that we are capable of making promises which we can keep. To dream of **the latter** deals with the binding or holding which can occur in situations and relationships. Depending on whether the dreamer is being bound or doing the binding, it shows submission to a greater force.

2 Depending on whether we are **giving or receiving** such promissory bonds, we need to consider our emotional commitment to ourselves and our own concerns. To be aware of being fettered, snared or held fast by chains indicates the possibility our emotional selves may be out of control.

3 The changing of conflict into law and order, of chaos into cosmic order. The Silver Cord.

BONES
– also see Limbs in Body

1 Bones appearing in a dream usually indicate that we need to be aware that which we consider to be basic material. We need to 'go back to basics'. To dream of a **dog eating a bone** means we need to consider our basic instincts. To dream of **finding bones** indicates that there is something essential we have not considered in a situation.

2 To dream of a full skeleton indicates that we need to reconsider the structure of our lives.

3 Bones are one of the integral parts of man. They often hold the key in terms of death and resurrection.

BONFIRE
– also see Fire

1 To be **lighting or tending** a bonfire in a dream indicates a need for cleansing some aspect of our lives. Such a fire can also represent passions that are not confined by rigidity and custom.

2 When we are conscious of **feeding a bonfire**, the passionate side of our emotional selves needs to be allowed freedom of expression. Old, outdated concepts and beliefs can be let go in order to create something new.

3 Spiritually, a bonfire reflects the power of the sun and encourages the power of good. It also represents Solar festivals.

BOMB

1 Bombs appearing in a dream usually indicate some form of explosive situation with which we need to deal. **Exploding** a bomb indicates the need for positive action, while **defusing** a bomb suggests taking care not to make a situation worse.

2 Psychologically we need to be aware that our own emotions are likely to get the better of us.

3 A bomb exploding is usually an unexpected event. Dreaming of one would suggest a fear of sudden death.

BOOK
– also see Novel

1 Our search for knowledge and the ability to learn from other people's experience and opinions, is symbolised in dreams by books and libraries. To dream of **old books** represents inherited wisdom and spiritual awareness. To dream of **account books** indicates the need or ability to look after our own resources.

2 Intellectually we are searching in our dreams for ways which will help us to handle what happens in our lives.

3 A book, particularly a sacred one such as the Bible or Koran, signifies hidden or sacred knowledge. Dreaming of one can represent our need to look into the realms of sacred knowledge or reassurance that we are going in the right direction.

BOUQUET

1 To be given a bouquet in a dream shows that we recognise our own abilities but also expect others to recognise them. To be **giving someone else** a bouquet indicates that we fully recognise their better qualities.

2 Very often a bouquet indicates, on a psychological level, that we have many gifts and talents available to us.

3 A bouquet, by virtue of its beauty and attachment to ceremonies can symbolise a spiritual offering.

BORDER
– also see Frontier

1 A border can appear in many different ways in a dream. To have our attention drawn to the **edge or border of material** can indicate changes we will make in the material world. To be standing on **a border between two countries** would show the need to be making great changes in life; perhaps physically moving our place of residence.

2 Psychologically we may need to make decisive changes in the way we think and feel.

3 Meeting a different aspect of the Self and thus a new experience in life. The dreamer needs to decide if the time is right to 'cross the border'.

BOTTLE

1 To a certain extent it depends on which type of bottle is perceived in the dream. **To see a baby's feeding bottle** would indicate the need to be successfully nurtured and helped to grow. **A bottle of alcohol** would show the need to celebrate, or to curb an excess, while **a medicine bottle** might symbolise the need to look at one's own health. **A broken bottle** could indicate either aggression or failure.

2 Opening a bottle could mean making available resources you have, but may have suppressed.

3 A womb symbol: the principle of containing and enclosure.

BOTTOM
– see Position

BOW

1 Since bowing is indicative of giving someone else status, to be **bowing to someone** in a dream would indicate our sense of inferiority. To perceive a bow, as in **Cupid's bow**, within a dream can indicate the need to be loved – the union of masculine and feminine.

2 While intellectually we may not need to feel inferior, on an unconscious level we may actually sense someone else's need to feel superior and acknowledge that in the dream state. To see a **bow made of ribbon** in a dream is making a connection to the feminine principle and beauty.

3 Variously a bow can indicate superiority, union of masculine and feminine, celebration.

BOWL

1 A bowl of food in a dream represents our ability to nurture and sustain others. **A bowl of flowers** can represent a gift or a talent, while a **bowl of water** represents our emotional capacity.

2 A bowl appearing in a dream has the same significance as a vase *(see Vase)*.

3 A bowl of water represents the feminine, fertility and the receptive principle.

BOX

1 To feel boxed in in a dream is to be prevented from expanding in an appropriate way. To dream of **packing things** in a box indicates that we are trying to get rid of feelings or thoughts with which we cannot cope.

2 Various types of boxes perceived in a dream may represent different aspects of the feminine personality.

3 The feminine containing principle.

BOY
– see People

BOYFRIEND
– see People

BRAIN

1 When attention is drawn to the brain in a dream, we are expected to consider our own or others' intellect. To dream of the **brain being preserved** indicates the need to take care in intellectual pursuits. We may be pushing ourselves too hard.

2 Since the brain is the seat of learning, we may psychologically need to consider our beliefs and ideals in the light of experience.

3 The seat of the soul.

BREAD
– also see Food

1 Dreaming of bread connects us with our need for basic emotional and biological satisfaction. To be **sharing bread** in a dream represents our ability to share basic experience.

2 If the bread in a dream is foreign or tastes bad we may be unsure of what we really need out of life. We may be doing the wrong thing in some area of our lives.

3 Bread is symbolic of life itself. It is food of the soul and can also represent the need to share.

BREAK

1 To dream of something being broken symbolises loss or damage. If a **favourite object** is broken, we must make changes and break from the past. If a **limb is broken** we may be prevented from moving forward or carrying out a certain action.

2 If the dreamer actually dreams of **breaking something**, appropriate action needs to be taken in order to break a bond or connection in the dreamers life.

3 Shattered idealism, hope and faith.

BREASTPLATE

1 In mythology, the breastplate was always considered to protect the knight. When we experience ourselves as wearing some form of protection around the heart, we are usually protecting our right to love unconditionally.

2 Psychologically we are at our most vulnerable where matters of the heart are concerned, and most often need protection in that area. To dream of **someone else wearing a breastplate** indicates their capacity to be hurt emotionally.

3 Our need to protect ourselves spiritually.

BREASTS
– also see Body

1 Considered to be one of the most often dreamed about parts of the body, it is the symbolism of the nourishment and love belonging to motherhood that is most often understood. For a **man to dream of breasts** usually indicates his unconscious connection with his

mother or the nurturing principle.
2 While intellectually we deny the need for mothering or 'smother-love', psychologically this need surfaces when we are under stress and usually comes up as the dream image of breasts.
3 Motherhood, protection and love.

BREATH

1 To become aware of **one's own breathing** in a dream indicates a deep connection with the process of life. To be aware of **someone else's breathing** indicates the need for empathy and understanding with that person.
2 Our own emotional state can very often have an effect on the rate at which we breathe which then becomes translated in dreams into, for instance, a panic attack. To be **breathing underwater** is an instinctive return to the womb-like state.
3 The Soul. Breath is the power of the Spirit and life giving power, without it we are nothing.

BREEZE

1 To dream of a breeze being meaningful indicates a contented state of mind. Wind is usually considered to belong to the intellect, so by association a gentle breeze indicates love, while a stiff breeze

indicates a degree of abrasiveness.
2 Psychologically for most people a breeze indicates happy times.
3 The old saying 'she's like a warm breeze' goes some way to explaining the symbolism of virginity, unconditional love and the Spirit.

BRIDE
– also see Marriage

1 When a **woman dreams of being a bride**, she is often trying to reconcile her need for relationship and her need for independence. She needs to have an understanding of the changes in responsibility. **In a man's dream,** a bride indicates his understanding of the feminine, innocent part of himself. To dream of **being at a wedding**, especially your own, indicates the integration of inner feeling and outer reality.
2 Psychologically, we are seeking union of the unintegrated part of ourselves. We may be looking for the innocent feminine within.
3 The spiritual need for, and recognition of love, receptivity and fertility.

BRIDEGROOM
– also see Marriage

1 To dream of a bridegroom usually indicates the desire to be married or to find a partner. It often shows the desire to be more responsible or to take on responsibility for someone else. It is a connection with, and an understanding of, the 'romantic' side of one's nature and indicates the need for integration of the intellect and the real world.

2 The need for partnership may be more intellectual than emotional, and we may need to make a connection with the drive of the masculine.

3 A bridegroom can represent the dreamer's need to take care of somebody or something, and maybe to exert a degree of control.

BRIDGE

1 The bridge is one of the most commonly found images in dreams and almost invariably indicates the crossing from one phase of life to another. The bridge may be depicted as weak or strong, sturdy or otherwise, which gives an indication of the strength of connection necessary to make changes in the dreamer's life.

2 The symbol of a bridge in a dream signifies the emotional connection between the dreamer and other people or various parts of his life.

3 Crossing the River of Life. The River Styx.

BRIDLE

1 To be **bridled in a dream, as in being yoked to something**, indicates the need for restraint and control. If the **bridle is made of flowers** it indicates a more feminine way of imposing control. If the bridle is harsher – such as **one of metal and/or leather** – we perhaps need to be harder on ourselves or on someone we love.

2 The bridle can indicate the need for focused attention on some aspect of our lives.

3 A degree of spiritual restraint or control may be needed.

BRIGHT

1 To experience brightness in a dream means that some part of our life needs illuminating, often by an external source.

2 We have the ability to use the brighter side of our personalities.

3 Dreaming of brightness symbolises the dreamer's move towards spiritual illumination.

BRINK

1 To be **on the brink of something** in a dream literally means we are on the edge of something. This will have a profound effect on our lives or of those around us.

2 We may have difficulty in sorting out what is rational or irrational behaviour.

3 There is the move towards darkness, and then there is the abyss. The dreamer should be careful – and aware – of a downward spiritual spiral.

BROADCAST

1 When we dream of **taking part in a broadcast** we are aware of needing to reach a wider audience. This may be risky since we have no means of measuring our audience's response. To dream of **listening to a broadcast** means we should be listening to the message that other people are trying to get across.

2 Psychologically, the performer in us needs some form of self-expression.

3 Widespread spirituality.

BROKEN
– see Break

BROTHER
– see Family

BROTHERHOOD

1 Dreaming of **belonging to a brotherhood** indicates our need to belong to a group of like-minded people. This could be something in the nature of a trade union, or of the Freemasons. We all need approval from our peers, and such a dream indicates the way we

handle ritualised group behaviour.

2 Any grouping of the masculine usually alerts us to the many sides and aspects of the masculine personality.

3 The Priesthood.

BROTHEL

1 If a **woman dreams of being in a brothel**, she has not yet come to terms with the sexually active side of herself. If a **man dreams of being in a brothel** it may show a fear of the feminine.

2 To dream of a brothel indicates the need for sexual liberation and freedom.

3 The darker side of femininity. It may also represent awareness of man's spiritual debt to woman.

BRUTALITY

1 To experience some form of brutality in a dream can be frightening until we realise that we are connecting into the darker, more animal side of ourselves. We may need to deal with fears associated with that side in order to make progress.

2 Unrestrained passion – whether sexual or otherwise – can appear as brutality and cruelty in our dreams.

3 Brutality can manifest itself in demonic acts of evil. Although rather severe, the dreamer should take note of this interpretation.

BUBBLE

1 We may dream of bubbles as part of our need to have fun in a childlike way. We often become aware of the temporary nature of happiness, and our need for illusion.

2 Bubbles as beautiful but fragile objects remind us of the transitory nature of human existence, that nothing is permanent.

3 A bubble represents the illusory elements of everyday life and, more specifically, the daydream.

BUFFER

1 In our dream imagery there may need for symbols which represent barriers and difficulties. To **run into a buffer** may indicate the need for caution.

2 In our most vulnerable emotional states we may need some sort of buffer between us and the rest of the world, and this may be experienced in dreams as an actual physical barrier.

BUCKLE

1 Dreaming of an **ornate buckle** has the same symbolism as that of a belt in that it can represent the holding of high office or status. It can also indicate honour and can be a symbol of loyalty or membership.

2 To be **fastening a buckle** in a dream shows that we accept responsibility for what we do.

3 A buckle can have a double meaning in this case. It can represent a protective element against the forces of evil; it can also help us take the strain and not 'buckle' under pressure.

BUD

1 To dream of a bud is to recognise the unfolding of a new way of life, new experiences or new emotions. To dream of a **bud dying** or shrivelling up indicates the failure of a project.

2 A new idea or way of thinking holds a great deal of potential, as yet untapped.

3 How the world unfolds before us – and how we can influence that – is symbolised here.

BUDDHA, BUDDHIST

1 There is a saying that goes 'If you meet the Buddha on the road, kill him.' In dreams the Buddha represents the denial or loss of ego. There needs to be a liberation from thinking and desiring.

2 If we dream of **being Buddhist,** we need to look at the difference between western and eastern religion.

3 Spiritual Clarity and all that it entails.

BUILDINGS

Buildings in dreams represent the constructions we make in our lives. They are attitudes and beliefs we have built from our experience, perception, and often from our family habits and customs. Where in real life we can learn a lot about a person from his personal environment, so in dreams a building can also reflect the dreamer's character hopes and concerns. The features of the building mirror the features of the dreamer's personality. Buildings in dreams can become composite, and therefore confusing. In understanding the dream, we should interpret the main appearance of the building first, as its main function, and the secondary appearance as qualities to be recognised.

Various buildings have distinct meanings:

Boarding house or Hotel - *also see individual entry in H* To dream of a boarding house or hotel indicates that we may not feel secure within our living conditions.

Castle, Fortress, Citadel The symbolism of the castle or fortress is that of the defended space and therefore can be taken to represent the feminine or the Great Mother.

Courtyard In dreams, the courtyard is a place of safety and often the shape will be relevant *(see Shapes)*.

Church, temple etc. – *also see Church Buildings in C and Church in Religious Imagery* As an environment for us to consider our system of belief, any religious building will suggest a place of sanctuary and refuge. Although we may not consciously adhere to any particular religion, most of us have principles by which we live, which will surface in dreams in recognisable images.

House If we are aware that **the house is not empty – that there is something in it (e.g. furnishings)** it shows some aspect of the dreamer. **Someone else in the house** suggests that the dreamer may be feeling threatened by an aspect of his own personality. If there are **different activities going on** it indicates there is a conflict between two parts of our personality, possibly the creative and the intellectual. **The front of the house** portrays the front we show to the outside world. **Going into/out of the house** We may have to decide whether we need at that time to be more introverted or more extroverted. **An impressive, awe-inspiring house** In a dream like this we are conscious of the Self or the Soul. **Moving to a larger house** There is need for a change in our lives, perhaps to achieve a more open way of life, or even for more space. **Being outside the house** The more public side of ourselves is being depicted. **A small house, or the house where the dreamer was born** The dreamer is seeking security, or perhaps the safety of babyhood, without responsibility. **If the smallness of the house is constricting** We are being trapped by our responsibilities, and may need to escape. **Work on the house; cementing, repairing, etc.** Relationships may need to be worked on or repaired, or perhaps we need to look at health matters. We may need to take note of the damage or decay that has occurred in our lives.

Igloo – *also see individual entry* Because of its shape, the igloo stands for completeness and sanctuary. It is warm on the inside and cold on the outside and therefore signifies the difference between the internal and the external.

Pyramid The pyramid is considered to be a focus for power, so for one to appear in a dream is to be concentrating on the power within.

Temple – *see Church Buildings in C and Church in Religious Imagery*

Tower (obelisk, steeple, lighthouse, etc.) Any image of a tower is representing the personality, and the Soul within. While there are obvious connotations that connect it with masculinity, it is more correct to perceive it as the Self within a wider context. When thought of in this way attention can then be paid to other attributes of the tower, such as where windows, doors and staircases are placed. This leads to a greater understanding of the Spiritual Self.

Warehouse The warehouse being primarily a storage place has the symbolism of being a repository either for spiritual energy or for spiritual rubbish.

Components of buildings
Balcony (or ledge, sill, etc.) We all have need for support within our lives and a balcony indicates both support and protectiveness. It can also represent the Mother in her protective aspect.

Construction or demolition of a building. We all have the ability within us to construct successful lives and equally an ability to self-destruct. A dream that highlights construction or demolition gives us access to those qualities and abilities within ourselves.

Doors *also see individual entry* Doors refer to the openings of the body and therefore, by default, one's sexuality. **The front door and back door** signifies the vagina and the anus respectively. **Breaking down the door** can be taken to indicate an inhibition over sex and an unwillingness to face the issues. It can also represent rape or abuse. **Opening and closing the door** While often taken to stand for intercourse, this can show the dreamer's attitude to sex. **Refusing to open the door** Although the dreamer may not technically be a virgin, for this to occur represents an innocent approach to their sexuality. **A door between the outer and inner rooms** shows there may be a conflict between the conscious and the unconscious. **Barring the door** This highlights the dreamer's need for self-protection. **If an animal or person forces his way in and destroys the lock** Our own protective mechanisms have let us down. **Escaping by another door** indicates the dreamer needs to find a new solution to the one he thought of to solve a problem.

Someone knocking on the door signifies that the dreamer's attention is being drawn to an external situation.

Hall/Passages Any passage can stand for the passages within the body, for instance the vagina or the anus. Equally, on a psychological level, it signifies how we allow our personal space to be penetrated. Passages also represent the transitions between the various stages of our lives.

Lift A lift usually indicates how we deal with information. For instance, a lift **going down** would suggest going down into the subconscious, while a lift **going up** would be moving towards the spiritual. It is believed that in the sleep state we leave our bodies. Thus, **descending in a lift and getting stuck** represents the entrapment of the spiritual by the physical body.

Rooms in a dream can describe various parts of our personalities or levels of understanding, but often signify either the womb or the mother figure. Thus the **kitchen** would be the home-making part of us whereas a **sitting room** would be the more relaxed, comfortable side. **A small room with only one door or a basement with water in it** is a direct representation of the womb, and may indicate a return to the womb-like state. **A series of rooms** This refers to the various aspects of femininity and often to the whole soul. **Anything in an upstairs room** An upstairs room usually signifies mental or spiritual attributes, so any object will represent an idea or concept. **The basement or cellar** This meaning can be ambivalent, since a cellar can represent the parts of ourselves that we have chosen to suppress. It can also represent family beliefs and habits, particularly if the basement is that of the parents. **Leaving one room and going into another** If this is a deliberate action in the dream, then it represents a change of state and of leaving something behind. **Empty rooms** Something, such as comfort or support, is lacking in our lives.

Stairs Stairs are often an indication of the steps we must take in order to achieve a goal. **Climbing the stairs** is indicative of the effort that we must make in order to have access to the more mystical, spiritual side of our being. It can more simply be the exertion we practise in our everyday life. **Going downstairs** Conversely, in order to have access to the hidden unconscious side of ourselves, we need to 'go down'

into the unconscious. **A golden staircase** This is such a basic image, with so many interpretations, that particular attention needs to be paid both to other aspects of the dream, and also the dreamers spiritual state at that specific time. Largely it represents a 'death', but not necessarily a physical death. It is more the realisation that we no longer need to be trapped within the physical, but can move towards a more fulfilling life. It is a way out of the mundane.

Walls A wall signifies a block to progress – a difficulty we have or will come up against. Often the nature of the wall will give some clue as to what the block is. For instance, **a wall which looks old** will signify an old problem, whereas **a glass wall** would indicate some difficulties with perception. **Walls closing in** could describe the remembered feelings of birth, but is more likely to represent a feeling of being trapped by the lifestyle we have. **A brick wall, rampart or dividing wall** all signify the difference between two states of reality, often the inner psychological state and the exterior everyday world.

Windows Windows will describe the means by which we appreciate the world we live in, the way we perceive reality. Dreaming that we are **looking outwards through a window** can suggest that we have a more extrovert view of ourselves and will tend to look at external circumstances. **Looking inwards through a window** indicates we are looking inwards at our own personality, and perhaps at our own motivation. **Opening a window** The interpretation depends on whether we are opening the window from the inside or the outside. If the former, we are dealing with our inner feelings which we may need to escape; the latter shows our attitude to outside opinion. **Breaking through a window (or glass door)** This can suggest the first sexual experience. **Stained glass windows** Because of the connection with churches, stained glass can be accepted as religious belief *(also see Colour)*.

BULL
– also see Animals

1 In dreams the bull represents the masculine principle and fertility. It also can indicate the way we handle male sexuality.
2 The bull appearing in a dream can point to the dreamer's own stubbornness.

3 The bull is connected with the moon goddesses and also represents Taurus in the Zodiac.

BULLET

1 To dream of bullets is to be aware of aggression and a desire to hurt. If the bullet is **being fired at** the dreamer, it may be considered to be a warning of danger. If, however, the dreamer is **firing the bullet,** there is an awareness of one's vulnerability.
2 There is a need to understand what ammunition the dreamer has available in the sense of resources to be used.
3 A bullet can represent the need for, and control of, sexual impregnation.

BURGLAR
– also see Intruder

1 When we become aware of a burglar or intruder in our dreams we are experiencing some form of violation of our private space. This may be from external sources or from inner fears and difficult emotions.
2 A part of our psyche may have been neglected, and intrude on our awareness, thus needing attention.
3 Penetration – either physical or material – is the symbolism here. Either way, the dreamer should look

at circumstances surrounding him

3 The Greater Good.

BURIAL

1 To have a dream about **being buried** indicates a fear of being overcome, possibly by responsibility, or of repressing parts of our personality in ways which are harmful.

2 To be **attending a burial** in our dreams shows the need to come to terms with loss.

3 The obvious spiritual symbols of death, loss and pain are relevant here. This is not necessarily a negative meaning, the dreamer should look at the resurrection and the positive elements that it can bring.

BUS
– also see Journey

1 If we dream of being **in a bus** we are coming to terms with the way we handle group relationships, and new directions we need to take in company with others.

2 We may be experiencing the need to be an individual, while at the same time belonging to a group with a common purpose.

BUTCHER

1 We see the butcher as one who mutilates, but provides for us at the same time, and this is reflected in dreams when he appears as someone who separates the good from the bad. He may also be a destroyer.

2 We may need to become aware of a destructive streak in ourselves.

3 The butcher has spiritual connotations with the Grim Reaper and death. The meat cleaver could be taken to represent the scythe.

BUTTERFLY

1 On a practical level when seen in dreams, the butterfly represents light-heartedness and freedom.

2 Psychologically, the butterfly indicates a lack of ability to settle down or to undertake a protracted task.

3 When seen in dreams or even meditation, the butterfly represents the freed soul and immortality. There is no need for the soul to be trapped by the physical body.

from

Caduceus *to* Cymbals

CADUCEUS

1 The Caduceus is the sign that is used by doctors and medical establishments as the sign of healing. To have this appear in a dream usually highlights health matters, which may be our own or other people's.

2 The body recognises and communicates in dream images its need and expectation of good health. On a psychological level, to dream of the Caduceus can mean that we need to create better conditions for achieving this.

3 Power in uniting opposites.

CAGE/CELL
– also see Prison

1 The cage normally represents some form of trap or jail. To dream of **caging a wild animal** alerts us to our need to restrain our wilder instincts. To dream that we are **in a cage** indicates a sense of frustration and perhaps of being trapped by the past.

2 We are being warned that we are enforcing too much restraint on our hidden abilities. We could be allowing others to hold us back in some way.

3 We should examine, and reconsider our negative images of religion or belief.

CAKES

1 When we dream of **celebration cakes** – such as a wedding or birthday cake – we are being shown that there is cause for celebration in our lives. This may be to do with the actual cause for celebration or to mark the passage of time. (**Candles on a cake** – *see Candle and Numbers.*)

2 Making cakes indicates our need to care for others or to nurture some inner need.

3 Sacrificial cakes, or buns, marked with the cross symbolise the round of the moon and its four quarters.

CALENDAR

1 If a calendar appears in a dream there can be more than one meaning. Our attention may be being drawn to the past, present or future and something significant in our lives, or we may be being warned of the passage of time in an important scheme.

2 Because time is a self-imposed limitation, when anything that marks time appears in a dream we are being warned of the potential for limitation.

3 We should become more aware of the timetable of festivals and celebrations.

CALF
– see Baby Animals and Animals

CAMEL

1 Depending on the environment in the dream the camel can represent the unusual or bizarre. It also represents available resources and obedience to a basic principle.
2 Psychologically the camel can represent stamina and self-sufficiency.
3 Dignity, the bearer of royalty.

CAMERA

1 The camera is a recording instrument. To be **using a camera** in a dream means we are recording events or occasions which we may need to remember or take note of more fully. **Being filmed** indicates that we need to look more carefully at our actions and reactions to certain situations.
2 There is a necessity to retain a mental picture of what is important to us.
3 There is a need to be watchful.

CANAL

1 Because a canal is a man-made structure, a dream about a canal usually indicates that we are inclined to be rigid insofar as the control of our emotions is concerned. We may be introducing too much structure into our lives at the expense of our creativity.
2 We need to structure our knowledge of ourselves to create a workable system.
3 Structure, definition, rigid belief.

CANCER

1 Cancer is one of the prime fears that a human being has to deal with, so to dream of a cancer indicates we are out of harmony with our body. It indicates fear of illness and equally can represent something 'eating away' at us – usually a negative idea or concept.
2 Intellectually we may have worked through our fears but still be left with attitudes and beliefs that cannot be cleared away. Very often this appears as cancer in dreams.
3 The Mother, the Moon and the astrological sign of Cancer.

CANDLE

1 In Pagan times, the candle or taper represented the dispersing of darkness and a way of worshipping power. To dream of candles indicates that we are trying to clarify something that we do not understand. **Candles on a birthday cake** can therefore indicate that we are marking a transition from the old to the new. **Lighting a candle** represents using courage and fortitude or asking for something which we need.
2 Since candles are now regarded

as old-fashioned, psychologically they can represent knowledge or wisdom that has not fully crystallised. They can also represent our control of personal magic.

3 Illumination, wisdom, strength, beauty.

CANE

1 Because many people associate the cane with some form of punishment or sadism, it can represent self-punishment, or masochism. It is more likely, however, that we are trying to come to terms with some form of childhood trauma.

2 Because a cane also represents pliability, we may be trying to achieve a balance between our willingness and our unwillingness to accept a situation.

3 The cane signifies self-flagellation.

CANNIBALISM

1 To dream of cannibalism usually represents unsophisticated or inappropriate behaviour. To be aware of **eating human flesh** may indicate our dislike of unsuitable foods or actions. There is often a part of ourselves we have not 'internalised' which we need to absorb.

2 Eating human flesh in a dream can mean that we are taking in wrong information.

3 Absorbing powers or qualities belonging to someone else.

CANOE

1 To dream of a canoe would indicate that we are handling our emotions in isolation. We are possibly making efforts to control the flow of our emotion. We are aware that we are capable of making changes but only by our own efforts.

2 We may be protected from our emotions, but also at risk. A degree of skill is necessary to enable us to move forward.

3 A lunar barque, the crescent moon.

CANOPY

1 When we dream of a canopy we are looking to be protected, sheltered or loved. In olden times a canopy was used to shelter those with special duties or powers, such as kings and queens or priests and priestesses. We still acknowledge on a deep internal level this privilege. If **we ourselves are being sheltered** we recognise our own abilities and potential for greatness.

2 A canopy protects the head which is the seat of intellect. We have a need to draw attention to higher ideals or aspirations.

3 Royalty or powerful people often

used a canopy with a special symbol either for spiritual protection or to signify their rank. We should consider how important we find such matters

CAP
– also see Hat in Clothes

1 The cap has the same significance as the hat in dreams and draws attention to status or spiritual powers. If we are **wearing a cap** in a dream, we may be covering up our creative abilities.

2 The cap shows the need for respect for a person's beliefs and wisdom or knowledge.

3 A cap signifies nobility and freedom.

CAPITAL
– also see Places and Money

1 To dream of one's **financial capital** would imply a need to conserve resources. **Dreaming of a country's capital city** indicates we should look at our attitude to the wider issues in that country or our connection with that city. We may also need to consider how we deal with large groups of people, particularly those whose customs and accepted behaviour is unknown.

2 To dream of capital letters could indicate that we need to pay more attention to important issues in

our lives. There is a matter which needs sorting out.

3 Spiritually, capital is the result of past actions.

CAR
– also see Journey

1 The car is very often representative of our own personal space, an extension of our being. To dream of **being in a car** usually alerts us to our own motivation, thus **driving the car** can indicate our need to achieve a goal, while **being a passenger** could indicate that we have handed over responsibility for our lives to someone else.

2 Dream scenarios involving cars are often more to do with what we are doing to ourselves on a psychological or emotional level. **Being alone in a vehicle** indicates independence, while dreaming of the **brakes** of a car shows one's ability to be in control of a situation. **The car engine** indicates the essential drives with which we have to deal. **A crashing vehicle** suggests fear of failure in life, while a **car on fire** denotes stress of some sort, either physically or emotionally. **To be in a car which is driven carelessly**, either by the dreamer or someone else, marks a lack of responsibility, while a feeling of being left behind would be shown by your car **being overtaken**. To dream of **reversing a car** registers a feeling that one is slipping backwards or having to reverse a decision.

3 A car stands for spiritual direction and motivation.

CARDS (GREETING)

1 To dream of **giving or receiving a card** such as a birthday card alerts us to the need for a specific kind of communication with the addressee. We may wish to celebrate our own or others' good fortune and luck.

2 Our subconscious may be registering concern, either about ourselves or others.

3 Visual communication, the ability to convey a message spiritually.

CARDS (PLAYING)

1 In a dream, playing cards highlights our ability to be open to opportunity or to take chances. The cards that one deals, or is dealt, in a dream may have significance as to number *(see Numbers)* or as to suit: **Hearts** indicate emotion and relationship. **Diamonds** represent material wealth. **Spades** represent conflict, difficulties and obstacles. **Clubs** represent action, work and intelligence. **The King** portrays human

success and mastery. **The Queen** indicates emotional depth, sensitivity and understanding. **The Jack** represents impetuosity, creativity or an adolescent energy.

2 On a psychological level, card playing in a dream can be seen as taking calculated risks and alerts us to potential danger.

3 The Tarot – our Inner Truth – can be used as images in dream work.

CARRIAGE
– also see Journey

1 Dreaming of a carriage, such as a **horse-drawn** one, could be suggestive of old-fashioned attitudes to modern thinking. **A train carriage** would indicate that we are taking a journey that is slightly more public in character than a car journey.

2 Any symbol which signifies our being moved in some way draws attention to our ability to make progressive changes in our lives.

3 The carriage is a symbol of majesty and power.

CARRIED/CARRYING

1 To be aware of **carrying an object** suggests we need to look at what is being accepted as a burden or difficulty. If we dream of **being carried,** we may feel that we are in need of support.

2 To dream of **carrying someone** registers the fact that we may be accepting responsibility for someone else and that this responsibility is a burden.

3 When we are prepared to 'carry' something we are taking Spiritual Responsibility.

CASK

1 Like most containers, a cask represents the feminine principle. Since a cask is usually hand-made, to dream of one indicates the care taken in dealing with one's own emotional make-up.

2 It is more likely to be the content of the cask which has meaning on a psychological level and indicates our ability to be creative with raw materials.

3 A bottomless cask represents needless effort.

CASTLE
– also see Buildings

1 Dreaming of a castle links us right back to the feminine principle of the enclosed and defended private space. It can represent the fantastic or perhaps difficulty in obtaining our objectives.

2 Before we can be fully open to other people, we normally have to let down our barriers, and being **trapped in a castle** may represent our difficulty in freeing our-

selves from old attitudes. **Trying to enter a castle** signifies that we recognise obstacles which have to be overcome.

3 Spiritual testing; overcoming obstacles in order to gain greater understanding.

CASTRATE
– also see Sex

1 In any dream that contains sexual trauma, we are usually being alerted to our inner fears. The violent act of castration in a dream indicates the damage we are doing to ourselves in denying such fears.

2 Conventionally, there may be some difficulty in coming to terms with the conflict between the masculine and feminine within oneself.

3 We are prepared to make a life sacrifice, to give up or control the sexual act in favour of celibacy.

CAT
– see Animals

CATACOMB/CRYPT

1 Many dreams contain images which are to do with space underground, and to dream of a crypt or a catacomb signifies a need to come to terms with subconscious religious beliefs or training.

2 Our subconscious fears or feelings connected with death can show in a dream as a catacomb or crypt.

3 As a place of hidden forces and occult power, in dreams the catacomb will represent the unconscious.

CATERPILLAR

1 The caterpillar appearing in a dream usually indicates that we are undergoing some form of major change. We may be being warned that we must undergo a complete metamorphosis. We must change and grow from what we are now into a greater potential.

2 To dream of caterpillars would indicate that we need to remain flexible in our attitude to change. Also, because of the caterpillar's association with creeping things, it may represent evil or difficulty.

3 The spiritual potential, largely unrecognised, which must transmute into something more beautiful.

CAULDRON
– also see Kettle

1 Almost universally the cauldron represents abundance, sustenance and nourishment. By association, the magic cauldron suggests fertility and the feminine power of transformation. To dream of a cauldron, therefore, reconnects us with our basic principles.

2 Psychologically, when a cauldron appears in a dream we may need to take note of our intuitive abilities, or of our ability to create new things from simple ingredients.

3 Spiritually the cauldron symbolises renewal and rebirth.

CAVE

1 As with the catacombs, the cave represents a doorway into the unconscious. While initially the cave may be frightening an exploration can reveal strong contact with our own inner selves.

2 Passing through the cave signifies a change of state, and a deeper understanding of our own negative impulses.

3 Spiritual shelter and initiation and rebirth.

CEMETERY

1 The cemetery and its association with death can have a double meaning in dreams. It can represent the parts of ourselves that we have 'killed off' or stopped using. It can also depict our thoughts and feelings about death and the attitudes and traditions surrounding it.

2 In dreams we can often allow our fears to come to the surface in an acceptable way. The cemetery can be a symbol of an appropriate way to handle these fears. In other words, we can legitimately allow ourselves to become frightened.

3 A cemetery is the place of the Dead but also of spiritual regeneration.

CENTAUR

1 Traditionally, the Centaur was half-man and half-beast, and is associated with the Zodiac sign of Sagittarius. To have a Centaur appear in a dream demonstrates the unification of man's animal nature with his qualities of human virtue and judgement.

2 The symbol of a Centaur in a dream represents our ability to unite two complete opposites in an acceptable way.

3 Vision and wisdom.

CENTRE
– also see Position

1 To dream of **being at the centre** of something, such as in the centre of a group of people highlights our awareness of our ability to be powerful within a situation; that everything revolves around us. To be **moving away** from the centre indicates that part of our lives may be off balance.

2 Psychologically, to be at the centre, or in the middle of a situation, shows we need to be aware of both our ability to control that situation and our ability to be flexible. **Moving towards the centre** shows our need for integrity in our day to day life.

3 Totality, wholeness, the origin and sacred space are symbolised.

CEREMONY/RITUAL
– also see Religious Imagery

1 When we dream of taking part in a ceremony or religious ritual we are conscious of a new attitude or skill that is needed or an important change which is taking place in our lives.

2 Any major life change has a profound effect on the dreamer and this is very often shown in dream form as a ceremony.

3 Ceremonies and rituals are used for initiation, deeper awareness and to establish new order.

CHAIN

1 To dream of chains in any form indicates a type of restriction or dependency. Just as we need strength to break out of chains, it is also needed in supporting chains. In becoming aware of what is holding us back, we also become appreciative of how to break free.

2 In dreams, we can become conscious of beliefs or mental attitudes – both in ourselves and others – which can create problems. The links in a chain can very often symbolise the communication that we need to free ourselves.

3 Bondage and slavery, dignity and unity are all symbolised by chains and highlight their ambiguity.

CHALICE

1 In dreams the chalice represents the feminine. Because of its religious significance, the chalice usually represents something that may seem to be unattainable except without a great deal of effort. It can also represent an important event or ceremony *(see Cup)*.

2 The chalice is associated with the symbolism of the heart, containing the lifeblood. In the chalice this is represented by wine – wine and blood having the same meaning.

3 The source of inexhaustible sustenance, abundance, the Holy Grail.

CHARIOT
– also see Journey

1 In modern times most people will dream about the car or other forms of transport. To dream of a chariot would possibly imply the necessity for old-fashioned methods of control within the situations surrounding the dreamer.

2 On a psychological level we may have to explore archetypal images

(see Archetypes) for an understanding of our own motivations. The chariot may represent basic urges before they have been altered by conditioning.

3 The Sun and the Divine are represented by the chariot in dreams.

CHARITY

1 To dream of **giving or receiving charity** has a lot to do with our ability to give and receive love. **A charity box** in a dream usually indicates an awareness of our own needs.

2 Charity has connections with our ability to care about others. To dream of a charitable act often alerts us to the wider issues that are important in our lives.

3 Charity comes from the word 'caritas' which means caring from the heart.

CHASED

1 Dreaming of **being chased or of trying to escape** is perhaps one of the most common dreams; usually we are trying to escape responsibility, our own sense of failure, fear or emotions we can't handle.

2 Being chased by shadows shows the need to escape from something previously repressed, such as past childhood trauma or difficulty. To be **chased by an**

animal generally indicates we have not come to terms with our own passion.

3 Spiritually the image of being chased or pursued suggests either fear of one's actions, or is a play on words, as in chaste.

CHASM

1 When we dream of a chasm or large hole, we are usually being made conscious of situations that contain some element of the unknown, or are in some way risky. We are going to have to make decisions one way or another.

2 We are being confronted by unknown or perhaps unrecognised negative elements in our own make-up; we have no previous experience by which to judge our actions or reactions.

3 We are faced by the Unconscious, the Void.

CHEMIST

1 To dream of a chemist is to link with that part of ourselves that is capable of altering the way we are. We are in touch with the wisdom – which is inherent in us all – about the Self.

2 The chemist on a psychological level is the part of us which looks after health concerns and self-healing.

3 The Alchemist is one who changes base material (basic spiritual knowledge) into spiritual gold.

CHESS
– also see Games

1 The game of chess originally signified the 'war' between good and evil. So in dreams it may still express the conflict within. It may also indicate the need for strategy in our lives.

2 Playing chess and losing indicates that we have undertaken an activity in our waking lives which cannot be successful. We have not got the wherewithal, or perhaps the knowledge, to pit ourselves against greater forces.

3 The conflict between the spiritual powers of light and darkness is highlighted.

CHEST/BOX

1 A chest or box appearing in a dream delineates the way we keep hidden or store our emotions. Our most important ideals and hopes may need to be kept secret. It may also show the best in us; our best insights.

2 Emotionally, we need to give some limitation to our feelings and secret desires. In dreams a box – whether plain or otherwise – will show how we handle life.

3 Pandora's Box and the story of

how negativity was released into the world is the best example of a box image on a spiritual level. We need to be aware that care must be taken when first exploring the spiritual.

CHILD/CHILDREN
– see People

CHIMNEY
1 When we dream of chimneys we are linking with a very old concept, that of escape from the mundane and ordinary into freedom. Any opening in a roof of a temple, tepee, tent, etc. represents the awareness of a change of state that may be an important part of growth.
2 Psychologically, a chimney and the passage of smoke portrays the channelling of energy in a more productive way than is presently occurring.
3 Dreaming of a chimney indicates that escape to the heavens through the solar gateway is possible.

CHISEL
1 The meaning of a chisel in a dream would depend on whether or not the dreamer is a craftsman in waking life. In such a case it will depict pride in achievement and specialist knowledge. If the dreamer

has no skill it will depend on other symbolism in the dream, but will probably indicate the need to use force in a situation known to the dreamer.
2 Intellectual drives may put us in a position of needing to break through a barrier in order to succeed in a favourite project.
3 In sacred architecture the chisel is the active, masculine principle in relationship with the passive and feminine.

CHOKE
1 When we find ourselves choking in a dream we are coming up against our inability to express ourselves appropriately. There is some conflict between our inner and outer selves, perhaps some indecision over whether we should speak out or remain silent.
2 We are being stifled by people or circumstances and are not in control of either.
3 Choking can indicate spiritual conflict and restraint. Choking in a dream therefore eventually has us learn when to speak and when to remain silent.

CHRISTMAS TREE
1 Because for most people the Christmas tree is associated with a time of celebration, to have one appear in a dream signifies the

marking of a particular period of time, perhaps a new beginning. It may also indicate a time of giving, and by association the ability to enjoy the present.

2 We may recognise in a Christmas tree the lightening up of a situation which has been either oppressive or depressive.

3 The tree of rebirth and immortality, because of its ever-green qualities.

CHRYSALIS

1 There are two ways in which a chrysalis can be interpreted within a dream. Firstly, as potential for action, which has not yet been realised, and secondly protection in a situation that must wait until the time is right.

2 Change is taking place within us, but on a very subtle level which is not immediately recognisable.

3 Metamorphosis and Magical Powers are symbolised by the chrysalis.

CHURCH BUILDINGS
– also see Church in Buildings and Religious Imagery

1 A church represents our feelings about organised religion. In dreams it can be a place of sanctuary, particularly in the sense that we can have a shared belief with other people. This may be as

much to do with a shared moral code as with a code of personal behaviour.

2 A church building may or may not be considered to be beautiful, but its image links with our appreciation of beautiful objects which mark and enhance our sense of worship. We link with the forces of life within us which enable us to live life more fully.

3 A church becomes a 'world centre' since it marks all that is holy and essential in our lives.

CHURNING

1 Most dreams in which there is a liquid being churned, boiled or made to move in some way links back to a very primitive sense of chaos (lack of order) This indicates we may need to reassess our creative abilities to make use of the energy available to us.

2 We very often need to become conscious of a very deep-rooted chaos in ourselves in order to become appreciative of our capacity for order.

3 Ultimately, chaos must give way to order. One school of thought is that form arose out of churning the chaos.

CIRCLE
– see Shapes

CIRCUMAMBULATION

1 To be walking around a building or a particular spot in a dream is to be creating a 'universe' in which action can take place. It is to be designating that place as having a particular significance.
2 Psychologically we all need to have a place which is ours alone, and to dream of circumambulation signifies taking responsibility for ourselves and our actions.
3 We symbolise creating the centre of our universe by circumambulation.

CIRCUMCISION
– *see Sex*

CIRCUMFERENCE

1 To be **held within** the circumference of a circle is to be made aware through dream images of the limitations we may have set ourselves. To be **shut out** of the circumference of a circle is to be unworthy, or perhaps unknowing.
2 We are on the edge of new knowledge or information and could move in either direction.
3 Spiritual limitation and the world in manifestation and enclosure are signified by the drawing of a circumference.

CITADEL
– *see Castle in Buildings*

CITY/TOWN

1 Dreaming of a city, particularly **one known to us** is to be trying to understand our sense of community; of belonging to groups. We will often, through dreams, give ourselves clues as to what we require in the mental and emotional environment in which we live, and a bustling city may show our need for social interaction. **A deserted city** may portray our feelings of having been neglected by others.
2 A city usually has a core community, and we sometimes represent the place of work or opportunity in this way.
3 A spiritual community to which we belong can be represented by a city, since a city was originally given status because it had a cathedral.

CLIFF

1 To be on **the edge of a cliff** in a dream indicates the dreamer is facing danger. It shows the need to make a decision as to how to deal with a situation, and possibly be open to taking a risk. We are often facing the unknown.
2 There may be a step we need to take which will psychologically put us either on edge or on the edge in such a way that we must overcome our own fears in order to proceed through our own limitations.

3 The cliff edge denotes a step off into the Unknown.

CLIMB

1 To dream of climbing is to dream of getting away from something, possibly to escape. We may be avoiding trouble.

2 We are trying to reach new heights in our lives, possibly having to make greater efforts than before to succeed.

3 Ascension, in the sense of climbing to achieve enlightenment, is an often perceived spiritual symbol.

CLOAK
– see Clothes

CLOCK

1 Largely, when a clock appears in a dream we are being alerted to the passage of time. We may need to pay more attention to our own sense of timing or duty, or may need to recognise that there is a sense of urgency in what we are doing.

2 The **clock hands** in a dream may be indicating those numbers that are important to us *(See Numbers)*. When an **alarm clock rings** we are being warned of danger.

3 The Realisation of Age and Time is signified by a clock.

CLOSE

1 To **be close** to someone in a dream can mean we are looking for intimacy, or perhaps protection. **To close a door** acknowledges the fact that we must make a decision to put the past behind us.

2 We can indicate to ourselves in dreams the fact that we are emotionally closed within a situation.

3 Spiritually to be close to someone is to have empathy with them.

CLOTHES

1 The clothes we wear in a dream can often depict the facade, or persona, we create for other people. We have certain roles that we adopt in response to other's reactions. Clothes which others are wearing in our dreams can also set the scene for an acting out of some of the confrontations which take place.

2 Clothes can often act as a protection against being touched. This protection may also be against having the real self violated. Clothes can conceal or reveal. In covering up nudity they conceal our perceived imperfections and, by implication, disguise our sexuality. In revealing certain parts of us our dreams may show in what ways we are vulnerable.

Getting undressed can suggest the shedding of old beliefs and inhibitions. **Losing one's**

clothes or being naked highlights our vulnerability and fears. **Dressing inappropriately, e.g. wearing formal clothes on a casual occasion and vice versa** When we find ourselves in this position in a dream, we are conscious of our own difficulty in 'fitting in' with other people. It will depend on the dream scenario whether we are surprised or distressed, and it is often the emotion that we experience which gives us the correct interpretation. We may be deliberately not conforming to others' perception of us, or trying to conform too much in adopting a certain role. **The colour of the clothing** is often significant *(see Colour)*. **Clothes being worn by someone to whom they do not belong** There is confusion in the dreamer's mind as to which roles are appropriate for each character. **A man wearing woman's clothing** The dreamer needs to be more conscious of their feminine side. **A uniform on a woman** The dreamer is highlighting the need to be aware of the more disciplined and masculine side of their personality. **Changing clothes** We are attempting to change our image. **Clothes that have been cut short** We may be outgrowing former pleasures and need to look to pastures new for our entertainment. **Pretty clothes** We have much to appreciate in our lives. **Clothes belonging to a particular person** We are being reminded of that person, even though we are aware that they cannot necessarily be with us.

Various articles of clothing are believed to have certain symbolic meanings:

Coat/Shawl (and especially a cloak) A coat can suggest warmth and love, but also protection. This protection can be either physical or emotional, and particularly in the case of a **cloak**, can be the spiritual protection of Faith. **A sheepskin coat** may emphasise this significance *(also see Sheep in Animals)*. **Fear of losing the coat** can suggest the fear of losing faith and belief. **The coat may be too short, or not thick enough** We may be fearful that our love, or the protection we have, is not adequate for our needs.

Gloves – *also see individual entry* The meaning of gloves can be ambivalent. They can represent covering and protecting oneself, but also 'showing one's hand' and challenging the status quo.

Hat/Cap A hat is a symbol of wisdom and the intellect and also of protection. It can also signify both spirituality and sexuality, depending on the other aspects of the dream.

Pyjamas/Nightclothes Pyjamas suggest relaxation and hence openness.

Raincoat A raincoat again holds the symbolism of protection, but this time against other people's emotional onslaught. Very occasionally it may suggest some kind of wish to return to a womb-like state.

Shirt A shirt can suggest appropriate action, but also, as in a **hair shirt**, grief and penitence.

Shoes Shoes signify our ability – or otherwise – to be grounded and in touch with everyday life. Recognising shoes that we, or others, are wearing in a dream are strange alerts us to an adjustment that needs to be made to our attitude to life. **Lacing up shoes** in a dream is supposed to be a well-known symbol of death as are **shoes on a table**.

Tie A tie in can have several significances in dreams. For some it can represent correctness and good behaviour, and for others, presumably because of its shape, it will signify the phallus.

Underclothes When we dream of underclothes – whether our own or other people's – we are considering hidden attitudes to self-image or sexuality.

Veil or veil-like garments *(also see individual entry)* When we, or others, are wearing a veil we are either trying to hide something, or are only partially accepting knowledge about ourselves or our relationship to others.

3 Clothes can suggest spiritual protection. For instance, certain types of clothes will highlight roles and status.

CLOUDS

1 Dreaming of clouds can have two meanings, depending on the other circumstances in the dream. It can either indicate uplifting or religious feelings, or can show that we are feeling overshadowed by someone or something. It can also warn of the possibility of difficulty or danger to come.

2 We may have a hidden depression which can be dealt with only after it has been given form in a dream.

3 Clouds were previously supposed to be the vehicle for Divine Power.

CLOVER

1 Traditionally the clover plant is considered to be lucky, so to find clover in a dream denotes good fortune is on its way.

2 We need to look at our ability to bring the various parts of our personality back into harmony with one another.

3 This is an example of body, soul and spirit, or any representation of the triad of divinity, Father, Son and Holy Spirit.

CLUB (PEOPLE)

1 When we dream of being in a club such as a **night-spot or sports club,** we are highlighting the right of every human being to belong.

2 Psychologically we are not able to be part of a group until we have a certain level of maturity, so to dream of being with a crowd can denote our awareness of ourselves.

3 Organised Ritual is an important part of the progression to spiritual awareness.

CLUB (WEAPON)

1 To dream of using a weapon to club someone denotes an inner violence that has remained unexpressed. It may also depict our violence against ourselves.

2 We have great strength at our disposal, for which we need to find an outlet.

3 The club signifies masculinity, although rather crudely expressed in this instance.

COCK
– also see Birds

1 The cock has always been a symbol of a new day, and of vigilance or watchfulness, so to have one appear in a dream forecasts a new beginning or warning to be vigilant in one's daily work.

2 We may need to be more up front and courageous in what we are doing.

3 Masculine principle, the Bird of Fame and the dawn are all perceived in the symbol of the cock.

COCOON
– see Chrysalis

COFFIN

1 When we dream of a coffin, we are reminding ourselves of our own mortality. We may also be coming to terms with the death of a relationship and feelings of loss.

2 We are perhaps shutting our own feelings away and therefore causing a part of ourselves to die.

3 Redemption, resurrection and salvation are all personified by the coffin.

COLD

1 To be conscious of cold in a dream is to be aware of feeling neglected, or of being left out of things.

2 We can very often translate our

inner feelings or our emotions into a physical feeling in dreams. To feel cold is one such translation.

3 Spiritual loss can be felt in dreams as extreme cold.

COLOURS

1 Colour is a vital part of symbolism. This is partly to do with the vibratory frequency which each individual colour has, and partly to do with tradition. Scientific experiments have now been carried out to ascertain what effect colour has, and have proved what occultists and healers have always known. In working with the colours of the rainbow, we discover that the warm, lively colours – which give back light – are yellow, orange and red. Cold passive colours are blue, indigo and violet. Green is a synthesis of both warmth and cold. White light holds all colour in it.

2 By working with one's own colour spectrum, it is possible to maintain health. Some meanings given to colours are

Black This colour holds within it all colour in potential. It suggests manifestation, negativity and judgement.

Blue It is the colour of the clear blue sky. This is the prime healing colour. It suggests relaxation, sleep and peacefulness.

Brown The colour of the earth, death and commitment.

Green This is the colour of balance and harmony. It is the colour of nature and of plant life.

Grey There is probably no true grey. It means devotion and ministration.

Magenta This is in some ways a colour which links both the physical and spiritual. It signifies relinquishment, selflessness, perfection and meditative practice.

Orange This is an essentially cheerful uplifting colour. The qualities associated are happiness and independence.

Red Vigour, strength, energy, life, sexuality and power are all connected with is colour. A beautiful clear mid-red is the correct one for these qualities; if there is any other red in dreams, the attributes may not be totally uncontaminated.

Turquoise The colour is clear greeny blue. This is supposed in some religions to be the colour of the freed soul. It means calmness and purity.

Violet This colour, while found by some to be too strong, means nobility, respect and hope. Its purpose is to uplift.

White This colour contains within it all colours. It suggests innocence, spiritual purity and wisdom.

Yellow This colour is the one which is closest to daylight. Connected with the emotional self, the attributes are thinking, detachment and judgement.

3 Colour affirms the existence of light. In spiritual terms, red is the colour of self-image and sexuality, orange is relationship – both with self and others. Yellow is the emotional self, green is self-awareness blue is self-expression and wisdom. Indigo is the colour of creativity, while violet depicts cosmic responsibility.

COMB

1 A comb is a many-toothed implement and often emphasises the need to neaten or tidy something up in our lives. We need to tidy up our thoughts. **In a man's dream,** it can indicate seduction or sensuality.

2 We may be conscious of the fact that we need to work with our self-image.

3 Fertility, the rays of the sun, entanglement and music are all represented by the comb.

COMET

1 To dream of seeing a comet is to recognise the possibility of circumstances arising very quickly over which we have no control. The outcome may be unavoidable.

2 The answer to a problem may come to us with the speed of light.

3 The coming of calamity, war, fire or danger can be seen in dreams as the comet.

COMPASS

1 Dreaming of a compass is often about an attempt to find a direction or activity. We need to be able to understand the differing directions offered to us, and to follow the one that is right for us.

2 Often having the same significance as the circle, the compass can represent the source of life, or sometimes justice.

3 Spiritually, when we are trying to find direction, and sometimes our own limitations and boundaries, we will dream of a compass.

CONCH
– also see Shell

1 The spiral convolutions on a shell have often been associated with perfection and therefore plenty. Dreaming of such an object would link with a primitive understanding of those things we can permit ourselves to have.

2 The conch shell was, and still is, used as a trumpet in certain societies, hence it may be seen as a warning.

3 The conch shell links with the spiral *(see Shapes)*.

CONVOLVULUS

1 When we are in a position of being hampered or smothered by circumstances or people round about us, we can often dream of being bound in some way. The convolvulus plant is one such symbol.

2 Convolvulus can represent uncertainty and difficulty in making decisions. Perhaps we have too many options.

3 Convolvulus is said to stand for humility and devotion.

COMPUTER

1 The computer and other high technology images are now such a part of people's lives that it very much depends on other circumstances in the dream as to the correct interpretation of this image. If one **works with computers,** it may simply be a means to an end whereas in other cases it will be a reminder of personal potential or abilities.

2 We are making a link with past memories or stored information which we may need to access in order to progress.

3 The computer can symbolise spiritual records and the past, present and future.

CONTRACEPTIVE

– see Sex

COOKING

1 To be cooking in a dream is to be preparing nourishment or to be satisfying a hunger, whether our own or other people's. This hunger may not be as straightforward as a physical hunger, but something more subtle such as a need to make use of the varied opportunities available to us.

2 To be able to move forward in our lives we may need to blend certain parts of our existence in new and original ways in order to succeed. Dreaming of cooking highlights this. We may need to nurture a new ability.

3 Cooking can symbolise creativity. There is a delightful fable which tells how God baked the various ethnic races into being.

CORD

1 Within any relationship there are certain restrictions or dependencies that become apparent, and these may be depicted in dreams as cords or ties. These emotional bonds can be both limiting and freedom-giving.

2 There is a need to be appreciative of the ties of duty and affection.

3 The Silver Cord – that subtle energy which holds the life force within the body.

CORN

1 Most dreams containing images of corn or wheat symbolise fertility or fruitfulness. They may also represent new life – either pregnancy or new developments in other ways.

2 To be **harvesting corn** is to be reaping the rewards of hard work. We may be linking with some very primeval needs and requirements.

3 The Great Mother in her nurturing aspect is always shown with corn.

CORNER

1 To turn a corner in a dream indicates that we have succeeded in moving forward into new experiences, despite what may have seemed to be obstacles in front of us. Turning a **right-handed corner** indicates a logical course of action, to turn a **left-handed** one indicates a more intuitive approach.

2 We are making available a hidden or little admitted aspect of ourselves. We no longer need to feel trapped or restricted. We can handle the unexpected or the new experience.

3 To turn the corner spiritually is to gain a new perspective on our own spiritual indecision.

CORNUCOPIA

1 Like the conch shell, to dream of a cornucopia can denote abundance, endless bounty, fertility and fruitfulness. It may be more than we are used to or can handle.

2 Within ourselves we have unlimited potential to create both an acceptable present and a sustainable future.

3 The Horn of Plenty is an image common in one form or another in all spiritual work. The abundance may be for us or the rest of the world.

CORRIDOR
– also see Hall/Passage in Buildings

1 When we dream of being in a corridor we are usually in a state of transition; possibly moving from one state of mind to another, or perhaps between two states of being.

2 We may be in an unsatisfactory situation, but not be able to make decisions except to accept the inevitable.

3 We are in a state of spiritual limbo.

COSMETICS
– also see Make-Up

1 To be using cosmetics in a dream can have two meanings. There is a need either to register the fact that we are covering up our features or that conversely we are enhancing our natural beauty. **If we are using cosmetics on someone else,** we literally need to 'make up' with that person.

2 Psychologically we may feel that we have a problem with our public image, and need to put on some sort of front before we can be seen by others.

3 The personality can show itself in many guises.

COUNTRYSIDE
– also see Places

1 When we dream of the countryside we are putting ourselves in touch with our own natural spontaneous feelings. We may have memories of the countryside that invoke a particular mood state or way of being. We can return, without feeling guilty, to a very relaxed state.

2 There is, in most peoples' minds, a type of freedom and openness about the countryside which is not necessarily available in towns and cities. It may signify a need to clarify our own feelings about our lifestyle.

3 The forces of 'nature' in us can be symbolised by scenes of the countryside.

COW
– see Animals

COYOTE
– see Wolf in Animals

CRAB

1 A crab appearing in a dream can indicate mothering, particularly of the 'smother love' type, but can also be the qualities of unreliability and self-interest. The crab can also, because of the way it moves, denote deviousness.

2 By word association the crab can represent sickness, or something eating away at us.

3 The Astrological sign of Cancer and the Great Mother *(see Introduction)* are represented by the crab.

CRADLE

1 To dream of a cradle can represent new life or new beginnings. As a **precognitive dream** a cradle can represent pregnancy, while **in a man's dream** a cradle can represent the need to return to a womblike, protected state.

2 An empty cradle can represent a woman's fear of childlessness or her fears of motherhood, depending on the other aspects of the dream.

3 The physical as opposed to the spiritual body is sometimes represented as a cradle.

CRACK

1 Dreaming of an article which is cracked indicates our recognition of something which is flawed in our lives. There may be a weakness or difficulty in the attitudes and defences we use to meet life's problems.

2 Psychologically a crack may represent the irrational or the unexpected. It may indicate our inability to hold things together mentally.

3 There may be a spiritual flaw in our make-up. A little thought should reveal it.

CRANE

1 When we dream of a **building crane** we are often being told of the need to raise our level of awareness in some matter. We need to make an attempt to understand the overall or universal implications of our actions.

2 We are capable of gaining control or status within a situation so we can build on it to our advantage.

3 As a **bird**, the crane is a messenger of the gods. It allows communion with the gods and the ability to enter into higher states of consciousness.

CRESCENT
– see Shapes

CRICKET
– see Games

CROCODILE
– also see Reptiles in Animals

1 To dream of crocodiles, or indeed any reptile, indicates we are looking at the frightening lower aspects of our nature. We may feel we have no control over these, and it would therefore be very easy to be devoured by them.

2 We are consumed by our fear of death, or the death process. We must, however, go through this process in order to overcome death – in order to be resurrected.

3 Liberation from the limitations of the world is symbolised by the crocodile.

CROOKED LINE

1 When a line appears in a dream as crooked, there is usually the need to register the oddity, as being out of balance or off-kilter. There may be some insincerity in our dealings with others. The line may be any sort of line, such as a queue of people, a line of cars or whatever.

2 We must acknowledge our own ability to be diverted from truth and honesty.

3 Deviance from the norm in a spiritual sense can be a falling away of the standards we have set ourselves. If we are aware of this on a spiritual level, a crooked line will often appear in a dream.

CROSS
– see Shape

CROSSING

1 To dream of **crossing a road** is recognising the possibility of danger, fear or uncertainty. We are perhaps pitting ourselves against the majority, or something that is bigger than us.

2 We may encounter something we cannot control, and which may control us. **To be crossing a field** shows we could have a false sense of security, or may need to bring our feelings out into the open.

3 Crossing a river or chasm often depicts death, not necessarily a physical death but possibly spiritual change.

CROSSROADS

1 Dreaming of cross-roads indicates that we are going to have to make choices in our lives, often to do with career or life changes. We perhaps need to be aware of where we have come from in order to make intelligent decisions. Often, to **turn left** at crossroads can indicate taking the wrong route, though it can indicate the

more intuitive path. To **turn right** can obviously mean taking the correct path, but can also mean making logical decisions.

2 We are in a situation where two opposing forces are coming together, not in conflict but in harmony.

3 A magical but dangerous space, since we can go in any direction which seems appropriate.

CROW
– see Birds

CROWD
– also see People

1 Dreaming of being in a crowd could be indicative of the fact that we do not wish to stand out, or that we do not have a sense of direction at present. We may wish to camouflage our feelings from others, to get lost or even to hide our opinions.

2 We need to retain our anonymity, to create a facade for ourselves, or to join a group of like-minded people.

3 A crowd in spiritual terms suggests popular belief, or common religious feelings.

CROWN

1 To dream of a crown is to acknowledge one's own success, and to recognise that we have opportunities that will expand our knowledge and awareness. We may be about to receive an honour or reward of some sort.

2 The crown can represent victory, and dedication, particularly to duty. We may have striven for something and our greatest victory has been against our own inertia.

3 A crown signifies victory over death and attainment.

CRUCIBLE

1 The crucible in a dream links in with receptivity, intuition and the creative side of the dreamer. As a container which is capable of withstanding great heat, it is the aspect which can contain change and make it happen.

2 Psychologically we all hold within ourselves great power which, when released, enables us to take responsibility for others as well as ourselves.

3 Manifestation of spiritual or psychic energy can be perceived as a crucible, a transforming receptacle.

CRUTCH

1 When we dream of crutches we are experiencing the need for support, although it may also be that we need to support others. We may find others inadequate and need to readjust our thinking.

2 We may disapprove of other people's shortcomings or weakness.

3 In developing spiritually we become aware of our various dependencies, whether these are alcohol, drugs, patterns of behaviour or people.

CRUCIFIXION
– see Religious Imagery

CRYSTAL
– see Jewels

CUBE
– see Shapes

CUCKOO
– see Birds

CUL-DE-SAC

1 When the dreamer finds that he or she is **trapped in a cul-de-sac** it symbolises futile action, but perhaps also a state of inertia. Circumstance may be preventing a forward movement, and it may be necessary to retrace one's steps in order to succeed.

2 We are stuck in old patterns of behaviour and may be being threatened by past mistakes.

3 A spiritual cul de sac represents futility.

CUP

1 The cup has much of the symbolism of the chalice, indicating a receptive state which accepts intuitive information. An offering is being made which the dreamer would do well to identify. Often the feminine is offering an opportunity from the unconscious.

2 Intuitively, if we are open to the more feminine side, we are able to both give and receive help and assistance.

3 The feminine awareness of the draught of life, immortality and plenty is intuitively and sensitively used.

CYMBALS

1 Cymbals are connected with rhythm and sound, so for them to appear in a dream is an indication of the need for and return to a basic vibration. Often there is a connection with sex and sexuality since, in some cultures, along with the drum and tambourine, they are used to induce an ecstatic state.

2 We are reconciling passion and desire.

3 Spiritually cymbals signify two inter-dependent halves – one cannot operate without the other.

D

from

Dagger *to* Dwarf

DAGGER

1 When a dagger appears in a dream, the meaning can either be aggressive or defensive. If the dreamer is **using the dagger** to attack someone then he may be trying to cut out some part of himself or trying to get rid of something he does not like. If the dreamer is **being stabbed,** he is highlighting his vulnerability.

2 Psychologically, to be penetrated by any sharp instrument is usually to do with one's masculine side and often refers to one's sexuality.

3 The dagger, if turned on oneself, represents an age-old instrument of sacrifice.

DAISY

1 Because of its connection with childhood (as in daisy-chains), to dream of daisies usually represents innocence and purity.

2 Often in dreams there can be a play on words and the 'days eye' can have particular significance for the dreamer and represent psychological awakening.

3 The daisy is a symbol of spiritual purity.

DAM
– also see Water

1 When we dream of a dam its significance may vary. We may be bottling up our own emotions and drive, or conversely we could be trying to stop somebody else's emotional outburst from happening. To be **building a dam** indicates we are likely to be putting up defences, whereas if a **dam is bursting** we may feel we have no control over emotional situations around us.

2 While on a conscious level we may need to exercise control over our emotions, in dream sequences we will often allow ourselves a natural expression of difficulty or frustration that can be symbolised by an overflow of water.

3 By word association – to be damned.

DANCE/DANCING

1 Dance has always represented freedom and been symbolic of other actions which were necessary for survival. To be dancing in a dream portrays the creation of happiness, feeling at one with the surroundings and possibly getting closer or more intimate with a partner.

2 Psychologically, dance can be a reinforcement of freedom of movement, strength and emotion.

3 Spiritually, dancing has always been taken to represent the rhythm of life. The patterns created are reputed to mirror the patterns of creativity. Dance also signifies the transformation of space into time.

DANGER

1 When we find ourselves in dangerous circumstances in dreams, we are often reflecting the anxieties and dilemmas of everyday life. We may be conscious that our activities could be harmful to us if we carry on in the same way.

2 Dreams can often point to a danger in symbolic form, such as conflict, fire or flood. We may need to have pitfalls represented in such a way in order to recognise them on a conscious level.

3 Dreaming of oneself in a dangerous or precarious position, can also indicate a Spiritual insecurity.

DARK

1 To dream of **being in the dark** usually represents a state of confusion or being in unknown and difficult territory. It may point to a secret part of ourselves or a part that we do not yet know.

2 Intellectually, we are in touch with the depressed, hidden side and may need to deal with the darker aspects of ourselves.

3 Spiritually, the dark side of oneself where chaos may reign, and where ultimately evil will prevail, unless some spiritual understanding can be attained.

DATE (DAY)

1 When a particular date is highlighted in a dream, we are either being reminded of something particularly significant – or possibly traumatic – in our lives or perhaps to consider the symbolism of the numbers contained in the date itself *(see Numbers)*.

2 Very often the psyche gives us information in dreams which is precognitive and it is possible to be alerted to particularly important events in dream form.

3 A certain date or day could point to information about a spiritual festival that the dreamer has sub-consciously retained and which may have relevance for them.

DATE (FRUIT)

1 Because dates are an exotic fruit, when we dream of dates we are becoming conscious of the need for the rare or exotic in our lives. Equally, we may need sweetness and nurturing.

2 We need to be cared for and looked after in a way that is different from normal.

3 Fruit, and particularly the date, is often associated with fertility and fertility rites. In Roman times dates, because of there luscious taste and spiritual connections, were often used as an aphrodisiac during pre-nuptial activities.

DAWN

1 To dream of a dawn or a new day represents a new beginning or a new awareness in circumstances around us. We are looking for different ways of dealing with old situations.

2 Psychologically we are aware of the passage of time, and perhaps the need to mark or celebrate this in some way.

3 A new dawn can bring a great sense of hope. As the new dawn fades that sense of hope grows stronger. A form of spiritual illumination is quite often felt within this type of dream.

DAY

1 When we dream of a day passing, or register that time has passed, we are alerting ourselves to the fact that we need to gauge time in some activity, or that action needs to be taken first before a second thing can happen.

2 Time has no real meaning in dreams, so to note that time is measurable suggests that we are actually looking at the length of our lives.

3 The old saying of 'a day is a long time in politics' goes some way to helping the dreamer understand that a day may also represent a much longer period of time than first thought.

DAY AND NIGHT

1 Dreaming of both day and night indicates the cycle of time or of changes that will inevitably take place. Sometimes indication is given of the nature of an aspect of timing.

2 We often differentiate between two states in dreams, and the contrast between day and night highlights this.

3 Day and night can represent opposites, as in black and white, boy and girl, etc. Indeed, any two opposites may have relevance, and it is up to the dreamer to decide what opposition there is in his or her life.

DEAD PEOPLE

1 Dead people we have known appearing in dreams usually refer back to strong emotions we have had about those people, whether they are negative or positive. For instance, there may be unresolved anger or guilt we still hold and the only way we can deal with it is within a dream sequence.

2 Memories can remain buried for years and often when people who have died appear in dreams, we are being reminded of different times, places or relationships which will help us to deal with present situations.

3 To dream of dead people may

suggest a link of a spiritual nature to our long-forgotten ancestors.

DEATH

1 Traditionally to dream of death indicated the possibility of a birth or a change in circumstances in one's own life or that of people around. Because in the past death held great fear, it also represented calamity, in the sense that nothing would ever be the same again. It was something that had to be experienced and endured rather than understood. In these present times, as peoples' attitudes change, death in a dream indicates a challenge we must confront. We need to adjust our approach to life and to accept that there can be a new beginning if we have courage.

2 On an intellectual level we are becoming conscious of potentials we may have missed or not expressed fully and because of this we are no longer able to make use of them. We need to be sensitive to our ability to resurrect these talents. A change of awareness is taking place, and we may be going through some 'rite of passage' such as puberty to adulthood, maturity to old age and so on.

3 The unseen aspect of life; omniscience, spiritual rebirth; resurrection and reintegration.

DEATH OF ONESELF

1 To dream of our own death is to be exploring our own feelings about death; the retreat from the challenge of life or the split between mind and body. Leaving the body is frequently an expression of this breach between the ego and life processes.

2 One's own death can often be used in dreams to explore others' feelings about us.

3 Death is a transition from an awareness of the gross physical to the more spiritual self.

DEEP

– also see Position

1 When we dream of the deep we are usually considering past family influences of which we may not be consciously mindful.

2 We may be trying to understand archetypal patterns which have not been recognisable in the past. There may be information available to us which we can only understand through being able to appreciate our own emotions.

3 The Unknown, and therefore the unfathomable, is often symbolised by depth in some way – deep water, deep underground etc.

DEFECATE

– see Excrement in Body

DEMOLITION

1 It rather depends on the circumstances in the dream whether demolition highlights major changes in the dreamer's life, or a self-inflicted trauma. If we are **carrying out the demolition** we need to be in control but if **someone else** is in charge we may feel powerless in the face of change.

2 We may be conscious of a build-up of emotional energy within ourselves which can only be handled by a breakdown of old attitudes and approaches.

3 Fanaticism and anarchy (a need to break down an old order), can be demonstrated by demolition in a dream.

DEPARTING

– also see Journey

1 To be departing from a known situation such as **leaving home** indicates a breaking away from old or habitual patterns of behaviour. We may need to give ourselves the freedom to be independent.

2 We may have a strong desire to get away from responsibility or difficulties, but must be careful how we handle it.

3 Conscious rejection of the past can be represented by departure in a dream.

DESCENT/ DESCENDING

1 When we dream of a descent, such as **coming down a mountain or steps**, we are often searching for an answer to a particular problem and need to be conscious of past trauma or something we have left behind and what we can learn from it.

2 We may fear a loss of status, and yet be aware of the positive aspects of such loss.

3 Going down into the underworld, the quest for mystic wisdom, rebirth and immortality are all shown in dreams by descent.

DESERT

1 To dream of **being alone in a desert** signifies a lack of emotional satisfaction, loneliness or perhaps isolation. Dreaming of **being in a desert with someone** else may show that particular relationship is sterile, or going nowhere.

2 We may need to consider a course of action very carefully if we are to 'survive' in our present circumstances.

3 A desert can symbolise desolation and abandonment, but also a place of contemplation, quiet and divine revelation.

DESK
– also see Table

1 If the desk we are dreaming about is an old one, such as our old **school desk or an antique one** we perhaps should be returning to old values, habits or disciplines. If it is a **work or office desk** we may need to consider the way in which we are carrying out our everyday life.

2 To dream of being at **someone else's desk** could indicate a lack of confidence in our own abilities.

3 Daily ritual and discipline can be relevant spiritual practices in our everyday lives *(see Altar)*.

DESTINATION
– also see Places

1 It is fairly common to dream of trying to get to a particular destination, and this would normally indicate a conscious ambition and desire If the **destination is not known to us,** we may be moving into unknown territory, or be attempting something new and different.

2 Destinations such as **exotic and faraway places** could signify our need for excitement and stimulation, or hopes we may have for the future.

3 A Spiritual goal or aspiration is signified in dreams by knowing what our destination is.

DEVIL
– also see Fiend

1 In previous times, the figure of the Devil was one to be feared and hated. As the wilder, more Pagan side of ourselves the conventional figure with horns and a tale will often appear in dreams. It is almost as though it has been given 'life' by the way that people concentrate on it. Once it is understood as something to be confronted, as something belonging to all of us, the Devil loses it potency.

2 As a personification of the evil side of ourselves, we often need to have an object to confront. In dreams, as in fantasies, the Devil allows us to do this. If we fear our own wrongdoing, that fear can also manifest as the Devil.

3 The Devil is the personification of Evil, or Lucifer.

DEVOUR

1 When we dream of **being eaten** we are facing our fear of losing our sense of identity; of being consumed by something such as an obsession, an overwhelming emotion or drive, or of having to deal with something we cannot control.

2 If **we ourselves are devouring something** we may need to consider the way we nurture ourselves.

3 Clearing evil – or taking in good – is symbolised as devouring it. Kali, as the keeper of the grave-yard, symbolises this as do the devouring Gods. It is a way of returning to source.

DEW

1 Dew or gentle rain falling in a dream can represent a sense of newness and refreshment we have perhaps not been able to obtain, except from an external source.

2 We may need to accept that gentle emotion can cleanse us of whatever is troubling us.

3 Spiritual refreshment, benediction and blessing are all symbols connected to dew.

DIADEM

1 The diadem or tiara in a dream often acknowledges the power of the feminine, or the ability to use the mental or intellectual abilities to obtain supremacy.

2 There is always a magical feeling or sense of wonder associated with the diadem, and it can be taken to represent the magical and unknown.

3 The diadem is perceived as an emblem of the Queen of Heaven and the circle of continuity. It often has twelve jewels which are said to represent the Twelve Tribes of Israel.

DICE/DIE

1 To be **playing with dice** in a dream emphasises the fact that we are playing with fate or taking chances in life which we really ought to be considering more carefully.

2 If **someone else is rolling the dice,** we are leaving our fate in the hands of other people and must therefore run our lives according to their rules.

3 A dice or die, through the play on words, is a way of taking chances which, in the spiritual sense, may be irrevocable.

DIGGING/ EXCAVATION
– also see Mines

1 Often when we begin the process of learning about ourselves we need to uncover those parts we have kept hidden, and this is shown in dreams as excavating a hole or digging up an object.

2 On a creative level we may have realisations which are hard to access and must be dug out.

3 Spiritually we need to have access to the characteristics of the unconscious.

DINOSAUR
– also see Prehistoric

1 When we dream of monsters or prehistoric animals we are touching into very basic images which have the power to frighten and amaze us. Because they are considered to be so large, we need to be aware of whether it is their size or their power which is frightening. Urges as basic as this can threaten our existence, by either their size or power.

2 We are in touch with an archaic or outmoded part of ourselves. Remembering that the dinosaur is extinct, and that for most people they are perceived as fossils, such a dream can recognise the part of ourselves that has become set in stone.

3 We all have within us a chaotic past which has been a huge part of our lives. Spiritual progress dictates that we understand that this part can be changed and our present selves can grow from that ability to change. Old standards have to break down.

DIRTY

1 We will dream of **being dirty** when we are not operating within our own principles or when someone else's action has put us in a situation which we find compromises us.

2 To be dirty in a dream may indicate that we are not at ease with our own bodily functions. If **someone we know has made us dirty,** it is an indication not to trust that person.

3 Evil or negative impulses are often shown in dreams as things or people being dirty.

DISK

1 A computer disk in a dream could suggest a great deal of information and knowledge is available to us. A **compact disc** can have a similar significance except that its content, being musical, is more recreational that work-oriented. This could indicate that, in waking life, we need to be aware of our need for relaxation.

2 The disk in a dream has the same significance as the sun, and represents perfection and the renewal of life.

3 Divinity and power are represented spiritually by the disk.

DISMEMBERMENT

1 Dismemberment of the body, or indeed any dream where some type of fragmentation takes place, is largely to do with being rendered powerless. A situation may be tearing us apart and violent action may be necessary before we can recover our equilibrium.

2 Psychologically we need to take our old feelings and ideas apart to make sense of what is going on. This process has to take place before a rebuilding of one's life can happen.

3 The death and rebirth symbolism of initiation; the death of the Self before reintegration and rebirth.

DISTAFF

1 This symbol will largely have been replaced in dreams by modern technological symbols, but usually represents the feminine attributes and may also represent the passage of time.

2 Most symbols dealing with thread or weaving and spinning are to do with the creation of an intuitive pattern within our lives.

3 Time, creation and fate have always been symbolised by the distaff.

DIVING

1 To dream of diving can represent the need for freedom within our lives, although we may associate freedom with taking risks. We may need to burrow into our unconscious to find the ability to face anxiety.

2 We need to be extremely focused and attentive to dive successfully and must bring these qualities into play in a situation we are in.

3 Diving suggests the taking of spiritual risk.

DIVORCE

1 Dreaming of divorce may actually refer to our feelings about that person in the dream, and perhaps our need to be free of responsibilities. It may also indicate the necessity to clarify our own relationship between the various facets of our personality.

2 We are becoming conscious of the need to express emotion if we are to maintain our own integrity. We are moving into a new way of life, perhaps without the old support systems we have used.

3 To dream of divorce would suggest a potential difficulty in understanding a loss of integration in our personality.

DOCTOR

1 When we dream of a doctor we are aware that we need to give way to a higher authority in health matters. For older people the doctor may also represent the professional classes.

2 It will depend what sort of doctor appears in our dream as to the correct interpretation. A **surgeon** would suggest the need to cut something out of our lives. A **physician** would indicate that careful consideration should be given to our general state, whereas a **psychiatrist** signifies the need to look at our mental state. If the doctor is **known to us** he may stand as an authority figure.

3 The personality of a doctor in dreams suggests the appearance of the healer within.

DOG
– also see Animals

1 Dreaming of a dog depends on whether it is one known to us (such as a childhood pet), when it then may represent happy memories; if **unknown** it may signify the qualities of loyalty and unconditional love associated with dogs.

2 To dream of a **pack of wild dogs** portrays emotions and feelings of which we are afraid.

3 A dog symbolises the guardian of the underworld. In Egyptian mythology this is depicted by Anubis, the dog-headed god.

DOLL

1 A doll can depict either how the dreamer felt as a child, or a need for comfort. It may also express an undeveloped part of the dreamer's personality.

2 We tend to learn through play, and for a doll to appear in a dream usually indicates the need to relearn some childhood lessons which we have forgotten.

3 The doll can be a representation of the soul of a particular person who can be helped, or harmed, by sympathetic magic or witchcraft.

DOLPHIN

1 Dolphins are perceived by sailors as saviours and guides, as having special knowledge and awareness, and this is the image which surfaces in dreams. Coming from the depths – the unconscious – the dolphin represents the hidden side of ourselves which needs to be understood.

2 Psychologically the dolphin may portray the more playful side of our personality, but at the same time may make us aware of the trickster. Dreaming of **swimming with dolphins** suggests putting ourselves in touch with, and appreciating, our own basic nature.

3 The dolphin now stands for Spiritual sensitivity and safety.

DONKEY
– see Horse in Animals

DOOR
– also see Buildings

1 A door in a dream signifies a movement between two states of being. It can represent entry into a new phase of life, such as puberty or middle age. There may be opportunities available to us about which we must make deliberate decisions.

2 If the door in the dream is **shut or difficult to open,** it indicates we are creating obstacles for ourselves, whereas if the door is **open** we can have the confidence to move forward.

3 Spiritually a door represents the sheltering aspect of the Great Mother *(See Introduction).*

DOVE
– see Birds

DRAGON

1 The dragon is a complex and universal symbol. Seen as both frightening and yet manageable, under certain circumstances it will represent in us our own untamed nature. We must come to terms with our own passions and chaotic beliefs. Often we can only achieve this through dreams, in an environment that has been suitably created.

2 There is a heroic part in each of us which must face dangerous conflict in order to overcome the lower side of our natures and reach our inner resources. Dreaming of a dragon allows us that conflict.

3 The dragon is traditionally the Guardian of Power. In conquering the dragon, spiritually we become custodians of our own future.

DRAGONFLY

1 To dream of a dragonfly is to appreciate the need for freedom, but equally to recognise that freedom can be short-lived.

2 We may be pursuing a dream, but without any real focus as to what we actually want out of life. Our reactions are instinctive rather than logical.

3 Though the dragonfly's physical existence is short, it symbolises immortality and regeneration.

DRAUGHTS/ CHEQUERS
– see Games

DRAUGHT

1 To **feel a draught** in a dream is to be aware of an external force which could affect us or a situation we are in. To **create a draught** is literally to be attempting to clear the atmosphere.

2 Traditionally, a **cold draught** when working psychically indicates a visitation by Spirit. In dreams it suggests a communication from a hidden part of ourselves.

3 The Holy Spirit manifested as a rushing wind to enable the disciples to spread the Gospel.

DRINK

1 To be drinking in a dream is to be

absorbing or taking something in. **What we are drinking** is also important, e.g. fruit juice would indicate we are aware of the need for cleansing and purity. The colour of what is being drunk is also important *(see Alcohol and Colours)*.

2 Drinking in a dream may indicate our need for comfort and sustenance. As a basic requirement for life, drinking symbolises the interplay between the inner need to sustain life and external availability of nourishment.

3 Spiritually there is a belief that the drinking of wine is, or symbolises, the imbibing of Divine life and power.

DROWNING
– also see Swimming

1 When we are drowning in a dream this usually indicates we are in danger of being overwhelmed by emotions we cannot handle. We are fearful of allowing our emotions free expression. Drowning may also indicate a perceived inability to handle a stressful situation around us at the time of the dream.

2 We have allowed ourselves to be put in a situation over which we have no control. We may be 'floundering around' with no way of being able to escape from a difficulty we are in.

3 Drowning symbolises an immersion in the Sea of Life, and therefore a loss of ego.

DRUGS
– also see Intoxication

1 When drugs appear in a dream – whether self-administered or not – this suggests that we may need external help to enable us to change our inner perceptions. **To be taking drugs** suggests we feel we have relinquished control of a situation in our waking lives and are having to rely on external stimuli. **To have an adverse drug reaction** could mean that we fear madness. **To be given drugs against our will** indicates that we are being forced to accept an unpalatable truth.

2 We may be attempting to avoid reality and drugs can enable us to do this. They can also be a healing agent in restoring balance. **To be given drugs by a qualified person** signifies that we have accepted someone else's greater knowledge. **To be sold drugs illegally** indicates that we are prepared to take unnecessary risks.

3 Certain drugs can be taken to induce a state of euphoria or a change of consciousness. This can be dangerous, since it is like using a crowbar – rather than a key – to open a door. Such practices can only be valid if done with knowledge and understanding.

DRUM
– also see Musical Instruments

1 To **hear a drum** in a dream indicates the basic rhythm needed to keep us sane and healthy. We need to be more in touch with our natural rhythms and primitive urges. To be **playing a drum** is taking responsibility for the rhythm of our own lives.

2 We may be seeking a more natural form of expression than the normal, everyday methods we use.

3 Sound. Divine truth, revelation.

DRUNK
– also see Alcohol and Intoxication

1 To be drunk in a dream means that we are abandoning ourselves to irrational forces. We want to be free from responsibility and from having inhibitions. **To make someone else drunk** is to be forcing our irresponsibility onto someone else.

2 Being drunk indicates the need to reconnect with a part of ourselves which can tolerate inappropriate behaviour. In previous societies it was an accepted part of life that, at certain times, drunkenness was allowed as a way of celebration or as a release of

tension – hence the term a 'Bacchanalian revel'.

3 Ecstasy is reputedly achieved after inhibitions have been removed through getting drunk.

DUCK
– also see Birds

1 As always, other circumstances in the dream may indicate the true relevance of the symbol. A **toy duck** may denote the childlike part of ourselves. To be **feeding the ducks** may show some kind of therapeutic or calming activity is important. To be **eating duck** suggests a treat or celebration in store.

2 We may need to allow the current of life to let us move rather than taking action ourselves.

3 The duck is said to be a symbol of superficiality, presumably because it floats on the water rather than in it.

DWARF/MAL-FORMED FIGURE

1 Any malformation in a dream indicates a part of our personality which has not been integrated or has been left undeveloped. In a dream a dwarf denotes a part of ourselves which has been left damaged by painful childhood trauma or a lack of emotional nourishment.

2 A dwarf may signify a small part of ourselves that needs consideration. This may be a stunted aspect of our personality which does not become apparent until we are prepared to take responsibility for it.

3 A dwarf symbolises the Unconscious and undifferentiated force of nature.

E

from

Eagle *to* Eye

EAGLE
– also see Birds

1 An eagle appearing in a dream signifies inspiration and strength. It may also indicate our need to ascend, in order to release ourselves from old ideas or attitudes. As a bird of prey, the eagle is capable of making use of all the opportunities available to it. Dreaming of one shows we can do likewise.

2 From a psychological point of view, we have the ability to use our intellect to succeed. We can take authority for our own lives. We may need to become objective and to take a wider viewpoint than we have done previously.

3 The eagle also represents a form of Spiritual victory.

EARTH

1 To dream of the **planet Earth** is to take account of the supportive network we have in place in our lives and the attitudes and relationships we take for granted. We are searching for some kind of parental love or social order. **Soft earth** particularly links with the need for mothering or tactile contact.

2 We have the need to be grounded and practical but need support to be so. If we find ourselves **under or trapped** by earth, it shows we need to be more aware of, and understand, our unconscious drives and habits.

3 Earth is the Great Mother and is synonymous with fertility.

EARTHQUAKE

1 Dreaming of an earthquake alerts us to an inner insecurity that we must deal with before it overwhelms us. There is great inner change and growth taking place which could cause upheaval.

2 Old opinions, attitudes and relationships may be breaking up and causing concern.

3 An earthquake, by way of its devastating after-effects, represents Spiritual upheaval.

EAST
– also see Position

1 Specifically dreaming of the East indicates we are looking at the mysterious and religious side of ourselves. We link with instinctual belief as opposed to logical reasoning.

2 We may be looking towards new life or a new beginning *(see Dawn)*.

3 The East in Spiritual terms suggests the spring, a time for hope and youth.

EASTER EGG

1 The Easter egg is a Pagan symbol of renewal and in dreams often takes us back to childhood feelings of promise and wonder. It may also alert us to the passage of time since the mind will often produce symbols of times and seasons rather than actual dates.

2 Dreaming of an Easter egg indicates there is a great deal of potential available to us on a mental level that needs releasing.

3 An Easter egg is associated with Spring, as in 'hope springs eternal'. Rebirth and resurrection.

EATING
– also see Devour, Food and Nourishment

1 To be eating in a dream shows that one is attempting to satisfy one's needs or hunger. Hunger is a basic drive and we need to realise that only once such a drive is met can we move forward to satisfying our more aesthetic needs.

2 Dreaming of eating may denote that we lack some basic nutrient or feedback in our lives. **To not eat or refuse food** indicates an avoidance of growth and change. We may be attempting to isolate ourselves from others or be in conflict with ourselves over our body image. **Being eaten** in a dream signifies we are aware of being attacked by our own – or possibly other people's – emotions and fears or by our internal drives.

Being eaten by a wild animal shows the likelihood of us being consumed by our more basic, animal nature.

3 We are reputed to become what we eat, so spiritually we should eat the best food possible.

ECLIPSE
– also see Moon and Planets

1 Dreaming of an eclipse signifies our fears and doubts about our own success. Others around us seem to be more important or able than we are, which does not allow us to shine or excel at what we are doing.

2 We are about to go through a period of difficulty when we could find ourselves unable to maintain our usual cheerfulness.

3 On a spiritual level, an eclipse can represent a loss of faith. By covering up a source of illumination and enlightenment, it can also represent a darkening of the light through external circumstances.

EDUCATION
– also see School and Teacher

1 To dream of a place of education, such as **a school or college** indicates that we should be considering our own need for discipline or disciplined action. We are perhaps inadequately prepared for a task we are to perform, and to access need more knowledge.

2 Since dreaming of education usually takes us back to a former state, we need to apply knowledge from the experiences we have had to enable us to deal with a present situation.

3 Education can be taken as a symbol of Spiritual Awareness.

EGG

1 The egg is the symbol of unrealised potential, of possibilities yet to come, so to dream of an egg indicates that we have not made fully conscious our natural abilities. To be **eating an egg** shows the need to take in certain aspects of newness before we can fully explore a different way of life.

2 We have a sense of wonder to do with the miracle of life, and a realisation that there is much to plan before we can enjoy life to the full. We may have to withdraw and contemplate before we can undertake new learning experience.

3 The life principle and the germ of all things is said to be contained in the cosmic egg, thus spiritually representing our potential and power to be perfect.

EGYPT
– also see Places

1 Although perhaps less so now, as travel becomes easier, faraway places in dreams usually signify the exotic. Egypt in particular is always seen as magical or connected with ancient knowledge, though this may depend on the dreamer's own knowledge of the country.

2 We are connecting with the magical and strange part of ourselves.

3 Egypt is a recognition of the hidden side of Self: the mysterious.

EJACULATION
– also see Sex

1 The dreamer's attitude to sex often becomes apparent in dreams through the sexual act, and to ejaculate in a dream may be an effort to understand negative feelings. It could also simply be indicative of the need for release, and the satisfaction of sexual needs.

2 The act of ejaculation may be the giving up of old fears and doubts about oneself and one's sexual prowess.

3 Ejaculation, quite literally, may signify a loss of power or 'the little death'.

ELECTRICITY

1 Electricity often represents power, and it will depend on the context of the dream which aspect of power is being highlighted. To dream of **electrical wires** is to be aware of the dreamer's capability, while to dream of **switches** is to be aware of the ability to control.

2 If in a dream we receive an **electric shock** it shows we are not protecting ourselves from danger, and need to be more aware of external events.

3 Electricity represents the greater Spiritual Power.

ELEPHANT
– see Animals

ELOPING/ELOPEMENT

1 Dreaming of eloping, particularly **with someone you know**, is trying to escape from a situation that could ultimately be painful. We must maintain a balance between the need for emotional and material security.

2 In a dream to be **planning an elopement** is creating circumstances where others do not understand the motives behind our actions. We are aware of our own need for some sort of integration within our personalities but cannot do this without people misunderstanding.

3 Elopement signifies a union – Spiritual or otherwise – particularly in adversity.

EMBRYO

1 To dream of an embryo or foetus is to become aware of an extremely vulnerable part of ourselves. We may also be making ourselves aware of a new situation in our lives, one which has not got beyond a germ of an idea.

2 We are linking back to conception, to a point where everything begins. We may need to look at the process of becoming consciously knowledgeable of all that we are or can be.

3 The core of being is the embryo, and therefore the centre of Creation.

EMERALD
– see Jewels

EMOTIONS

1 Within the framework of a dream our emotions can be very different to those we have in everyday life. They may be more extreme, for instance, almost as though we have given ourselves freedom of expression, or we may be able to notice that there are strange swings of mood.

2 Occasionally in order to understand a dream it is easier to ignore the symbols and simply work with the moods, feelings and emotions that have surfaced. Doing this will very often give us a clearer interpretation of what is going on inside us, rather than confusing ourselves by trying to interpret myriad symbols.

3 Our emotional requirement, particularly responsiveness, to something which is a more subtle energy permits us to begin the process of development.

EMPLOYMENT

1 Dreams about employment are often more to do with what we consider our proper work to be. So if a **housewife dreams of being a businesswoman,** it may be showing that she needs to apply business methods in doing her job, whereas the other way round may indicate her secret yearnings to be a housewife. Since employment can also represent the way that other people think and feel about us, such a dream will tend to be about us assessing our own worth.

2 When we are fully employed our attention is very focused on what we are doing. To dream of **being employed** can suggest that we need to focus our attention on work that creates satisfaction and gives us the lifestyle that we want.

3 Spiritual employment suggests using our talents and gifts effectively for the Greater Good.

EMPTY

1 To experience emptiness in a dream indicates there is a lack of pleasure and enthusiasm. We could be suffering from a sense of isolation, or perhaps of not having anything to hold on to. We may have had expectations which cannot be realised.

2 We may need space to be ourselves in order to come to terms with what is occurring in our lives. To be in an **empty house or building** denotes the fact that we have left behind old attitudes and habits.

3 Spiritually, any sort of experience which brings about an emptiness signifies the Void.

ENCHANTRESS
– also see Introduction

1 The enchantress is such a strong image within both the masculine and feminine psyches that she can appear in dreams in many guises. She is the feminine principle in its binding and destroying aspect; the evil witch or the beautiful seductress. She has the power to create illusion, and the ability to delude others.

2 As the negative aspect of the feminine, the enchantress can appear in dreams as a woman meets her self-destructive side. She is to be understood rather than feared.

3 An enchantress exudes the destructive side of the Feminine, as represented by Lilith.

ENCLOSED/ ENCLOSURE

1 In dreams, the defence mechanisms we put in place to prevent ourselves from deeply feeling the impact of such things as relationships, love, anxiety or pain can often manifest as an enclosed space. Restraints and constraints can appear as actual walls and barriers.

2 Aspects of ourselves which are too frightening to be allowed full expression are often perceived as enclosed spaces.

3 Spiritually, any enclosure represents the protective aspect of The Great Mother *(See Introduction)*.

END

1 To dream of there being an end or an ending to something signifies the reaching of a goal, or a point at which things must inevitably change. We need to decide what we can leave behind, and what must be taken forward. We must decide what we value most.

2 A situation which may have given us problems is coming to a successful conclusion.

3 To be at the end can mean the subconscious and death.

ENGINE
– also see Car and Piston

1 The motivating drive or energy that we need within a situation can be perceived in dreams as an engine *(see Car)*. When the dream seems to concentrate on the mechanical action of the engine, we may need to be looking at the more dynamic pragmatic ways of dealing with our lives. To be **removing the engine** could indicate a serious health problem.

2 Depending on the type, the engine can represent the sexual act. To perceive a **diesel or railway engine** may be putting us in touch with our own inner power or principles.

3 An engine is symbolic of our own Spiritual inner motivations and drives.

ENGINEERING

1 To dream of engineering is to link with our ability to constuct. This is our ability to create a structure which will allow us either to move forward or will make life easier for us. To dream of engineering works – as in **roadworks** – is to recognise the need for some adjustment in part of our lives.

2 Engineering suggests ability to use forces which are not normally available to us through techniques and mechanical means. To dream of engineering in this way highlights our ability to take control of power which is external to us. We are able to manipulate in order to achieve.

3 Spiritual engineering signifies gaining control of our own inner power and being able to make use of it.

ENTER/ENTRANCE

1 An entrance in a dream has the same significance as a door *(see Door)*, representing a new area of experience, or the new experience itself. Such a dream often signifies the need to make changes, to create new opportunities, perhaps to explore the unknown.

2 When we need to be in touch with the hidden side of ourselves, the intuitive or more 'knowing' side, and have the knowledge and ability to experience ourselves in new ways, we will often dream of a secret entrance.

3 Because of the symbolism of moving from the external to an inner enclosed space, an entrance signifies the Eternal Feminine.

ESCAPE

1 When we dream of escape we are trying to move beyond – or to avoid – difficult feelings. We may be trying to run away from responsibility or from duty.

2 It is possible that anxiety or past trauma puts us in a position where we are unable to do anything other than try to escape from the situation itself.

3 Escape also represents our own need for spiritual freedom.

EVAPORATION

1 To be aware of water in a dream and then realise that it has evaporated is to recognise the transformation which can take place once emotion is dealt with properly.

2 By raising one's consciousness, the energy within a situation can be changed for the better. We have it within our power to create opportunities for transformation.

3 Fire and water combined is an alchemical symbol for the transformative power of the Spirit.

EVERGREENS

1 Dreaming of evergreen trees can represent the need for vitality and freshness, for youth and vigour and sometimes for cleansing.

2 To be **walking in woods of evergreen trees** indicates a need for peace and tranquillity.

3 Evergreens because of their ability to survive any conditions signify everlasting life.

EVENING

1 When we are aware of it being

evening in a dream we need to recognise the fact that we need time for ourselves – perhaps relaxation and quiet peace.

2 The evening can be a synonym for twilight and the boundaries of our conscious mind. There may be apparitions around of which we do not become aware until we start working with the unconscious.

3 Evening signifies old age and many years of Spiritual experience.

EVIL

1 To experience evil in a dream is usually to be conscious of our own urges, which we have judged to be wrong. Other aspects of evil, such as inappropriate action by others, may be experienced as dread and disgust.

2 Evil is that which cannot be explained away, and any violent action can be interpreted as evil. Any darkness can also be seen as evil.

3 By association, evil walks hand in hand with the Devil and Satan.

EXAMS/BEING EXAMINED
– also see Tests

1 Dreaming of examinations (particularly educational ones) is usually connected with self-criticism and the need for high achievement. We may be allowing others to set our standards of morality and success for us. **Being examined by a doctor** indicates concerns over our own health.

2 We may be in the habit of setting ourselves tests of self-value, or habitually be concerned with our accomplishments. There are many instances recorded of people having been abducted by 'aliens,' of having been examined, and then returned to earth. Opinions vary as to whether these were dreams or not.

3 There is a recognition of the need for Spiritual examination.

EXCREMENT
– also see Body

1 When we dream of faeces or excrement we are returning to an infant level of expression and enjoyment. Experiences we have had may have been relevant at the time but we now need to let them go.

2 There are certain aspects of our lives which we have used up and need to expel.

3 The power of the person is said to be contained in his excrement.

EXPLOSION

1 An explosion in a dream usually indicates a release of energy in a forceful way which will allow us to make changes in the way we express ourselves. Usually the emotion behind the explosion will be considered negative and we may have suppressed it for some time.

2 The forceful explosion of anger, fear or sexual release can accomplish a cleansing. A dream may be a safe space in which to accomplish this.

3 An explosion in a spiritual sense would suggest a revelation of some sort.

EYE
– see Body

from

Fabulous Beasts *to* Future

FABULOUS BEASTS

such as Griffins, Unicorns, Minotaurs

1 In dream imagery, in order to draw the dreamer's attention to certain qualities, animals may be shown as having characteristics belonging to other creatures. Archetypally, there are many combinations which are possible and which will give unlimited potential to the creative abilities within the dreamer *(see Archetypes)*. The dreamer is being shown that there is freedom from conventional principles.

2 Given the freedom to create, the mind can produce both the fantastic and the grotesque. Such fabulous beasts are the result of trying to reconcile these two polarities.

3 Fearsome and terrifying powers of nature are represented in this interpretation. The dreamer should be aware of his own 'animalistic' power and whether he can control it.

FACE

1 To concentrate on **somebody else's face** in a dream is an attempt to understand the outward personality. To be **looking at our own face** means that we may be trying to come to terms with the way we express ourselves in the ordinary, everyday world. When the **face is hidden** we are hiding our own power, or refusing to acknowledge our own abilities.

2 We learn most about people from their faces, so we may be seeking knowledge or information not otherwise available to us.

3 Elemental powers.

FAILURE

1 Failure in a dream may not necessarily be personal. If, for instance, **lights fail or refuse to work,** we may need to be aware of a lack of energy or power. **Personal failure** can indicate a degree of competitiveness or can offer alternatives in the way we need to act.

2 The fear of failure is an almost universal fear, and to dream of failure may give us the opportunity to face that fear in an acceptable way.

3 Depression or spiritual frustration. The failure we may feel at the hands of a greater power.

FAIRY

1 Because fairies are representations of elemental forces, for them to appear in a dream signifies our connection with those forces within ourselves. It could be that the lighter side of our nature is being highlighted, or it may be the more malign side as in goblins and elves.

2 Fairies are known to be

capricious, and on a psychological level they may represent the side of our being that does not wish to be controlled, and wishes to have the freedom to react and be spontaneous.

3 Fairies are reputed to have magical powers and, as Shakespeare's Oberon found, there is also a need for control, otherwise the mischievous side will run riot.

FAIRGROUND

1 To dream of **being in a fairground** may represent a reconnection with the light-hearted childlike side of ourselves. We can afford to be less inhibited in public. To be **attending a carnival or fiesta** means we can drop whatever constraints or restraints we may impose on ourselves or others.

2 The fairground has a dreamlike quality of its own. It is a sort of enclosed world, and to dream of one indicates we are becoming aware of the more hedonistic side of our nature. We are more wrapped up in our own pleasures.

3 Life's merry-go-round and its spiritual 'ups and downs'.

FALCON
– also see Birds

1 To dream of a falcon or any trained bird can represent energy focused on a particular project

with freedom to act. Such a dream may allow us to concentrate on our aspirations, hopes and desires.

2 The power that we have to succeed must be used in a contained way. A falcon – as a trained bird – can depict this.

3 Ascension and freedom from Spiritual bondage are represented by the falcon.

FALL

1 A fall in a dream outlines the need to be grounded, to take care within a known situation. We may be harmed by being too pedestrian.

2 If we forget who we are or where we come from, we will surely fall.

3 Spiritual fear is symbolised here, particularly the Fall from Grace and its attendant consequences.

FALLING

1 To dream of falling shows a lack of confidence in our own ability. We may feel threatened by a lack of security, whether real or imagined. We fear being dropped by friends or colleagues.

2 Falling has come to be interpreted as surrender (particularly sexual) and with moral failure, of not being as one should.

3 We may feel we are slipping away from a situation, essentially we are losing our place. This can be because of others' negative influence.

FAME

1 Dreaming of **being famous** or of **achieving fame within a chosen field** signifies that we ourselves need to recognise and give ourselves credit for our own abilities. In waking life we may be relatively shy, but in dreams we can often achieve things of which we would not believe we were capable.

2 The Ego *(see Introduction)* is a very powerful tool and the human being's need for recognition arises from this. If we are trying to make decisions as to how to move forward within our lives, we have to recognise our potential to stand out in a crowd – or not as the case may be – and to dream of fame allows us to crystallise our attitude to this.

3 Spiritually, fame suggests the need to accept our own integrity.

FAMILY

1 The family is the first basic security image that a child has. Often, through circumstances not within that child's control, that image becomes distorted, and dreams will either attempt to put this image right or will confirm the distortion. Thus we may dream of **an argument with a family member**, but the interpretation will depend on both the circumstances of the dream and our everyday relationship with that person. All future relationships are influenced by the ones we first develop within the family.

2 Psychologically the struggle for individuality should take place within the safety of the family unit. This, however, does not always happen. In dreams we are able to 'manipulate' the images of our family members, so that we can work through our difficulties without harming anyone else (It is interesting to note that one person working on his own dreams can have a profound noticeable effect on the interactions and unconscious bondings between other members of his family). Almost all of the problems we encounter in life are reflected within the family, so in times of stress we will dream of previous problems and difficulties that the family has experienced.

3 The Spiritual Triangle. A group in which we feel safe.

Since relationships in the family are so important, dreams containing family members can have extra significance. Some typical dreams are:

A man's mother being transformed into another woman A man's first close relationship with a woman is with his mother. Depending on the circumstances of the dream, such a transformation can be either positive or negative. It can be a sign of growth for him to realise, through dream, that he can let mother go. This transformation indicates some change in his perception of women *(see Anima)*. **A woman's father, brother or lover turning into someone else** Similarly, a woman's first relationship with the male is usually with her father. She must learn to walk away from that relationship in order to progress onto fuller relationships. When she can handle her Animus *(See Introduction)*, she is ready for that transformation. **A man's brother or a woman's sister** appearing in a dream often represents the Shadow *(See Introduction)*. Often it is easier to project the negative side of our personalities onto members of the family. If this projection is allowed to continue, it can cause difficulty with family relationships in later life. Often the solution will present itself in dreams to enable us to come to terms with our own projections. The pattern of aggressions between family members is fairly typical, but oddly is often easier to

work through in dreams than in everyday life.

Dreams about the family figure so prominently because most of the conflicts and problems in life are experienced first within that environment. It is as though a pattern is laid down which, until it is broken willingly, will continue to appear. **Confusion of family members e.g. mother's face on father's body** suggests that we may be having problems in deciding which parent is most important to us. **Family members suffering from injury or trauma** or appearing to be distorted in some way may reflect the dreamer's fear for, or about, that person. **A family member continually appearing in dreams or, conversely, not appearing when expected** The relationship with that person (or the dreamer's concept of that person) needs to be better understood.

Dreaming of an incestuous relationship may indicate that the dreamer has become obsessed in some way with the other person. The dream has occurred in order to highlight either the importance – or the potential danger – of such a relationship.

Dreamer's parents crushing

the dreamer and thus forcing rebellion. This suggests that the dreamer needs to break away from learnt childhood behaviour and develop as an individual. **Dreaming of a parent's death** can also have the same significance. **When a parent appears in our own environment,** we will have learnt to change roles within the parent/child relationship and perhaps will accept our parents as friends. **Parents behaving inappropriately** can indicate our need to recognise that they are only human, and not as perfect as we had first perceived. **Dreaming of rivalry with one parent** When a child is first born, it moves through extreme self-involvement to an exclusive relationship, usually with mother. Only later does he or she become aware of the need for a different relationship with a third person. Often this relationship causes the child to question his or her own validity as a person. When this question is not resolved successfully it may persist in the dream image of conflict with a parent. **Dreaming of conflict between a loved one and a member of one's family** The dreamer has not fully differentiated between his needs and desire for each person. Learning how to love

outside the family is a sign of maturity. **The figure of a family member intruding in dreams** suggests that family loyalties can get in the way within the dreamer's everyday life. **Rivalry between siblings in dreams** usually harks back to a feeling of insecurity and doubt, possibly as to whether we are loved enough within the family framework.

Individual members and their position within the family can symbolise the various archetypes. Thus, father can represent the masculine principle and authority, whereas mother represents the nurturing, protective principle.

Brother As already stated, a brother can represent both feelings of kinship and of rivalry. **In a man's dream** an **older brother** can represent experience and authority, while a **younger brother** suggests vulnerability and possibly lack of maturity. **In a woman's dream,** a **younger brother** can represent a sense of rivalry, but also of vulnerability, whether her own or her brother's. An **older brother** can signify her extrovert self.

Daughter When the relationship with a daughter is highlighted in dreams, it often represents the outcome of the relationship between husband and wife. **In a woman's dream**, the relationship with the daughter usually suggests a mutually supportive one – although rivalry and jealousy can arise and needs to be dealt with. Sometimes this can safely be done in dreams. **In a man's dream** his daughter may represent his fears and doubts about his own ability to handle his vulnerability.

Extended family (such as cousins, aunts, uncles) Members of the extended family usually appear in dreams either as themselves, or as typifying various parts of ourselves which are recognisible.

Father If the relationship with father has been successful in waking life, the image of father in dreams will be a positive one. Father represents authority and the conventional forms of law and order. **In a man's life** father becomes a role model, whether appropriate or not. It is often only when the individual realises that he is not being true to his own nature that dreams can point the way to a more successful life. **In a woman's life**, father is the 'pattern' on whom she bases all later relationships. When she appreciates that she longer need use this pattern, she is often able to work out in dreams a more appropriate way to have a mature relationship. If the relationship with father has been a difficult or negative one, there may be some resistance to resolving the various conflicts which will have arisen. Often this can be accomplished in dreams.

Grandparents Grandparents appearing in dreams can highlight our attitude to them, but also to the traditions and beliefs handed down by them. It could be said that grandparents do not know whether they have done a good job of raising their children until their sins and daughters have children of their own.

Husband/Live in partner Crucial within the husband/wife relationship are the wife's feelings about her own sexuality and intimacy of body, mind and spirit. Her view of herself will have been formed by her connection with her father, and any subsequent partnering will be coloured by that attachment. If her doubts and fears about validity are not properly expressed, they will surface in dreams about the loss, or death, of her husband. They may also be projected onto other women's husbands.

Mother A child's relationship with mother is pivotal in its development. Largely it is the first relationship which the child develops, and should be perceived by the child as a nurturing, caring one. If this does not happen, fears and doubts may arise. **In a man's life** this may result in continually developing dependent relationships with older women, or denying his right to a relationship completely. **In a woman's life**, her relationship with her mother will colour all other relationships. She may find herself pushed into nurturing the needy male, or in forming relationships with both men and women which do not satisfy her basic needs. There are many ways through dreams of working through relationships with mother, and much can be gained by daring to take this step. Provided one has come to terms with this relationship, much material and spiritual success can be achieved.

Sister The sister in dreams usually represents the feeling side of ourselves. We have the ability to make links with that side of ourselves through being able to understand our sister's personality. **In a man's dream if she is older**, the sister can represent the potential for persecution, but also of caring. If she is **younger** then she can epitomise the more vulnerable side of him. **In a woman's dream if the sister is younger**, she can represent rivalry. If **older** she stands for capability.

Son The son in dreams can signify the dreamer's need for self-expression and for extroversion. He can also signify parental responsibility. **In a mother's dream** he may represent one's ambitions, hope and potential. **In a father's dream** he can highlight unfulfilled hopes and dreams. **Wife/Live in partner** The wife/husband relationship is based on how the man perceives himself to be. If he has previously formed a good, if not successful relationship with his mother, he will attempt to prove himself a good husband through his dreams. He will experience potential loss and death of his partner in the same way as he experienced the 'loss' of his mother.

FAMOUS PEOPLE/ FILM STAR

1 Most of us are capable of creating an ideal person on whom to project our fantasies and wishes. We are not at this stage particularly in touch with reality. In dreams a film, pop star or public figure will represent the Animus or Anima *(See Introduction)*. A young person dreaming of a film star may not be ready for the responsibility of a real relationship.

2 Famous people, pop or film stars may also serve in dreams as a projection of the type of person we would like to be. We may, for instance, in real life be shy and withdrawn, but need to be admired and loved.

3 Spiritually, as we reach for perfection we need to 'work through' various aspects of our personality. Sometimes we are able to reject such aspects as not being appropriate for the life we live. For instance, we may realise that the destructiveness of a public life would take its toll within our own lives.

FAN

1 Dreaming of a fan connects with the feminine side of one's nature and the intuitive forces. Particularly **in a woman's dream** a fan can represent sensuality and sexuality.

2 The fan can be used as a symbol for openness to, and a willingness for, new experiences and creativity. **Waving a fan** is reputed to clear away evil forces.

3 Lunar changes.

FARE

1 To be **paying a fare** in a dream is acknowledging the price that is paid in order to succeed. A **taxi-fare** would imply a more private process than a **bus fare**.

2 Demands may be being made on us and we have to decide on their appropriateness.

3 A fare paying dream often occurs when one feels that past actions have not been paid for, and that we have a need to come to terms with them.

FARM/FARMYARD
– also see Animals

1 To be in a farmyard in a dream (if it is not a memory) shows us as being in touch with the down-to-earth side of ourselves. There are many facets of behaviour which can be interpreted in animal terms and often this type of dream has more impact than one including people.

2 Our natural drives such as a need for physical comfort, herd behaviour and territorial rights are best expressed in a safe, conserving environment.

3 A farmyard is an enclosure in which we may feel safe and, to some extent, looked after. Dreaming of one shows that we are within safe Spiritual boundaries.

FASTING

1 To be fasting in a dream may be an attempt to come to terms with some emotional trauma, or to

draw attention to the need for cleansing in some way *(see Eating)*.
2 If we have a grievance, fasting may be a way of making it known.
3 Fasting is a way of changing consciousness, and also a move towards realisation through resistance to temptation.

FAT

1 To dream of being fat alerts the dreamer to the defences used against inadequacy. Equally, we may also be conscious of the sensual and fun side of ourselves we have not used before.
2 Depending on how we think of our bodies in the waking state, we can often use the dream image of ourselves to change the way we feel.
3 A choice part of Spiritual knowledge.

FATHER
– see Family

FATIGUE

1 Feeling fatigue in a dream may indicate that we should be looking at health matters, or that we are not using our energies in an appropriate way.
2 If others appear fatigued in a dream we may need to recognise our ability to drive people too hard.
3 Spiritual inertia.

FAX/FAX MACHINE

1 Messages from a hidden source or part of ourselves are often brought to us in dreams in a totally logical way. Thus, while the message itself may be unintelligible, how it is initially received is not.
2 We may be aware that someone is trying to communicate with us but, because we are distanced from them, the transmission has to be mechanical.
3 In a dream, a fax machine can have spiritual undertones in that can be a way of transmitting messages from 'beyond'. We need to be open to this.

FEATHER

1 Feathers in a dream could denote softness and lightness, perhaps a more gentle approach to a situation. We may need to look at the truth within the particular situation and to recognise that we need to be calmer in what we are doing.
2 Feathers often represent flight to other parts of the Self, and because of their connection with the wind and the air, can represent the more spiritual side of ourselves. To see feathers in a dream perhaps means that we have to complete an action before allowing ourselves to rest.
3 The Heavens. The Soul.

FEATHERED SUN

1 This symbol appears in a number of religious images and indicates the universe and the centre of ourselves. It indicates that we ourselves are the centre of our own universe and must accept responsibility for that.

2 Drawing together the symbols of the Sun and the Eagle, this image represents our ability to move into other areas of perception and knowledge.

3 The Centre. Solar Power.

FEET/FOOT
– see Limbs in Body

FENCE

1 When we dream of fences we are dreaming of social or class barriers or perhaps our own need for privacy. We may be aware of boundaries in relationships which can prevent us from achieving the proper type of connection we need. We may have difficulty in expressing ourselves in some way.

2 When we come up against a fence or a barrier there is extra effort which is needed in order for us to overcome whatever that barrier represents.

3 A fence can represent spiritual boundaries. The dreamer needs to look at what is restricting him in his spiritual quest.

FERMENTATION

1 To dream of the process of fermentation indicates that events are occurring in the background of which we are aware but we must wait for them to develop.

2 A process of fermentation allows us to transform and transmute ordinary aspects of our personality into new and wonderful characteristics.

3 Spiritual transformation and transmutation. The dreamer should welcome this symbol in a dream and be prepared to move forward.

FERRY

1 To dream of **being on a ferry** indicates that we are making some movement towards change. Because the ferry carries large numbers of people it may also represent a group to which we belong needing to make changes, needing to change its way of working and take responsibility for moving as a group rather than as individuals.

2 The ferry is one of the oldest symbols that is associated with death. The old idea of being ferried across the River Styx, the boundary between life and death, gives an image of making major change.

3 A spiritual 'death' or change of some kind. The dreamer needs to be aware that he may, spiritually, be moving on from his present knowledge.

FIELD

1 When we dream that we are in a field, we are actually looking at our field of activity, what we are doing in everyday life. It may also be a play on words in that it is to do with the feeling state and is to do with the freedom from social pressure.

2 We need to be aware of the wider spaces in which we can operate our lives, to be aware of what is more natural to us, and perhaps to get back to basics.

3 The Earth Mother, the Great Provider and quire possibly a 'field of dreams'. The dreamer should make use of what is available to him on a practical level to further himself spiritually.

FIEND
– also see Devil

1 To dream of a fiend or devil usually means that we have got to come to terms with a part of ourselves which is frightening and unknown. We need to confront this part and make it work for us rather than against us.

2 We may be afraid of our own passions, anger and fear.

3 It is said that there is sometimes little difference between 'friend' and 'fiend'. The dreamer may find it worthwhile to look close to home if examining some kind of evil or wrong-doing for the answers to Spiritual problems.

FIG, FIG TREE OR PIPAL

1 Often because of its shape, the fig is associated with sexuality, fertility, masculinity and prosperity. To dream of **eating figs** may well be a recognition that some kind of celebration is necessary although equally that a situation holds more potential than at first thought.

2 The fig tree in dreams usually suggests that we are in touch with a deeper spiritual awareness of which we have previously had no conscious knowledge. This is because of its associations with the Tree of Knowledge, the beginning of duality, and with masculinity and femininity.

3 Psychic ability and a direct connection with beginning of physical life.

FIGHT

1 If we dream that we are **in a fight**, it usually indicates that we are confronting our need for independence. We may also need to express our anger and frustration and the subconscious desire to hurt a part of ourselves. We also may wish to hurt someone else, although this would be unacceptable in the waking state

2 To fight back is a natural defence mechanism, so when we are feeling threatened in our everyday lives, we will often dream of taking that situation one stage further and fighting it out.

3 Quite literally a spiritual conflict. The dreamer should try to work out where, and why, there is a conflict and perhaps deal with it in a more subtle way than with 'all guns blazing'.

FILE

1 In modern times to dream of files or filing and thus to put order into our lives, is to make sense of what we are doing and how we are doing it. To be **filing things away** would perhaps indicate that we no longer need to be aware of a particular situation but need to retain the knowledge that an experience has given us.

2 Dreaming of an **abrasive file** – such as a metal file – would indicate that we need to be aware that we can make mistakes in being too harsh with other people.

3 A chaotic situation in our lives can now be dealt with in an orderly manner.

FILM

1 To dream of being at a film – as in the cinema – indicates we are viewing an aspect of our own past or character which needs to be acknowledged in a different way. We are attempting to view ourselves objectively or perhaps we may be escaping from reality.

2 Film as recording images is an important part of modern man's make up and to be put in a position of viewing film within a dream is to be creating a different reality from the one we presently have. This usually applies to the waking self, rather than to the sleeping self. If we are making a film, when this is not our normal occupation, we may need to question the reality we are creating, but may also be being warned not to try to create too many realities.

3 The Akashic Records, the past.

FIND

1 If we dream of finding something, such as a precious object, we are becoming aware of some part of ourselves which is, or will be, of use to us. We are making a discovery or a realisation, which depending on the rest of the dream scenario may be about us or about others.

2 The mind has an uncanny knack of drawing our attention to what needs to be done to enable us to achieve our aims. It will use hiding, searching and finding as metaphors for effort we must make in the waking state. So to find something without having to make too much effort would show that events will take place which will reveal what we need to know.

3 We may be close to finding something within our spiritual search which will enable us to move forward.

FINGER
– see Hand in Body

FIRE

1 Fire in a dream can suggest passion and desire in its more positive sense, and frustration, anger, resentment and destructiveness in its more negative. It will depend on whether the fire is **controlled** or otherwise on the exact interpretation. To be more conscious of **the flame** of the fire would be to be aware of the energy and strength which is created. Being aware of the **heat** of a fire is to be aware of someone else's strong feelings.

2 Psychologically, fire often appears in dreams as a symbol of cleansing and purification. We can use the life-giving and generative power to change our lives.

Sometimes fire indicates the need to use our sexual power to good effect. To dream of **being burnt alive** may express our fears of a new relationship or phase of life. We may also be conscious of the fact that we could suffer for our beliefs.

3 Baptism by fire signifies a new awareness of spiritual power and transformation.

FIRE BUCKET

1 As a symbol, the fire bucket indicates that we may have a situation around us which is out of control. It is only by a display of 'dampening' emotion that there can be any progress. Someone may have gone over the top and need help.

2 As with any hollow vessel, the fire bucket can represent the feminine principle. It will be important within the context of the dream whether the bucket is full or empty.

3 Passionate emotion.

FIREWORKS

1 Fireworks are generally accepted as belonging to a happy occasion or celebration, though they may also be frightening. When we dream of fireworks we are hoping to be able to celebrate good fortune, although there may be a secondary emotion associated with that celebration.

2 Fireworks can have the same significance as an explosion. A release of energy or emotion can have quite a spectacular effect on us, or on people around us.

3 There is an excess of spiritual emotion which needs to be channelled properly in order to prevent it shooting off in all directions.

FISH

1 Dreaming of fish connects with the emotional side of ourselves, but more our ability to be wise without being strategic. We can often simply respond instinctively to what is going on, without needing to analyse it.

2 The Collective Unconscious as Jung has called it – that part of life everyone shares, the common experience, awareness and knowledge which we all have – is becoming available to us.

3 Fish signify temporal and spiritual power. When pictured as two fish swimming in opposite directions, it is recognised as the sign of Pisces.

FISHERMAN

1 Whenever one of our dream figures is carrying out a specific action we need to look at what is represented by that action. Often a fisherman will represent a provider, or perhaps bravery, as with a **deep-sea fisherman,** whilst a **fresh water fisherman** may indicate the need for rest and recuperation.

2 Within a situation in our lives we may be trying to 'catch' something, such as a job or a partner.

3 Because of its Christian connection a fisherman can suggest a priest in dreams.

FLAG

– also see Banner

1 A flag in a dream will have the same meaning as a banner – that is, a standard or a place round which people with common aims and beliefs can gather. It may represent old-fashioned principles and beliefs.

2 The national flag will signify a degree of patriotism which may be necessary, or possibly the need to be more militant.

3 Spiritual crusades often require standards of behaviour.

FLAIL

1 Any instrument used to beat us in dreams is a recognition that someone has power over us, and can use force rather than giving us the power to act for ourselves.

2 The flail would reinforce our ideas about authority. In older times the Jester would use a pig's bladder to flail the king to remind him of his humility.

3 A flail also sometimes represents

spiritual supremacy and Supreme power which may be available to us.

FLAME
– see Fire

FLEAS

1 Fleas are an irritation, and in dreams signify just that. There may be people or situations in our lives which are causing us difficulty, or that we feel are being parasites, and we need to go through a process of decontamination in order to be free.

2 We may be aware that we are not being treated properly and that people who should be our friends are not being fair.

3 Fleas are symbolic of the type of evil which is likely to hurt, rather than destroy – such as gossip. The dreamer should be aware that he has the ability to deal with it.

FLEECE

1 We may be word-associating as in the sense of being 'fleeced' or cheated. The **fleece of a sheep** also represents security, warmth and comfort and will often signify those creature comforts we are able to give ourselves.

2 Dreaming of a fleece, as opposed to the sheep itself,

signifies a return to an older set of values. It links with the tasks which are given us when we set out on our Hero's journey *(See Archetypes)*. We may fear that what we are about to do is impossible, but our sense of self-preservation will not allow us to give up.

3 We may be in line for a spiritual reward. In this case the message would be 'keep up the good work'. Our task will bring us success.

FLEUR-DE-LIS

1 As a symbol, the fleur-de-lis is very much connected with the French in people's minds, and so may be taken as this in dreams. It also represents the right to power.

2 As illustrative of fire and light we may need to look for greater clarity.

3 The right to rule, by association with spiritual power.

FLIES

1 Flies are always associated with something nasty, which does not allow for the fact that they also devour rotten material. So to dream of flies is to be aware that we have certain negative aspects of our lives which need dealing with. To dream of **a swarm of flies** is to dream of the sort of purposeful behaviour which occurs when there are large numbers of insects. Where one insect may appear to be moving aimlessly, large numbers do not. Often we can only succeed in changing matters by group behaviour.

2 Insects of any sort usually link us to primal instinctive behaviour, that of survival against all odds. Whatever threatens us does so on a very basic level, and we may have no defences, except those of our own nature.

3 Some form of spiritual contamination may have taken place. Hopefully it can be dealt with easily, and steps can then be taken to keep it away.

FLIGHT/FLYING
– also see Journey

1 Conventionally to dream of flying is to do with sex and sexuality, but it would probably be more accurate to look at it in terms of lack of inhibition and freedom. We are releasing ourselves from limitations which we may impose on ourselves.

2 To be **flying upwards** is to be moving towards a more spiritual appreciation of our lives, while to be **flying downwards** is to be making an attempt to understand the subconscious and all that entails.

3 Spiritual Freedom.

FLOATING

1 Floating in a dream was considered by Freud to be connected with sexuality, but it is probable that it is much more to do with the inherent need for freedom. Generally we are opening to power beyond our conscious self; when we are carried along apparently beyond our own volition. We are in a state of extreme relaxation and are simply allowing events to carry us along.

2 Because we are not taking charge of our own direction, we are being indecisive and perhaps need to think more carefully about our actions and involvements with other people.

3 Out of Body Experiences.

FLOCK

1 To dream of a flock – for instance of **birds or sheep** – is to recognise the need to belong to a group, to have a common aim or way of being.

2 When we dream of belonging to a group, our personal behaviour can quite often be different from that of others, and we may be alerted to this by dreaming of a flock.

3 A flock can be symbolic of our spiritual beliefs, and our faith in that what we are following is the correct path.

FLOGGING

1 Any violent act against the person usually indicates some form of punishment. To dream of **being flogged** would indicate that we are aware that someone is driving us beyond our limits, often in an inappropriate manner. **Flogging ourselves** would highlight a type of masochism in our own personality.

2 Flogging someone else means we have to be careful that we are not attempting to impose our will on that person. While painful there is also a degree of encouragement and stimulation present.

3 Atonement of sins.

FLOOD
— also see Water

1 Flood dreams are fascinating, because while frightening, they often indicate a release of positive energy. Usually it is an overflow of repressed or unconscious feelings which needs to be got out of the way before progress can be made. To be **in the middle of a flood** indicates we may feel we are being overwhelmed by these feelings, whilst **watching a flood** suggests we are simply watching ourselves. Often a flood dream can indicate depression.

2 If we are not good at expressing ourselves verbally, dreaming of a flood may allow us to come to terms with our anxieties and worries in an appropriate way.

3 The end of one cycle and the beginning of another. Old grievances and emotional 'cobwebs' are washed away, leaving a clear head and a clear way forward.

FLOWERS

1 Flowers in a dream usually give us the opportunity to link to feelings of pleasure and beauty. We are aware that something new, perhaps a feeling or ability is beginning to come into being and that there is a freshness about what we are doing. **To be given a bouquet** means that we are being rewarded for an action – the colour of the flowers may be important *(see Colours)*. In folklore, each individual flower had a meaning in dreams: **Anenome** Your present partner is untrustworthy. **Arum Lily** An unhappy marriage or the death of a relationship. **Bluebell** Your partner will get argumentative. **Buttercup** Your business will increase. **Carnation** A passionate love affair. **Clover** Someone who is in need of finance will try to get in touch. **Crocus** A dark man around you is not to be trusted. **Daffodil** You have been unfair to a friend, look for reconciliation.

Forget-me-not Your chosen partner cannot give you what you need. **Forsythia** You are glad to be alive. **Geranium** A recent quarrel is not as serious as you thought. **Honeysuckle** You will be upset by domestic quarrels. **Iris** Hopefully, you will receive good news. **Lime/Linden** This suggests feminine grace. **Marigold** There may be business difficulties. **Mistletoe** Be constant to your lover. **Myrtle** This gives joy, peace, tranquillity, happiness and constancy. **Narcissus** Don't mistake shadow for substance. **Peony** Excessive self-restraint may cause you distress. **Poppy** A message will bring great disappointment. **Primrose** You will find happiness in a new friendship. **Rose** Indicates love, and perhaps a wedding, within a year. **Snowdrop** Confide in someone and do not hide your problems. **Violet** You will marry someone younger than yourself.

2 The feminine principle is often represented in dreams by flowers, as is childhood. The bud represents the potential available, while the opening flower indicates development.

3 Spiritually flowers signify love and compassion, both that which we may receive and that which we give to others.

FLUTE
– also see Musical Instruments

1 Many musical instruments – particularly wind instruments – indicate extremes of emotion, enticement and flattery. Because of the shape the flute is often taken as a symbol of masculine virility, but could also be taken to stand for anguish.

2 As a way of expressing the sound of the spirit, and therefore harmony, the flute can be used as a symbol of happiness and joy.

3 Celestial music.

FLY WHISK

1 The fly whisk is a tool for removing an irritant, and may be interpreted as our need to deal effectively with aspects of our lives which no longer please us.

2 In many cultures the fly whisk represents authority and power, and has the same symbolism as the flail or fan. Interpreting the symbol will therefore depend on the dreamer's ethnic and cultural background.

FOG

1 To dream of being in a fog marks our confusion and inability to confront, or often even to see, the real issues at stake in our lives. We are often confused by external matters and the impact they may have on us emotionally.

2 To be **walking in a fog** is often a warning that matters we consider important can be clouded by other people's judgement and it may be wiser to sit still and do nothing at this time.

3 A degree of spiritual doubt and a feeling of directionless wandering – which is probably only temporary – is symbolised here.

FOLLOW

1 If we are **following someone** or something in a dream we may need a cause or crusade to help give us a a sense of identity. We are looking for leadership or are aware that we can be influenced by other people. It also indicates that, particularly in a work situation, we are perhaps more comfortable in a secondary position rather than out in front.

2 When we dream of **being followed** we need to identify if what is following us is negative or positive. If it is negative, we need to deal with past fears, doubts or memories. If positive, we must recognise our need to take the initiative, or to identify what drives us.

3 The dreamer is aware of either the need for, or the recognition of, 'discipleship' in his life.

FOOD
– also see Eating and Nourishment

1 Food signifies a satisfaction of our needs whether those are physical, mental or spiritual. It is something we might take or are taking into ourselves. Frequent dreams about eating suggest a great hunger for something.

2 Our need – or enjoyment – of food fulfils certain psychological needs. The meanings of various foods are as follows; **Bread** We are looking at our experiences and our basic needs. **Cake** This signifies sensual enjoyment. **Fruits** Represent in dream form the fruits of our experience or effort, and the potential for prosperity. The colour can also be significant *(see Colour)*. **Ham/Cured Meat** Our need for preservation is represented by cured meats. **Meals** Depending on whether we are eating alone or in a group, meals can indicate acceptance and sociability. **Meat** Physical or worldly satisfaction or needs are shown often in dreams as meat. **Raw meat** can supposedly signify impending misfortune. **Milk** As a basic food, milk will always signify baby needs and giving to oneself. **Onion** The different layers of oneself are often shown as an onion *(also see individual entry)*. **Sweets** These tend to represent

sensual pleasure. **Vegetables**
Vegetables represent our basic
needs and material satisfaction.
They also suggest the goodness we
can take from the Earth and situations around us. The colour may
also be important (See Colour).
3 Spiritual Sustenance.

FOOTPRINTS

1 To see footprints in a dream
indicates that we are needing to
follow someone or their way of
being. If those footprints are
stretching in front of us, there
is help available to us in the future,
but if they are **behind us** then
perhaps we need to look at the way
we have done things in the past.
They usually indicate help in
one way or another and certainly
consideration.
2 If we see footprints **going in
opposite directions,** we need
to consider what has happened in
the past and what is going to
happen in the future. We also need
to consider what actions we have
initiated in the past to enable us to
move into the future. We are, as it
were, standing in the present and
are considering the confusion of
the present and how it may affect
our future.
3 We may be aware, on a subconscious level, of a Divine presence.

FOREIGN COUNTRIES
– see Places

FOREST
– also see Trees and Wood
1 Dreaming of forests or a group
of trees usually means entering the
realms of the feminine. A forest
is often a place of testing and initiation. It is always something to do
with coming to terms with our
emotional self, of understanding
the secrets of our own nature or of
our own spiritual world.
2 The dark or enchanted forest
which very often appears as an
image in fairy tales is a threshold
symbol. It is the soul entering the
areas it has never explored before,
and is looking at having to work
with intuition and with one's own
ability to sense and feel what is
going on around us. We may find
that it has a lot to do with being
lost *(see Lost)* and unable to find
direction.
3 The psyche. The Feminine.

FORK
1 A fork, particularly a three-
pronged one, is often considered to
be the symbol of the Devil and
therefore can symbolise evil and
trickery. In dreams, a fork denotes
duality and indecision.
2 Psychologically, the fork can

signify the same as a barb or a goad – something which is driving us, often to our own detriment.

3 We may have come to a fork on our spiritual path and development and need guidance as to which direction to take.

FORGE

1 When the forge and the blacksmith were a part of normal, everyday life this particular dream would indicate some aspect of hard work or desire to reach a goal. Now it is more likely to mean a ritual action.

2 The forge represents the masculine and active force. It also represents the power of transmuting that which is base and unformed into something sacred. To dream of a forge indicates that we are changing internally and allowing our finer abilities to be shown.

3 Sacred fire.

FORTRESS
– see Individual Entry for Castle and in Buildings

FOUNTAIN

1 To dream of a fountain means that we are aware of the process of life and 'flow' of our own consciousness. Because of its connection with water *(see Water)*, it also represents the surge of our emotions, and often our ability to express this. The fountain can also represent an element of play in our lives and the need to be free-flowing and untroubled.

2 In dreams the fountain often represents the mother figure or perhaps the source of our emotions.

3 The Fountain of Immortality. Eternal Life

FOX
– see Animals

FRAUD

1 When fraud appears in a dream, particularly if the dreamer is **being defrauded**, there is the potential to be too trusting of people. If the dreamer is the one **committing fraud**, he or she runs the risk of losing a good friend.

2 If we accept that the various figures appearing in a dream are parts of our personality, we should guard against being dishonest with ourselves.

3 We should look at our true spiritual aims and be true to them, whilst guarding against complacency and contrived goals.

FRIEND

1 Friends appearing in our dreams can signify one of two things.

Firstly we need to look at our relationship with that particular person, and secondly we need to decide what that friend represents for us (for instance security, support and love).

2 Often friends highlight a particular part of our own personality that we need to look at, and perhaps understand or come to terms with, in a different way.

3 We can continue on our spiritual search in the knowledge that we are being supported.

FROG
– also see Animals

1 Many people associate the frog with a visible growth pattern which mirrors the growth to maturity of the human being. In dreams, to see a frog at a particular stage of its growth depicts the feeling we have about ourselves. For instance, to see it at the stage where it has grown its back legs would suggest that we capable of moving forward in leaps and bounds.

2 The frog is a symbol of fertility and eroticism. In dreams it is also representative of an aspect of character that can be changed, something nasty that can be changed into good. This image is seen in myths and legends where the frog becomes a prince.

3 Transmutation.

FRONT
– see Position

FRONTIER
– also see Border

1 To dream of **crossing a border or frontier** from one place to another represents making great changes in life, actively instigating a change from one state to another, perhaps taking ourselves from the past to the future, or causing other people round us to make those changes.

2 Psychologically when we cross from one way of life to another – such as changing from puberty to adulthood or from middle age to old age – we need to depict this by creating an actual marker. In dreams for a frontier to appear is crossing a barrier within ourselves.

3 Spiritually, we have a new experience ahead of us which we can use on our way towards enlightenment.

FRUIT
– also see Food

1 To dream of fruit, particularly in a bowl, very often indicates the culmination of actions that we have taken in the past. We have been able to 'harvest' the past and to make a new beginning for ourselves.

2 Psychologically, when we have worked hard we ought to be able to recognise the fruits of our labour. Dreaming of fruit in this way indicates that we have succeeded in what we set out to do.
3 Creativity.

FUNERAL
– also see Mourning

1 To dream of **being at a funeral** indicates that we need to come to terms with our feelings about death. This may not necessarily be our own death but the death of others. It may also indicate a time of mourning for something that has happened in the past and this time of mourning can allow us to move forward into the future. To dream of our **own funeral** can indicate a desire for sympathy. It may also indicate that a part of us is dead and we have to let it go.
2 Dreaming of our **parents' funeral** indicates a move towards independence, or of letting go of the past, which may be painful. We may need to let our childhood – or childhood experiences – go and mark that by some ritual or ceremony.
3 Rites of Passage.

FURNITURE/ FURNISHINGS

1 The furniture which appears in our dreams, particularly if it is drawn to our attention, often shows how we feel about our family and home life, and what attitudes or habits we have developed. It also can give an indication as to how we feel about ourselves. For instance, **dark heavy material** would suggest the possibility of depression, whereas **brightly painted objects** could testify to an upbeat mentality.
2 Sometimes the furniture which appears in a dream can highlight our need for security or stability, particularly if it is recognisable from the past.

Different articles can represent different attitudes:

Bed/mattress This can show exactly what is happening in the subtle areas of our close relationships. We can get an insight into how we really feel about intimacy; and sexual pleasure. For some people the bed is a place of sanctuary and rest, where they can be totally alone. **Carpet** Often when carpets appears in a dream we are looking at our emotional links with finance. The colour of the carpet should also be noted *(see Colour)*. **Chair** A chair can indicate that we need a period of rest and recuperation. We may need to deliberately take time out, to be open to other opportunities and openings.

Cupboard/Wardrobe
Cupboards and wardrobes may depict those things we wish to keep hidden, but may also depict how we deal with the different roles we must play in life. **Table** For a table to appear in a dream is often to do with communal activity, and with one's social affiliations *(also see individual entry and Altar)*.
3 Revered objects.

FUTURE

1 There are several aspects to dreaming about the future. We may be aware within the dream itself that the events will take place in the future of our dream, and in which case they are usually to do with actions we need to take in waking life. We also may have precognitive dreams, which is when we dream of events before they take place, and then recognise that we already have the information – we 'knew' about it. The theory behind this is that the past, present and future co-exist side by side as it were, and that it is possible to 'read' these records in the dream state. Our experience of them is subjective, although we are in the position of observers.

2 Psychologically, if we are to be in control of our lives, we often need to feel that we must be aware of the future, and dreams can give an insight into how we can or will act in the future. Dreams allow us to play out certain scenarios, to explore possibilities without coming to any harm.
3 Spiritual Manifestation, as in 'all things must pass'.

G

from

Gall *to* Guru

GALL

1 To dream of **being galled** in a dream means to connect with feelings of bitterness that we may have about something that is happening in our life. Bringing that feeling to the surface and allowing it to come through in dreams gives us the opportunity to express it and to work it through.

2 To dream of a **gall bladder**, or of a **gall bladder operation**, often represents the need to give up some activity that is not doing us any good at all. We are assimilating the wrong information, which is causing us problems and we need to get rid of bitterness, difficulty or even guilt.

3 To find aspects of a dream galling is symbolic of a form of evil. We may want to turn away in disgust, but eventually we must face up to the effects and deal with it appropriately.

GALE

– also see Hurricane and Wind

1 Being in a gale indicates that we are being buffeted by circumstances that we feel are beyond our control. We are allowing those outside circumstances to create problems for us when actually we may need to look at what we are doing and either take shelter – to withdraw from the situation – or battle through to some form of sanctuary.

2 Since wind in a dream often denotes spiritual matters, we may be taking ourselves too seriously. We are allowing those forces within ourselves, which will lead us forward to something else, to have too much meaning.

3 A gale can be symbolic not only of the spirit we have within us, but also the spiritual side of things, particularly the Spirit.

GAMES/GAMBLING

1 Playing a game in our dream indicates that we are taking note of how we play the game of life. If we are **playing well** we may take it that we are coping well with circumstances in our lives. If we are **playing badly** we may need to reassess our abilities and identify which skills we need to improve in order to do things better. Games and gambling can also represent not taking life seriously. They can show how we work within the competitive field and give us some kind of insight into our own sense of winning or losing.

3 Specific games such as **football, baseball, rugby and cricket** which are **team games** represent for many the strong ability to identify with a 'tribe' or a group of people. Because they are mock fights they can be used as expressions of aggression against other people, in the way that wars and tribal localised fights were used previously. They indicate the way in which we gain identity and how we connect with people. In dreams, games which require the power of thought and strategy – such as **chess or draughts –** often give some idea of how we should be taking a situation forward *(see Chess)*. Decisions may need to be made where we have to gauge the result of our action and take into account our opponent's reaction. To dream of **gambling** indicates that we may need to look at something in our lives that is figuratively a gamble; we may need to take risks, but in such a way that we have calculated the risks as best we can.

3 Ritualised fighting between two opposing forces.

GARAGE
– also see Workshop

1 A garage appearing in a dream may indicate how we store our own personal abilities. It is the workshop from which we need to move out into the world in order to show what we have done We are looking at our reserves of drive and motivation and possibly at our abilities.

2 A car repair garage –

remembering that a car represents the way we handle our external life – can indicate the need for personal attention and perhaps bodily maintenance.

3 We all have spiritual tools which we can call upon at certain times. A garage is a symbolic reminder that we have these in storage, and they can be utilised at any time.

GARBAGE

1 Garbage in our dream creates a scenario where we are able to deal with those parts of our experience or our feelings which are like garbage, and need to be sorted in order to decide what is to be kept and what is to be rejected. To be **collecting garbage** can indicate that we are making wrong assumptions.

2 Very often, garbage is the remains of food preparation. Often we are being alerted to what we need to do in order to remain healthy – how we need to treat our bodies and how we need to create space in order to act correctly.

3 We may need to dispose of spiritual rubbish, and a dream about garbage can alert us that now is the time to do that.

GARDEN

1 Dreaming of a garden can be fascinating, because it may indicate the area of growth in our own lives, or it can be that which we are trying to cultivate in ourselves. It often represents the inner life of the dreamer and that which we totally appreciate about our own being.

2 The garden is often the symbol of the feminine attributes and the qualities of wildness which need to be cultivated and tamed in order to create order. **Closed gardens** particularly have this significance and can represent virginity.

3 A garden can represent a form of paradise, as in the Garden of Eden. The dreamer should look to some spiritual relaxation.

GARDENER

1 Whenever a person appears in our dream in a certain role it is important to look at what he is actually doing. The gardener can represent the insights which we have gathered through our experience in life and can equally represent wisdom, but of a particular sort. Often the gardener indicates someone on whom we can rely, who will take care of those things with which we do not feel capable of dealing.

2 If we find ourselves **looking after a garden** within a dream then we are looking after ourselves. We are nurturing those

aspects of ourselves that we have carefully cultivated and which we need to keep 'tidy', in order to get the best out of ourselves.

3 A gardener helps us identify with the wiser aspects of ourselves. We need to tend to these gifts of wisdom and not let them become stagnant.

GARLAND

1 Depending on the type of garland in the dream we are recognising some distinction or honour for ourselves. If we are **wearing the garland**, such as a **Hawaiian flower garland**, we are looking at various ways of making ourselves happy. We are looking at dedication, and at some way of setting ourselves apart from others.

2 Psychologically, a garland can represent honour and recognition and can link us to the people who presented us with the garland.

3 A garland is symbolic of the need for dedication, either spiritually or physically. It may also represent an element of the dreamer's subconscious Holiness, which he will need to acknowledge.

GARLIC

1 Garlic in olden times had much significance. Because of its shape and its many parts it was often seen as a symbol of fertility; because of its smell it was seen as protection. Dreaming of garlic may therefore link back to either of these meanings.

2 Garlic as the protective amulet is important against evil. Physically it protects the heart area and therefore protects one against fear.

3 Magic.

GAS

1 Gas can have the same significance as air and wind but usually is taken to be slightly more dangerous. So to be dreaming of gas in some way – e.g. **a leak** – indicates we may be looking at some difficulty in controlling our own thoughts feelings and abilities.

2 Gas as a means of assistance or as a tool has the same significance as breath *(See Breath)*.

3 The spirit, as an unformed entity, can be symbolised by gas. We should be aware of its ability to float in and out of our lives.

GATE

1 Dreaming of a gate usually signifies some kind of change, often in awareness. We are passing a threshold in our lives, perhaps trying something different or moving from one phase of life to another.

2 Often the awareness of change is highlighted by the type of gate.

For instance a **farm gate** would tend to indicate a work change, whereas a **garden gate** might represent pleasure.

3 The gate between the physical and spiritual realms has a long established existence It is used as a 'gateway' for communication, and can be utilised as such if the dreamer so wishes.

GAZELLE
– see Deer In Animals

GENITALS
– also see Body

1 To dream of **our own genitals** has a direct reference to our own sexuality. To dream of **being mutilated** could refer to either past or present abuse.

2 Dreaming of **someone else's genitals** either indicates our involvement with that person's sexuality, or, if of the opposite sex, our need to understand the hidden side of ourselves.

3 Our awareness of the physical self within a spiritual framework.

GEMS
– see Jewels

GHOST

1 Actually dreaming of a ghost links us to old habit patterns or buried hopes and longings. There is something insubstantial in these, possibly because we have not put enough energy into them.

2 We may be resurrecting old memories or feelings in order to understand our own actions. By putting ourselves in touch with what is dead and gone we can take appropriate action in the here and now.

3 If a ghost appears in a dream we may be alerted to our past states of being – in which case we should try to identify these, and acknowledge that we have moved on.

GIANT

1 Dreaming about giants may mean we are coming to terms with some of the repressed feelings we had about adults when we were children. They may have seemed larger than life or frightening in some way.

2 Giants and ogres often represent the emotion of anger, particularly masculine anger. This can be confronted in dreams where perhaps we cannot do this in waking life.

3 Primordial power.

GIFT
– also see Present

1 To **receive a gift** within a dream is to recognise our talents and abilities. Depending on the circumstances, we are acknowl-edging what we receive from others.

2 Each of us has a store of unconscious knowledge which from time to time becomes available to us and may appear in dreams as gifts.

3 In a spiritual sense, dreaming of a gift may be pointing us towards our creative talents, of which we may not yet be aware.

GIG

1 In modern times the gig, concert or rave has taken the place of the dance or tea party. In dreams, therefore it can represent a social occasion or a gathering of like-minded people.

2 A gig offers us an opportunity for freedom and movement, so to be at one in a dream represents a need in us to 'let go'.

3 Spiritually, a gig can symbolise our need for abandonment in the form of ecstatic liberation from the norm, if only for a short time.

GIRDLE

1 In a woman's dream the girdle may depict her sense of her own femininity, for instance when she feels bound or constricted by it. **In a man's dream** it is more likely to show his understanding of his power over his own life.

2 The girdle can represent the inevitability of life and death.

3 A girdle also represents wisdom, strength and power. The dreamer should make note of this, as spiritually he is progressing in the right direction.

GIRL
– see People

GIRLFRIEND
– see People

GIVING

1 Giving is all about the internal relationship with oneself or the environment and with others. So to dream of giving somebody something in a dream indicates our need to give and take within a relationship – our need to give of ourselves, perhaps to share with others what we have, and to create an environment that allows for give and take.

2 It is one of the fundamental needs of the human being to be able to share with other people. Psychologically this represents our ability to belong to others, to have others belong within our lives and to assume responsibility for other people. So to dream of giving in this way indicates our own innate abilities.

3 The dreamer should acknowledge the gifts he has and use them appropriately, lest they be taken away.

GLASS

1 Dreaming of glass indicates the invisible but very tangible barriers we may erect around ourselves in order to protect ourselves from relationship with other people. They may also represent the barriers that other people put up and also be those aspects of ourselves which we have built up in our own defence.

2 To dream of **breaking glass** is to be breaking through those barriers *(see Break)*. We are shattering the emotions that keep us trapped and moving into a clearer space where we do not allow barriers to build. **Frosted or smoked glass** can indicate a desire for privacy or our obscured view of a particular situation within our lives.

3 The barrier between life and the life hereafter.

GLASSES/ SPECTACLES
– also see Lens

1 For glasses or spectacles to stand out in a dream indicates a connection with our ability to see or to understand. Equally, if **someone is unexpectedly wearing glasses**, it is to do either with our lack of understanding or perhaps their inability to see where we are coming from.

2 Psychologically, when we are able to wear glasses we are more able to look at that which is external to ourselves rather than turning inwards and becoming introspective. So, in dreams, glasses can represent the need for extroversion within a situation.

3 Spiritually, a dream of glasses or spectacles may be urging us to take a different viewpoint – on a physical as well as spiritual level.

GLOBE
– also see World

1 To dream of looking at a globe, particularly in the sense of a **world globe**, indicates our appreciation of a wider viewpoint. We can cultivate the ability not only not to be narrow minded but to be more globally aware. If we are looking at, for instance, **a glass globe** we may be looking at a lifestyle that is complete, but which is contained. The globe is a representation of the wholeness of life.

2 Dreaming of a globe is to dream of power and of dignity. We have certain powers within us that will enable us to create a sustainable future, and for this we need to be able to understand and take a world view.

3 A globe symbolises our need for wholeness or, for someone much further along the spiritual journey, the approach to wholeness.

GLOOM

1 If there is gloom around in a dream, it can indicate difficulty in being able to see or comprehend things from an external viewpoint. There may be negativity around of which we have to be aware in order to be able to dispel it – to create light and clarity – so that we can continue with our lives.

2 If we find ourselves **enclosed in gloom**, while others appear to be in the light, we may be being warned of a certain type of melancholy that is affecting us, but not affecting them. Conversely if we are **in light while other people are in shadow** we may have information which will help them to enhance their lives.

3 Gloom usually indicates a presence of evil, which will be lifted as soon as the gloom descends to its murky beginnings.

GLOVES
– also see Clothes

1 Often in previous times the glove had greater significance than it does nowadays. Because it was so much part of social etiquette it represented honour, purity and evidence of good faith. Now being aware of gloves in a dream often represents some way in which we are hiding our abilities from people around us. To **take off the glove** signifies respect and an act of sincerity. To dream of **boxing gloves** could indicate that we are trying too hard to succeed in a situation where there is aggression.

2 Gloves represent the ability to challenge people, and the ability to hide our own awareness from other people so that we can challenge them in their beliefs and belief system.

3 Spiritually, since hands may be representative of our creativity, gloves can symbolise the need to protect our creative ability. They may also be an impediment to full creative expression.

GOAD

1 The goad can be shown in many ways. Often if **we are goading somebody** to do something they do not want to do, we must take care that we are not creating circumstances which could turn around and control us. We may be trying to force people to take action to move forward but we must also be aware that we need to be in control of that particular movement.

2 Psychologically, we are all goaded by our own more aggressive and negative parts. Often a dream can reveal how we are making things difficult for ourselves and can represent which parts of ourselves are taking authority over the other.

3 Power and Spiritual authority often act as a goad so we can improve our knowledge.

GOAL

1 To dream of **scoring a goal** may indicate that we have set ourselves external targets. In achieving those targets we may also recognise that the goals which we have set ourselves in life are either short or long term and we may need to adjust them in some way. **To miss a goal** indicates that we have not taken all the circumstances within a situation into account and need, perhaps, to reassess our abilities to achieve.

2 To set life goals – or to be conscious of doing this in a dream – indicates that we are in touch with our own internal sense of our ability to achieve. The external is often a reflection of the internal and goals can indicate that we instinctively know how much, and what, we are capable of doing.

3 Our spiritual aspirations are being highlighted. If we are aware of our goal, then we can make terrific inroads towards attainment.

GOAT
– see Animals

GOBLET

1 In dreams the goblet has similar significance to the chalice *(See Chalice)*. It represents the feminine, receptive principal and our ability to achieve enjoyment in different ways. We may be able to make a celebration out of something that is quite ordinary. To be **drinking from a goblet** indicates allowing ourselves the freedom to enjoy life to the full.

2 To dream of **a set of goblets** as in wine glasses indicates several different ways in which we can make our lives enjoyable and fun.

3 The feminine principal.

GOD/GODS
– also see Religious Imagery

1 When we dream of God we are acknowledging to ourselves that there is a higher power in charge. We connect with all humanity, and therefore have a right to a certain set of moral beliefs. We all have needs for love and approval which can only be met through our understanding of our childhood. **In a woman's dream**, dreaming of mythical gods will help her to understand various aspects of her own personality. **In a man's dream** he is linking with his own masculinity and his sense of belonging to himself, and therefore to the rest of humanity.

2 The powerful emotions we sometimes experience may be connected with our tremendous childhood need for love and parental approval. Often these emotions can be personalised and recognised in the figures of mythical gods. **Adonis** signifies health, beauty and self-adoration. **Apollo** signifies the Sun, and taught **Chiron** the art of healing. It is interesting that although **Heracles** was taught the art of healing by Chiron, when he accidentally shot Chiron the latter was not able to accept healing from him. **Jehovah**, in the sense of a vengeful god, alerts us to the negative side of power. **Mars** as the god of war symbolises the drive we require to succeed. **Mercury (or Hermes)** suggests communication, often of a sensitive sort. He is the patron of magic. **Zeus** is the king of the gods and signifies fathering in both its positive and negative forms.

3 Spiritually, we are aware of a greater power. Christian belief holds to one God, although manifesting in three forms – Father, Son and Holy Ghost. Other religions attribute the powers to various Gods. As we grow in understanding, we can appreciate the relevance of both beliefs and can begin to understand God as an all-pervading energy.

GODDESS/ GODDESSES

– also see Religious Imagery

1 Dreaming of **mythical goddesses** connects us with our archetypal images of femininity *(see Archetypes)*. **In a woman's dream** a goddess will clarify the connection through the unconscious that exists between all women and female creatures. It is the sense of mystery, of a shared secret, which is such an intangible force within the woman's psyche. In the waking state it is that which enables women to create a sisterhood or network among themselves in order to bring about a common aim. To dream about goddesses therefore is to accept our right to initiation into this group. **In a man's dream** the goddess figure signifies all that a man fears in the concept of female power. It usually also gives an insight into his earliest view of femininity through his experience of his mother.

2 There are many goddess figures in all cultures. There are those perceived as being destructive such as **Kali, Bast** and **Lilith**, and also beneficent ones such as **Athena** and **Hermia**. The beneficent ones which women most closely relate to are given here: **Aphrodite**, goddess of love and beauty, moves women to be both creative and procreative. She governs a woman's enjoyment of love and beauty. **Artemis**, who is the goddess of the moon, personifies the independent feminine spirit whose ultimate goal is achievement. She is often pictured as the hunter. **Athena** is goddess of wisdom and strategy. She is logical and self-assured and is ruled by her mental faculties rather than her emotions. **Demeter**, the maternal archetype and goddess and fertility, highlights a woman's drive to provide physical and spiritual support for her children. **Hera**, the goddess of marriage, denotes the woman who has her essential goal of finding a husband and being married as paramount and any other role as secondary. **Hestia**, goddess of the hearth, manifests the patient woman who finds steadiness in seclusion. She emits a sense of wholeness. **Persephone**, who is ultimately queen of the underworld but only through having rejected her status as Demeter's daughter, gives expression to woman's tendency towards a need to please and be needed by others. Her submissive behaviour and passivity must change to an ability to take responsibility for who she is.

3 Spiritually, women are able to make intuitive links with the essential aspects of her own personality. She then achieves a greater understanding of her own make up, and is able to use all facets of her being within her normal everyday life.

GOGGLES
– also see Glasses and Mask

1 Goggles in a dream can have the same significance as spectacles and also the mask. The meaning can be ambivalent since goggles can be used, either to cover up the eyes – often believed to be the seat of the soul, or to enable us to see better. Under most circumstances it can be taken as the latter, but equally we need to be certain that we are not using the dream image of goggles to indicate the protection that we may need in real life. Perhaps we may feel that what we are seeing is going to harm us in some way.

2 For a woman to dream that she meets a man with goggles generally means she cannot trust that man to be honest with her.

3 We may be covering up, or denying the existence of, evil. This can only be a negative feeling and should be dealt with appropriately.

GOLD

1 Gold in dreams suggests the best, most valuable aspects of ourselves. **Finding gold** indicates that we can discover those characteristics in ourselves or others. **Burying gold** shows that we are trying to hide something – perhaps information or knowledge – that we have.

2 Gold in dreams can also represent the sacred, dedicated side of ourselves. We can recognise incorruptibility and wisdom, love, patience and care. Interestingly, in this context it seldom stands for material wealth, being more the spiritual assets that one has.

3 The old saying of 'everything that glitters isn't gold' certainly doesn't apply in the spiritual sense. To dream of gold symbolises Spirituality on a supreme level.

GOLF
– also see Games

1 The game of golf can represent many things in a dream sequence. As with many games, it can represent belonging to a team, but conversely it can also represent our own individual achievement. To be playing such a game indicates that we need freedom of movement and clarity of vision.

2 Playing golf can often represent our need to show our prowess, to be able literally to drive as far as we can, and often is used within the context of business acumen.

GONG

1 To **hear the sound of a gong** in a dream is to be aware that some limitation has been reached, or conversely that some permission has been given for further action. **To strike the gong** may represent the need for strength and the need to be able to achieve a particular quality of sound or information within a waking situation.

2 In older religions the gong is often used to alert people's attention to something that needs recognising. It is this symbolism which is often apparent in the circumstances of the dream.

3 Our awareness to Spirituality is symbolised by a gong. It is literally 'waking us up' on a spiritual level.

GOOSE

– see Birds

GOSSIP

1 To be gossiping in a dream can mean that one is spreading information, but in a way that is not necessarily appropriate. To be in a group of people and **listening to gossip** generally means that we are looking for some kind of information, but perhaps do not have the ability to achieve it for ourselves. We have to use other people to enable us to achieve the correct level of information.

2 Within the framework of personal development, there is often what could be called the 'gossip' in the background – the chatterbox – that which is part of our personality but which prevents us from moving away from previously held ideas and behaviour. Thus, to be gossiping in a dream may mean that we have to complete certain actions before moving on.

3 'Spiritual static'.

GOURD

– also see Vase

1 Both as a carrier of water and of sustenance, the gourd appearing in a dream may be a great deal to do with our own view of femininity and our ability to nurture. It is also the ability to link into untapped information and knowledge.

2 The gourd is often a symbol of mystery. As something unusual it can denote secret information, sustenance or nurturing. Because it is is used as a carrier after it has fruited, it can often represent the physical body.

3 A gourd can symbolise the mystery surrounding spiritual progression. At this time we may feel that there is little to go on.

GRAIL

1 The Holy Grail is such a basic image that in dreams it can appear as something miraculous, something which fulfils our wish and allows us to move forward into our full potential. Often it represents the achievement of spiritual success, but can also represent the cup of happiness. The grail appearing in a dream would indicate that we can expect some form of satisfaction and change to occur within our lives.

2 We are searching for something which we may feel at this particular moment is unattainable, but that by putting ourselves through various tests we may eventually achieve.

3 The Holy Spirit.

GRAIN

1 Dreaming of grains such as wheat, oats, barley, etc. can indicate some kind of a harvest. We have created opportunities for ourselves which can now come to fruition. Provided we look after the outcome of these opportunities, we can take that success forward and create even more abundance.

2 To dream of **grain growing in a field** can indicate that we are more or less on the point of success, that we have tended our lives sufficiently to be able to achieve growth.

3 Grain can represent the very seeds of life and our need to discover the hidden truth.

GRAMMAR

1 When we become conscious of grammar in dreams we are aware of our own or others difficulty in communicating.

2 There may be a need for precise information in a situation in our lives.

3 Accurate communication is essential on all levels; physical, mental and spiritual.

GRANDPARENTS
– see Family

GRAPES
– also see Fruit

1 To see grapes in a dream generally indicates that there is a need for celebration. The grape is the fruit most closely associated with Bacchus or, in his Greek form, Dionysus who was the god of conviviality. To dream of grapes indicates the searching for fun, laughter and creativity in our lives.

2 Grapes appearing in a dream

can represent sacrifice. We need to give something up in order to achieve what we are really looking for. Wine is often taken to represent such sacrifice since it has a close affiliation with blood.

3 Grapes, representative as food of the Gods, can symbolise wisdom and immortality.

GRASS
– also see Drugs

1 Grass is often a symbol of new growth, and of victory over barrenness. In old dream interpretations it could represent pregnancy, but is now more likely to signify new ideas and projects.

2 Grass can often denote our native land or surrender of deeply held beliefs.

3 Changes of Spiritual awareness can be indicated by grass appearing in a dream.

GRASSHOPPER

1 The grasshopper is a symbol of freedom and capriciousness, and in dreams it can often indicate a bid for freedom.

2 A grasshopper mind (one which flits all over the place), shows an inability to settle to anything and can actually be seen in dreams as a grasshopper.

3 In Chinese history the grasshopper is often associated with enlightenment. Thus, it represents some form of Spiritual freedom.

GRAVE
– also see Death

1 Dreaming of a grave is an indication that we must have regard for our feelings about, or our concept of, death. Such a dream may also be attempting to deal with our feelings about someone who has died.

2 Part of our personality may, quite literally, have been killed off, or is dead and buried to the outside world.

3 Spiritually, we may fear not just physical death but also its consequences.

GRAVEL

1 Often our attention is drawn to the size of an article within a dream. Gravel in this context is simply an indication of small particles. Such a dream may also bring back memories of a particular time or place, and remind us of happier times, such as those of childhood.

2 **Skidding on gravel** signifies that we should avoid taking risks in everyday life.

3 The microcosm.

GREASE/GREASY

1 Grease in a dream makes us

aware that we perhaps have not taken as much care in a situation as we should have done. We have created circumstances which do not give us an advantage and could be 'slippery' or uncomfortable.

2 We should use better judgement before putting ourselves at risk. Grease may also signify making things easier for ourselves.

3 Grease has two spiritual meanings in dreams. It may represent either simplicity or contamination. It will be up to the dreamer, depending on the other circumstances in the dream to decide which applies.

GREYHOUND
(or any trained dog)
– also see Dog in Animals

Dreaming of any trained dog will highlight the qualities we need in order to remain focused on a particular goal.

GROWTH

1 The changes in us which bring about new ways of relating to other people, who we ourselves are or situations around us, are all stages of growth. They can be pictured in dreams as the growth of a plant or something similar.

2 Often when we dream of childhood we are able to put ourselves in touch with the growth process.

3 Growth in a dream can be the recognition of a new Spiritual maturity, from which the dreamer should take heart.

GUILLOTINE

1 A guillotine in a dream indicates something irrational in our personality. We may be afraid of losing self-control, or of having part of our personality amputated. We could be aware of an injury to our person or to our dignity.

2 There is the potential for us to lose contact with someone we love, or with the part of ourselves which is capable of love.

3 By way of its physical action, a guillotine represents a severance of some kind. We may have become severed from our spiritual yearnings.

GUITAR

1 Guitar music in a dream can foretell the possibility of a new romance, but can also indicate the need for caution. **If the dreamer is playing the guitar** he or she is making an attempt to be more creative.

2 Any musical instrument characterises our need for rest and relaxation and for harmony in our lives.

3 We may feel the need for harmony in both our spiritual and physical worlds.

GULLS
– see Seagull in Birds

GUN
– also see Weapons

1 In dreams the gun has an obvious masculine and sexual connotation. **If a woman is firing** a gun she is aware of the masculine, aggressive side of her personality. **If she is being shot at** she perhaps feels threatened by overt signs of aggression or sexuality.

2 It will depend on the other circumstances in the dream how we interpret the use of a gun. We may be using it to protect those things we feel are important to us.

3 The symbolism here reverts to a more base attribute – that of overt masculinity.

GURU

1 A guru appearing in a dream is a representation of the wisdom of the unconscious. As that wisdom becomes available we often bring it through to conscious knowledge by the figure of the Wise Old Man *(See Introduction)*.

2 Psychologically, we all need a symbol for a father or authority figure and this is one such representation. In searching for knowledge of a specific sort, we need an external figure with whom to relate. In Eastern religions, this is the guru – who performs the same function as the priest in Western religion.

3 For many of us, God is too remote for us to be able to have a personal relationship with him. A guru therefore becomes the personification of all wisdom made available to us through his perception. He will assist us to access our own inate wisdom.

H

from

Hail *to* Hyena

HAIL

1 Hail in a dream, because it is frozen water *(see Ice)*, signifies the freezing of our emotions. It would appear that the danger and damage created by these frozen emotions comes from outside influences rather than internal feelings.

2 Hail has a particular part to play in the cycle of nature. We need to appreciate that there are times when numbing our emotions may be appropriate. It does not, however, need to be a permanent state of affairs.

3 Emotions connected with spirituality sometimes have to be held in check, and this can be symbolised for us in dreams by hail.

HAIR
– see Body

HAIRDRESSER

1 For many women, her hairdresser is someone with whom she can communicate freely. In dreams the hairdresser may appear as the part of ourselves which deals with self-image and the way we feel about ourselves. We perhaps need to consider ways in which we can change our image.

2 Psychologically and intellectually, the hairdresser can represent the healer within us. An intimate yet objective relationship can be important within our lives. A hairdresser appearing in dreams would signify this relationship.

3 In terms of spirituality the connection between self-image and beauty is obvious. We cannot grow spiritually unless we like ourselves.

HALF

1 Dreams can often have a very peculiar quality in that our image may only be half there or we perhaps only experience half an action. This usually indicates an incompleteness in us, being a sort of in-between state which means that we have to make decisions. Often it is about either going forward into the future or back into the past: completion or non-completion. For instance, we may have half-completed a task and be aware of this, but do not know how to finish it. Often the dream images that appear can show us how to do this. Conversely, if in a dream we have only **partially completed a task** and are left feeling dissatisfied with what has happened, we perhaps need to consider in waking life what needs to be done to enable us to complete the action in the dream. What would we have done had we been able to complete it?

2 To have only half of what

we feel we should have – for instance in quantity – perhaps only to have half of the food or drink we had expected, indicates that we are possibly selling ourselves short. We are not allowing ourselves to have what we need. To dream of being **half way up a hill or a mountain or halfway down a river** would indicate that there is some indecision. We are not as motivated as we should, or could, be to continue with the task we have in hand. We have made an initial effort but greater effort is needed in order to be where we want to be. This type of dream is very often to do with either motivating ourselves or others. To continually dream of **slipping back**, until we are only halfway through our task, to be repeating it over and over again, would indicate that we do not have the ability to complete it. There is perhaps an extra skill that we need to enable us to achieve success.

3 A degree of spiritual indecision is also indicated here. The dreamer should look at where he wants to be spiritually.

HALLUCINATIONS

1 When dreaming, there is an hallucinatory quality about everything that we see. We usually accept what we experience as real and in the actual dream state do not question. Scenes can change as quickly as the blink of an eye, faces can change, we can be looking at one thing then a few seconds later realise we are looking at something completely different. This is totally acceptable within the dream reality. It is only when we consider the dream afterwards that we realise how odd this may be. During dreams, things can take on qualities of other objects and of other feelings. Dreams can create a reality of their own, they do the unexpected – which in normal waking life would be totally illogical and surreal. Within this dream world we need to take a note of what is happening. We do not watch these with amusement, it seems simply that we observe what is going on. Even our own actions can take on an oddness. We may be doing things in a dream which in waking life we would never expect ourselves to do. Freed from the logical quality that mentors our ordinary everyday life, we can be liberated to create a totally different awareness of our own abilities, of our thought patterns and even our own past. We can often dream that we have done things in the past which we have never done, or we can prepare ourselves to do things in the future which again we would never expect to do.

2 Psychologically freeing the mind so it can 'roam' under its own speed allows hidden memories, images and thoughts to surface in such a way that we can handle the input when perhaps in real life we may not have been able to do so. We create a reality which suits an action, rather than creating an action which suits the reality. For instance, an abused child may displace the activity into some kind of response that would be acceptable, not allowing the reality of the abuse to come through until such times as he or she was able to come to terms with it.

3 The hallucination that we experience in dreams can also be direct messages from the unconscious.

HALTER

1 The halter shares the symbolism of bonds, since under normal circumstances it often controls the head. We are dreaming about reigning back on the intellect, instead of allowing the creative energy to flow freely. We are not allowing ourselves the freedom to create to the best of our ability. It usually represents restriction of one form or another, although interestingly enough it may indicate acceptable restriction.

2 When we are moving into new areas of growth we sometimes need to be shown the way, and the halter is a symbol of this leading forward into new creativity. We are, as it were, being taken by the head and shown what we need to see.

3 We may be also experiencing some spiritual restraint. If so, we should take time to look at what we want most spiritually.

HAM
– *see Food*

HAMMER

1 Dreaming of hammers or blunt instruments highlights the more aggressive and masculine side of our nature. There may be the feeling that their is an aspect of our personality which needs to be crushed or struck for us to be able to function properly.

2 While aggression may be necessary it may be more that the judicial application of force is appropriate.

3 The hammer also has a double-sided symbolism – these are justice and vengeance. The dreamer needs to be aware which of these apply in his own spiritual domain.

HAND
– *see Body*

HANDCUFFS

1 Dreaming of **being in handcuffs** denotes that we have been restrained in some way, often by an authority figure.

2 If we are **putting handcuffs on someone**, we may be attempting to bind that person to us. We may be being overly possessive.

3 Handcuffs are a binding symbol and spiritually would suggest that we are being hampered, probably by our own doubts and fears.

HANGING
– also see Noose and Rope

1 Hanging is a violent act against a person, therefore if we are **present at a hanging** we are being party to violence and perhaps need to reconsider our actions. If **we ourselves are being hanged**, we are being warned of some difficulty ahead.

2 If we are conscious in our dream of **something hanging up**, there may be word association, in that literally there is a 'hang up' in our lives. If something is **hanging over us**, then we are being threatened by circumstances around us.

3 Spiritual suppression could be at work here. If so, the dreamer needs to find out where the suppression originated and then handle the situation from there on in.

HARE
– see Animals

HAREM

1 For a man to dream that he is in a harem shows that he is struggling to come to terms with the complexities of the feminine nature. **For a woman to have the same dream** shows that she is understanding her own flamboyant and sensual nature. On a different level, she is recognising her need to belong to a group of women – a sisterhood.

2 Any group of women appearing in dreams will signify femininity in one form or another. It will depend on whether the dreamer relates to a particular person in the scenario for a deeper interpretation.

3 The Great Mother in her more playful aspects.

HARNESS

1 Like the halter, the harness indicates some form of control or restraint. It may be that we are actually being restrained by our own limitations, or that we are being controlled by external circumstances. To be **wearing a harness** often takes us back to periods in childhood when we were not allowed the freedom we would have liked.

2 Harnessing energy is an important way of using power that we have. To **harness something** is to make it usable in a controlled fashion, so in dreams to be aware of this type of control implies the restraint that is necessary to enable the correct things to happen.

3 Spiritually, we need to harness energy. This means using what we have available in the most efficient way possible. When we have done this, we are then able to control the wilder side of our personality.

HAT
– see Clothes

HARP

1 The harp as a musical instrument indicates the correct vibration that we need in order to create harmony within our lives. We ourselves are very much in control of this and since the harp is also a national symbol of music, rhythm and harmony we often link back to our own basic selves.

2 To **harp on about something** in a dream – that is, to keep repeating what is going on is to recognise the need for acknowledgement perhaps in some activity we are undertaking.

3 The ladder to the next world, represented by the harp, is an image which can be used both in dreams and meditation.

HARVEST

1 To be dreaming about a harvest indicates that we are going to reap the rewards of previous care we have taken. We can create a store for ourselves by, for instance, doing good and then achieving some kind of reward later on. We are able to work hard, and in working hard we take care of the future. So, to dream of a harvest can actually have two meanings. It can mean looking back into the past and reaping the rewards, or it can mean looking towards the future in order to use what has happened previously. The other circumstances in the dream will indicate which interpretation needs to be used.

2 To be **taking part in a harvest or perhaps a harvest festival**, indicates that we are celebrating our own life energy – that energy we have available to us – to be used in achieving those dividends we feel are ours by right.

3 Any kind of a harvest represents fruitfulness and fertility, particularly spiritual.

HASH
– also see Drugs

1 When we dream of **'making a**

hash' of things, we are making things difficult for ourselves, and are perhaps creating a problem where there isn't one. We are making things difficult for people around us, and not really doing and planning our actions carefully in an appropriate way.

2 To dream of **hash, as in marijuana**, indicates we are using substances to raise consciousness and we may need to recognise that we should look at things from another direction.

HAY

1 In previous times, for many the hayfield represented fun, relaxation and irresponsibility. Nowadays it is more likely to represent irritation – as in hay fever – and an unknown quality. To dream of hay is probably to be looking at a practical aspect within ourselves. It may be the ability to provide shelter and sustenance for others.

2 Happy memories and good feelings may be represented in dreams by stereotyped romantic scenarios where those feelings need to be reproduced.

3 Summer and the feeling of warmth and happiness it generates are connected with spiritual progress.

HEAD
– see Body

HEARSE

1 To dream of a hearse indicates that we are probably recognising that there is a time limit, either on ourselves or on a project we are connected with. Often we need to come to terms with our feelings about death on order to understand ourselves.

2 We may be aware that a part of ourselves is no longer 'alive' and it is better to let it go rather than resurrect it.

3 A hearse will always symbolise death, but it can also mean an ending of some sort.

HEART
– see Body

HEARTH

1 To dream of a hearth or fireplace is to recognise the need for security. This may be of two different types. One is knowing that the home, our place of existence, is secure. The other is recognising the security of the inner self, the interior feminine which gives warmth and stability.

2 We may be, or need to be, linking with our passionate wilder nature – the seat of our passions

3 The Anima, and that part of

ourselves which guards the feminine spirit, can be symbolised by the hearth.

HEAVEN
– see Religious Imagery

HEDGEHOG
-see Animals

HEEL
– see Body

HELL
– see Religious Imagery

HELMET

1 In dreams, it will depend on whether the helmet is **being worn by someone else** or by the dreamer. If the former, it may have the same symbolism as the mask *(see Mask)* in that it prevents the wearer being seen. If the latter, then it is a symbol of protection and preservation.

2 In olden times, the helmet was the attribute of the warrior or hero. Even today – as with the motorcycle helmet – it is still largely a representation of the masculine.

3 Protection by the Spiritual Self.

HEN
– see Birds

HERMAPHRODITE
– also see Sex

1 When we dream of a hermaphrodite, we may be having uncertainties about our own gender, or about our ability to adjust to the roles played by our own sex. Interestingly, as we learn more about ourselves, we attempt to achieve a balance between the logical and the sensitive sides of our nature. This can appear as hermaphrodism in a dream.

2 As a child grows, he begins to understand that certain behaviour is appropriate or acceptable. This may mean that other natural reactions are suppressed and can surface later on. These may confuse the dreamer and be perceived in dreams as hermaphrodism.

3 Perfect balance.

HERMIT

1 There is a kind of loneliness within many people which prevents us from making relationships on a one-to-one basis. This may manifest in dreams as the figure of the hermit.

2 There are two types of hermit. One withdraws from life in order to live an entirely spiritual existence and knows that others will care for his bodily needs. The other travels throughout the world using his knowledge and expertise to help others. In dreams if **we meet the hermit**, we are discovering the dimension in ourselves which has a spiritual awareness.

3 A holy man, or the Wise Old Man *(see Introduction)* will often appear in dreams as the hermit.

HERO/HEROINE
– see Archetypes

HEXAGRAM
– also see Shapes

1 Technically, the hexagram is a figure of six lines and represents the union of two forces, the Yin (feminine) and the Yang (masculine). For this to appear in a dream represents the principle of 'as above, so below'.

2 When we attempt to reconcile two forces – the spiritual and the physical – we may experience that union in the form of patterns, one significant group of which are hexagrams.

3 The union of the spiritual and physical worlds is represented by the hexagram.

HIGH
– see Position

HILL
– also see Mound

1 To be **on top of a hill –** and therefore high up – indicates we are aware of our own expanded vision. We have made an effort to achieve something and are able to survey the results of what we have done, to assess the effect on our environment and the people around us. We have achieved those things that we previously thought impossible, and are able to undertake further work in the light of knowledge we have attained.

2 To be **climbing a hill in the company of others** often indicates that we have a common goal, that a journey we possibly thought was ours alone, is actually connected with other people. We can use their knowledge and comradeship to take us to the heights of our being. To dream that we are **going downhill** would indicate we are feeling as if circumstances are pushing us in a certain direction. We may be moving from a level of attainment and now feel that – with relaxation of effort – we are not so much in control of our own abilities.

3 Effort is needed in order to achieve the clarity necessary for us to continue to progress spiritually.

HISTORIC

1 To have a dream which is set in history – such as in the Elizabethan or Victorian times – is to link with our past feelings and with that part of ourselves which has passed into history. It links with the person we were at some previous time in our lives and perhaps links with outdated beliefs and ways of living.

2 The human being continually assesses both their, and the historic, past. History is perhaps an objective assessment of a subjective way of being. Sometimes to dream in this way is to dream of the person we might have been.

3 Old beliefs and life patterns need to be considered in the light of present knowledge.

HIVE

1 The hive usually represents an area of work where there is considerable industry and activity going on, and where the best use is made of all possible resources. To dream of **being near a hive** can represent the effort that is needed to be made to create fertility – or fertile situations – for ourselves. The hive can also represent protective motherhood.

2 The old belief that one told one's sorrows to the bees *(see Bee)* still manifests in dreams. The hive may represent the activity that is needed to get ourselves out of a situation.

3 The feminine power in Nature is represented by the hive. The

symbol of a hollow vessel holding nurture or sustenance links with Mother Earth *(See Introduction)*.

HOLE

1 A hole usually represents a difficult or tricky situation. It can also be a place where we may hide, or feel protected in. To dream of **falling into a hole** indicates that we are perhaps getting in touch with our unconscious feelings, urges and fears. To **walk round a hole** suggests we may need to get round a tricky situation. We may also need to become aware of the other parts of ourselves that are buried beneath our surface awareness.

2 A hole can very often represent the feminine and the emptiness one feels as one moves towards an understanding of the Self. **A hole in the roof of any sacred building**, or any hole which allows steam or smoke to escape, is the opening upwards to the celestial world and is the door or gateway to other dimensions. It is interesting that, as central heating and living in flats becomes more commonplace, we feel more and more enclosed without aspect to that spiritual awareness.

3 A round hole represents the Heavens, a square hole represents the Earth.

HOLIDAY

1 To be on holiday in a dream indicates a sense of relaxation and of satisfying ones own needs without having to take care of others.

2 Our need to be independent and to be responsible often comes across in dreams as a holiday. Quite literally, the word means holy-day – a day set apart and we may need to heed the warning that we need time off to create space for ourselves.

3 Spiritual replenishment, rest and relaxation are all part of a holiday.

HOLLOW

1 Dreaming of **feeling hollow** connects with our feelings of emptiness, lack of purpose and inability to find a direction in our lives. To dream of **being in a hollow** would indicate that we need some kind of protection from what is going on around us in our ordinary everyday life.

2 Hollowness can come across in a dream in several ways. We can be conscious of our being hollow inside – for instance, 'it felt as though I had hollow legs', or that we are in a hollow state – a state similar to the void *(see Abyss)*. We are in a position where nothing is happening, where we do not feel in control and need to take control of the space we have been given.

3 Hollowness can indicate a lack of motivation, particularly on our spiritual journey.

HOLY COMMUNION
– see Religious Imagery

HOME

1 The human being has certain basic needs such as shelter, warmth and nourishment. The home, and particularly the parental home, can stand for all of these things. To dream of **being at home** signifies a return to the basic standards we learnt as a child.

2 Psychologically we all need to integrate our own primary personality traits with learnt behaviour. Dreaming of a safe environment – such as home – allows us to do this.

3 Sanctuary, that is a place where we can be ourselves without fear of reprisal, is contained in this image. Spiritualists speak of 'going home' when they are approaching death since the physical state is a temporary one.

HOMOSEXUALITY
– also see Sex

1 Dreaming of **having intercourse with somebody of the same sex** as oneself usually indicates a conflict or anxiety about our own gender. We may find ourselves attracted to someone of the same sex in dreams because we are looking for parental love. We may also be looking for love of a different sort – a nurturing rather than sexual love.

2 Very often, to dream of a homosexual affair is an attempt to come to terms with opposite aspects of oneself. It is understanding that, through the integration of a part of ourselves, we are making ourselves more whole and therefore more able to go onto successful relationships of any sort.

3 Unification on an internal level is a sign of spiritual maturity.

HONEY

1 Honey almost inevitably represents pleasure and sweetness. To dream of honey – and particularly **eating it** – can be to recognise that we are needing to give ourselves pleasure. Equally, it can indicate the essence of our feelings, that we have been through some kind of joyful experience which can now be assimilated as part of ourselves.

2 Honey is supposed to impart fertility and virility. To be dreaming of honey would indicate that we are perhaps entering a much more actively sexual or fertile time.

3 Immortality and rebirth are two

symbols which belong to honey. As a healing substance it has the power to regenerate.

HORSE
– see Animals

HORSESHOE

1 The horseshoe is always taken as a lucky symbol and, traditionally, if it is **turned upwards** it represents the moon and protection from all aspects of evil. When **turned downwards,** the power is reputed to 'drain out' and therefore be unlucky. The horseshoe is also connected as a lucky symbol to weddings. Customarily to dream of a horseshoe may indicate there will shortly be a wedding in your family or peer group.

2 In ordinary everyday life, symbols which have a long history become fixed in, and used by, our unconscious – often to represent other happier times or times when there has been more happening.

3 Spiritually, we can link the horseshoe with a talisman or amulet which protects us and our personal space.

HOOD

1 A figure wearing a hood in a dream will always appear to be slightly menacing. While not necessarily being evil, there may be a part of us which has been threatened. The hood can also represent part of ourselves which, if we have withdrawn, we are creating a problem. An aspect of our personality may be invisible to us and may need to be uncovered in order for us to function in an acceptable fashion.

2 Traditionally, **for a woman to be wearing a hood** suggests that she is being deceitful. If a **man is wearing a hood**, it suggests that he is withdrawing from a situation. Equally, in its more advanced sense, the hooded figure of a monk can indicate the more reflective side of us as it begins to become more evident in our everyday lives.

3 Death and invisibility were formerly represented by the hood. It would now indicate that certain aspects of knowledge are held invisible until the time is right.

HOOK

1 When we dream of a hook we are are generally understanding that we have the ability to draw things towards us that are either good or bad. It can equally indicate that we are being hooked by someone, and thus not being allowed the freedom to which we feel we have a right.

2 In childhood dreams the hook can represent the hold that a parent or authority figure has over us. This symbolism can continue into adulthood, depicting the way that we allow people to take control within our lives.

3 We need to be clear not to get 'hooked' into religious beliefs and practices just for the sake of it.

HORNS
– also see Antlers

1 Horns appearing in dreams hark back to the idea of the animal in the human. The god Pan, who represents sexuality as well as life force, wore horns. A horn also represents the penis and masculinity. Because it is penetrative, it can also signify the desire to hurt. Protectiveness is also a quality of horns since the male animal will use his horns to protect his territory. A **musical or hunting horn** suggests a summoning or a warning in dreams.

2 Horns in a dream suggest superiority, either earned or conferred. It is interesting that horns are supposed to bestow the powers of the animal on the wearer. In Pagan times, as well as some tribes today, the donning of horns signifies a particular senior position within the tribe. In Chinese medicine, **rhinoceros horn** is reputed to be an aphrodisiac. This is possibly because of its association with masculine power.

3 In a spiritual sense, because horns are associated with the head, they represent intellectual as well as supernatural power. Because they rise above the head, they also symbolise Divinity and the power of the soul.

HOSPITAL
– also see Operation

1 Depending on our attitude to hospitals, when one appears in a dream it can either represent a place of safety, or a place where ones very being is threatened and we become vulnerable. Taken as a **place of healing**, it represents that aspect within ourselves that knows when respite is necessary from cares and troubles – when we can allow ourselves to be cared for and nurtured and put back into one piece. If we find **hospitals threatening**, it may be that we are conscious of the fact that we have to 'let go', to put ourselves at the mercy of others and allow things to happen for us, in order that a situation can be improved.

2 Dreaming of **being in a hospital** may be mentally creating a transition period between something that has not gone well, and an improved attitude where things can get better. To be **visiting**

someone in hospital indicates that we are aware that a part of ourselves is perhaps not well, is 'dis-eased' and needs attending to in order to give us clarity.

3 A healing environment where things can be brought into a state of balance is signified by a hospital.

HOSTILITY

1 When we experience **hostility within ourselves** in a dream, it is the direct expression of that feeling. It is safe to express it in a dream whereas we may not dare do this in waking life. If however, someone is being **hostile towards us**, it very often means that we need to be aware that we are not acting appropriately, that others may feel we are putting them in danger.

2 Hostility is one of those emotions that can be worked through in a dream. If we can identify what is making us feel hostile in a dream, then we can usually draw a parallel in our waking lives and deal with whatever the problem is. If we can identify the feeling as being appropriate in a particular situation, then we can deal with the feeling.

3 Spiritual opposition – or rather opposition to our spiritual beliefs – can generate a tremendous amount of hostility. We need to be aware that others may not necessarily agree with our spiritual beliefs.

HOT

1 Pleasurable feelings can be translated in dreams to a physical feeling. To dream of **being hot** indicates warm – or perhaps passionate – feelings. To be conscious of the fact that **our surroundings are hot** indicates that we are loved and cared for.

2 Occasionally, extreme emotion can be interpreted as a physical feeling – so anger, jealousy or other such feelings can be experienced as heat. Experiencing **something as hot which should be cold** – e.g. ice – indicates that we are perhaps having difficulty and experiencing confusion in sorting out our feelings.

3 Spiritual passion is a deeply held feeling. It can be experienced as in a dream as heat.

HOTEL
– also see Boarding House/Hotel in Buildings

1 Dreaming of being in a hotel can mean that we need to escape from a situation in our lives for a short time. Conversely, it can also mean that a situation we are in will only last for a limited amount of time.

2 To dream of **being a guest in a hotel** can indicate that we are unsettled and feel we can only settle down temporarily. Being forced into a position of **living in a hotel** signifies a basic restlessness in the dreamer's character, who may be attempting to escape from himself.

3 Temporary sanctuary, or the need to be in a safe environment is depicted by a hotel.

HOURGLASS

1 In dreams, time is irrelevant. To experience something which measures time is often to alert us to the need for measuring our thoughts and activities. When such a symbol is old fashioned – as in an hourglass – our perception of time and its management may be old-fashioned. We need to use different, and more precise, ways of measuring those activities.

2 When we are particularly under stress we can be overly aware of the running out of time, that it can become an enemy. This is often symbolised as an hourglass.

3 In former times, the hourglass was frequently taken as a symbol of death. More properly it is now seen as a symbol for the Passage of Life.

HOUSE
– also see Buildings

1 A house nearly always refers to the soul, and they way that we build our lives. The different rooms and parts of houses in dreams indicate the various aspects of our personality and experience. For example, **Attic** Dreaming of being in an attic is to do with past experiences and old memories. Interestingly, it can also highlight family patterns of behaviour and attitudes which have been handed down. **Basement/cellar** The cellar most often represents the subconscious and those things we may have suppressed through an inability to handle them. A basement can also highlight the power that is available to us provided we are willing to make use of it. We may not have come to terms with our own sexuality and prefer to keep it hidden. **Bathroom** In dreams our attitude to personal cleanliness and our most private thoughts and actions can be shown as the bathroom or toilet. **Bedroom** The bedroom portrays a place of safety where we can relax and be as sensual as we wish. **Chimney** As a passage from one state to another and a conductor of heat, in dreams the chimney can indicate how we deal with our inner emotions and warmth. **Hall** The hallway in a dream is illustrative of how we meet and relate to other people. **Library** Our minds, and how we store the information we receive, can appear as a library.
2 A house represents security and safety, and therefore signifies protection and the Great Mother.
3 The house is popularly known as the seat of the soul, and in spiritual terms links us to the way we are in the world.

HUNGER

1 Experiencing hunger in a dream indicates that our physical, emotional or mental needs are not being properly satisfied. It is possible that the dreamer is actually hungry, and this is being recognised in the dream.
2 Every human being has needs which require satisfaction. While that lack of satisfaction may not be acknowledged in the waking state, it can be translated into dream symbolism and become hunger.
3 Seeking Spiritual satisfaction and fulfilling a need is one aspect of hunger.

HUNT/HUNTSMAN

1 Dreaming of **being hunted** is mostly taken to be to do with one's sexuality. Its even older meaning is linked with death, particularly a death containing an aspect of ritual killing or sacrifice. By association therefore, to dream of a hunt is to register the necessity for a change of state in everyday life.

2 To dream of **being a huntsman** alerts us to the part of ourselves which can be destructive and vicious.

3 Death and destruction, but in a ritualised setting is part of the spiritual journey. We must 'kill off' that part of ourselves which prevents us from going forward.

HURRICANE
– also see Gale and Wind

1 When we experience a hurricane in a dream, we are sensing the force of an element in our lives which is beyond our control. We may feel we are being swept along by circumstances – or possibly someone's passion – and are powerless to resist.

2 A hurricane can represent the power of our own passion, or passionate belief, which picks us up and carries us along. We may not know how to handle the results of that passion, and feel it could be disastrous for others.

3 The intensity of our spiritual belief is depicted here – dependant on the other circumstances in the dream.

HUSBAND
– see Family

HYENA
– see Animals

I

from

Ibis *to* Ivy

IBIS
– see Birds

ICE

1 When we dream of ice we are usually looking at the emotions. We are aware that perhaps we are colder than we should be, shutting off any display of warmth and compassion. We are thereby enclosing ourselves in a situation from which it may be difficult to free ourselves.

2 Ice is also a representation of rigidity, of the brittleness that comes from not understanding what is going on around us, of creating circumstances where people cannot get – or be – in touch with us. Depending on how the ice appears in a dream, it can indicate a state of impermanence.

3 Spiritually, ice symbolises a part of ourselves which has become frozen and needs to thaw out before we can progress.

ICE-CREAM

1 Ice-cream appearing in a dream is a great deal to do with the sensual tastes that one has. Under normal circumstances it is a pleasurable experience and very often reminds us of childhood and happier times. To be **eating ice-cream** indicates that we may be accepting pleasure into our lives in a way that we have

not been able to do before. To be **giving other people ice-cream** indicates that we are giving other people pleasure.

2 Ice-cream can also depict the state of mind where one has reached conclusions that nothing is permanent – that the pleasure we have can melt away.

3 Ice cream is an image which can be used to signify impermanence, particularly insofar as pleasure is concerned. We need to decide if we wish to go for transitoriness or permanence.

ICICLES

1 Often in dreams icicles can appear to hang in a certain fashion – it is the pattern that is important as much as the icicle itself. We may be aware that we are having problems with our environment and that it is not supporting it in a way we would expect – thereby creating difficulties.

2 To see **icicles melting** indicates that the troubles that have been around us will literally disappear within a short space of time. Whether the fault is our own or other people's, it would appear that outside circumstances give the ability to overcome whatever has been troubling us.

3 Spiritual isolation– that is, existing in isolation because of the way our lives have gone – can be symbolised by icicles.

ICON
– also see Religious Imagery

1 Dreaming of any religious symbol usually indicates our very deep connection with old ideas and principles. The icon usually symbolises the microcosm within the macrocosm – that is the small world reflecting the larger world. The human being often needs something tangible to represent what is simply a principle or a concept, and the icon performs this purpose.

2 Usually, icons are representations of a belief system and therefore portray the way we feel about a number of other issues. In a dream, when an icon appears to have a religious picture but in actual fact it contains pictures of one's own family, it indicates the ability to idolise the family.

3 The icon is a small spiritual picture which symbolises a greater whole.

IGLOO
– also see Buildings

1 The igloo is interesting as a symbol in dreams. It can equally represent a cold exterior containing a very warm interior, or the coldness of the construction itself.

It can appear as though someone is uncaring and therefore creating an unloving home environment, although in fact there is warmth within that person.

2 The igloo can often represent the feminine and the womb. Sometimes, it represents frigidity, but at other times the ability of a woman to relax and be herself once her barriers have been overcome.

3 The feminine principle, in the sense of sheltering and nurturing, is depicted in the igloo.

ILLNESS
– also see Sick

1 Whatever life has to offer, we may be left with painful memories, feelings of anger and difficulties. In a dream these memories and feelings can surface as illness. Sometimes such a dream can foretell real illness, but most of the time it represents the way we deal with things. It means that we are not putting ourselves in touch with a force that can help us to overcome difficulties.

2 Often when we are ill in a dream we are grappling with part of our personality. Rather than the whole being ill, part of us is sick and perhaps needs to be dealt with. Often the dream will give the method of dealing with it – perhaps by taking medication, having surgery or a combination of both. It also often represents our fears of not being looked after properly.

3 Lack of spiritual clarity can often be experienced in dreams as illness.

IMITATION

1 To dream of **being imitated** is ambivalent. It can mean that we are aware that whatever we have done is the correct thing to do and that other people can learn from our example. It can equally mean that other people are seeing us as being leaders, when we ourselves do not necessarily feel that it is the correct role for us.

2 If we are **imitating someone else**, we are usually conscious of the fact that we have the ability to be as they are. To be **imitating one's superiors** is to recognise their greater knowledge. However, to be imitating someone in negative action – **mimicking** – may show that we doubt our own integrity and need to look at whether we are happy with our own actions.

3 The microcosm of the macrocosm, the small imitating the large.

IMMERSION

1 To dream of being **totally immersed** in water generally indicates the way we handle our own emotions, that we are attempting to find the more innocent part of ourselves which does not need to be affected by external circumstances. We are attempting to clarify situations and to cleanse ourselves, perhaps of ideas and attitudes that have been suggested to us by other people.

2 To be totally immersed – **totally focused** – on something in a dream indicates we very definitely need to be able to concentrate entirely on one particular thought or idea to help us understand ourselves.

3 Transformation and rebirth can only be accomplished by a total immersion in spirituality.

IMMOBILITY
– also see Paralysis

1 Immobility in a dream can be extremely frightening. This feeling very often occurs as the dreamer is beginning to learn more about themselves. A feeling of oppression and of not being able to move usually indicates that the dreamer needs to, quite literally, sit still and be immobile within their ordinary everyday lives. They need to achieve a kind of stillness which is foreign to most people, and therefore initially frightening, while later on it can be a state of peace and tranquillity.

2 To be immobilised in a dream usually indicates that we have created circumstances around us which are now beginning to trap us. We need to remain absolutely still until we have decided what the appropriate action needs to be, and then we can move forward in an appropriate way. Often such a dream comes when we are facing the darker side of ourselves – that which could be called evil. A superhuman effort needs to be made to overcome what is holding us down.

3 The Unconditioned State, the Liberated Self. Immobility in this sense is dynamic stillness.

IMP

1 An imp appearing in a dream usually foretells disorder and difficulty. The imp often has the same significance as the Devil *(See Devil)* in its aspect of tormenting one, of creating difficulty and harm within one's life.

2 The imp can represent the uncontrolled negative part of ourselves, that part that instinctively creates chaos and takes great joy in doing so. It is perhaps an aspect of loss of control.

3 The Devil as the Tempter can appear in dreams as an imp, or as a manifestation of a particularly irritating type.

IMPRISONED

– also see Prison

1 Being imprisoned in a dream usually means that we are trapped by circumstances, often those we have created through our own fear or ignorance. We feel that other people are creating circumstances around us which will not allow us to move forward. We will often need to negotiate our freedom.

2 When we experience imprisonment in a dream, we are usually becoming conscious of old attitudes and beliefs which are imprisoning us.

3 Spiritual imprisonment can suggest that we are too introverted or self-involved. We need to 'open ourselves up' to new influences. We may need assistance in doing this – and have to look to an outside influence to release us.

INAUGURATION

1 We have many opportunities to make new beginnings, and inauguration – in that it indicates a change of status – is one such symbol. This may be important to us in terms of either personal growth or within the work situation. To dream that we are being given such an honour means we can receive public acclaim for something that we have done, for our ability to make the transition from the lesser to the greater.

2 Often a ceremony is necessary to mark the fact that we have succeeded in one thing and can now move on, putting that knowledge to the test in the outside world. To be dreaming of such a ceremony indicates that we can be pleased with ourselves and what we have achieved, that we have literally inaugurated a different way of being, and can now move forward into the future.

3 A ceremony in a spiritual sense can mark a new beginning. In this case it marks the taking of new spirituality, perhaps Cosmic Responsibility.

INCENSE
– also see Religious Imagery

1 Physically, incense is designed to perfume a room. In dreams, it is possible to be aware of the smell of incense, particularly if it has associations for the dreamer. For instance, it may hold childhood memories of church or religious buildings.

2 Incense is used in order to raise consciousness, or to cleanse atmospheres and sacred spaces. In dreams, when we become aware of it being used in this way, we need to consider how best to improve ourselves or our environment.

3 Spiritually incense is used as a

vehicle for prayer and as a symbol for the subtle body or soul. In dreams we can become aware of our need to use spiritual symbolism in our work.

INCEST
– also see Sex

1 Incest is such a taboo subject that to dream of it seldom actually refers to the physical act. It usually represents the need and desire we have to be in control, either of ourselves or of our relationships within the family. It is possible that incest occurs because the child has not yet been allowed, or had the opportunity to sort out, his or her feelings so far as the family are concerned.

2 Since self-image and sexuality are so closely connected, incest in dreams is much more likely to be an effort to sort out our feelings about ourselves. We are attempting to make a link with the part of our own personality most closely reflected by that person. We can only do this within the safety of a dream.

3 In legend and myth, incest among the gods and goddesses was an attempt to maintain the purity of the energy. Spiritually therefore when we dream of incest, we are attempting to purify or keep clear our own power.

INCOME

1 The income we earn is an important part of our support structure, so any dream connected with this will tend to signify our attitude towards our wants and needs. To dream of an **increased income** shows we feel we have overcome an obstacle in ourselves and can accept that we have value. A **drop in income** signifies our neediness, and perhaps our attitude to poverty.

2 In trying to look after ourselves we are aware of what people have to offer us, and also what we have to do in order to be rewarded for our efforts. Dreaming of receiving a private income – such as **a trust fund** – suggests we perhaps need to look at our relationships with other people.

3 The giving of alms is the belief that what one has one shares, and is a meaningful part of income. It does not matter whether this is in the material sense, or in the giving of time and effort.

INDIGESTION

1 To be **suffering from indigestion** in a dream shows that there is something in our lives which is not being tolerated very well. Equally, it may indicate that we are actually suffering from indigestion, and this is recognised

in the dream state. There is a belief that certain foods can trigger off lurid dreams.

2 If **something is indigestible** in a dream, it may be that we recognise that we have some sort of mental block on our own progress. Perhaps we need to do things in a different way, or perhaps in smaller steps.

3 Spiritual knowledge that has not been properly assimilated can be represented by indigestion in a dream.

INFECTION

1 Dreaming of having an infection suggests that there is the possibility of us having internalised negative attitudes from other people. Depending on where in the body the infection appears, there is information as to the type of 'infection'. For example, an **infection in the leg** may indicate that we feel we are being prevented from moving forward quickly enough in waking life.

2 When we are made uncomfortable by external circumstances in waking life, this may appear as an infection in a dream.

3 In spiritual development, and particularly when dealing with outside influences, we can become contaminated – or infected – by ideology and spurious beliefs. We need to be aware of the possibility that we can be 'taken over' by wrong thought and negativity.

INITIATION
– see Religious Imagery

INJECTION
– also see Syringe

1 To dream of **being given an injection** is to be feeling that one's personal space has been penetrated. Other people's opinions, needs or desires may be forced on the dreamer leaving him little option but to co-operate. To dream of **giving an injection** suggests that we are attempting to force ourselves on other people. Obviously, this may have sexual connotations.

2 An injection may be an attempt to heal, or to make one better. We may feel that we need external help in order to function more successfully. It will depend on our attitude to conventional medicine whether this is seen as co-operation or resistance.

3 Spiritually, to find ourselves accepting an injection indicates that we are prepared to create circumstances within ourselves which will help us to progress. More negatively, an injection can indicate short term pleasure rather than long term gain.

INK
– also see Pen

1 Since very few people now use fountain pens, the significance of ink on a physical level is no longer quite so valid. Formerly in dreams it suggested the ability to communicate in a lucid fashion. It was also an instrument of 'torture' for children and would often appear in dreams in later life.

2 On a more intellectual level, ink signifies the ability to transcribe and understand knowledge in a more sophisticated way.

3 More spiritually, ink has significance, particularly in magical practices, when it was used to reflect powers which were outside the norm. In written magical spells it was necessary to use particular inks in order to achieve the required results.

INSECTS

1 Insects in dreams can reflect the feeling that something is irritating or bugging us. It may also indicate our feeling of insignificance and powerlessness. It will depend on the particular insect in the dream as to the interpretation. Thus, a **wasp** might indicate danger, whereas a **beetle** could mean either dirt or protection.

2 Psychologically, insects can represent feelings we would rather do without. This could be something niggling at our consciences, or guilt. Insects tend to signify negative feelings.

3 Psychically, insects can appear in dreams as some kind of threat. This is one reason why they are often used in psychological thrillers and science fiction. More positively, insects can appear in dreams as reminders of instinctive behaviour.

INSCRIPTION

1 Any inscription in a dream is information which will need to be understood. **Reading an inscription** can suggest that something is understood already, whereas **not being able to read an inscription** suggests that more information is required in order to complete a task.

2 An **inscription appearing on**, for instance, a rock would suggest old knowledge or wisdom. An **inscription appearing in sand** would suggest that the knowledge is either impermanent, or must be learnt quickly.

3 The image of an inscription often appears in dreams as we reach a certain stage of development. Spiritually, this usually indicates the type of knowledge that can be passed onto other people.

INSOMNIA
– see Introduction

INTERSECTION

1 An intersection which appears in a dream – such as a **T junction** – indicates there is a choice of two ways forward. Two opposites may be coming together in our waking lives, and we are able to make changes and move forward in a more focused way.

2 If we are conscious of an intersection – perhaps in a pattern which appears in a dream – we are being offered choices, and perhaps have to differentiate between right and wrong.

3 When we meet an intersection in dreams, we are putting ourselves in a position of having to make choices which may have a greater impact on others than they do on us.

INTESTINES
– see Abdomen and Excrement in Body

INTOXICATION
– also see Alcohol, Drunk and Drugs

1 When we are intoxicated in a dream it can be important to decide what has caused us to become intoxicated. **Being drunk** can indicate a loss of control, whereas a **change of state brought about by drugs** can represent a change in awareness.

2 The changes that occur in consciousness through intoxication can be mirrored in a dream. Sometimes that change can be depressive – suggesting a need to explode the negative in our lives; sometimes they can be euphoric – showing our ability to reach a state similar to a kind of mania.

3 There is a type of euphoria which is experienced at certain stages of spiritual development. This usually occurs as we move from one level of awareness to another, and is to do with the sudden influx of new energy.

INTRUDER
– also see Burglar and People

1 As human beings, we are very conscious of our own personal space. Dreaming of an intruder indicates that we are are feeling threatened in some way. Often in dreams the intruder is masculine, and this generally indicates a need to defend ourselves.

2 To dream of an intruder has an obvious connection with sex and threats to one's sexuality.

3 Spiritually it is possible to put ourselves in danger of being open to desecration. Our Self is a sacred space, but until we understand that it is inviolable, we can be open to challenge. The intruder is that part of ourselves which does not handle our fears and doubts.

INVENTOR

1 Dreaming of an inventor or professor type links us with the more creative sides of ourselves. Usually this is more the thinker rather than the doer: someone who is capable of taking an idea and making it tangible.

2 When we dream of an inventor, psychologically we are linking with that side of ourselves which is wiser, but at the same time perhaps more introverted than our waking selves.

3 The inventor in us is the part that takes responsibility for our progress. He often signifies our ability to 'create' new ways of being, but needs assistance from us on a conscious level.

INVISIBLE

1 Actually **becoming invisible** in a dream – disappearing – would indicate either that we are not ready to face the knowledge that understanding would bring us, or that there is something we would rather forget.

2 When we are conscious that **something is invisible** in a dream, it indicates that we simply need to be aware of the image's presence, without necessarily having to interpret it immediately. Sometimes a figure (either a man or woman) seeming to be invisible can represent the Shadow *(see Introduction)*.

3 Spiritually, the invisible is the Undefined. Often described as God Unmanifest, it is invisible because it is not experienced by sight alone.

IRIS
– see Flowers

IRON

1 When the metal **iron** appears in dreams, it usually represents our strengths and determination. It can also signify the rigidity of our emotions or beliefs. We should consider being more flexible.

2 When we dream of using an **clothes iron** we are attempting to make ourselves more presentable to the outside world. We may also be trying to 'smooth things over'.

3 Iron in a dream can signify the part of ourselves which requires discipline. Before being tempered by fire and made into hard steel, iron requires protecting against corrosion. It is this quality of protection against spiritual 'corrosion' that needs to be dealt with so we can progress.

ISLAND

1 Dreaming of an island signifies the loneliness one can feel through isolation, self imposed or otherwise. We may feel out of touch with others or with situations around us. An island can also represent safety in that, by isolating ourselves, we are not subject to external pressures.

2 Occasionally we all need to recharge our batteries, and to dream of an island can help, or warn us, to do this. Dreaming of a **desert or treasure island** indicates there is something to be gained by being alone and exploring our ability to cope with such a situation. We may actually function better in some way.

3 In dreams an island can signify a spiritual retreat – somewhere that is cut off from the world – which will allow us to contemplate our own spiritual Self.

IVORY

1 Previously, ivory was a precious and valuable substance. In today's more environmentally friendly society, however, it is something which must be preserved. Thus, to dream of ivory is to be looking within ourselves to discover what we consider worth preserving.

2 Psychologically, the ivory tower

symbolises the fact that woman is not easily accessible, unless she herself gives permission. To dream of an ivory tower can signify the way we shut ourselves off from communication.

3 Ivory can symbolise the feminine principle. This is in many ways odd, since the most recognisable form of ivory – tusks – are, because of their shape, penetrative in character.

IVY

1 Dreaming of ivy harks back to the old idea of celebration and fun. It can also symbolise the clinging dependence which can develop within relationships.

2 Because ivy has the symbolism of constant affection, we can recognise that, psychologically, we are in need of love and affection.

3 Spiritually, ivy symbolises immortality and eternal life.

J

from

Jackal *to* Justice

JACKAL
– see Animals

JACKDAW
– see Birds

JAGUAR
– see Animals

JAIL
– see Prison

JAILER

1 To dream of a jailer will indicate we feel we are being restricted in some way, maybe by our own emotions or by somebody else's personality or actions. There will be a sense of self-criticism and of alienation which makes it difficult to carry out our ordinary, everyday tasks.

2 When we are in a situation from which we cannot escape, the personality that appears in our dream often gives us a clue as to how we have got ourselves into that situation. For instance, to experience **ourselves in prison – and at the same time being unfairly treated by our jailer** – would indicate that not only may we have been party to the entrapment, but also that we have become victims of our own circumstances.

3 The dreamer may be feeling a degree of spiritual difficulty.

JAR
– also see Vase

1 A jar very often represents the feminine principle, perhaps some aspect of mothering or of conservation which we recognise within our lives. It often has the same symbolism as the vase – that is, the receptacle for something beautiful or necessary.

2 To be conscious of being jarred – of **being shaken** in some way – indicates that we are not controlling the way we are moving forward. We are putting ourselves in a position where we can be knocked about or hurt.

3 The receptacle for the Soul.

JAW
– see Body

JESUS
– see Christ in Religious Imagery

JEWELLERY

1 Jewellery usually indicates that we have, or can have, something valuable in our lives. **Being given jewellery** suggests that someone else values us; **giving jewellery** signifies that we feel we have something to offer to other people. Those qualities we have learnt to value in ourselves through hard experience are those that we display most easily to other people.

Jewellery can also indicate love given or received. For **a woman to be giving a man jewellery** usually indicates that she is attracted to him and perhaps is able to offer him her own sexuality and self-respect.

2 Very often, jewellery can represent our own feelings about ourselves. For it to appear in a dream – either as something which is very valuable or as something we know to be false (such as **costume jewellery** which masquerades as something valuable) – gives an indication of our own self-esteem. It may also give an indication as to how others feel about us.

3 Jewellery represents honour and self-respect without the usual vanity.

JEWELS

1 Jewels appearing in dreams almost invariably symbolise those things which we value. These may be personal qualities, our sense of integrity, our ability to be ourselves, or even our very essential being. When we feel we know what we are looking for, we are aware on some level of its value to us or others. When we simply register that we are **looking for jewels**, sometimes up a mountain, otherwise in a cave, we are attempting to find those parts of ourselves that we know will be of value in the future. **Counting or in some way assessing them** would suggest a time of reflection is needed.

2 If the **jewels are set** – made up into wearable articles – we are aware of some of the uses of whatever the jewel signifies. For instance, to find an **emerald ring** might suggest that we have completed a stage of growth towards immortality. There are different interpretations for each gemstone, and opinions do vary as to the correct ones. A little consideration will usually tell the dreamer what each stone means for him. One system suggests: **Amethyst** promotes healing and influences dreams; **Diamond** signifies human greed, hardness of nature and what one values in a cosmic sense; **Emerald** highlights personal growth; **Opal** suggests the inner world of fantasies and dreams; psychic impressions; **Pearl** signifies inner beauty and value; **Ruby** informs on emotions, passion and sympathies; **Sapphire** highlights religious feelings.

Other meanings of some well known jewels and gems are:

Agate (**black**) symbolises wealth, courage, assurance and vigour; (**red**) peace, spiritual love of good, health, prosperity and longevity. **Amber** represents crystallised light and magnetism. **Amethyst** is the healing gem. Connecting the dreamer with the spiritual, it represents the influence of dreams. Also humility, peace of mind, faith, self-restraint and resignation. **Aquamarine** embodies the qualities of hope, youth and health. **Beryl** is believed to hold within it happiness, hope and eternal youthfulness. **Bloodstone** holds the qualities of peace and understanding. It is also reputed to grant all wishes. **Carbuncle** holds determination, success and self-assurance . **Carnelian** highlights friendship, courage, self-confidence, health. **Cat's eye** influences longevity, the ability to sustain and the waning moon. **Chrysolite** represents wisdom, discretion, tact, prudence. **Chrysoprase** symbolises gaiety, unconditional happiness, the symbol of joy. **Corundum** influences and helps create a stability of mind. **Crystal** symbolises purity, simplicity, and various magical elements. **Diamond** has a number of influences: light, life, the sun, durability, incorruptibility, invincible constancy, sincerity, innocence. **Emerald** embraces immortality, hope, youth, faithfulness, and also the beauty of Spring. **Garnet** can help energy

levels and indicates devotion, loyalty and grace. **Hyacinth** symbolises fidelity and the truth within, but also the gift of second sight. **Jacinth** holds within it humble qualities, verging on modesty. **Jade** 'All that is supremely excellent', the yang power of the heavens, and all its accompanying delights. **Jasper** holds the qualities of joy and happiness. **Jet** Although usually associated with darker emotions such as grief and mourning, jet also controls safety within a journey. **Lapis Lazuli** A favourable stone said to evoke divine favour, success and the ability to show perseverance. **Lodestone** holds within it the qualities of integrity and honesty; also said to influence virility. **Moonstone/Selenite** The moon and its magical qualities, tenderness and the romantic lovers. **Olivine** influences simplicity, modesty and happiness within a humble framework. **Onyx** represents degrees of perspicacity, sincerity, spiritual strength, and conjugal happiness. **Opal** not only represents fidelity, but also religious fervour, prayers and assurance of spiritual beliefs. **Pearl** symbolises the feminine principles of chastity and purity, and also the moon, and waters. **Peridot** represents consolidation of friendships. Also, so to speak, the thunderbolt, with which we may be 'hit' at unlikely times. **Ruby** represents all that is traditionally associated with Royalty; dignity, zeal, power, love, passion, beauty, longevity and invulnerability. However, some people may consider these interpretations to be slightly ironic. **Sapphire** holds within it worldly truth, heavenly virtues, celestial contemplation and the feminine side of chastity. **Sardonyx** represents codes of honour, renown, brightness, vivacity, and aspects of self-control. **Topaz** holds the beauty of the Divine; goodness, faithfulness, friendship, love, sagacity. A topaz also symbolises the sun. **Tourmaline** inspiration and imagination are represented by the tourmaline. Friendship also comes under the same influence. **Turquoise** symbolises courage – physical and spiritual – fulfilment, and also success. **Zircon** Much worldly wisdom is held within zircon, as well as the virtues of honour, and the glories (or otherwise) of riches.

3 From a spiritual point of view, jewels and their understanding can enhance personal development. In most dreams it is the better-known stones which appear, but when the lesser-known ones are seen, there is much benefit to be gained by learning more on a conscious level.

Many stones have healing properties, and this is a whole subject in itself. The reader is referred to the many good books on this subject.

JOURNEY

1 The image of a journey is a very potent one in dream work. Any time the idea of a journey becomes apparent, it is to do with the way that we carry on our everyday lives and how we move forward. Every step that we take towards understanding ourselves and the world we live in can be pictured in terms of a journey, and the dreams that a person has reflect that movement. In our ordinary everyday speech we use idioms to suggest our understanding. We speak of the ups and downs of life, of being at a standstill and so on. Each moment is totally unique, and that uniqueness is reflected in our dreams. Mostly dreams are about the here and now and give a snapshot picture as to what is happening at this particular moment. The images will reflect how we are feeling, what obstacles there are, possible courses of action and what our ultimate goal should or may be. The dream will bring in images from the past or recognisable scenes to help us interpret what is going on and move forward to meet our destiny.

Any sense of having **completed a journey** – arriving home, touching down and so on – indicates the successful completion of our aims. **Collisions** represent arguments and conflicts which are often caused by our own aggression. **A difficult journey now behind us** means we have come through the difficulties and setbacks of the past. **The obstacles ahead** indicates we are aware of the difficulties which may occur. We do need to be aware that we ourselves create the problems. Our own attitude to life is perhaps responsible. **Turning a corner** shows we have accepted the need for a change of direction. We may have made a major decision. **Avoiding an accident** means we are able to control our impulses. **Stopping and starting** suggests there is conflict between laziness and drive. **At a standstill/in a traffic jam** indicates we are being prevented, or are preventing ourselves, from moving forward. This needs handling with care, since to stop may be appropriate. **Departing (departures from airports, stations, etc.)** Formerly all departures were interpreted as death. Nowadays the symbolism is much more of a new beginning. We are leaving the old life in order to undertake something new. When someone in our lives leaves us, we may dream of departures and the grief that parting causes. In certain circumstances, to dream of **wanting to leave but not being able to** suggests that there is still further work to be done. To be **conscious of the time of departure** might suggest that we are aware of a time limit within an area of our lives.

The destination, when it becomes apparent, will give some ideas about the aims and objectives we have. Our declared hopes and ideals may not correspond with those we subconsciously have – our inner motivation may be totally different to our outer behaviour – and dreams will highlight this discrepancy. The exact nature of our objective is often not known to us until after we have confronted the obstacles and challenges along the way. It is often enough just to have an aim for that particular section of the journey.

Driving The whole of the symbolism of driving in dreams is particularly obvious. It represents our basic urges, wants and needs. If **we are driving** we are in control. If **we are not happy when someone else is driving** we may not trust that person and may not wish to be dependent on them. When

someone else takes over, we are becoming passive. If we are **overtaking the car in front**, we are achieving success, but perhaps in a competitive manner. When **we are overtaken**, we may feel someone else has got the better of us. Once again the way we are in everyday life is reflected in the dream. Our drives, aggressions, fears and doubts are all reflected in our driving.

Engine This represents the sexual impulse or instinctive drives, one's basic motivation.

Passenger It will depend if **we are a passenger** in a vehicle or **are carrying passengers**. If the former, we may feel that we are being carried along by circumstances, and have not really thought out our own way forward. If the latter, we may have knowingly or inadvertently made ourselves responsible for other people. **Travelling with one other passenger** suggests we may be considering our relationship with that person.

Road The road in a dream suggests our own individual way forward. Just as each individual vehicle demonstrates the dreamer's body and external way of being, so the road reflects the way of doing. Any **obstacle in the road** will reflect difficulties on the chosen path. **Any turns in the road** will suggest changes of direction. **Crossroads** will offer choices, while a **cul-de-sac** would signify a dead end. If a **particular stretch of road** is highlighted it may be a period of time, or may mean an effort. **Going uphill** will suggest extra effort while **going downhill** will suggest lack of control.

Traffic accidents and offences These may all be to do with sexuality or self image; perhaps we are not being careful to ensure that our conduct is good. **A collision** might suggest a conflict with someone. **Road rage** would signify not being in control of our emotions and so on.

2 The **type of transport** may suggest how we are moving through this particular stage of our lives. Previously the horse was used as an image to depict how we dealt with life. Nowadays the car, the aeroplane and so on have been substituted. **The vehicle** which appears in our dreams often conforms with the view we hold of ourselves. For instance, we may be driving a very basic type of car or a Rolls Royce (One dreamer described an image he had as a 'Rolls Royce that thinks it's a Mini'). Such an image may represent either our physical body or our personality. **If the dreamer**

is driving he perhaps feels more in control of his own destiny. **If he is a passenger** he may feel others are trying to control his life. If he is **with friends** he may be aware of a group goal. If **he does not know the other people** he may need to explore his ability to make social relationships.

Aeroplane *(also see individual entry)* An aeroplane suggests a swift easy journey with some attention to detail. We may be embarking on a new sexual relationship. **An airman or pilot** This is a romanticised picture of either the Animus or of the Self *(see Introduction).*

Bicycling This suggests youth and freedom, and perhaps the first stirrings of sexual awareness.

Boats (and sea voyages) It will depend on what kind of boat is in the dream. A **small rowing boat** would suggest an emotional journey but one done alone. A **yacht** might suggest a similar journey done with style, whereas a **large ship** would suggest creating new horizons but in the company of others. What the boat does in the dream will have relevance as a reflection of our waking life, e.g. **running aground, pulling into harbour** etc. **Making a long journey** This suggests leaving friends and family as would **running away to sea**.

Disembarking The end of a project, successful or otherwise. **Missing the boat** We have not paid enough attention to detail in a project in our waking lives. **Any narrow waterway or river** suggests the birth experience. **Ship** A ship is usually taken as feminine because of its capriciousness. **Ferry, rowboat** This holds all the symbolism of the journey across the River Styx after death. It is the giving up of selfish desires. After this we may be 'reborn' into a better life, or way of life.

Bus *(also see individual entry)* A bus journey is that part of our lives where we are conscious of the need to travel and to be with other people. We perhaps have a common aim with them. **Trouble with timetables, missing the bus, arriving too early, missing a connection** We are not in control of our lives and perhaps should sit down and replan how we wish to continue our lives. **Getting on the wrong bus, going the wrong way** There are conflicting desires and we need to listen to our own intuition. This is usually a warning of a wrong action. **Not being able to pay the fare** We do not have enough resources to set out on a particular course of action. It may be that we have not paid attention to detail.

Car (carriage, cart, chariot) *(also see individual entries)* The car is a reflection of the dreamer and how he or she handles life. It reflects the physical body, so anything wrong with the car will alert us to a problem. For instance **if the engine is not working properly** we are not able to get up enough energy to go on. If **the starting motor was not working** this would suggest that we need help to start a project. It is for us to be able to translate the symbolism into our own lives. Even in everyday life it can be seen that a car is a reflection of a person's self image and possibly sexuality. Any part of the car will have significance. The **back tyres** might suggest the dreamer's support system, the **steering wheel** the way we control our lives and so on. If the **brakes are not working** we are not exercising proper control over our lives. **Too many people in the car** would suggest that we feel overloaded by responsibility.

Lorry A lorry in a dream will have the same significance as a car, except that the drives and ambitions will be connected more with our work and how we relate on a business basis to the world in general.

Motorbike, motorcycle The motorbike is a symbol of masculine youth and daring. In dreams it is an image of independent behaviour, and is often a symbol for the sexual act. It can also be a symbol of freedom. A **Hell's Angel** would suggest some kind of anarchical behaviour.

Trains A train will often highlight the dreamer's attitude to social behaviour and relationships with other people. It will also clarify his attitude to himself. A **steam train** would suggest that we feel ourselves to be outdated and obsolete, whereas an up-to-date **electric turbo** might suggest speed and efficiency. **Catching the train** shows we have successfully been able to have outside circumstances co-operate with us in achieving a particular goal. **Missing the train** We do not have the resources to enable us to succeed in an appropriate way, either because we have forgotten something, or because we have not been sufficiently careful. We fear that we will miss an opportunity. Equally, we may feel that external circumstances are imposing an element of control over us. Often dreams of missing a train and then catching either it or a later one, suggest that we are managing our inner resources better. Dreams of **missing a train alternating with those of catching one**

shows we are trying to sort out our motivation. **Getting off the train before its destination** We are afraid of succeeding at a particular project. This can also signify premature ejaculation. We do not appear to be in control. **Getting off the train before it starts** The dreamer has changed his mind about a situation in waking life. Railway lines and tracks will have significance as ways of getting us to our destination. Being **conscious of the way the track runs** ahead may give us an inkling as to what direction we are going. **Recognising the signals up ahead** would have the same significance. **Coming off the rails** might suggest doing something inappropriate or of not being in control. **Not wanting to be on the train** might indicate we feel we are being unduly influenced by outside circumstances. **Arriving at a station** indicates we have completed a stage of our life journey. We may be ready for a new relationship with the world in general. **The carriages** on a train suggest the various compartments or sections of our lives and the way we feel about them. For example, if a carriage is **untidy or dirty**, we are aware that we need to 'clean up' an aspect of our lives.

Walk If in our dreams we are aware of having to walk, it usually suggests that we are capable of making a part of our life journey by ourselves without any help. **Going for a walk** We can enjoy the process of recharging our batteries and clearing our minds.

3 The image of a journey becomes more apparent as time goes on and death approaches. We become more aware of reaching our final destination.

JUBILEE

1 The time of a jubilee represents a fresh start. This has significance in that it is the 49th part of the life cycle. After 7 x 7 years, the fiftieth year becomes sacred and gives a new beginning. To be dreaming of a jubilee or jubilee celebrations would indicate a rite of passage – a passing from the old into the new.

2 Dreaming of a jubilee or jubilant occasion can represent the natural spontaneity with which we greet changes.

3 A sacred start to Spiritual celebration.

JUDGE
– see Authority Figures in People

JUNGLE

1 The jungle in dreams is an image belonging to mysticism and fairy tales. It can often represent chaos. This chaos can be either positive or negative depending on the circumstances of the dream. It is the eruption of urges and feelings from the unconscious, perhaps from those areas which could be considered to be uncivilised. In myths the jungle symbolises an obstacle or barrier that has to be passed through in order to reach a new state of being. With this meaning it has the same significance as the enchanted forest *(see Forest)*.

2 To be **trapped in a jungle** indicates that we are trapped by negative and frightening feelings from the unconscious with which we have not yet come to terms. To be conscious of **having come through a jungle** would indicate that we have passed through, and overcome, those aspects of our lives which we have never dared approach before. Psychologically, without the ordering of information that we receive, our minds can simply become a jungle of information. We need to use logic to apply order so that we can make sense of ourselves and our environment.

3 The jungle can symbolise spiritual chaos due to its unpredictability. Spiritually for the dreamer it may be 'a jungle out there'.

JUMPING

1 The act of jumping can be somewhat ambiguous in a dream. It can indicate either **jumping up** – attempting to attain something better for ourselves – or **jumping down**, which can mean going down into the unconscious and those parts of ourselves where we may feel we are in danger. **Jumping on the spot** can indicate joy and has the same significance as dance *(See Dance)*.

2 Repetitive movement of any sort in a dream usually indicates the need to reconsider our actions, to look at what we are doing and perhaps to express ourselves in a different way. On a psychological level, jumping up and down in a dream may indicate being caught up in a situation without having the power to move either forwards or backwards.

3 In certain religions, spiritual ecstasy is induced by jumping. This is a way of employing the physical in order to reach the spiritual.

JURY

1 When a jury appears in a dream we are usually struggling with an issue of peer pressure. We may fear that others will not understand our actions, that they could judge us and find us wanting. **2** If **we are a member of the**

jury, it depends on the circumstances of the dream whether we agree with the group or not. We may not feel we can go along with the group decision. We might have to decide to 'go it alone' and make a unilateral decision. Such a dream would probably reflect a situation in our everyday lives.

3 Often in the process of personal development we may have to make judgements which are not popular. Provided we adhere to our own inner truth, we cannot be judged.

JUSTICE
– also see Authority Figures in People Section and Jury

1 Very often in a dream we do not seem to be capable of expressing our right to be heard, to articulate those things we believe are correct. Therefore, to dream of either **justice or injustice** can indicate that the unconscious mind is trying to sort out right from wrong. This is usually on a personal level, although it can have a wider implication as to what is morally right and the norm within society.

2 Often when we are attempting to balance two different states or ways of being, the figure of justice can appear within a dream. This is to alert us to the fact that we may need to use both sides of ourselves successfully. To be **brought to justice** can signify that we must pay attention to our actions or to our attitude to authority.

3 In spiritual progression there needs to be a balance between our more spiritual selves – what might be called ideal behaviour – and the physical. This balance can be difficult to both attain and maintain.

K

from

Kaleidoscope *to* Knot

KALEIDOSCOPE

1 A kaleidoscope connects us with our childlike selves, and the patterns that such a toy creates reminds us of the mandala *(see Mandala)*. We are able in dreams to appreciate the beauty of basic patterns. Just as a child is fascinated by the pattern that a kaleidoscope creates, so the dream image can introduce us to the creativity which can often become trapped.

2 The magnification of the pattern created by small objects harks back to the sense of wonder that is felt in being human. We become aware of our own 'smallness' within the larger scheme of things.

3 A kaleidoscope can symbolise the patterns that we make for ourselves in times of spiritual self-doubt.

KANGAROO
– see Animals

KEEPSAKE

1 A keepsake in olden times was something which was often exchanged by lovers. To be conscious of having such an object in a dream signifies our ability to love and be loved. Any object which links with the past reminds us of what we have been capable of doing or being.

2 Romantic memories figure largely in dream imagery. To dream of something which is very precious to us, and has been given by someone else, allows us to recognise the beauty held within.

3 A keepsake in the spiritual sense is an object which, because of the high regard the owner has for it, is sacred. It will probably have been blessed in some way.

KETTLE
– also see Cauldron

1 Because a kettle is such a mundane everyday object, to dream of one indicates our more practical, pragmatic side. If the kettle is unusual – such as an **old fashioned copper kettle** – it denotes outworn, but still appreciated, beliefs.

2 A kettle is often taken to symbolise transformation and change. To dream of one in this context suggests that we need to accelerate a process of learning and growth.

3 A kettle by way of its association with a cauldron (but also by its own strength) can symbolise magic and magical forces working for the Greater Good.

KEY
– also see Lock and Prison

1 Keys often appear in dreams. They represent fresh attitudes, thoughts and feelings which are capable of unlocking memories, experiences and knowledge which we have previously hidden. To dream of a **bunch of keys** suggests the need to open up the whole of our personalities to new experiences.

2 When we experience ourselves as trapped, the key to freedom can often appear as if by magic. We hold within us many of the answers to our difficulties, but often need a down-to-earth mundane symbol to trigger off our ability to work out solutions.

3 A key can represent the dreamer's need for liberation from a stressful situation and then initiation of a positive move. **Silver and gold keys** represent – respectively – temporal and spiritual power.

KEYHOLE

1 When we dream that we are **peering through a keyhole**, we are conscious of the fact that our ability to see and understand is somehow impaired. Conventionally, the keyhole has been taken to represent the feminine, so that impairment could result from our attitude to the feminine.

2 Since a key usually requires a keyhole, to dream of one without the other indicates some kind of confusion between the inner and outer self.

3 A keyhole symbolises the dreamer's tentative entry into the Sublime.

KICK

1 Aggressiveness can be represented in many ways, and to dream of **kicking someone** often allows the expression of aggression in an acceptable way. We would not necessarily do this in waking life. To dream of **being kicked** highlights a propensity to be a victim.

2 **Kicking a ball** around in a dream signifies our need for self-control, but also our control of external circumstances.

3 A kick can be taken symbolically as a need for spiritual motivation; it may be the kick that we need in order to continue (or maybe even begin) the spiritual journey.

KIDNAP

1 If we find ourselves **being kidnapped** within a dream, we are conscious of the fact that our own fears and doubts can make us victims. We are being overcome by our own 'demons', which have ganged up on us and caused us to become insecure.

2 In dreams we may find ourselves **trying to kidnap someone else** and this would indicate, at its simplest level, that we are trying to influence someone else. It may also suggest that we are trying to absorb some quality from the other person which is not freely available.

3 Some sort of psychic theft may be symbolised here, or on a darker level a thread of spiritual vampirism may be running through the dreamer's subconscious. It is up to the dreamer thoroughly to define this image.

KIDNEYS
– see Body

KILL

1 To dream of **being killed** represents the dreamer coming under an influence – usually external – which is making him, or an aspect of his personality, ineffective in everyday life. **Killing someone** in a dream is attempting to be rid of the influence they have over the dreamer.

2 Killing is an extreme answer to a problem. It is such a final act that in dreams it can often represent the dreamer's perception of the need for violence, particularly against himself. Perhaps the only way a solution to a problem can be reached is by 'killing off' part of himself. There is no denying in this case the potential for violence,

although ultimately the impulse may not be correct.

3 A spiritual slaying and therefore sacrifice is represented here. The dreamer will need to be aware that what he considers worthy may need further nurturing, lest it be relinquished.

KING
– see People

KINGFISHER
– see Birds

KISS

1 When we dream about kissing someone, it can suggest an acceptance of a new relationship with that person. Such an act can also signify that, on a subconscious level, we are seeking to develop a quality belonging to that other person in ourselves.

2 We are sealing a pact – perhaps coming to some sort of agreement. This agreement may be sexual, but it could also be one of friendship. We may also be moving towards unity. **Being kissed** indicates that we are appreciated and loved for ourselves.

3 A single kiss (particularly on the forehead) has often had spiritual and religious undertones, and here the image symbolises a blessing of a spiritual kind.

KITCHEN

1 For most people, the kitchen represents the 'heart' of the house. It is the place from which we go out into the world and to which we return. In dreams, the kitchen can often represent the mother, or rather, the mothering function. It is the place which is usually busiest and therefore the place where many relationships are cemented, and where many exchanges take place.

2 The kitchen is a place of creation, and usually of warmth and comfort. It has therefore come to represent the nurturing aspect of woman.

3 There are folk tales in most cultures to do with the kitchen, and spiritually it represents transformation and transmutation. This is much more to do with desired transformation, rather than one which is enforced. The rituals associated with the hearth and with fire were, and still are, a significant part of spiritual development. Even in today's climate of convenience foods there is the sense of work in the kitchen being an offering.

KITE

1 In Chinese lore, the kite symbolised the wind – and even today it represents freedom. So, to dream of flying a kite can remind us of the carefree days of childhood when we were without responsibility. Often the colour is important *(see Colour)*, as may be the material from which it is made.

2 While flying a kite, we are at the mercy of the wind unless we have a fair degree of expertise. In dreams it is recognisable that we have some expertise in our everyday lives.

3 A kite represents the dreamer's need for, or recognition of, forthcoming spiritual freedom. To be free of constraints and to be 'pulling our own strings,' as it were.

KNAPSACK

1 When we discover that we, or someone else, is wearing a knapsack in a dream, we are dreaming either about the difficulties we are carrying – for instance, anger or jealousy – or about the resources we have accumulated.

2 In Tarot imagery, the Fool carries in his knapsack the lessons he has to learn in life. If one believes in reincarnation, the knapsack is also reputed to carry those things one has brought forward from a previous life. These can also be the resources which one has in order to deal with problems.

3 Spiritually the knapsack suggests those qualities which are external to ourselves, and which we must learn to handle. These may be negative or positive – it depends on how we handle them.

KNEE/KNEELING
– see Body

KNIFE
– also see Weapons

1 A cutting instrument in a dream usually signifies some kind of division. If we are **using a knife** we may either be freeing ourselves or trying to sever a relationship. If we are **being attacked with a knife**, it indicates either violent words or actions may be used against us. **In a woman's dream** this is probably more to do with her own fear of penetration and violation, whereas in a **man's dream** it is highlighting his own aggression.

2 It can be important in a dream about a knife to notice what type is being used. For instance, a **table knife** would be interpreted very differently to a **Swiss Army knife**. Both are functional, but the former would only be appropriate under certain circumstances, whereas the latter might have a more universal application.

3 A symbol of division. Possibly a 'joy division' in the spiritual sense. That is, although we are on our way to achieving what we want at this time, it is not making us particularly happy, so there is confusion as to which road we should have taken.

KNIGHT

1 A knight appearing in a dream, particularly a woman's, can have the obvious connotation of a romantic liaison – the knight in shining armour. This actually is a manifestation of her own Animus *(see Introduction)* – her own inner masculine – and is to do with her search for perfection. In a man's dream it indicates he may be searching for the Hero *(see Archetypes)* in himself.

2 Psychologically, the knight in a dream signifies the guiding principle. He is that part of ourselves which is sometimes known as the Higher Self, the spirit guiding the physical. The **black knight** is the embodiment of evil. It is interesting that often the **white knight** appears with his visor up, whereas the black knight appears with his visor down.

3 Initiation, in order to develop one's finer qualities.

KNITTING

1 The first symbolism connected with knitting is that of creating something new out of available material. A project or idea which is being worked on is beginning to come together. To be **unravelling knitting** suggests that a project that is being worked on needs reconsideration.

2 Often it is worthwhile taking note of the colour of what is being knitted *(see Colour)* in order to make sense of why the image of knitting should appear in a dream. It may well be that the dreamer is working at creating a relationship, or working on emotions.

3 Knitting can symbolise a form of creativity, which we may not have fully realised we have available to us.

KNOB

1 To be dreaming of a knob such as a **doorknob** can indicate some kind of turning point in one's life. A noticeable contrast between the door and the knob can present the dreamer with certain insights. For instance, **a very plain knob on an ornate door** may indicate that the process of moving forward from a situation is very easy. To dream of any other sort of knob is often to do with one's hold on a situation.

2 Since many people still have difficulty in calling 'private parts' by their correct name, a knob appearing in a dream can represent the penis or, if the dreamer is a man, his masculinity.

3 Spiritually, a knob can suggest changes occurring in the way we access our subconscious self.

KNOCK

1 To **hear knocking** in a dream generally alerts us to the fact that our attention needs to be refocused. We may be paying too much attention to one part of our personality. For instance, we may be too introverted when in fact we need to be paying more attention to external matters.

2 If **we ourselves are knocking** on a door, we may be wanting to become part of someone's life. We are waiting for permission before moving forward.

3 We are being given permission from our spiritual self to progress on our current spiritual journey.

KNOT

1 A knot is one of the most interesting symbols to appear in dreams, since it can have so many meanings. Negatively, if it is seen as a **tangle**, it can represent an unsolvable problem or difficulty. The answer can only be 'teased out' gradually. Positively, a knot can represent the ties that one has to family, friends or work.

2 A **simple knot** seen in a dream could represent the need to take a different direction in a project. A

more complex knot could indicate that we are bound to a situation by a sense of duty or guilt. It may well be that, ultimately, the only way to escape from such restraint is by loosening the ties in our relationship with someone else, or with a work situation. **3** Spiritual continuity or connection.

from

Label *to* Lynx

LABEL

1 Often dreaming of labels links with the human being's need to name things. Our sense of identity comes from the name we are given, and our label is much to do with the way that others see us and understand us.

2 To dream of having **the wrong label** suggests that we are aware that we are not perceiving something in the correct way. To be **re-labelling something** suggests that we have rectified a misperception.

3 In the spiritual sense a label can give us a sense of Identity *(see Name)*.

LABOUR

1 To be labouring at something in the sense of working hard, suggests that we have a goal we wish to achieve. To dream of **'hard labour'** will alert us to an aspect of self-flagellation or self-punishment in what we are doing.

2 If a woman dreams of **being in labour** she should look at her wish and desire to be pregnant.

3 The twelve labours of Hercules are reputed to represent the passage of the sun through the twelve signs of the Zodiac. They are also the hardships and effort man uses to attain self-realisation.

LABORATORY

1 Dreaming of **working in a laboratory** indicates that we need to be more scientific in our approach to life. We may have certain talents which need to be developed in an objective fashion, or we may need to develop our thinking faculty further.

2 A laboratory can suggest a very ordered existence, and it will depend on whether we are working in or are specimens in a laboratory how we interpret the dream.

3 Dreaming of a laboratory indicates we need to make an objective assessment of what is going on in our lives.

LABYRINTH
– also see Maze

1 On a purely practical level, the labyrinth appearing in dreams signifies the need to explore the hidden side of our own personality. With its many twists, turns and potential blind alleys it is a very potent representation of the human being. Within the labyrinth one meets and overcomes the difficulties in life which could impede progress.

2 Psychologically, in undertaking our own heroic journey, we must at some point go through some kind of labyrinth experience. It is undertaken at a point when we must travel into the differing areas of our subconscious and come to terms with our fears and doubts, before confronting our own Shadow *(See Introduction)*. In dreams the labyrinth can be suggested by any dream which has us exploring a series of underground passages. It is held by some to be an exploration of the hidden feminine.

3 Spiritually the labyrinth experience marks a watershed. It is a symbol for the transition stage between the physical and practical world and a deeper understanding of all mankind. The route in one type of Labyrinth is 'unicursal' – that is, it goes by a straightforward route which covers maximum ground straight to the centre and out again. The second type is designed with the intention to confuse, and has many blind alleys and unexpected twists. This represents spiritual progress, through having to work out the key or code. Many trials and tribulations are met and overcome or negotiated on the path to attainment. Each individual will undertake his or her own route to the centre of his existence.

LADDER

1 The ladder in dreams suggests how secure we feel in moving from one situation to another. We may need to make a considerable effort to reach a goal or take an opportunity. Often this dream occurs during career changes, and so has obvious connotations. If the **rungs are broken** we can expect difficulty. If **someone else is carrying the ladder** it could suggest that another person, perhaps a manager or colleague, has a part to play in our progression.

2 The ladder denotes our ability to break through to a new level of awareness, moving from the physical to the spiritual, but also being able to move downwards again. It also suggests communication between the physical and spiritual realms as a stage of transition. Occasionally it may also represent death, though this may be the death of the old self, rather than a physical death.

3 In a dream, the rungs of the ladder are often either seven or twelve in number, these being the stages of growth towards spirituality.

LAGOON/LAKE
– also see Water

1 A lagoon or lake represents our inner world of feeling and fantasy. It is the unconscious side which is a rich source of power when it can be accessed and understood. If **the lake is contaminated** we have taken in ideas and concepts which are not necessarily good for us. **A clear stretch of water** would indicate that we have clarified our fears and feelings about ourselves.

2 Often thought to be the home of the magical feminine and of monsters, the lagoon stands for the darker side of femininity. This is seen clearly in the legends of King Arthur and this type of image will appear in dreams as we lose our fear of that particular part of ourselves.

3 The unconscious and the primordial substance are often pictured as a lagoon. The Chinese concept of a kind of soup from which came all existence, links with the lagoon.

LAMB
– see Animals

LAME

1 Dreaming of being lame suggests a loss of confidence and strength. If **we ourselves are lame** there can be a fear of moving forward or a fear of the future.

2 To be aware that **someone else is lame** has two meanings. **If the person is known** to us, we need to be aware of their vulnerability and uncertainty. **If they are not known**, it is more likely to be a hidden side of

ourselves which is insecure.

3 Lameness in the spiritual sense suggests the imperfection of creation, when an imperfect world is formed.

LANCE

1 A lance – **as in a Knight's lance** – in a dream suggests an aspect of masculine power, penetration and therefore sometimes the sexual act.

2 A lance as **a surgical instrument** is also penetrative, but has a more healing connotation, as it is designed to release the negative. We may need to take short, sharp action in order to improve a situation.

3 A phallic image of solar power.

LAMP
– also see Light

1 In dreams a lamp or a light can represent life. To be **moving towards a lamp** suggests a clarity of perception, which may be slightly old-fashioned. The lamp in its most practical aspect in dreams signifies the intellect and clarity.

2 The lamp in dreams often signifies guidance and wisdom. It can also represent previously held beliefs which may need to be updated.

3 Spiritually the lamp can suggest the idea of a personal light in darkness. The hermit in the Tarot demonstrates this in his need to be able to move forward despite the darkness around him. The lamp can also signify the light of the Divine and immortality.

LANDSCAPES

1 The landscape in a dream can be an integral part of the interpretation. It usually mirrors feelings and concepts that we have and therefore reflects our personality. A **rocky landscape** would suggest problems, whereas a **gloomy landscape** might suggest pessimism and self-doubt. **A recurring scene** may be one where in childhood we felt safe, or may reflect a feeling or difficulty with which we have not been able to come to terms. Landscapes do tend to reflect habitual feelings rather than momentary moods.

2 Dream landscapes can have a bizarre quality about them in order to highlight a particular message. For instance, there may be **trees made of ice, or rocks made of sugar**. The plot of the dream may be important in arriving at the correct interpretation of these symbols *(see Introduction)*. The landscape in a dream can also indicate how we relate to other people. To be **in a desert** might represent loneliness, whereas to be **in a jungle** might represent a very fertile imagination.

3 Spiritually, the landscape in a dream can suggest improvements which we can make in handling our own moods and attitudes. **If the landscape changes** between the beginning and end of the dream, we perhaps need to make corresponding changes in everyday life.

LANGUAGE

1 Hearing **foreign or strange language** in dreams illustrates some kind of communication, either from within or from the Collective Unconscious. It has not yet become clear enough for us to understand it.

2 As we become more open to possibilities, the various facets of our personality can achieve their own method of communication with us. This is often experienced in dreams as strange language, and often comes across as sleep-talking.

3 In Spiritualism, hearing language is communication by discarnate beings.

LARDER
– also see Refrigerator

1 A larder, being a repository for food, usually indicates sustenance or nurturing in a dream. It will depend to a certain extent what is in the larder as to the interpretation of the dream. In previous times it would have referred to having harvested *(See Harvest)* food, but it may be significant here if the dreamer registers that a particular food is missing.

2 As life moves on, many people no longer have larders, this image being replaced by the refrigerator or fridge freezer. All these images indicate that conservation is necessary. This may be conservation of energy, resources or power.

3 A larder in spiritual terms suggests gifts or talents.

LARGE
– see Size

LARK
– see Birds

LATE
– see Time

LAUGH

1 Being laughed at in dreams suggests we may have a fear of being ridiculed, or may have done something which we feel is not appropriate. We may find ourselves embarrassing. It can also be seen as a sign of rejection.

2 If we ourselves are laughing we may be experiencing a release of tension. Often the object of our amusement will give a clue to the

relevance of the dream in everyday life. **To hear a crowd laughing** suggests a shared enjoyment.

3 Laughter in the spiritual sense signifies pure joy.

LAUREL/BAY LEAVES

1 The laurel or bay tree is less likely to appear in dreams nowadays, unless the dreamer is either a gardener or has particular knowledge of symbolism. In former times, it would have represented a particular type of success. Traditionally the laurel or bay is difficult to grow, so it would have symbolised triumph over difficulty.

2 The laurel wreath is often used to indicate triumph and victory, and therefore is an acknowledgement of success. It also suggests immortality.

3 The laurel or bay tree signifies chastity and eternity.

LAVA
– see Volcano

LAVATORY
– see Toilet

LEAD (METAL)

1 The conventional explanation of lead appearing in a dream is that we have a situation around us which is a burden to us. We are not coping with life as perhaps we should be, and it is leaving us heavy-hearted. Lead, as in a **lead of a pencil**, has obvious connections with the life force and masculinity.

2 Lead as a substance is less used nowadays than it used to be, but still has the connotations of a base metal. In dreams it can indicate that the time is ripe for transformation and transmutation. We need to instigate changes to give a better quality to our lives.

3 Lead in spiritual symbolism stands for bodily consciousness. It is the metal of Saturn and we should look at how that planet may help us progress.

LEAD AND LEADING

1 Dreaming of a **dog lead** *(also see Harness and Halter)* would symbolise the connection between ourselves and our lesser nature. To have **lost the dog lead** would indicate a loss of control. **Leading someone** in a dream pre-supposes that we know what we are doing and where we are going. **Being led** suggests that we have allowed someone else to take control of a situation around us.

2 Leadership qualities are not necessarily ones that everybody will use. Often we can surprise ourselves in dreams by doing things that we would not normally do, and taking the lead is one of them.

3 We are able to take authority by virtue of our spiritual knowledge. This can be done with humility and without ego.

LEAF/LEAVES

1 A leaf very often represents a period of growth and can also indicate time. **Green leaves** can suggest hope and new opportunities, or the Springtime. **Dead leaves** signify a period of sadness, barrenness or Autumn *(see Autumn)*.

2 When looking at our lives as a whole, leaves can give some indication of a particular period of our lives – perhaps a period that has been meaningful and creative. Following a dream about leaves we may need to assess how to go forward in order to avail ourselves of the opportunities offered.

3 Leaves signify fertility and growth. Since each leaf is completely unique, we may be being alerted to the beauty of creation.

LEAK
– also see Water

1 Dreaming of a leak suggests we are wasting or losing energy in some way. If it is a **slow leak** we are perhaps not aware of the drain on our energies. If it is **gushing**

we need to look at 'repairing' the leak, perhaps by being more responsible in our actions.

2 A leak can indicate carelessness. We may not be paying attention to necessary repairs either on a physical, emotional or mental level.

3 A leak of any sort suggests wastefulness on some level.

LEATHER

1 At its basic meaning, and depending upon the circumstances in the dreamer's life, leather can be associated with self image. Often it is connected with protection, and subsequently uniform. For instance a **motorcycle rider's leather suit** will make him easily identifiable, but will also protect him in all weathers. Dreams will often throw up an image that has to be considered very carefully.

2 Leather can also be connected with sadistic methods of torture, and thus can become connected with the wider issues of sexual behaviour, either ours or others which we may or may not find appropriate.

3 Self-flagellation.

LEFT
– *see Position*

LEG
– *see Limbs in Body*

LENS
– *also see Glasses and Goggles*

1 Just as in everyday life a lens helps to focus the attention, so in dreams it can signify our need to perceive something very clearly.

2 When a lens appears in a dream we need to be clear as to whether it is enlarging the object being looked at, or is intensifying it. A proper interpretation can only be made in the light of other circumstances in the dream.

3 Visionary clarity.

LEMON
– *see Fruit*

LENDING

1 If in a dream we are **lending an object** to someone, we are aware that the quality that object represents cannot be given away ,that it is ours to have, but that we can share it. If **someone is lending us an article** then we are perhaps not responsible enough to possess what it represents on a full-time basis. Conversely, we may only need it for a short time.

2 If we are **lending money**, we are creating a bond of obligation within our lives. If we are being **lent money** we need to look at the way we are managing our resources, but more importantly what help we need to do this.

3 In spiritual terms, the concept of lending is connected with healing and support.

LEOPARD
– see Animals

LEPER

1 To dream of a leper suggests that we are aware of some aspect of ourselves that we feel to be unclean. We feel that we have been rejected by society without quite knowing why. We may also feel that we have been contaminated in some way.

2 If we are **caring for a leper** we need to attend to those parts of ourselves we consider unclean, rather than trying to dispose of them. If **the leper is offering us something**, it may be that we have a lesson to learn about humility.

3 Spiritually, a leper in a dream can suggest that we are having to deal with a moral dilemma which takes us away from compassion and caring.

LETTER
– also see Address

1 If we **receive a letter** in a dream we may be aware of some problem with the person it is from. It is possible that the sender is known to be dead, in which case there are unresolved issues with that person or the situation connected with them. If we are **sending a letter** we have information we feel may be relevant to that person.

2 Often we dream about a letter without knowing the contents. This suggests some information which is at present being withheld. If a particular **letter of the alphabet** is highlighted, we may understand more if we can name someone with that initial.

3 Hidden information can often become acceptable if we have made the effort to understand.

LEVEL

1 Usually a level surface suggests ease and comfort. Dreaming of **a road being level** would indicate our way ahead is fairly straightforward. **A level crossing** suggests that we are approaching a barrier which requires our attention. We may not yet have enough information to take avoiding action.

2 There are many levels of understanding which are available to us in the dream state. It will depend on our stage of advancement at which level we choose to interpret our dreams.

3 A level in sacred architecture represents knowledge out of the norm.

LIBRARY
– also see House

1 A library in a dream can often represent the storehouse of our life's experience. It can also represent our intellect and the way we handle knowledge. A **well-ordered library** would suggest the ability to create order successfully. A more **chaotic, untidy one** would suggest that we have difficulty in dealing with information.

2 At a certain stage in psychic and spiritual development, the library is an important symbol. It suggests both the wisdom and skills that we have accumulated, but also the collected wisdom available to all humanity. As we are able to look more objectively at our lives we have more access to universal knowledge.

3 A library represents the Collective Unconscious – all that is, was, and ever shall be. It is often taken as the Akashic records – that is, the spiritual records of existence.

LICE
– see Insects

LIFEBOAT
– also see Sea in Water

1 Dreaming of a lifeboat could indicate that we have the feeling that we need to be rescued, possibly from our own stupidity or from circumstances beyond our control. If we are at **the helm of a lifeboat** we are still in control of our own lives, but are perhaps aware that we need to offer assistance to someone else. Because the sea can represent deep emotion, in dreams a lifeboat may be of help in handling our own emotions.

2 Since a lifeboat requires a degree of dedication from the members of the crew, we may be alerted to the need for such selfless dedication in our lives. We may also be being made aware of the degree of skill we require to navigate life's difficulties.

3 Spiritually we can only be 'rescued' by a greater knowledge and wisdom. There is always risk in undertaking a difficult task.

LIGHT
– also see Lamp

1 Light in a dream usually means illumination. For instance, 'light at the end of the tunnel' suggests coming to the end of a difficult project. 'He saw the light' means recognition of the results of actions. It is much to do with confidence. To **feel lighter** signifies feeling better about ourselves.

2 When light appears in dreams we are usually in process of trying to improve who we are. A **very bright light** often symbolises the development of intuition or insight. There are various techniques using candle flames and other sources of light which can be used in the waking state to enhance this faculty.

3 Spiritually in dreams a bright light symbolises the manifestation of divinity, truth or direct knowledge. Often this knowledge is beyond form and therefore appears as energy which the dreaming mind translates as light.

LIGHTHOUSE

1 A lighthouse is a warning system, and in dreams it tends to warn us of emotional difficulties. It will depend on whether we are aware in the dream of being on land or at sea. If we are **on land** we are being warned of difficulties to come, probably from our own emotions. If we are **at sea** we need to be careful not to create misunderstandings for ourselves by ignoring problems.

2 A lighthouse can act as a beacon and can lead us into calmer waters. It can often have this significance in dreams whether emotionally or spiritually. A lighthouse can also take on the symbolism of the tower (see Tower).

3 Spiritually a lighthouse high-lights the correct course of action to help us achieve our spiritual goals.

LIGHTNING

1 Lightning in a dream denotes unexpected changes, which are taking place or are about to take place. These may come about through some type of realisation or revelation. Often such a revelation has the effect of knocking down the structures we have built in as safeguards in our lives. Alternatively, we may have to make changes in the way we think while leaving our everyday structure and relationships in place. Lightning can also indicate strong passion – such as love – which may strike suddenly but be devastating in its effect.

2 When we dream of lightning we are marking a discharge of tension in some way. There may be a situation in our everyday lives which actually has to be blasted in order for something to happen which will change the circum-stances. This may seem like a destructive act on our part, but is nevertheless necessary. If we take all the known facts into account, our intuition will make us aware of the correct action.

3 Spiritually, lightning denotes some form of spiritual enlightenment. This may be the sudden realisation of a personal truth, or of a more universal awareness. Literally something which had not 'struck us' before. In dreams **a lightning flash** can also represent the Holy Spirit.

LILY

1 Because of their connection with funerals, for some people lilies can symbolise death. They can, however, also symbolise nobility and grace, and the interpretation needs to be carefully thought out. If we are **planting lilies** we are hoping for a peaceful transition in some area within our lives. If we are **gathering lilies**, particularly in **a woman's dream** we are developing a peaceful existence.

2 One symbol of lilies is that of purity and, particularly in a teenager's dream, lilies can suggest virginity. Lilies in dreams, other than the white funerary arum lily, can suggest aspects of femininity.

3 Spiritually lilies are a symbol of resurrection and of everlasting life. They are often used in religious ceremony to denote this.

LINE

1 A line in a dream often marks a boundary or denotes a measurement. In dreams, it can also signify a link between two objects to show a connection which is not immediately obvious. **A line of people or queue** would suggest an imposed order for a particular purpose. If the dreamer is **waiting in line**, the purpose of the line will be important.

2 Psychologically, we tend to need boundaries or demarcation lines, and those lines can be demonstrated in dream symbolism in ways which might not be feasible in everyday life. For instance, **jumping over a line** would suggest being brave enough to take risks. A **line of objects** might signify the choices we are offered.

3 Spiritually in dreams a line can have great significance. The **straight line** can represent time and the ability to go both forward and back. When **horizontal**, the line is the earthly world and the passive point of view; when **vertical**, it is the spiritual world, the active aspect and the cosmic axis.

LINEN

1 Linen in dreams on a purely practical level can suggest an appreciation of fine things. **Linen tablecloths**, for instance, may suggest some kind of a celebration in the sense of only using the best. **Linen bed sheets** might signify sensuality.

2 In today's world, where everything is done as quickly and as easily as possible, linen appearing in a dream would suggest a slowness of pace and caring which enables us to appreciate our lives better.

3 Spiritually, fine linen signifies purity and righteousness. It was the cloth used to wrap Christ with in the tomb, and therefore suggests reverence and love.

LION
– also see Animals

1 The lion in dreams signifies both cruelty and strength.

2 In psychological terms, the lion represents all those qualities it shows – majesty, strength, pride, courage and so on. It is easier to recognise the necessity for such qualities in ourselves when symbolised in something else.

3 Spiritually the lion symbolises all those attributes that belong to the fiery principle. It is an ambivalent symbol, since it represents both good and evil. It plays a part in the recognition of the four elements – Fire, Earth, Air and Water – and represents fire.

LIQUID

1 Liquid in dreams can have more than one meaning. Because it is always connected with 'flow', it can represent the idea of allowing feelings to flow properly. The colour of the liquid in the dream *(see Colour)* can be important since it can give an indication of exactly which feelings and emotions are being dealt with. **Red** might represent anger, whereas **violet** might signify spiritual aspiration.

2 When **something is unexpectedly liquid** in a dream, we need to be aware that in everyday life we are in a situation which may not remain stable. At that point we need to be ready to 'go with the flow' in order to maximise the potential within that situation. One of the symbols of liquid is to do with liquidity – that is, having assets or possessions which can be realised. This can be on either a physical or emotional level.

3 A strong symbol in spiritual development is golden liquid which can represent both power and energy.

LIVER
– see Body

LIZARD
– see Reptiles in Animals

LOAF/LOAVES

1 In less sophisticated times bread, because it was made from grain, was also a fit offering for the gods. It was formed into loaves which then became symbols of fertility, nourishment and life. This symbolism remains visible today at Harvest and Jewish festivals. In dreams, loaves can represent our need for nourishment.

2 The Biblical parable of five loaves and two fishes signifies the principle of being fed through caring. In most cultures, the sharing of a loaf denotes friendship. It can have the same significance in dreams.

3 Spiritually the loaf represents the Bread of Life, the love of God and charity in the sense of caring.

LOCK/LOCKED
– also see Key and Prison

1 It is very easy to lock away the emotions, supposedly to keep them safe. A lock appearing in a dream may alert us to the fact that we need to free up whatever we have shut away. **To force a lock** would indicate that we need to work against our own inclinations to lock things away in order to be free of inhibitions. **To be mending a lock** suggests that we feel our personal space been trespassed upon and we need to repair the damage.

2 To recognise in a dream that a **part of our body has become locked** suggests that we are carrying extreme tension. We need to release that tension in a physical way in order to be healthy. To realise **a door is locked** suggests that somewhere we thought of as sanctuary is no longer available to us. It may also be that a course of action is not right.

3 Spiritually, a lock can represent that either a new freedom is being offered to us or that the way forward is barred. Our actions are not appropriate.

LOCUST

1 The image of a plague of locusts is so strong in Western thought that even in dreams it has come to represent retribution for some misdemeanour.

2 As a flying insect the locust can signify scattered thought, and concepts which have not been properly thought out and marshalled. Put together they may be a very powerful tool, but should be used wisely.

3 Spiritually locusts signify divine retribution, but also a misuse of resources.

LOOM

1 A loom in dreams will obviously have a different significance if it is a work tool, or if one is a creative artist. By and large a loom suggests creativity, whether more mechanical or craft-oriented. We all have the ability within ourselves to create beautiful objects and the loom is one of these symbols.

2 A loom picks up on the symbol of weaving and the idea of creating our own lives. We have certain basic materials which can lay down an elementary pattern, but we must add our own touches which give the individuality to the overall woven object. The loom is the tool we need to achieve the right pattern.

3 The loom in spiritual terms suggest fate, time, and the weaving of destiny.

LORRY
– see Journey

LOST

1 To have **lost something** in a dream may mean that we have forgotten matters which could be important. This may be an opportunity, a friend or a way of thought which has previously sustained us. To suffer loss suggests that part of ourselves or our lives is now dead and we must learn to cope without it.

2 To experience ourselves as **being lost** denotes confusion on whatever level is depicted in the dream. It may be emotionally or mentally as much as physically. We have lost the ability or the motivation to make clear decisions.

3 The search for the **lost object or the lost chord** epitomises the search for enlightenment. In spiritual terms we do not know what we are looking for until we have found it.

LOTTERY

1 A lottery – particularly in today's climate – suggests the idea of gaining through taking a risk. To dream of **winning a lottery** would suggest that one has either been lucky or clever in waking life. To dream of **losing** might suggest that someone else was in control of our destiny.

2 A lottery can highlight all sorts of belief systems, some valid and some not. The idea of random selection – particularly mechanically – links with belief in a mechanistic universe. The lottery also denotes one's attitude to greed and poverty and to the principle of winning through luck rather than effort.

3 Spiritually the lottery represents the ability to take chances, to rely on fate rather than good judgement.

LOW
– see Position

LUGGAGE

1 Luggage in a dream can be slightly different to baggage in that luggage will symbolise what we feel is necessary to have us go forward. It can be those habits and emotions which have helped us in the past, but which can now be reappraised before being 'repackaged'.

2 When luggage appears as a symbol in our dreams we should perhaps look at whether it is **ours or someone else's**. If ours, it signifies those views, attitudes and behaviours which we have brought through from the past. If it is someone else's, then we may be looking at family or global concepts which no longer are useful to us.

3 Spiritually if we are to travel 'light' we must often find a way of unburdening ourselves. Luggage in a dream can help us to envisage this.

LUNGS
– see Body

LYNX
– see Animals

M

from

Machine *to* Mystic Knot

MACHINE

1 When a machine of any sort appears in a dream, it is often highlighting the body's automatic functions such as breathing, heart beating, elimination – those mechanical drives towards life that help us to survive. It is usually to do with some kind of mechanical, habitual form – that is, the ordinary everyday things that take place. The 'mechanics' of the body are an important part of our well-being and often when we perceive a **machine breaking down** in dreams, it warns us that we need to take care, that perhaps we are over-stressing a particular part of our being.

2 The machine is very often to do with the brain and the thinking processes, so psychologically it is the process of thinking that is important. If a machine seems **large and overpowering**, we perhaps need to reassess what we are doing to ourselves.

3 A machine may well represent the machinations of life, which would be interpreted as The Life Process.

MAD

1 When we are confronted by madness in a dream, we are often meeting those parts of ourselves that have not been integrated within our present situation. We are facing a part of ourselves that is out of control and which, under certain circumstances, can be frightening.

2 Being mad in a dream represents the uncontrollable aspects of extreme emotion. If we are conscious of being at odds with other people, and therefore considered to be mad, we are not integrating fully within society or the group to which we belong.

3 Madness can also be translated into feelings of Spiritual ecstasy. The old saying 'in the comforts of madness' is appropriate here.

MAGGOTS

1 Maggots appearing in dreams in their correct context can represent the feelings we have about death. If a **fisherman was using maggots** we would be referring to power and energy, but if someone else was using maggots, their use of nastiness might be in question.

2 Maggots can represent impurities in the body and the sense of being eaten up by something – of having something within our body – such as an idea or feeling – that is alien to us and can therefore overtake and overcome us.

3 Maggots in dreams may reflect our own fears about death and illness.

MAGIC

1 When we are using magic in a dream, we are using our energy to accomplish something without effort or difficulty. We are capable of controlling the situation that we are in, to have things happen for us and to create from our own needs and wants.

2 Psychologically, when there is magic in a dream it is to do with our ability to link with our deepest powers. They can be the powers of sexuality or the powers of control, or of power over our surroundings.

3 Magic has always had an appeal. This may well be due to the mystery that surrounds it, and the idea of something which is beyond our own understanding.

MAGISTRATE

– also see Authority Figures in People

1 Whenever an authority figure appears in a dream, it is very often harking back to our relationship with our father, with the need to be told what to do, or perhaps to have somebody who is more powerful than we are take control within our lives. Since a magistrate imposes the laws of society, it is also to do with our willingness to submit to authority on behalf of the Greater Good. Throughout life, we learn to belong to groups and to act in a way that is more in keeping with the needs of those groups.

2 Authority figures are part of our make up. It may well be that part of our being knows best what we should be doing, and our conscious, everyday working self is not operating in keeping with that inner authority.

3 Spiritual authority coupled with spiritual knowledge is often represented by a dream of a magistrate. It signifies the dreamer can be susceptible to both.

MAGNET

1 We all have within us the ability to attract or repel others, and often a magnet appearing in a dream will highlight that ability. Since of itself the magnet is inert, it is the power it has that is important. We often need to realise the influence that we have over other people comes not only from ourselves, but also from our interaction with them.

2 The magnet has the ability to create a 'field' round itself, a field of magnetic energy. Often the magnet appearing in a dream alerts us to the intrinsic power that we have, which is inert until such times as it is activated by situations around us.

3 A magnet will suggest a degree of charisma within the dreamer which can be used in various ways, depending upon the dreamer's inclinations.

MAGNIFYING GLASS

1 When anything is magnified in a dream it is being brought to our attention. **To be using a magnifying glass** indicates that we should be making what we are looking at conscious. It needs to be made part of our everyday working life and we do have the power to create something out of the material that we have.

2 Where it strikes us that the magnifying glass itself and not what we are looking at is important, we are recognising our own abilities, our own power within a situation.

3 Making Spirituality manifest would initially mean being more aware of our own actions. We need to examine ourselves minutely.

MAGPIE
– see Birds

MAKE-UP
– also see Cosmetics

1 Make-up normally indicates our ability to change the impression we make on others. If we are **making ourselves up** it can very often indicate a happy occasion. We need to put on a facade for people

– we may even need to put on a facade for ourselves – so that we feel better about our own self-image. If we are **making someone else up**, then often we are helping them to create a false – or perhaps better – impression.

2 To be dealing with make-up means that we have a choice as to the sort of person we want to be. We can choose our outward appearance and can create an impression that perhaps is different from the one we naturally make use of.

3 Spiritually we must be aware of the way we are 'made-up' (constructed) and must be conscious of the facade we present to other people and whether it differs greatly from the person we feel ourselves to be.

MANDALA
– also see Mosaic

1 The mandala is a sacred shape which is so powerful that it is found in one form or another in most religions. Typically, it is a circle enclosing a square with a symbol in the centre representing the whole of life. It is mostly used as an aid to meditation. The principle is that one travels from the outer circle (which stands for the whole of existence) through the creation of matter – the square –

to the centre of existence – the central figure. Finally, one moves back out to take one's place in material existence again. It is often consciously depicted as an eight-pointed star, and represents both man's aspirations and his burdens. It often appears in dreams in this form, and can then become a personal symbol of the journey from chaos to order. It has also been found that, in a healing process, this symbol will occur over and over again. It is seen more frequently in Eastern religions, often as ornate pictures or patterns.

2 Jung judged this figure to be an important part of psychological wholeness. The word means 'circle', and he saw the mandala as being an archetypal expression of the soul. In dreams this figure often appears without the dreamer knowing what it represents. It is only when it is drawn afterwards that it is recognised as a mandala. This would suggest that it is a true expression of the dreamer's individuality and of his connection with Unity, whatever he sees this to be.

3 When ego and individuality are understood, the soul searches for representation. The expression of wholeness and yet separateness in this figure moves us into a space which enables us to create a whole new concept of the principles of existence. Often, by creating and recreating this figure, we move towards and experience a wholeness and tranquillity which would not otherwise be available. The particular shape, number of sides, and colours in the mandala will be significant *(see Shape, Numbers and Colour)*. The mandala seen in dreams can become a gauge for spiritual progression.

MALLET

1 The mallet is a symbol of authority and masculine force. For something like a hammer *(See Hammer)* or a mallet to appear in a dream indicates that we may be using undue force or power to achieve a certain outcome.

2 The mallet is also the directing will, and to have such an item in a dream indicates that we may be attempting to make things happen in a way that is not necessarily appropriate for that particular situation.

3 A mallet suggests a form of spiritual power and energy. However, because of the symbolic qualities of the mallet, we need to be aware of how the power and energy is being channelled.

MANDRAKE

1 In olden times the mandrake

root was taken to symbolise man. It was often used in magical ceremonies, and thus became significant in the same way that a voodoo doll can be significant. When the mandrake root or a manikin is recognised in a dream, we are linking in with our own wish to harm other people and with our conflict with someone else. Interestingly enough, the mandrake root is also a symbol of the Great Mother *(see Introduction)*, and therefore represents feminine aspects. So, in witchcraft, the witch was in fact linking with the destructive powers of her own Self.

2 The significance of mandrake within a dream is that perhaps of word association. We are not necessarily dreaming of the root itself, but are trying to make sense of some aspect of the personality around us that appears not to be fully formed in some way.

3 The power of life and death in spiritual terms is our right to exist in a way that is commensurate with our own beliefs.

MANNA

1 Manna represents food and therefore has the same significance as bread. It is food for the soul and food which is in some way miraculous. For this to appear in a dream usually represents the ability we have to transmute something from the ordinary to the sacred.

2 When we are seeking something, perhaps to change our lives in some way, we often need external help when everything around us is going wrong and we are beset by problems. The symbolism of manna – of the miraculous bread appearing – is something which makes us realise that we can in fact carry on. This symbol of the miraculous appears in many religions and therefore represents the aspect of ourselves that links with the Divine.

3 The Grace of God and his goodness is implicit in manna. We are in the right place at the right time for the right reasons.

MANSION
– see House

MANTIS

1 As with most insects, the mantis often represents something devious within our lives, that trickster part of us that can create problems when things are effectively working out for us. It is that aspect of our personality which perhaps preys on the other parts and will not take its place within our overall integration.

2 In dreams, we often translate a quality or a situation we are struggling with into an object. To be aware of the mantis may indicate that on some level we are aware of trickery around us.

3 The dreamer should look carefully at the appearance of a mantis as it represents deviousness, particularly of an emotional kind.

MANTRA

1 The Mantra is the creation of a sound, corresponding to a name or an aspect of god, and is a creative vibration. Often it is three syllables long, and is an aid to becoming closer to the centre of both oneself and the universe. In dreams it is frequently first heard as the sound of one's own name *(See Name)*, and can be developed from there. It is (or rather becomes) the personal 'key' to universal knowledge.

2 The intense concentration and repetition needed to fill the mind with one concept of whichever God one believes in – coupled with a sense of spiritual union – is a conscious activity designed to achieve a state of restful alertness. If dreams are considered to be alert restfulness, the use of Mantra can have a profound effect on the dream state in allowing us to be more focused in our dreaming. We are thus able to accept the spontaneity of the images evoked by Mantra when they also appear in dreams.

3 Spiritually, sound repeated over and over induces a change of consciousness and awareness. Mantra permits this to be positive and opens up possibilities for enhanced wisdom and knowledge.

MANURE

1 Some of the experiences which we have to go through can be painful or downright unwholesome. If we do not manage to understand what has happened to us and make use of it as part of our growth process, we can often find that those experiences remain within our subconscious and cause difficulty later on. These bad experiences may appear as manure within a dream and alert us to the fact that we should be breaking down our problems and making positive use of them.

2 Manure can represent something which is disintegrating in our lives. To be aware for instance, of a pile of **manure in an inappropriate position** would indicate that we have something in our lives which will have to disintegrate, to change form before it can be used properly.

3 Manure can be seen also as the prelude to spiritual breakdown. This does not have to be a negative thing as a rebuilding process is often what is required to enable us to find solutions to current problems.

MAP

1 For a map to appear in a dream often indicates the clarification of the direction we should be taking in life. We may feel that we are lost and need something to indicate the way forward, particularly so far as ambition or motivation is concerned. **A map that has already been used** by other people would therefore indicate that we are capable of taking a direction and learning from those people.
2 When we first set out on the journey of discovery which makes us grow into capable human beings, we often need clarification of the way that we must undertake the journey. In dreams this often appears as a map. The **direction we are being shown to take** *(See Position)* is important; i.e. forwards, backwards, left or right and we are often helped by the idea of having a course to follow.
3 A map can obviously help us in our quest to find the spiritual way forward. It is worth remembering that we would need to read the map ourselves, and therefore we are our own guides.

MARBLE

1 Because it is a fine substance, marble appearing in a dream often indicates age or perhaps permanence. We all need some quality of permanence within our lives and marble can symbolise this.
2 When we are in trouble, it can often seem that we are 'between a rock and a hard place'. Marble in a dream – because it is a beautiful substance – can reconcile us to the fact that we must move forward in an appropriate way.
3 Marble can represent spiritual firmness.

MARE
— see Horse in Animals

MARIGOLD
— see Flowers

MARKET/ MARKETPLACE
— also see Shop

1 Dreaming that we are **in a market** indicates our ability to cope with everyday life, of being able to relate to people, but particularly to relate to crowds. It is also the place of buying and selling and therefore often gives us some sort of indication as to how we value our various attributes, whether we have something to sell or whether we are buying.

2 A market is a bustling, happy place and to dream of one may indicate that we need to look after ourselves more and to spend time with more people. It could also suggest that we need to become more commercial in the work that we are doing, or perhaps to be more creatively influenced, rather than doing something purely and simply because it is commercial – thus it has quite an ambivalent meaning.

3 A marketplace can be viewed as a place of spiritual exchange in dreams. We can establish a balance between our everyday reality and our spiritual or inner world.

MARRIAGE/ WEDDING

1 A marriage or a wedding in a dream often indicates the uniting of two particular parts of the dreamer which need to come together in order to create a better whole. For instance, the intellect and feelings – or perhaps the practical and intuitive sides – may need to be united. Often a marriage or wedding can be precognitive in that one may subconsciously be aware of a relationship between two people, but it has not yet registered on the conscious level. So, **to be attending a wedding** may indicate that one is aware of such a relationship. To be dreaming of **wearing a wedding dress** is to be trying to sort out one's feelings and hopes about relationships and weddings. To be **dressing someone else in a wedding dress** can indicate one's feelings of inferiority – 'always the bridesmaid, never the bride'.

2 Because the human being is always looking for someone to complement him- or herself, to dream of a wedding can give some indication of the type of person we are looking for as a partner. We may, for instance, dream that we are **marrying a childhood friend** – in which case we are looking for somebody who has the same qualities as that person. We may dream we are **marrying a famous figure** and again the qualities of that particular person will be important.

3 Spiritually there is a process of integration which needs to come about. Firstly the masculine and feminine sides of our personality need to unite, then the physical and spiritual sides need to harmonise. This is usually known as a Mystic Union.

MARROW

1 To dream of a **marrow – the vegetable** – has either sexual or childhood connotation and can indicate our attitude to our own sexuality. Because the **marrow of the bone** also indicates the life-force, vitality or strength within a person, to be dreaming of this type of marrow also indicates the quality of life that we wish to give ourselves.

2 We may be aware of some imbalance within ourselves, some difficulty that we may be having and to dream of marrow is to indicate that imbalance.

3 Just as the physical bone marrow suggests the life force, so in dreams marrow can suggest Spiritual Strength.

MARSH
– also see Swamp

1 When we dream of a marsh or a swamp, it can indicate that we are feeling 'bogged down'. We feel that we are being held back in some-thing we want to do, and perhaps we lack either the self-confidence or emotional support that we need to move forward. A marsh or a swamp can also indicate that we are being swamped by circum-stances, being trapped in some way by the circumstances round us.

2 Dreaming of marshy ground very often represents difficulty on an emotional level. Perhaps we are creating emotional difficulties for ourselves – or even having them

created for us – which make it difficult for us to feel secure.

3 Spiritual and emotional conflict. We may be spiritually on 'dodgy ground' so to speak.

MARTYR

1 Actually experiencing ourselves in dreams as **playing the martyr** highlights our tendency to do things without being sufficiently assertive to say no, and to act from a sense of duty. When we are aware of **someone else being a martyr** we may have too high expectations of that person.

2 Dreaming of a **religious martyr** often means we need to question our own religious beliefs and upbringing. We are perhaps allowing excessive enthusiasm to guide us.

3 We may feel the need, spiritually, to become a sacrificial victim and hence give our life some meaning. However, this should be looked at closely, as it may not be necessary.

MASK

1 Most people have a facade they put on for others, particularly at a first meeting. To dream of a mask often alerts us to either our own or other people's facade. When we are not being true to ourselves we can often experience this in dreams as a 'negative' or frightening mask.

2 When we are trying to protect ourselves and prevent other people knowing what we are thinking or feeling, we 'mask' ourselves. A mask appearing in a dream can therefore represent concealment. Additionally, in primitive cultures, **to wear a mask** such as that of an animal gave the wearer the powers of that animal. In Shamanism that is still accepted today.

3 The Death Mask, either our own or another's, can appear in dreams as a signal that it is time to put an end to a spiritual game we are playing.

MASTURBATION
– see Sex

MASOCHISM
– see Sex

MATTRESS
– also see Bed in Furniture

1 Similar to a bed, to dream of a mattress indicates the feeling we have about a situation we have created in our lives, whether it is comfortable for us or not. We are aware of our own basic needs and are able to create relaxed feelings that allow us to express ourselves fully.

2 Sexual comfort is important to most people. To dream of a mattress can very often indicate the way we handle our own sexuality – whether we are comfortable with it, or whether we find it an uncomfortable thing to deal with.

3 As sexual comfort is important, so is spiritual. The dreamer should not neglect this important aspect of learning.

MAYPOLE

1 A maypole in a dream can very often represent the masculine and may indicate the 'dance' which one goes through when coming to terms with one's own universe. It is the central pole of the world that we create for ourselves; thus to dream of a maypole may have sexual connotations, but also may indicate the way in which we handle our own lives.

2 Psychologically, festivals, celebrations and occasions for ceremony are necessary for the human being to be at ease with himself. Often, the maypole may be one such symbol – of celebration, of new life. It may also represent time in a dream, and the way in which a dream indicates the type of timing that is necessary within certain situations.

3 The maypole in a spiritual sense is a representation of the phallic, of masculine spirituality and of life-giving energy.

MAZE
– also see Labyrinth

1 A maze often represents a confusion of ideas and feelings. There are conflicting urges and opinions and we often discover that in attempting to find our way through the maze we have learnt something about our own courage, our own ability to meet problems. Often there is the apparently irrational fear and doubt that arises from not being able to find our way in and out of the maze. This can allow us to release feelings of self-doubt and fear.

2 Psychologically, the maze may represent the variety of opinions and authoritative beliefs that we come up against in our ordinary, everyday world. We may be trying to find our own way through this mass of detail and we picture it in a dream as actually trying to find our way through a maze.

3 The path to the Divine. The feminine. The way to the feminine is a strange route, and all the roads that lead there are winding, but the end result has worthy consequences.

MEANDER

1 In a dream, to have a path or the road in front of you meandering – that is, not going in any particular direction – suggests that we very often have to 'go with the flow', to simply follow what happens without actually thinking of the direction in which we are going. Sometimes the meandering has a kind of purpose, in that by moving about in an aimless fashion we are actually finding out more about ourselves or the circumstances we are in.

2 Water moves in its own way, and often to be conscious of a **river or a road meandering** around us indicates that we should be more aware of our own emotions, that we are capable of dealing with these emotions in a much gentler way than by being very direct. This may also refer to our relationship with other people. It could be that we need to recognise that other people cannot be as straightforward as we are.

3 The Spiritual Spiral. The dreamer must look at whether it is a downward spiral, an aimless wandering or a purposeful – if indirect – exploration.

MEDAL

1 A medal is often a reward for good work or for bravery, so when one appears in a dream, it is a recognition of our own abilities. If we are **giving someone else a medal** then we are honouring that part of ourselves represented by the other person.

2 Human beings both like and need to feel good about themselves. A medal in a dream acknowledges our talents and/or successes – not just in the immediate moment – but gives a permanent reminder of what we have done.

3 A badge of honour reflecting our attunement with the Spiritual code can be symbolised in dreams by a medal.

MEDICINE

1 To be taking medicine in a dream suggests that on some level we are aware of part of ourselves which needs healing. Often we are aware of what the medicine is for and are thus alerted either to a health problem, or to a situation which can be changed from the negative to the positive.

2 Sometimes an experience which we have in waking life can be unpleasant in the immediate moment, but ultimately is good for us. In dreams, medicine can stand as such a symbol.

3 The spiritual need for a healing influence in our lives is indicated by medicine appearing. The dreamer can look at what his own requirements are in this domain.

MEDITATION

1 Interpreting the act of medita-tion will depend on whether the dreamer meditates in real life. In someone who does, it will suggest a discipline that is helpful to the dreamer putting him or herself in touch with intuition and spiritual matters. In someone who does not, it may indicate the need to be more introverted in order to understand the necessity to be responsible for oneself.

2 Often on an unconscious level we are aware of the need to change consciousness or attitude, and to dream of meditating can highlight this for us. We can access the more creative, spiritual side.

3 The dreamer has to come to terms with discipline of a spiritual nature if he is to succeed in his spiritual goal.

MEDIUM

1 Dreaming of **visiting a medium** very often means that we are looking for some kind of contact with our own unconscious, or with the dead. We may also be attempting to alert our own intuition and use it differently to a way we have done previously.

2 To dream of **being mediumistic** would indicate that we are aware of greater powers than we believe we have in ordinary everyday life.

3 Mediumistic aspects in a dream

can represent the dreamer's wish to be in contact with the dead. This does not necessarily have to be dead in literal terms, it can merely be what is 'dead' in the dreamer's life, that which he may wish to resurrect.

MELT

1 To see **something melting** in a dream is an indication that our emotions may be softening. We are perhaps losing the rigidity we have needed to face the world with previously. We are undergoing a change and are becoming softer.

2 When we **feel ourselves to be melting** we may be becoming more romantically inclined and less likely to drive ourselves forward. We perhaps need to sit and simply let a situation develop around us to the point where it is safe for us to give up control.

3 On a spiritual level 'melting away' has sometimes had connections with evil, or badness.

MEMORIAL

1 To see a memorial such as **a war memorial** in a dream takes us back to a previous time, to a memory which may be 'cast in stone'. We need to be able to come to terms with this memory in order to be able to move on.

2 A memorial may simply be a recognition of a happier time which needs to be remembered.

3 A memorial is a tangible representation of homage and esteem.

MENSTRUATION
– also see Blood

1 To dream of menstruation may be linking with the creative side of ourselves which can conceive new ideas and can create new and more wonderful 'children' out of simple material. We are linking with the mystery of life and with the procreative drive.

2 Since menstruation is such an integral part of the feminine life, it can indicate in **a woman's dream** her acceptance of her own emerging sexuality. In a **man's dream** however, it can alert him to his fear surrounding relationships and union with the feminine. It can also indicate his own feminine side and his need to understand his own sensitivity.

3 The Cycle of Life and all that is mysterious in women can be symbolised by menstruation. It is only in a patriarchal society that it is seen as unclean.

MERMAID/MERMAN

1 Traditionally, the mermaid or merman belongs to the sea as well as being able to exist on land. This symbolically represents an ability to be deeply emotional and also entirely practical. Until these two separate parts are properly integrated, the human being cannot fully exist in either realm.

2 Mermaids and mermen are feminine and masculine representations of the link between the darker forces – which we do not necessarily understand – and the conscious self. Many stories exist of the human's attempt to mate or link with these creatures of the sea. Most end in hurt and distress for one party or the other. This is an example of how difficult it is to integrate the two sides of our nature.

3 Each individual must bring about integration between the spiritual self and the emotional self before there can be wholeness.

METAL

1 Any metal appearing in dreams represents the restrictions of the real world. It can represent basic abilities and attributes, but also can be hardness of feeling or emotional rigidity.

2 Most metals have symbolic meanings. They can also be connected with various planets: Sun is represented by gold, the Moon by silver, Mercury by quicksilver, Venus by copper, Mars by iron, Jupiter by tin, Saturn by lead.

3 Spiritual elements and how they can enhance our progression.

MICROSCOPE

1 A microscope in a dream very often indicates that we need to pay attention to detail. Also we may need to be somewhat introspective in order to achieve a personal goal.

2 We have the ability to look at things in dreams in much finer detail than we would necessarily do in the waking state. While the mind can be creative it sometimes also needs to apply scientific and perhaps logical thought to a problem, and the symbol of a microscope can draw attention to this.

3 A degree of detailed introspection is called for, either spiritual or physical.

MILK
– *see Food*

MILL/MILLSTONE

1 A mill extracts what is useful from the crude material it is fed. It is this quality that is symbolised in dreams. We are able to extract from our experiences in life what is useful to us and can convert it into nourishment.

2 There is a transformation which occurs when a material is ground, and any dream containing a mill will signify that transformation.

The two stones are said to signify will and intellect, the tools we use in transformation.

3 Transformative energy, turning the crude into the usable.

MINES
– also see Digging

1 Dreaming of mines signifies bringing the resources of the unconscious into the light of day. We are able to use the potential we have available. Interestingly in dreams mines can also represent the workplace.

2 This is one of those symbols which can actually be a word play. The things in the dream are 'mine'.

3 Mines spiritually suggest the ability to 'mine', or learn from the emerging unconscious.

MINOTAUR
– See Fabulous Beasts

MIRROR
– also see Reflection

1 Dreaming of a mirror suggests concern over one's self-image. We are worried as to what others think of us, and need self-examination in order to function correctly. There may be some anxiety over ageing or health.

2 To be **looking in a mirror** can signify trying to look behind us

without letting others know what we are doing. We may have a concern over past behaviour. We may also need to 'reflect' on something we have done or said. When the **image in the mirror is distorted** we are having a problem in understanding ourselves. When the **mirror image speaks to us** we should be listening more closely to our inner selves.

3 The mirror suggests self-realisation which reflects wisdom. As a means of understanding oneself on a deeper level, we can set up a dialogue in real life between one's mirror image and oneself. Many of the insights gained can be quite startling.

MISCARRIAGE

1 Dreaming of a miscarriage **whether our own or someone else's** suggests that we are conscious of the fact something is not right. **In a woman's dream** it will depend on whether she has suffered a miscarriage, since nowadays she will may not have given herself time to grieve properly.

2 Dreaming of a miscarriage can also suggest the loss of work, a project or even a part of ourselves, and we need time to acclimatise.

3 A miscarriage can represent aspects of early death and the fear it can engender.

MIST

1 Mist is a symbol of loss and confusion – particularly emotionally – so when this image appears we may need to sit down and reconsider our actions.

2 Mist in a dream can indicate a transition state, a way from one state of awareness to another and will often manifest to signify this.

3 Mist can symbolise initiation.

MISTLETOE
– also see Flowers

1 Conventionally, mistletoe represents a time of celebration, love and partnership. It obviously is most often dreamt of around Christmas.

2 As a parasite, mistletoe has the ability to draw strength from its host, but also to be useful in its own right. It can therefore symbolise relationships where there is a dependency on one partner.

3 Mistletoe represents the Essence of Life. It is a divine healing substance.

MOAT

1 A moat is a representation of our defences against intimacy. In dreams we can see for ourselves how we build or dig those enclosures. We can also decide what steps we need to take to remove them.

2 When we need to contain our own emotions we will often create a way of monitoring to whom we need to relate. A moat can be a symbol for this ability.

3 A moat can be an emotional barrier or defence.

MOLE
– see Animals

MONEY
– also see Wealth

1 Money in dreams does not necessarily represent hard currency, but more the way in which we value ourselves. This symbol appearing in dreams would suggest that we need to assess that value more carefully, and equally to be aware of what we 'pay' for our actions and desires.

2 Money can also represent our own personal resources – whether material or spiritual – and our potential for success. In some circumstances a dream of money can be linked with our view of our own power and our sexuality.

3 Spiritual currency and also spiritual 'change', small or otherwise.

MONK
– see High Priest in People

MONKEY
– see Animals

MONSTER

1 Any monster appearing in a dream is something that we have made larger than life. We have personalised it so that whatever is worrying us appears as a creature. It usually stands for our negative relationship with ourselves and fear of our own emotions and drives.

2 When, in everyday life, events get out of proportion we often have to suppress our reactions. In dreams we cannot do this and so our minds create some way of dealing with the problem. Often the colour of the monster (*see Colour*) will give us some indication of what the problem is, thus a **red** monster would indicate anger (possibly uncontrolled), whereas a **yellow** one might suggest resentment.

3 Fear of death and all that goes with it. A monster can highlight a more childlike fear, and can be looked at thus.

MOON

– also see Planets

1 The moon has always represented the emotional and feminine self. It is the intuition, the psychic, love and romance. To dream of the moon, therefore, is to be in touch with that side of ourselves which is dark and mysterious. Often in dreams the moon can also represent one's mother or the relationship with her.

2 It has always been known that the moon has a psychological effect on the human being. In Pagan times, it was suggested that she ruled men's emotions and guarded women's intuition. Even today, that symbolism still stands. **In a man's dream** when the moon appears, he either has to come to terms with his own intuitive side or with his fear of women. **In a woman's dream** the moon usually indicates her inter-relations with other women through their collective intuition.

3 The Great Mother, the darker, unknown side of Self, is symbolised by the moon. It is also symbolic of the unapproachable.

MORNING

– see Time

MORTUARY

1 In everyday life, a mortuary is a frightening place, connected as it tends to be with the trauma of death. When a mortuary appears in a dream, we are usually having to consider our fears and feelings about death.

2 If we are **viewing a dead body** we may be having to consider a part of ourselves that has died, or perhaps a now defunct relationship. If **we are the body in the mortuary**, we may have induced a state of inertia which does not allow us to enjoy life properly.

3 Death and dying, again not necessarily the final calling, but possibly new spiritual awareness.

MOSAIC
– also see Mandala

1 Any intricate pattern appearing in dreams usually signifies the pattern of our lives. We probably need to consider life as a whole, but also to understand and respect the many separate parts of it.

2 Within a mosaic, made up of many small parts, there is a deliberate act of creation. When such a symbol appears in dreams we are being alerted to our abilities as creator. The colours and shapes used will be important *(see Colours and Shapes)*.

3 The Kaleidoscope of Life with its many facets is a potent spiritual symbol represented in dreams by the mosaic.

MOSES
– see Religious Imagery

MOTH

1 The moth is largely associated with night-time and therefore connects with the hidden side of our nature. Also, because the moth

can be self-destructive when there is light around, it tends to symbolise our dream self and the more transient side of our personality.

2 As the butterfly is taken as the symbol for the soul, so the moth symbolises the darker side of us which uses fantasy. The **moth emerging from darkness** signifies the recognition of self we must all achieve to survive.

3 The moth symbolises the Self, but perhaps in its darker sense.

MOTHER
– see Family and Archetypes

MOTORBIKE
– see Journey

MOUND
– also see Hill

1 Traditionally, any mound appearing in a dream is supposed to link back to our very early childhood needs and the comfort that mother's breast brought.

2 Emotionally, man's need for comfort and sustenance continues throughout his life. At the same time, he needs to come to terms with his dependence on the feminine. Often to dream of mounds helps him to understand this.

3 The mound symbolises the Earth Mother or the entrance to the Underworld.

MOUNTAIN

1 In dream sequences the mountain usually appears in order to symbolise an obstacle which needs to be overcome. By daring to **climb the mountain** we challenge our own inadequacies and free ourselves from fear. To **reach the top** is to achieve one's goal. To **fall down the mountain** indicates carelessness.
2 We all have difficulties to face in life. Often it is how we face those difficulties that is important. The symbol of the mountain offers many alternatives and choices. This means we can work out, through dreams, our best course of action in everyday life.
3 Representing the centre of our existence in earthly terms, the mountain is an image that can be worked on over and over again.

MOURNING
– also see Funeral and Weeping

1 The process of mourning is an important one in all sorts of ways. We not only mourn death but also the end of a relationship or a particular part of our lives. Since sometimes mourning or grieving is seen as inappropriate in waking life, it will often appear in dreams as a form of relief or release.
2 In many cultures less emotionally repressed than our own, the period of mourning is seen as a way of assisting the departing soul on its way. In dreams we may find that we are helping ourselves to create a new beginning through our mourning for the old. Psychologically, we need a period of adjustment when we have lost something, and need to grieve for ourselves as much as for what we have lost.
3 Grief. We may need to look at how we deal with grief on both a spiritual and physical level.

MOUSE
– see Animals

MOUTH
– see Body

MOVEMENT

1 Movement in dreams is usually highlighted to make the dreamer aware of progress. **Moving forward** suggests an acceptance of one's abilities, while **moving backwards** signifies withdrawal from a situation. **Moving sideways** would suggest a deliberate act of avoidance.
2 The way we move in dreams can indicate a great deal about our acceptance of ourselves. For instance, to be **moving briskly** would suggest an easy acceptance of the necessity for change, whereas **being moved** – such as

on some kind of moving walkway – would signify being moved by outside circumstances or at the wish of other people.

3 A movement towards Spiritual Acceptance can be undertaken when the time is considered to be right.

MUD

1 Mud in a dream suggests that we are feeling bogged down, perhaps by not having sorted out practicality and emotion (earth and water). Mud can also represent past experiences or our perception of them which has the ability to hold us back.

2 Mud represents the fundamental substance of life which, handled properly, has a tremendous potential for growth but handled badly can be dangerous. Other circumstances in the dream will indicate what we should be doing.

3 Spiritually mud represents the very basic material from which we are all formed, and the need to go 'back to basics'.

MUMMY (EGYPTIAN)

1 There is an obvious connection between Mummy and mother is a play on words. In many ways our mother must 'die', or rather, we must change our relationship with her, in order for us to survive. The Egyptian mummy in dreams can also symbolise our feelings about someone who has died.

2 The Egyptian mummy symbolises death, but also preservation after death and therefore the afterlife. We may be trying to understand such a concept in real life, or we may realise that life has got to continue on a more mundane level.

3 The Self, the unbending Mother and self-preservation are all symbolised in the mummy.

MURDER/ MURDERER

1 We may be denying, or trying to control, a part of our own nature that we do not trust. We may also have feelings about other people which can only be safely expressed in dreams. If we ourselves are **being murdered** a part of our lives is completely out of balance and we are being destroyed by external circumstances.

2 To be angry enough to kill suggests that we are still holding some kind of childhood anger, since it is quite natural for a child to wish somebody dead. If we are **trying to murder somebody else** in a dream, we first need to understand what that person represents to us before recognising the violence of our own feelings.

3 Wilful destruction is the relevant symbol here. Spiritually we need to take a look at what is in our path.

MUSEUM

1 A museum in a dream denotes old-fashioned thoughts, concepts and ideas. We may need to consider such things but perhaps more objectively than subjectively.

2 A museum can represent a place where we store our memories and therefore can represent the subconscious – it is that part of ourselves which we will usually only approach in an effort to understand who we are and where we came from.

3 The past as an interesting relic that can be observed at some length, and then moved away from in order to progress.

MUSIC/RHYTHM
– also see Orchestra

1 Music and rhythm are both an expression of our inner selves and of our connection with life. To **hear music** in a dream suggests that we have the potential to make that basic association. Music can equally represent a sensuous and sensual experience.

2 **Sacred music** such as chanting, drumming and **pipe playing** is used to induce an altered state of consciousness, and this can be represented in dreams

by the hearing of music.

3 Sacred sound has always been used in acts of worship, as has dancing *(see Dance)*.

MUSICAL INSTRUMENTS
– also see Drum, Flute, Organ and Piano

1 Musical instruments in a dream often stand for our skills and abilities in communication. **Wind instruments** tend to suggest the intellect. **Percussion instruments** suggest the basic rhythm of life.

2 Sometimes in dreams, musical instruments can suggest the sexual organs and therefore one's attitude to one's own sexuality.

3 Ways of self-expression (for example, playing a musical instrument) are offerings of our own creativity and are spiritual acts.

MYSTIC KNOT

1 Traditionally, the mystic knot had no beginning and no end. Its basic meaning suggests an unsolvable problem. We probably need to leave such a problem until it is solved by time.

2 The mystic knot usually appears as we are attempting to understand ourselves and our relationship with the spiritual.

3 The mystic knot suggests Infinity.

N

from

Nail *to* Nymphs

NAIL

1 Dreaming of nails, as in **woodworking**, suggests our ability to bond things together. The holding power of the nail may also be significant. **Finger and toe nails** usually suggest claws or the capability of holding on.

2 The penetrative power of the nail may be significant if the dreamer is having difficulty with issues of masculinity or sexuality.

3 Spiritually the nail represents necessity and fate. In Christianity, nails also signify ultimate sacrifice and pain.

NAKEDNESS
– see Nude

NAME

1 Our name is the first thing we are conscious of possessing. It is our sense of self and of belonging. If we **hear our name called** in a dream, our attention is being drawn specifically to the person we are. There is a suggestion that parents name their child so that the meaning of the name carries the biggest lesson that the child has to learn in life. For instance, Charles means 'man', and Bridget means 'strength'.

2 When we are aware of **other people's names,** we are probably also aware of the qualities that

person has and it is those qualities we need to look at. When the **name of a place** comes up in a dream, we are considering the way we feel about that place, or something we know about it. There may also be some word-play on the names.

3 Spiritually, when something is named it then has form and therefore meaning. The name allows us to link with the Essential Self.

NARROW

1 When we dream of anything which is narrow, we are aware of restrictions and limitations. Sometimes we have created them ourselves, sometimes other people will have created them for us. A **narrow road** would perhaps suggest some kind of restriction, and a warning that we must not deviate from our path.

2 We should take care not to be narrow-minded and judgmental in our dealings with other people. We may be intolerant and parochial in our opinions. A **narrow bridge** might suggest a difficulty in communication, perhaps in putting our ideas across.

3 One-pointedness and bigotry are not qualities which are particularly spiritual, but self-discipline may require us to keep to the 'straight and narrow.'

NATIVES

1 Any dream which contains 'natives' – that is, people from another culture and possibly with a tribal system – is making us aware of a very simple structure to life. Our natural feelings can come to the fore in a way that expresses our wilder, rather less civilised selves.

2 Within man, however civilised he may be, there is a part which holds to a basic simplicity. Native culture is perhaps in some ways more free – and less restricted – than Western culture. It therefore allows for not only an easier expression of emotions on a personal level, but also a structured management of power both in a tribal and spiritual sense. It is understood, for instance, that only those who have been trained can become witch-doctors and can deal with the spirits. Everyone is aware of his or her task. It is this aspect which may be relevant in dreams about natives.

3 In the spiritual sense, natives represent a closeness to the earth and to nature – something we need if we are to understand our own spirituality.

NAUSEA

1 Nausea in a dream usually indicates the need to get rid of something which is making us feel uncomfortable. It may be a reflection of our physical state, but since the stomach is the seat of the emotions, it may be a representation of an emotion that is distressing us.

2 The body often has its own way of alerting us to difficulties, and it may be that nausea in a dream indicates a problem before it manifests in the physical.

3 Nausea can also suggest an awareness of something spiritually rotten or putrid.

NAVEL

1 To be conscious of the navel, whether **our own or another's**, is to be aware of the way in which we connect our inner-self with the rest of the outside world. It is the way in which the baby in the womb first becomes aware of its physicality. In dreams we often need to be aware of our bodily image, which will help indicate the way we see ourselves, which in turn enables us to work out the way we fit in to the everyday world.

2 The navel in a dream can signify our dependency on others, particularly our mother. The navel is our emotional centre, and also, as adults, initially the seat of our power. Often in nightmares we become conscious of something, perhaps a Devil sitting on our navel, and this can be a personification of our own fears.

3 The navel or solar plexus is spiritually the point of connection between the spiritual and the physical.

NEAR

1 When we are conscious of being near someone or something in a dream we are on the point of recognising them in waking life. We may be becoming emotionally closer or more able to handle whatever is happening.

2 When an object or image in a dream is near us – that is, when we are passive within the dream situation – we are often alerted to the fact that something will happen quickly. Spatial awareness can give us a concept of time.

3 Conscious Awareness of those aspects of life which are spiritual often manifest as a nearness.

NECKLACE
– also see Jewels

1 A necklace suggest a special object, and thus translates into special qualities or attributes. There is a richness to be acknowledged. This may be of feeling or of emotion. An old interpretation of a man giving a woman a necklace was that he would soon ask for her hand in marriage.

2 Necklaces arose from the wearing of a chain of office and therefore in dreams suggests a dignity or honour which has been conferred on the wearer.

3 The necklace is an acknowledgement of honour and power. The rosary is a special kind of necklace which aids one in prayer.

NEEDLE

1 In dreams needles suggest irritations, but can also signify the power to heal through penetration. A concept or knowledge has to be introduced from the outside, which may hurt, but will ultimately make us better from the inside.

2 The ability to have some penetrating insights about our own state can help us to cope with everyday life. It will depend if the needles are being used by us or on us.

3 The needle can suggest masculine sexuality, but also the type of penetrating insight which changes our view of life.

NEIGHBOUR
– see People

NEPHEW
– see Extended Family in Family

NEST

1 The nest symbolises safety and perhaps home life. We may be emotionally dependent on the people around us and afraid of 'leaving the nest'.

2 It is perhaps interesting to note that just before giving birth many women have a nesting instinct. This will sometimes emerge in dreams before it is recognised in waking life.

3 Security within one's known environment.

NET/NETWORK

1 A net in dreams usually indicates that we are feeling trapped and entangled in a scheme or situation. **In a woman's dream** she will be aware of her own seductive power, whereas **in a man's dream** he will be conscious of his fear of women.

2 Women are often more able to create a network of 'sisters' through the use of intuition, and often will symbolise this in their dreams as a tangible bonding.

3 Unlimited Relationship.

NETTLE

1 A nettle in a dream suggests that there is a difficult situation which will have to be avoided. There may be irritation, particularly if we are not interacting with others or with the environment we are in. **A patch of nettles** could also suggest difficulty in communication if we are in the middle of it. Others round us may be using words or circumstances to hurt us. Nettles in a dream can also signify a worthless transaction: 'I got stung'.

2 Nettles are wild plants with the quality of irritating the skin. This symbolism can come across in dreams as having allowed ourselves to be over-stimulated by a display of wild behaviour. This may be sexually, but could be in other ways as well, such as through dance. There is a point at which there is loss of control. Nettles can also suggest a kind of healing, both through the vitamins and minerals they contain when eaten, and also because they can be used to stimulate the system through external application. Folk medicine often suggested applying poultices of nettles to stimulate the blood supply.

3 In spiritual terms, nettle is supposed to be a specific against danger. It is also used in purification rituals. Fresh nettles are reputed to aid a sick person's recovery.

NEW

1 Dreaming of something which is new suggests a new beginning, a new way of looking at or dealing with situations, or perhaps even a new relationship. Thus, **new shoes** might suggest either a different way forward or a way of connecting with the earth. A **new hat** might suggest a novel intellectual approach, whereas **new spectacles** indicate a fresh way of seeing things.

2 To be **doing something new** in a dream highlights the potential in a fresh learning situation. We are stimulated and excited initially. When we move into a new situation in real life our dreams can highlight our fears and difficulties. We may often dream of possible scenarios where we are not functioning as well as we should, or of actions we might take to enhance our performance.

3 The new, within the spiritual, is information which comes to us at the right time to enable us to progress. What is new to us may not actually be new but has impact because we have not previously known it.

NEW YEAR

1 To dream of the New Year is to recognise the need for a fresh start. It may also signify the measurement of time in a way that is acceptable, or a time when something can happen.

2 Psychologically, when there is a need for renewal or a new growth in understanding we need to acknowledge the effort we must make. This is often symbolised as a New Year, a new beginning.

3 Spiritually, in any culture, the New Year with its attendant celebrations can signify enlightenment or new knowledge becoming available. We are no longer in the depths of darkness.

NEWSPAPER

1 Largely in dreams a newspaper will suggest knowledge which is publicly available. It may be information that we require in order to make sense of the world around us, or it may be something which is specific to us. A **tabloid newspaper** may suggest sensational material, whereas **a quality one** would suggest better researched data. **A Sunday newspaper** may suggest that we have the ability to assimilate the knowledge we need in periods of rest and relaxation. **A local newspaper** signifies that the facts we require are close to hand.

2 Newspapers in dreams signify new information available to us which is now conscious, rather than being held subconsciously. It is information which we need. A **blank page** can have two meanings. Firstly, the information may not be available to us for various reasons. Secondly, it may be for us to provide the information for other people to make use of.

3 Spiritually, we should be aware that what we do needs to be for the Greater Good. We need to be more publicly visible.

NICHE

1 Everyone has a basic need to belong and often we are conscious in dreams of finding our particular place. It manifests itself in dreams as a place where we are protected on all sides except from the front. It has been suggested that this is a return to the childhood state prior to the age of four when the child begins to realise that he is vulnerable from the rear. A niche is therefore our 'spot' – the place where we are safe.

2 In new situations we have a need to understand the world we are entering. Often our dream scenarios can open up possibilities by showing us where we belong – what niche we need to find for ourselves. Not only must we find the space where we belong but we must know which external factors are going to help us and which will hinder. Dream images connected with the niche will give us such information.

3 In religious imagery, the niche is consecrated so that it is a fit place to contain the Divine. It then symbolises the holiness and special powers relevant to the particular deity. If an icon *(see Icon)* is placed within the niche, then the god or goddess is there also.

NIECE
– see Family

NIGHT
– also see Time

1 Night signifies a period of rest and relaxation. It can, however, also suggest a time of chaos and difficulty. It is a time for 'ghosties, ghoulies and things that go bump in the night'. More positively, it is a period which allows us to create a new beginning with the dawning of the new day. Used constructively, night is therefore the fallow period before fresh growth.

2 Physiologically night is a time when the body is supposed to be renewing itself. In Chinese medicine, certain hours of the night correspond with the renewal of certain organs in the body. Madness would eventually ensue if the body were not able to repair itself properly *(see Sleep Deprivation in Introduction)*.

3 Night symbolises the darkness that occurs before rebirth or initiation. There is a disintegration which has to occur before there can be enlightenment. Night can also signify death or drastic change.

NIMBUS
– also see Aura

1 The force field – or electro-magnetic energy – that emanates from each of us has a particular quality in those who have undertaken to develop themselves spiritually. To the clairvoyant eye it can appear as a type of mother-of-pearl radiance.
2 The charisma which many world and spiritual leaders have is felt by many. The nimbus is usually slightly more subtle, and therefore more far-reaching, than the normal person's aura.
3 The nimbus is often portrayed in religious pictures as the halo or divine radiance around Christ-like or saintly people.

NO

1 To be aware of saying no in a dream may be an important part of our growth process. We are capable of making decisions which go against the wishes of other people, without feeling that we are going to be punished. We are coming to terms with rejection and are no longer fearful. We are capable of standing on our own two feet.
2 The right to refuse is an important aspect of making choices. We may have no coherent reason for refusal, except the right to say no. In terms of relationships, saying no in a dream suggests that on some

level we know what is right for us.
3 Saying no in spiritual terms entails rejecting that which is not compatible with our progress.

NOOSE
– also see Hanging and Rope

1 A noose in a dream suggests that we have a fear of being trapped, perhaps by others' actions. We are aware that we can create a trap for ourselves, thereby 'putting a noose round our own necks'. Traditionally, a drawing of a **hangman's noose** was a threat of death and it can still have that significance in dreams. As always, this death may be of part of our personality.
2 A noose, like the halter, harness and other symbols of restraint, suggests the taming of something wild. So, for a **young man about to be married** to dream of a noose might indicate a fear of being restrained unduly. For a **young woman wishing to leave home,** a noose might represent a fear of becoming trapped in the parental home. A noose can also imply the prevention of self-expression.
3 At its simplest, the noose represents a traumatic death. In a more complex sense it can represent the binding of spiritual intent, the harnessing of spiritual energy.

NORTH
– see Position

NOURISHMENT/ NURTURING
– also see Food

1 In dreams, all symbols of nourishment are associated with basic needs. Firstly, we require warmth and comfort; secondly, shelter and sustenance. Initially we experience this as coming from mother. Any dream in which we become aware of our needs then links with our relationship with mother. If our need for nourishment and nurturing is not met we experience rejection and hurt. In dreams the two become interchangeable.

2 All symbols of containment (the vessel, cup, cauldron, bowl etc.) are symbols of nurturing and femininity. Food-producing animals are also associated with the nourishing aspects of the mother and therefore of Mother Earth.

3 The suggestions of nourishing the soul and conferring immortality all belong to the nurturing of the Mother Goddess.

NOVEL
– also see Book and Reading

1 Strictly, a novel represents a different way of looking at things. If we are aware in dreams of reading such a book, we need to ascertain what kind of a novel it is. The storyline may have relevance in our lives at that particular moment. For instance, a **historical novel** might suggest we need to explore the past, whereas a **romantic novel** would suggest the need to look at relationships.

2 Novel also means new, and psychologically we are often searching for stimulation. In dreams, therefore, there can be a play on words to indicate that we should be looking for some new way of dealing with our lives.

3 New spiritual learning can often be explained in terms of a story or a myth.

NUCLEAR EXPLOSION
– also see Atom Bomb

1 A nuclear explosion can be accidental (as, for instance, was Chernobyl). Such an accident can unintentionally have very far-reaching effects. To dream of a nuclear explosion can highlight our anxiety about great change in our lives. We do not yet know what effect that change may have. We do, however, know we must undertake radical change, but would prefer it to be a more gradual process.

2 When we have suppressed certain parts of our personality rather than handling them, there may be some type of synergy (combined energy) which can become destructive. We would be alerted to this by dreaming of causing a nuclear explosion.

3 Spiritually, a nuclear explosion would suggest a discharge of power which, if not handled properly, could be destructive.

NUDE

1 Freud assumed that dreaming of being nude was linked with sexuality. It is, however, more to do with self-image. We have a desire to be seen for what we are, to reveal our essential personality without having to create a facade. To interpret a dream of **walking down a street naked** will depend on whether we are **seen by other people** or not. If we are seen by others, there may be something about ourselves which we wish to reveal. If we are **alone** we may simply have a wish for freedom of expression.

2 Nudity signifies innocence. It may be that there is a situation in our lives which requires honesty and truth. If we are sufficiently secure within our own self-image, we will not be afraid of being 'stripped' in public. Dreaming of appearing nude, for instance in a **strip show**, could suggest we

have anxiety about being misunderstood. We are conscious of the fact that we are prepared to be open and honest, but others may not understand.

3 Nudity can suggest a new beginning, a rebirth. It is the paradise state and the state of natural innocence we all, at one time, had. It can also represent renunciation of the material world.

NUGGET

1 More often than not a nugget is made of gold and therefore signifies the best part of a situation. In dreams we may find that there is a piece of information or knowledge that is represented by a nugget.

2 Precious metals are usually found in nuggets in a raw state. Often **gold** will represent the masculine, and **silver** the feminine. So, to find either in a dream signifies finding a part of ourselves that we did not know existed. It may be in a rough state, but with work can be made into something beautiful.

3 Spiritually a nugget will represent knowledge, power and psychic ability. It is the kernel of an idea or concept.

NUMBERS

1 When numbers are drawn to our attention in dreams they can have either a personal or a symbolic significance. Often a number will appear which has personal meaning, such as a particular date, or the number of a house we have lived in. Our minds will often retain the significance of the number even though we do not necessarily consciously remember it ourselves.

2 Symbolically numbers have some kind of significance in all systems of belief and religions. Below are the most often found meanings, which have been divided into three sub-sections.

a) Supposed practical everyday interpretations of numbers as seen in dreams:

One You will have outstanding skill in the work you do. **Two** Business or personal relationships need handling carefully. **Three** Your ideas for stability and success will materialise. **Four** A secure and sheltered home is yours for the asking. **Five** You are about to make an important discovery which will bring about changes. **Six** A loving relationship is available to you. **Seven** With personal effort you can solve your problems. **Eight** Your life holds the potential for a wonderful offer. **Nine** Take care not to overreach yourself. **Zero** The cipher holds within it all potential.

b) Summary of qualities represented by primary numbers:

One Independence, self-respect, resolve, singleness of purpose. Intolerance, conceit, narrow-mindedness, degradation, stubbornness. **Two** Placidity, integrity, unselfishness, gregariousness, harmony. Indecision, indifference, lack of responsibility, bloody-mindedness. **Three** Freedom, bravery, fun, enthusiasm, brilliance. Listlessness, over-confidence, impatience, lackadaisical behaviour. **Four** Loyalty, stolidity, practicality, honesty. Clumsiness, dullness, conservatism, unadaptibility. **Five** Adventurousness, vivaciousness, courage, health, susceptibility, sympathy. Rashness, irresponsibility, inconstancy, unreliability, thoughtlessness. **Six** Idealism, selflessness, honesty, charitableness, faithfulness, responsibility, superiority, softness, impracticality, submission. **Seven** Wisdom, discernment, philosophy, fortitude, depth, contemplation. Morbidness, hypercriticism, lack of action, unsociability. **Eight** Practicality, power, business ability, decision, control, constancy. Unimaginativeness, bluntness, self-sufficiency, domination. **Nine** Intelligence, discretion, artistry, understanding, brilliance, lofty moral sense, genius. Dreaminess, lethargy, lack of concentration, aimlessness.

c) The more esoteric interpretations are:

One Oneself, the beginning, the
first, unity. **Two** Duality, indecision, balance, male vs female, two
sides to an argument, opposites.
Three The triangle, freedom.
Four The square, strength,
stability practicality, the earth,
reality, the four sides of human
nature – sensation, feeling,
thought, intuition; earth, air, fire
and water. **Five** The human body,
human consciousness in the body,
the five senses. **Six** Harmony or
balance. **Seven** Cycles of life,
magical, spiritual meaning;
human wholeness. **Eight** Death
and resurrection, infinity. **Nine**
Pregnancy, the end of the cycle
and the start of something new,
spiritual awareness. **Ten** A new
beginning; the male and female
together. **Eleven** Eleventh hour,
the master number. **Twelve**
Time, a full cycle or wholeness.
Zero The Feminine, the Great
Mother, the unconscious, the
absolute or hidden completeness.

3 Spiritually, as we progress we put
ourselves in a position to make the
best use of the vibratory effect of
numbers. It has long been
accepted that by combining
numbers in certain ways, influence
can be brought to bear on the
dreamer's environment.

NUN
– see Carers in People

NURSE/NURSING
– see Carers in People

NUT

1 To dream of a metal nut, as in
nuts and bolts, is highlighting
our ability to construct our lives in
such a way that it will hold together.
In the old-fashioned sense a nut
was considered to be feminine,
and the screw masculine.

2 Edible nuts, because of their
shape, have significance as inner
nourishment. It was thought that
they fed the brain, thus giving
wisdom. They can still have this
significance in dreams. Again,
because of their shape, there is a
connection with masculine sexuality and fertility. To dream of nuts
may suggest that we are trying to
de-personalise issues to do with
sexuality.

3 Nuts were reputed to be the food
of the Gods, and so spiritually
enhance the psychic powers.

NYMPHS

1 Nymphs are personifications of
feminine universal productivity.
They have an innocent and carefree energy which is naive and
clear. They tend to be guardians of
sacred spaces such as woods,

mountains and lakes. In dreams, therefore, they are connected with a woman's sense of beauty and her own femininity.

2 Psychologically the nymph most clearly has associations with the princess *(see Princess in Archetypes and People)*. She is the carefree, fun-loving aspect of energy which glories in movement and light. As pure energy, when we work with dreams, the nymph allows us the opportunity to connect to the qualities of purity and grace.

3 Nymphs are Earth spirits that deal with pure energy. Their charm is their youthfulness, beauty and vitality. Each group of nymphs has their particular own role and guardianship of specific areas, such as forests and lakes, woods and valleys, mountains and grottoes. Dryads, for instance, do not mingle with others nymphs. Their significance spiritually is that they epitomise most of the feminine qualities in their purest states.

from

Oak *to* Oyster

O

OAK
– *see Trees*

OAR

1 The oar is a tool that enables a boat to move forward successfully, but its use requires some skill. Thus it stands for our own set of personal skills. We have certain skills which help us to 'navigate' our lives.

2 To put one's oar in indicates our ability to interfere with other people's lives. **To lose an oar** indicates the loss of an ability we have formerly valued.

3 An oar can suggest a Spiritual Tool, by nature of its guiding qualities, though ultimately it is we ourselves who have control over the direction we take.

OASIS

1 Most people see an oasis as a place of refuge in a desert. Because of its association with water, in dreams it becomes a place where we can receive whatever emotional refreshment we require.

2 When people are in difficulty, they need a place where they can express themselves – or perhaps renew their own strengths and ability to cope. In dreams an oasis, particularly when we are lost *(See Lost)*, represents such a place. It highlights a particular type of sanctuary.

3 An oasis in spiritual terms represents refreshment, and the idea of being able to slide away from old oppressions.

OATS

1 Oats in the form of **porridge** signify an almost 'magical' food. Because they have been used since time immemorial as a staple food, they represent warmth and comfort.

2 Wild oats obviously have a connection in people's minds with sexual satisfaction and freedom. To dream of **sowing grain** suggests that we are expecting to reap a benefit from a situation at a later date.

3 Because oats are a very 'humble' yet also a very satisfying food, to dream of them indicates the need for spiritual sustenance, and perhaps the desire to revert to a more simplistic outlook on life.

OBEDIENCE

1 When in dreams we **expect obedience from someone**, we are acknowledging our own power and authority over others. To dream of having to be **obedient to others** indicates we are aware of their greater authority and knowledge, and also of the disempowerment that has occurred.

2 If we find ourselves in the

position of **being obedient to someone we know** in an unexpected situation, we can often expect to have an easier relationship with them in the future, perhaps because we are able to acknowledge them in a different way.

3 To be obedient, in the spiritual sense, suggests a submission to the Greater Good, and after much struggle, to the spiritual side of oneself.

OBELISK

1 Any carved stone appearing in a dream suggests we are considering how we have shaped our own basic nature. The simpler it is, the more room we have for improvement; the more ornate it is, the more successful we are at using our creative energy.

2 An obelisk often represents a marker outlining a particular area – such as a sacred space. It can also represent old instinctive knowledge.

3 An obelisk is often representative of a Sacred Stone, and therefore the dreamer needs to be clear regarding his spiritual beliefs.

OBLIGATION

1 When we find ourselves **under an obligation** to one of our dream characters we are being reminded of our innate sense of duty. We may feel that we have done, or need to do, something for them which, in our heart of hearts, we do not feel is appropriate for us.

2 If we are conscious of **others' obligation to us** we need to be certain we are not forcing our will within a situation.

3 To feel obliged in a dream may lead us to the performance of a spiritual task or duty that we may, subconsciously, have been putting off.

OBSCENITY

1 Often dreams will link with the lower aspects of ourselves, those parts we will not normally face in waking life. To have obscenity appear in a dream allows us to deal with these impulses safely, in a non-judgmental way.

2 Often obscenity is connected with our perception of ourselves. If we are **performing obscene acts**, we need to be aware of suppressed impulses. If such acts are **performed against us**, we need to decide how we are being victimised in our daily lives.

3 Obscenity is sometimes associated with acts of evil. If the dreamer identifies with this link, then he may need to be aware of his own interpretations of evil and evil-doing.

OBSESSION

1 Obsession is an unnatural focusing on a feeling, belief or object, and may simply indicate that we need to take time to work a difficulty through. There is often anxiety about some past occasion or deed, with which we have not been able, or allowed, to deal. When such an unnatural feeling appears in dreams we can appreciate how harmful this can be.

2 Obsessive or repetitive behaviour in dreams is often used to ensure that the dreamer has fully understood the message being conveyed by the unconscious.

3 Obsession can come in the shape of spiritual possession. However, possession by a spirit does not necessarily indicate evil. It will be up to the dreamer to decide on which side of the Spiritual coin the obsession lies.

OBSTACLE

1 Obstacles in dreams can take many forms – a wall, a hill, a dark forest, etc. Largely, we are aware that these obstacles need to be overcome. How we do this in a dream can often suggest how to tackle a problem in everyday life.

2 Indecision and self-doubt can often translate themselves in dreams into actual physical objects. At times, our own inhibitions and anxieties cannot be faced unless we give them tangible forms.

3 Difficulty, indecision and doubt are the three main blocks one will come up against in this particular spiritual 'obstacle course'. The dreamer will have to scale each one if he is to finally achieve his spiritual goal.

OCCULT

1 Occult actually means 'hidden', so for someone to dream of the Occult when they have no knowledge of the subject usually suggests the need to come to terms with all their hidden fears. Most people tend to think of the Occult in its negative sense, as in black magic or Satanism, and thus may link with the egotistical side of their natures.

2 If the dreamer has Occult knowledge it may be important to apply that awareness in an everyday situation. The rule is always then 'harm no-one'.

3 In dreams, the Occult, due to its many strange facets, may well be alerting the dreamer to an as yet untapped arcane wisdom.

OCEAN
– see Water

OCTOPUS

1 Because the octopus has eight

legs, it picks up on the symbolism of the mandala *(see Mandala)*. Often the tentacles can have particular significance, indicating that we can be drawn into something that we find frightening and from which we cannot escape.

2 Creatures that are unusual and are not familiar to us appear in dreams to alert us to certain qualities within ourselves. The octopus is capable of moving in any direction and it is this symbolism we need to be aware of.

3 An octopus can represent the unrestricted movement of the Spirit.

ODOUR
– also see Perfume and Smell

1 If there is an odour in a dream it is usually highly significant and will highlight whatever is happening. If it is a **pleasant one** it suggests good times; if a **bad one** then it is more likely to be a warning of bad things.

2 Our sense of smell is extremely delicate, but just as the use of other senses is suspended or transmuted into something slightly different, an odour in a dream may be a way of reminding ourselves of another time or place.

3 A sweet odour in spiritual terms always signifies saintliness and spirituality.

OFFENCE
1 To take offence in a dream is to allow a display of emotion and feeling about our own sensitivity which may not be appropriate in waking life. **To give offence** to someone in a dream is to recognise that we are not as aware of other people's feelings as we should be.

2 To be committing an offence suggests that we are not, either consciously or unconsciously, following our own code of moral behaviour. We have put ourselves outside the norms of society.

3 A suggestion of spiritual wrongdoing may be relevant. It is, however, for the dreamer to assess the seriousness of the offence and then to act accordingly.

OFFICE
1 Often our work or office situation gives an environment in dreams with which we feel comfortable. It is slightly more formal than our home, and often deals with our feelings about, or our relationship with, work and authority.

2 To be in an office, particularly if it is not known to us, would suggest some kind of order or bureaucracy is necessary in our lives. **To be in office**, in the sense of holding a post, signifies taking responsibility for what we do.

3 An office in spiritual terms suggests having taken responsibility for who we are.

OFFICER/OFFICIAL
– also see Authority Figures in People

1 To be dreaming of an officer, unless we have a relationship with that person in real life, is to be looking at that part of ourselves which co-ordinates and directs our lives. Any official figure, and particularly one in uniform *(see Uniform)*, alerts us to that part of our being which needs to belong to an organised group. On a conscious level we may rebel, but there is a part of ourselves which recognises that we must fit in some way.

2 Often, if our father has been particularly strict or overbearing, we picture him in dreams as an officer. We learnt in childhood to conform to authority. Interestingly, different armed forces will represent different aspect of our personality. The **Army** will signify the more down-to-earth practical side, the **Air Force** the intellectual, and the **Navy** the freedom-loving, more emotional side.

3 The need for Spiritual Authority may well be represented here. The dreamer is seeking a higher guidance, and needs to be 'told' what to do.

OGRE
– see Archetypes

OIL

1 It will depend on which type of oil is being used in the dream. **Cooking oil** will often signify the removal of friction, or a way of combining different components. **Massage oil** suggests caring and pampering, whereas **engine oil** will highlight our ability to keep things moving.

2 Psychologically, we may recognise that a situation can only be dealt with by removing the stress, e.g. 'Pour oil on troubled water.'

3 Consecration and dedication.

OINTMENT

1 Dreaming of ointment means we need to be aware of the part of ourselves that either needs, or is capable of, healing. The kind of ointment will often give information as to what we need. For instance, to be dreaming of a **well-known brand** can suggest a non-specific type of healing, whereas an ointment that has been **prepared specifically for the dreamer** suggests a more focused approach.

2 Since Pagan times, ointments have been used to preserve and to prevent decay. Often the use of ointments was a mark of respect, and this symbolism can still apply in dreams today.

3 Ointment can point to our Spiritual need to care and heal, or alternatively, our need to be cared for.

OLD/ANCIENT/ ANTIQUE

1 When we dream of old things, we are touching into the past and perhaps need to bring some kind of knowledge forward, so that we can make use of it in the present day. Dreaming of **historical figures** usually means we are aware of the qualities that those people possessed. Perhaps we need to develop those qualities within ourselves.

2 Old people in dreams tend to suggest traditional thought or wisdom arising from experience *(see People)*. We may also need to consider our attitude to death. **Old buildings** can signify a past way of life which we thought we had left behind. **Antiques** will often represent elements of our past experience which might be worth keeping.

3 The **Wise Old Man** *(see Introduction)* is a part of ourselves which is not always consciously available to us. An old man appearing in our dreams puts us in touch with this part of ourselves.

He can also represent our feelings about time and death.

ONION
– also see Food

1 Oddly enough, the onion can appear in dreams and meditation as a symbol of wholeness, but a wholeness which is many-layered. **Peeling an onion** can suggest trying to find the best part of ourselves, or of somebody else. It may also indicate attempting to understand the various facets of our personality.

2 Chopping onions can signify an attempt to increase the energy available to us in some way.

3 The Cosmos, revelation.

OPAL
– see Jewels

OPERA

1 To be attending an opera in a dream suggests observing the 'drama' of a situation around us (it may be more appropriate to observe rather than take part). To **be taking part** in an opera highlights our need for some kind of dramatic input into our lives.

2 When we find ourselves **singing in an opera**, we should be able to express ourselves in a more dramatic and tutored way within everyday situations.

3 The Drama of Life.

OPERATION
– also see Hospital and Surgery

1 An operation in hospital is frightening and invasive. In dreams it can signify our awareness of our own fears of illness and pain, but also a recognition of our need to be healed.

2 If we are performing an operation we are recognising our own level of skill within a situation in waking life. **If the operation is being performed on us** we are attempting to access some inner knowledge but are possibly fearful of the outcome.

3 Incisive Healing.

OPTICIAN

1 To be **visiting an optician** in a dream probably indicates that we do not feel we can see a situation clearly – we need assistance. It may also indicate that we need to develop a new way of looking at things.

2 The optician in a dream may suggest that we need to understand the skill of seeing. This may also signify clairvoyance.

3 This dream indicates our ability to enhance our perceptions.

ORACLE

1 Most of us like to know what is going to happen to us and also like to be told what to do, so dreaming of an oracle links us with that part of ourselves which knows what our next moves are. Often an oracle can appear as a person, for instance as a goddess or wise old man, or we can dream that we are using one of the many systems of prediction which are available in everyday life.

2 The need to know is very strong and the assumption is that an oracle has more information than we do. Often that information has to be unscrambled, since it is presented in odd ways and sometimes it cannot be made sense of until such time as we have considered it in waking life.

3 Prediction and Hidden Knowledge.

ORANGE
– see Colour and Fruit

ORCHARD

1 In dreams an orchard may represent our attempts to look after ourselves. It will depend on whether the trees are showing flowers or fruit. If they are showing **flowers** then this will represent the potential we have for success; if they are showing **fruit** we are being reassured as to the harvest we may gather.

2 Any collection of trees can

represent our own fertility. As an orchard tends to be more ordered than, for instance, a forest, dreaming of one indicates we are appreciating the more structured side of our personalities.

3 Fertility.

ORCHESTRA
– also see Music, Musical Instruments and Organist

1 We all have certain aspects of our personality which must work in harmony with one another for us to function properly. Dreaming of an orchestra represents ways in which we can bring all those aspects together and make a coherent whole.

2 When we wish to orchestrate something, we want to make it happen. This occasionally means that we must take action which enables us to be heard and to have people understand us. When we find we are **conducting an orchestra** in a dream, we feel we can accept we are in control. When we are a **member of an orchestra** we are simply part of a greater task.

3 We are capable of operating in spiritual harmony.

ORE

1 Ore is a crude material which needs refining in order to make it usable. In dreams this can represent the resources we have available, although this may be initially rather crude. It can also represent new ideas, thoughts and concepts which have not yet been totally understood.

2 Whenever any basic material – such as ore – appears in a dream, the unconscious is asking us to 'dig for information'. It may not present itself as usable material to begin with but will need working on to enable us to make use of the information we have.

3 Basic spiritual knowledge can be revealed.

ORGAN

1 The various organs of the body can represent the different aspects of the self. In dreams they can signify diverse weaknesses and strengths. A **musical organ** will tend to highlight the dreamer's views and feelings about religion. In slang terms, the organ suggests the penis.

2 In Chinese medicine, the different organs of the body represent different qualities. For instance, the gall bladder deals with the ability to make decisions, while the liver is the seat of irritability. In dreams, therefore, being conscious of a bodily organ would require us to be aware of what is bothering us and dealing with it in an appropriate manner.

3 Spiritually, perfect health of mind and body would be possible provided we understood the workings of the physical body. If we know what perfect is, then self- healing would ensure proper working of the organs.

ORGANIST
– also see Orchestra

1 The organist as an image is the part of us which knows how to make use of the various vibrations of which we are formed. When we dream of such a figure we are appreciative of the fact that, as with an orchestra, the various notes that we play can be brought into harmony. This, however, requires some skill in making the sounds available.

2 Expressing ourselves successfully is a learnt skill. The organist represents that part of us which is prepared to be disciplined and determined in order to enable us to be listened to and heard properly.

3 The Higher Self.

ORGY

1 An orgy relates to a tremendous release of energy which can take place when we give ourselves permission to access our own sexuality. This permission will often be given subconsciously first, and can be expressed in dreams more fully than we would allow ourselves to do in everyday life. To dream of an orgy can also highlight the way we relate to other people. The need for other people to love and understand us is quite strong and, when seen as an orgy, can perhaps indicate that we are afraid of loss of control.

2 Often our dreams will express a difficulty or blockage we may have in any one area of our lives. Since most people's self-image is very much connected with their sexuality, dreaming of an orgy can indicate the way in which we can release the blocked energy. Behaviour which would not necessarily be appropriate in ordinary everyday life can be used in dreams to balance the difficulty.

3 Spiritual excess.

ORIENT

1 For many people the Oriental or Eastern way of life is seen as being very exotic. Dreaming of this may give us access to that part of us which becomes suppressed by the demands of everyday life.

2 The Oriental way of life appears to be more gentle and perhaps more intuitive than the Western. In dreams we tend to link with that side of ourselves which has access to wisdom and clarity. This tends to be quite a feminine way of working, so the figure often appears as an oriental woman *(also see Woman in People)*.

3 Transcendental wisdom.

ORNAMENT

1 It will depend on whether the ornament seen in a dream belongs to us as to what the interpretation is. Dreaming of **personal ornamentation** *(see Necklace and Jewels)* suggests an attempt to enhance something that we have and value, but that we want to make more valuable. In dream terms this can represent either our feelings, emotions or ideas.

2 To be conscious of ornaments in a dream tends to indicate that our personal space can be used more fully and therefore bring us greater success. We are not simply going back to basics but are actively improving our situation.

3 Tangible and recognisable spirituality.

ORPHAN

1 To dream of an orphan indicates that we may be feeling vulnerable and possibly abandoned and unloved. If we are **looking after an orphan** we are attempting to heal that part of us that feels unloved. If we experi-

ence ourselves as **having been orphaned** it may indicate that we need to be more independent and self-sufficient.

2 We have to come to terms with our ability to grow up and to move away from our parents. When our lives force us into losing them, either by death or other circumstances such as moving away, we may experience the feeling of being orphaned.

3 Spiritual desertion.

OSTEOPATH

1 In dreams an osteopath would signify our need to manipulate the circumstances of our lives to a point where we are comfortable. Because an osteopath heals, for one to appear in a dream would suggest concern over health matters and how the body works.

2 Oddly enough, because an osteopath manipulates the physical body, such a person appearing in a dream could alert us to manipulation that is going on in everyday life. Psychologically, any healing treatment is going to have an effect on the energy within the body and we often need to be conscious of the subtle changes necessary in our lives.

3 On a spiritual level an osteopath may represent a kind of spiritual manipulation or change.

OSTRICH
– see Birds

OTTER
– see Animals

OUIJA BOARD

1 The use of the ouija board holds within it certain inherent dangers. Dreaming of one may simply be a way that the psyche has of alerting us to further exploration of those things we do not understand. To be **playing with the ouija board** in dreams – as well as in waking life – denotes being prepared to take certain risks, particularly with our own peace of mind. When the **ouija board seems frightening** we are touching in on our deep fear of the unknown.
2 Psychologically, we all need some way of making contact with the unconscious side of ourselves. To dream of the ouija board alerts us to different ways of accessing the unconscious. It may be a symbol for all we have suppressed and refused to recognise.
3 Spiritually, the ouija board was – and indeed still is – a rather crude way of communicating with the spirit world. In dreams, it shows we may be aware of the need to communicate with spirit, rather than have the spirit world communicate with us.

OUROBOROS

3 Spiritually the ouroboros represents completion. Usually depicted as a serpent which is eating its own tail, it denotes never-ending energy and everlasting power. It will usually appear in dreams when the dreamer is ready to deal with, and understand, complete spiritual self-sufficiency.

OUTLAW

1 Inherent in the figure of the outlaw is someone who has gone against the laws of society. In dreams therefore, that part of ourselves which feels that it is beyond the law will appear as the outlaw. To be **shooting the outlaw** is attempting to control our wilder urges.
2 Psychologically, we all have a part in us that is anarchical or wishes to rebel. Occasionally this can appear as a **person of the opposite sex**, in which case we are dealing with the Anima/Animus *(see Introduction)*. If however, the outlaw is of the **same sex** as the dreamer, then we are dealing with the Shadow *(see Introduction)*.
3 To put ourselves beyond the reach of spiritual law, wide-ranging though it may be, is to play a dangerous game which may have to be paid for in various ways in the future.

OVAL
– see Shapes

OWL
– see Birds

OVEN
- Also See Baker

1 An oven is representative of the human ability to transfer raw ingredients into something palatable. In dreams, therefore, this can suggest the ability to transform character traits and behaviour from something coarse to the more refined.

2 As a hollow object, in dreams an oven can also represent the womb. With its ability to change ingredients into something else, the oven can also represent the process of gestation and birth.

3 The oven represents the transmutation of base qualities, and thus suggests spiritual transformation.

OX
– see Animals

OYSTER

1 The oyster is reputed to be an aphrodisiac food. In dreams it can therefore represent the sexual act or anything associated with sex.

2 The oyster is almost unique because of its ability to transform a grain of sand into a pearl. It is this quality which tends to be brought to notice in dreams to demonstrate how we can change an irritant into something beautiful.

3 The oyster represents spiritual transformation. We can build on negative qualities in our lives without trying to eradicate them completely.

P

from

Packing *to* Pyramid

PACKING
– also see Wadding

1 When we dream of **packing suitcases**, as though going on a journey, we are highlighting the need to prepare carefully for the next stage of our lives. There is a need, or want, to get away from past ideas and difficulties. To be **packing a precious object** very carefully, indicates we are aware of the intrinsic value to ourselves, or others, of what is represented by that object.

2 We need to establish some kind of order in our lives. To dream of packing suggests an internal selection process must be undertaken in order to decide what is important to us.

3 We need to make a choice about relevant spiritual information and decide what needs to be retained.

PADLOCK

1 Dreaming of **locking a padlock** suggests that we are attempting to shut something (perhaps a feeling or emotion) away. This may either be through fear or possessiveness. Conversely, if we are **opening a padlock** we may be trying to open up to new experiences.

2 Often when our security is threatened, a symbol which reinforces our need for defence mechanisms appears, and the padlock comes into this category.

3 We are preserving our spiritual integrity.

PAGODA
– see Temple in Buildings

PAINTING

1 Often in waking life we will not recognise our own creative ability, and **to be painting** in a dream may alert us to other talents we have not realised we possess. We may not actually have the ability to paint successfully in everyday life. **To be looking at paintings** in dreams indicates that we are questioning or paying attention to ideas and concepts of which we have not been consciously aware. **Painting as in decorating** suggests we are making recognisable changes how we think and feel.

2 Because painting has such a lot to do with self-expression, the way that we are painting in a dream may be important. If, for instance, we are **painting miniatures** we may need to concentrate on detail. If we are painting **large pictures** we may need to adopt a more global perspective. Colour in a painting is also important *(see Colour)*.

3 We are creating a spiritual scenario.

PAIRS

1 The unconscious mind appears to sort information by comparing and contrasting. Particularly when we are aware of conflict within ourselves, we may dream in pairs (e.g. old/young, masculine/feminine, clever/stupid). It is almost as though there is some kind of internal pendulum, which eventually sorts out the opposites into a unified whole.

2 A dream clarifying the masculine side of ourselves may be followed by a dream clarifying the feminine. The juggling that goes on in this way can take place over a period of time. Often in dream interpretation looking at the opposite meaning to the obvious can give us greater insight into our mental processes.

3 The use of pairs in dreams is trying to achieve a Spiritual balance.

PALACE
– see Castle in Buildings

PALM

1 To see a palm tree in a dream is most often to do with rest and relaxation. Previously the palm was associated with honour and victory, but as foreign holidays have become more available it has largely lost that significance.

2 The **palm of the hand** is significant as a symbol of generosity and openness.

3 The palm in spiritual terms suggests blessings and goodness.

PAN, POT

1 In dreams a pan or a pot signifies nurturing and caring. It can also suggest a receptive frame of mind.

2 Just as a cauldron can be taken to indicate the transformative process, so a pan can suggest the ability to combine several 'ingredients' to make something completely different.

3 As always, any receptacle suggests the containing Feminine Principle, usually the nurturing side.

PANTHER
– see Animals

PANTOMIME

1 For many people the pantomime is a happy childhood memory, and often appears in dreams as a reminder of happier times. It can also suggest the more spontaneous, humorous side of our nature.

2 Because the images associated with pantomime are often exaggerated and larger than life, the pantomime can be used in dreams as a setting to draw our attention to something of which we need to be aware.

3 Most images connected with the theatre suggest the idea of life being a play. In the case of pantomime it is a very surreal image.

PAPER

1 Paper is one of those images which, in dreams, is dependent on the circumstances in the dreamer's life. For instance, in a **student's** life, paper would suggest the need to pay attention to the studies. In a **postman's** life there may be job anxieties, whereas **festive wrapping paper** could indicate the need for, or the possibility of, celebration.

2 Blank writing paper points to a lack of communication, or need to communicate with someone, but can also suggest a new beginning. **Brown paper** can highlight the utilitarian side of the dreamer's nature.

3 There is potential for Spiritual growth through both learning and creativity.

PARACHUTE

1 Dreaming of a parachute suggests that, whatever is happening to us in real life, we have protection that will see us through. It may also indicate that we are able to face our anxieties and still succeed – at least in part.

2 Parachuting as a sport has become very popular, and such a sense of freedom and adventure can easily become apparent in dreams.

3 There is intellectual freedom in the image of parachuting. We have the ability to rise above the mundane.

PARADISE

1 To dream of Paradise is to link with the dreamer's innate ability to be perfect. We can experience total harmony within ourselves, and be totally innocent.

2 Psychologically, Paradise is that part of ourselves which is enclosed within and does not need to be available to anyone else. It is separate and the part from which we can develop perfect union with the universe.

3 To dream of Paradise is to be aware of the perfect Soul. In this state there is no right and no wrong, only completion.

PARALYSIS
– also see Immobility

1 When paralysis is felt in a dream we are probably experiencing great fear or suppression. Feelings that are emotionally based are experienced as paralysis in order to highlight the physical effect those feelings can have.

2 Imagination can often play tricks

on us, and we experience as real some kind of reaction we would not normally allow ourselves. Paralysis is one such reaction.

3 Paralysis can signify spiritual inadequacy, inability to create movement, and inertia. There is a condition which sometimes occurs during development when we are forced into facing our own fears, and this can be experienced as paralysis.

PARASITES

1 Parasites such as **lice, fleas or bugs** in a dream suggest that we may be aware that someone is attempting to live off our energy in some way. Our lifestyle may, to them, appear to be exciting and more interesting than their own or provide them with amusement.

2 We may feel unclean in some aspect of our lives which makes us ashamed or uncomfortable. We are aware that we cannot exist without support.

3 We realise that we are not satisfied with our own lives and why we may be living vicariously.

PARCEL, PACKAGE
– also see Address

1 When we **receive a parcel** in a dream, we are being made aware of something we have experienced but not explored. At this stage, we

do not quite know what the potential of the gift is, but by exploration can find this out. When we are **sending a parcel or package** we are sending our energy out into the world.

2 Parcels and packages in dreams can also represent the gifts that one receives from others. It can often be important to note who is actually giving us the gift, whether it is being directly received from the person concerned or whether we are simply aware who the donor is and that it is something that we can receive with joy.

3 Parcels and packages can suggest latent potential and gifts or skills.

PARENTS
– see Family and Archetypes

PARLIAMENT

1 Dreaming of parliament often alerts us to that part of ourselves that is involved in decision-making. The higher aspects of Self have a degree of authority over us and are, if you like, the part of ourselves that deals with the Greater Good. Parliament thus represents those parts that connect us with the rest of the world.

2 Any gathering of people is important in a dream, since it shows us how we relate to that group. To dream that we are in the

Houses of Parliament represents that we are in a decision-making place; we may not be capable of making decisions which affect other people, but we do have access to that space.

3 Parliament should stand for Spiritual Clarity.

PARROT
– see Duck in Birds

PARTY

1 When we find we are **attending a party** in a dream, we are often alerted to our social skills – or lack of such skills. In waking life we may be shy and dislike such gatherings, but in dreams if we are coping with the groups involved, we have a greater awareness of our own belonging. To belong to a **political party** would indicate that we are prepared to stand up for our beliefs, that we have made a commitment to a particular way of life.

2 The human being often has need of celebration in his or her life. To be attending a party in a dream can indicate our need for celebration, for joining with other people to create a potentially happy atmosphere.

3 When a group celebrates a belief, which can be spiritual, it is an occasion for a party or festival.

PARSLEY

1 In Pagan times parsley was considered to have mystic powers. Like all herbs, it was used very specifically in teas and flavourings to achieve certain results. We still, at some level of awareness, hold this knowledge, so when parsley appears in a dream we are linking with this information.

2 One of the qualities of parsley is as a cleanser, or purifier, and it is as this that it may appear in dreams. We are aware that we need to get rid of something which is contaminating us.

3 Parsley is a symbol for the Feminine Principle and occult awareness.

PASSAGE
– see Hall/Passages in Buildings

PASSPORT

1 The passport is normally taken to prove one's identity. In waking life, we may experience difficulty in maintaining a good self-image and in dreams may reassure ourselves by producing a passport.

2 Often the passport can appear as a symbol of the permission we need to obtain from ourselves or others to move on to new things or situations.

3 A passport to a better life can be achieved by Spiritual Awareness.

PATH

1 A path in a dream signifies the direction one has decided to take in life. The type of path, e.g. whether it is **smooth or rocky, winding or straight**, may be just as important as the path itself.
2 Often a path can represent the way we feel a relationship or situation is developing. It can also suggest a way of following up a concept or line of enquiry. In waking life, it is often the way a clairvoyant 'sees' the way in which the enquirer's life is changing.
3 A path in a dream can indicate a Spiritual direction.

PATTERN
– see Shape

PAWN-SHOP

1 Dreaming of a pawn-shop can indicate that we are not being sufficiently careful with the resources, whether material or emotional, that we possess. We may be taking risks which we need to consider more carefully.
2 We are aware that certain attributes and characteristics we have are being appropriated by other people, leaving us with nothing of value.
3 Spiritually, a pawn-shop may represent an inappropriate use of the resources that we have. We

may not be creating a correct exchange of energy.

PEACOCK
– see Birds

PEARL
– see Jewels

PEDESTAL

1 When we become conscious in a dream that something has been placed on a pedestal we have obviously attempted to make that thing special. We have elevated it to a position of power.
2 Most human beings have a tendency to idolise or worship certain characteristics. Dreams will often show the appropriateness – or otherwise – of such an action.
3 Putting someone or something on a pedestal suggests spiritual worship and idolatry, which can impede one's spiritual journey if that worship is misplaced.

PELICAN
– see Birds

PEN/PENCIL
– also see Ink

1 If a pen or pencil appears in a dream we are expressing or recognising the need to communicate with other people. **If the pen will not work** we do not understand information we have been given. **If we cannot find one** we do not have enough information to proceed with an aspect of our lives.

2 We all have an ability to learn but need to have some way of transmitting our learning to other people. A pen would suggest the learning would be more permanent than a pencil.

3 The powers to transcribe spiritual knowledge and to keep a record of that information are a necessary part of development. Dreaming of a pen or pencil may suggest that we could attempt automatic writing.

PENDANT
– see Necklace

PENGUIN
– see Birds

PENTACLE/ PENTANGLE/ PENTAGRAM
– see Star in Shapes

PEOPLE

1 The people who appear in dreams are the characters with which we write our 'play'. Often they appear simply as themselves, particularly if they are people we know or have a relationship with

in the here and now. We may introduce them in order to highlight a specific quality or characteristic. We may also permit them into our dream scenario as projections of our inner life or state of being. Finally, they may signify someone who is more important than the dreamer.

2 In order to disentangle the various types of 'information' which each character brings to the dreamer, it is often necessary to decide what or who each one makes us think of. That way we will reveal the deeper meanings and connections.

An individual from the past could link us with that period of our lives and with specific memories which may, or may not, be painful. **A neighbour** or close associate usually appears in a dream to highlight a particular quality in that person. **Somebody else's mother, father, brother etc.** may suggest our own family members or possibly jealousy. Sometimes, rather than trying to decipher the meaning of the dream it is enough to look at what bearing the dream character's actions have on the dreamer's everyday life. To interpret why the dreamer has adopted a particular role we would need to know a little bit more about his lifestyle. When there is some conflict within the dreamer between love and aversion for a particular person, we are more likely to dream about them. Often in dreams there may be a noted difference between two of the participants to illustrate two sides of the dreamer's thoughts and feelings. Similarly, there may be a marked contrast in the way the dreamer handles a situation with two of his dream characters. It is as though two options are being practised. **Composite characters** As with composite animals, the composite character will emphasise one characteristic or quality in order to draw the dreamer's attention to it. The fact that it is not just one person emphasises the many-faceted human being. Every character who appears in our dreams is a reflection of a facet or part of our own personality and can often be better understood if we put ourselves in the position of that person. **Adolescent** To dream of **oneself as adolescent** focuses on our undeveloped side. Dreaming of an **adolescent of the opposite sex** usually means dealing with a suppressed part of our development. The emotions associated with adolescence are very raw and clear and such emotions are accessible often only

through dreams. There may be conflict over freedom.

Ancestors Our customs, ways of behaving, morality and our religious feelings are all handed down from generation to generation. When we become conscious of our ancestors in a dream we are focusing on our roots. We may understand ourselves through our relationship with the past.

Authority Figures *(such as magistrates, teachers etc. – also see individual entries)* Our concept of authority is first developed through our relationship with our father or father figure. Depending on how we were treated as children, our view of authority will be anything from a benign helper to an exploitative disciplinarian. Most authority figures will ultimately lead us back to what is right for us, although not necessarily what we might consider good for us. Authority figures in dreams initially appear to have power over us, though if worked with properly will generate the power to succeed. Dreaming particularly of **police** can indicate a kind of social control and a protective element for us as members of society. Often a policeman will appear in dreams as one's conscience. We may feel that our wilder, more renegade side needs controlling.

Baby To dream about a **baby which is our own** indicates that we need to recognise those vulnerable feelings over which we have no control. We may be attempting something new. If the **baby is someone else's** in the dream, we need to be aware of that person's ability to be hurt, or that they may be innocent of something. Psychologically we are in touch with the innocent, curious side of ourselves, with the part which neither wants nor needs responsibility. Dreaming of a baby can indicate that, on a spiritual level, the dreamer has a need for a feeling of purity.

Boy To have a dream about a boy shows the potential for growth and new experience. If the **boy is known** he reflects recognised qualities in the dreamer. Psychologically, we may need to be in touch with ourselves at that age and with the innocent youthfulness and enthusiasm that a boy has. We are contacting our natural drives and ability to face difficulties.

Boyfriend To dream of a boyfriend, **whether present or former**, connects with the feelings, attachments and sexuality connected with him. To dream of having as a boyfriend **someone whom you would not anticipate**, indicates the need to have a greater understanding of the way you relate to men. Consideration may need to be given to the loving, nurturing side of masculinity. We are still searching for the ideal lover.

Carers such as nurses, nuns etc. This suggests the more compassionate, nurturing side of ourselves. Often it is that side of us which has been 'called' or has a vocation. Usually there is, for men, a non-sexual relationship.

Child (who could be one of the dreamer's own children) Dreaming of a child gives us access to our own inner child. We all have parts of ourselves which are still child-like and curious. When we are able to get in touch with that side of ourselves we give ourselves permission to clarify a potential for wholeness which we may not previously have recognised.

Crowd Crowds in dreams can indicate how we relate to other people, particularly in a social sense. They may indicate how we can hide ourselves, or indeed how we hide aspects of ourselves and do not single out any one attribute. We may also be attempting to avoid responsibility. A **huge crowd** suggests information which we may not be able to handle.

Dictators (Hitler, Stalin etc.) If the dreamer has had an

353

overbearing father, a known dictator may appear in dreams as representing that relationship.

Emperor or Empress – *see Authority Figures and also King and Queen*

Ethnic minority Any aspect within ourselves which is out of the ordinary or different can manifest in dreams as a member of another race.

Girl When a girl of any age appears in our dreams we are usually attempting to make contact with the more sensitive, innocent side of ourselves. Those qualities of intuition and perception may be somewhat undeveloped but can be made available. If the girl is **known to us** we probably are aware of those qualities, but need to explore them as though we were approaching them from the girl's point of view. If **she is unknown**, we can acknowledge that a fresh approach would be useful.

Girlfriend When a girlfriend or ex-girlfriend appears **in a man's dream** there are usually issues to do with masculinity and femininity involved. There may be fears to do with sexuality. If a girlfriend appears **in a woman's dream**, there can either be a concern about her in the dreamer's mind, or she (the dreamer) needs to search for – and find – qualities belonging to the friend in her.

Hero or any heroic figure *(also see Archetypes)* **In a man's dream** the figure of the hero can represent all that is good in him, the Higher Self. **In a woman's dream** he will suggest the Animus *(see Introduction)*. **When the hero is on a quest** We are struggling to find a part of ourselves which is at this time unconscious *(also see Quest)*. It is important that the darker forces are vanquished – but not killed – since they cannot be totally annihilated without harming the Wise Old Man *(see Introduction)*. In other words, our eventual integration still needs the challenge of the negative. **The hero's failure may be brought about inadvertently** We all have a weak point through which we can be attacked. To have such a dream indicates that we are not paying attention to the details in our lives or to that part of ourselves we tend not to have developed. We may be being warned of an element of self-neglect. **The death of the hero** can often suggest the need to develop the more intuitive side of ourselves, to be born again to something new. A **conflict between the hero and any other dream character** suggests a basic disharmony between two facets of our own character. The hero often appears in dreams as an antidote to some hated external figure within the dreamer's everyday life.

High Priest, Astrologer, or anyone with similar esoteric knowledge *(also see Archetypes and Authority Figures in this section)* Any character within our dreams who appears to have knowledge of magical practices or similar types of knowledge is usually first introduction to the Higher Self. It is as though we can only become privy to this deeper knowledge by meeting our teacher first.

Inadequate Person It is a lot easier to confront our own inadequacies in the dream state where we are safe. Often this is the first opportunity we have to meet the Shadow *(See Introduction)*. We ignore this aspect of ourselves at our peril and cannot afford to dismiss such an image when it appears. We must acknowledge this dream figure as a reflection of ourselves in order to deal with a learnt sense of inferiority. If we do not, we are continually faced in life by our own sense of inferiority.

Intruder *(also see individual entry and Burglar)* The intruder **in a woman's dream** is often a personification of her own Animus *(see Introduction)*. **In a man's dream** it characterises his Shadow *(see Introduction)*. In either case it suggests the need for a change in attitude in order for the dreamer to be able to have a full and meaningful relationship with himself.

King Almost invariably a king appearing in a dream represents the father or father figure. A personality such as **an emperor** may indicate that some of the father's attitudes are alien to the dreamer, but should perhaps be accepted. When **the king is old or on the point of dying** the dreamer will be able to reject outworn or old-fashioned family values.

Ministers of all Religions *(also see Authority Figures in this section and Archetypes)* Ministers of all religions hold a special place in the dream hierarchy, since their authority is given to them not by man alone, but to all intents and purposes by God or an ultimate power. There is therefore an 'otherness' about them.

Man Any man appearing in a dream shows an aspect or facet of the dreamer's character in a recognisable form. Each of us has a repertoire or portfolio of behaviours, some of which are acceptable and some of which are not. In dreams those behaviours and characteristics can be magnified so that they are easily identified, often as personalities. By working with the characteristic, more energy and power becomes available. Even when we are threatened by a negative character trait, we can still access room for improvement. A **man in a dream** can identify the Shadow for a man, and the Animus for a woman *(see Introduction)*. An **older man** (if the man is white-haired or holy) can represent the innate wisdom we all have. Such a person can also signify the father in dreams. When a **large man** appears in our dreams we are usually appreciating the strengths, certainties and protection which our basic beliefs give us. A **man in a woman's dream** signifies the more logical side of her nature. She has, or can develop, all the aspects of the masculine which enable her to function with success in the external world. If the **man is one she knows or loves** she may be trying to understand her relationship with him. **An unknown man** is generally that part of the dreamer's personality which is not recognised. In a woman's dream it is the masculine side of herself, and in a man's dream it is the Self *(see Introduction)*.

Old People *(also see Man and Woman)* In dreams, old people can represent either our **ancestors or grandparents**, hence

wisdom accrued from experience. If the old person is **male** – depending on the gender of the dreamer – he will stand for either the Self or the Animus *(see Introduction)*. If **female** then she will signify the Great Mother or the Anima *(see Introduction)*. All father figures, or representations of the father, will often appear old as if to highlight their remoteness. **A group of old people** often appears in dreams. Usually this signifies the traditions and wisdom of the past – things sacred to the 'tribe' or family. Older people usually stand for our parents even though the dream figures may bear no relationship to them.

Pirate Dreaming of a pirate suggests there is an aspect of our personality which destroys our emotional connection with the soul.

Prince (Hero) and Princess *(also see Archetypes)* These figures represent those parts of ourselves, or others, who exist by right; that is, those aspects which have been brought into conscious awareness and authority. As the hero has taken responsibility for his own journey, so the prince and princess take responsibility for the lives they live.

Queen (Not only the present queen, but a historical one

such as Victoria) This usually represents the dreamer's relationship with his mother, and thus with women in authority generally.

Stranger *(also see Shadow in Introduction)* The stranger in a dream represents that part of ourselves which we do not yet know. There may be a feeling of awe or of conflict with which we need to deal before we can progress.

Twins (including the mirror-image of a figure in the dream) *(also see individual entry)* Twins in a dream can suggest two sides of our personality. If they are **identical** we may be recognising our ambiguous feelings about ourselves. If **not identical** they suggest the inner self and the outer reality. Twins may also signify our projections into the world of our own personalities.

Woman In a woman's dream a woman, such as **a family member or friend** is often representative of an aspect of her own personality, but often one she has not yet fully understood. **In a man's dream** such a figure denotes his relationship with his own feelings and with his intuitive side. It may also show how he relates to his female partner. **A goddess or holy woman** signifies the highest potential for working with the Greater Good that the

dreamer has. **Oriental women** appearing in dreams usually suggest the mysterious side of the feminine. **In a man's dream** such a figure will often reveal his attitude to sexuality, while **in a woman's dream** it will reveal more about her own intuitive transcendent powers. **An older woman** mostly represents the dreamer's mother and her sense of inherited wisdom. **An unknown woman** in dreams will represent either the Anima *(see Introduction)* **in a man's dream**, or the Shadow *(see Introduction)* **in a woman's**. It is the qualities of surprise and intrigue which allow us to explore further the relevance of that figure. We can gain a great deal of information because the figure is unknown.

3 When we begin to work spiritually with ourselves, there is a gargantuan store of knowledge which can be worked on, and with, to enhance our lives.

PEPPER

1 Pepper as a spice has the ability to 'spice something up' and it is this quality which is most symbolised in dreams. We need to liven up a situation we are in.

2 To dream of pepper suggests we are changing our tastes. We may, in everyday life, be reacting to something in a relationship or particular situation that is not to our liking. It is this symbolism that often comes across when we need to make radical changes.

3 Pepper in dreams suggests spiritual warmth and love.

PERFUME
– also see Odour and Smell

1 When we dream of **smelling perfume**, we are often being reminded of particular memories. Smells can be extremely evocative and we may need to recapture a certain emotion associated with that specific perfume.

2 Certain perfumes may remind us of people we have known. We may have a good – or bad – reaction to that smell. Just as people appearing in dreams remind us of our own qualities, so also can perfumes.

3 Intuitive information can often recognised because of a particular perfume.

PERSPIRE

1 When we experience fear in a dream, the physical manifestation in the dream state itself – such as rapid heartbeat and sweating – can actually be absent. It is only on awakening that we realise that we have reacted physically.

2 When we realise we are perspiring in a dream, we are acutely aware of our reactions to external

stimuli. We are alerted to the need to handle our own emotions and fears.

3 Spiritual effort can manifest as a physiological reaction such as perspiring, which indicates the amount of energy being expended.

PET
– also see Animals

1 Whereas in the waking state we may not be aware of our need for love and affection, when a pet appears in a dream we are reacting to a natural drive in ourselves to give or receive love.

2 On a subliminal level we may be aware that someone else has control over our lives. We can only do what is expected of us. Conversely, if we **own a pet in a dream** we perhaps need to question our ability to look after something or someone more vulnerable than ourselves.

3 Unconditional love which is without dependency often comes from our pets. They are often sensitive to our immediate emotional distress or pain.

PETROL

1 Petrol is a form of energy and in dreams it is recognised as a requirement that we may have in order to keep us going. For instance, to be **putting petrol**

into a vehicle would indicate that perhaps we need to be taking more care of our bodies. Petrol is also explosive and dangerous, so to be **using petrol in a dangerous way** would indicate that we are creating problems for ourselves within a situation in ordinary everyday life.

2 The energy we use in making decisions and in creating opportunities for ourselves can often be turned to drive. When we are handling petrol in a dream we are producing motivation, either for others or for ourselves. When we are at **a petrol station, being given or buying petrol**, we are taking energy from something external to ourselves.

3 Spiritual energy and power can both be symbolised by petrol.

PHEASANT
– see Birds

PHOENIX
– see Birds

PHOTOGRAPHS
1 When we dream of **looking at photographs** we are often looking at an aspect of ourselves, perhaps our younger self or a part of ourselves that we no longer feel is particularly valid. To be **given a photograph of oneself** would indicate that we need to be taking an objective view of situations round us or perhaps of ourselves within that situation. We need to stand back and look very clearly at what is going on.

2 Obviously photographs represent memories, past occasions, perhaps past difficulties. To be looking at photographs of **someone from the past** is to be looking at that person's qualities – perhaps bringing them forward into our own lives – and making use of those same qualities within.

3 Photographs in dreams can be used to represent a spiritual need to understand the past.

PHYSICIAN
– see Doctor

PIANO
1 Piano playing is something which satisfies all the aesthetic senses. The piano appearing in dreams is a symbol of our own creativity. Just as in everyday life we need to learn and practise playing the piano, so we also need to learn and practise using our creativity.

2 One of the aspects of piano playing is that we are creative with someone else's work. Few of us actually compose our own music. It may be that we need to look at our workaday situation in the light of making something happen in order to use our best potential.

3 Creative sound is a vital aspect in spiritual development, and our appreciation of music can often give an indication of spiritual progression.

PICTURE

1 A picture in a dream is usually an illustration of something which is part of our lives. It will depend on whether it is **painted**, or a **print of another picture**, as to the interpretation. For instance, in a dream, a **picture that we have painted** might have more emotional impact than an Old Master (An Old Master can also suggest our attitude to the past).

2 The condition of the picture may be important, as may also the colours in the picture *(see Colours)*. The subject matter may give us suggestions as to what we should be 'looking at' in our lives.

3 A picture is an icon, or alternatively a representation of spiritual significance.

PIER

1 Dreaming of a pier would suggest happy times and memories to most people. We may have an association with a particular town or it may simply be that a seaside pier signifies rest and relaxation.

2 A pier as a point of embarkation or arrival may suggest to us new opportunities or the end of a journey *(see Journey)*.

3 A pier signifies both a beginning and an ending and also moving to a new level of spiritual understanding.

PIG
– see Animals and Boar

PIGEON
– see Birds

PILL
– also see Tablet

1 For most people, taking a pill suggests doing something to make themselves feel better. In dreams, taking such a course of action will signify putting ourselves through an experience we need in order to improve our performance or potential.

2 On a psychological level we may be aware of our ability to heal ourselves. **Taking a pill** in a dream may alert us to that capability. We may also be conscious of the necessity for taking care over what we put in our mouths, particularly if **someone else is giving us the pill**.

3 Spiritual or alternative methods of healing may be appropriate in a given situation.

PILGRIM/
PILGRIMAGE

1 When we are **undertaking a pilgrimage** in a dream we are recognising the purposeful, directed side of our personality. We have a goal in life, which may require faith to achieve.

2 A pilgrim can often represent the hermit or Wise Old Man *(see Introduction)* within. That part of our personality which is secure and may not need much input from others has the ability to direct our lives provided we create the correct circumstances.

3 A seeker of Spirituality must always undertake a journey of some kind. This is often represented by a pilgrimage to a holy place.

PILLAR

1 One symbolism of a pillar is phallic, but another one is probably more accurate. We are able to create stability and to stand firm in the presence of difficulty. In dreams, to find that we are a **pillar of the community** suggests that we should be taking more responsibility for our actions.

2 Pillars mostly indicate a sort of support, so to become aware of **supporting pillars** indicates that the structure that we have given our lives may need some attention. Esoterically, for there to be **two pillars** in a dream highlights the difference between the masculine and the feminine. The **left pillar** represents the feminine, and is often seen as being black. The **right** is masculine, and is seen in dreams as white.

3 The contrast between spiritual and material power is seen as two pillars in dreams.

PILLOW

1 In ordinary everyday life a pillow or cushion can offer support or comfort. So, in a dream, being conscious of a pillow may suggest such a need. Sometimes **what the pillow is made of** is important, and may have relevance in the interpretation of the dream. For instance, **a feather pillow** would suggest gentle support, whereas **a stone pillow** would represent a degree of rigidity.

2 Sometimes, when the dreamer is going through a period of self-denial, he will deny himself any comfort symbolism and so his pillow may disappear. To dream of **a pillow fight** indicates a mock conflict.

3 Spiritual comfort and ease are represented by the pillow.

PIMPLE

1 For most people the way they see themselves is important. To be overly conscious of something like a pimple in a dream is to suggest some worry as to how one comes across to others. A pimple can also represent some kind of blemish in our characters which at some time or another will have to be dealt with.

2 Since a pimple usually suggests the body's inability to throw off toxins, such a symbol in dreams indicates our inability to throw off infection or negativity. It has only come partly to the surface of our consciousness.

3 A pimple can suggest a spiritual blemish – that is, something which causes ugliness in our lives.

PIN

1 It depends whether the pin is holding something together or is being used to pierce us, or an object, in our dreams. If it is **holding something together** it indicates the emotional connections or bonds we use. If it is **piercing an object** a trauma is suggested, although it may be quite small.

2 Occasionally in a dream we are reminded of a feeling we have in everyday life. To experience **a feeling of pins and needles** in our dream suggests that we are not ensuring an adequate flow of energy in a situation around us.

3 We may not be able to solve a spiritual difficulty immediately. A temporary solution may be necessary and this can be symbolised by the use of a pin.

PINE CONE

1 If the pine cone does not have a personal connection for the dreamer – such as a childhood memory – it will denote fecundity and good fortune.

2 The shape of the pine cone and the fact that it contains many seeds gives an obvious connection to the phallus and masculinity.

3 A pine cone is an attribute of Dionysos, and therefore is a symbol of good times.

PIPE

1 On a purely practical level a pipe can symbolise many things. A **water pipe** can give information as to how we might handle our emotions (the size and type in this case will be significant). A **tobacco pipe or chillum** might suggest a means of escape, whereas a **musical pipe** indicates our connection with the rhythm of life.

2 When we are in difficulty in everyday life, a simple symbol such as a pipe will indicate how making connections between the various aspects of a situation will help resolve it.

3 A pipe suggests some kind of spiritual conduit.

PIRATE
– see People

PISTOL
– see Gun and Weapons

PISTON
– also see Engine

1 A piston in a dream can be taken to mean sexual drive or activity. In this context it is more of a mechanical action than a loving act, and may show the dreamer's attitude to sex. **In a woman's dream** a piston may reveal her fear of being hurt sexually. She may also be aware that she is simply being used, and that there is no tenderness. **In a man's dream** such an image may indicate his sense of identity and masculinity. If the **piston is not rigid** a man may fear impotence, whereas a woman will feel perhaps that she cannot trust her partner.

2 A piston may also represent a person's drive for success. The dreamer may need to assess the amount of effort that is necessary for him or her to be able to achieve their goals. They may need to recognise that concentrated effort – which is fairly mechanical – may, at this stage, achieve more than creative flair. The piston, being only part of an engine, requires the rest of the components to operate successfully. Often a great deal of help can be gained by considering the way in which the piston works. In other words, when at a particular stage of development our actions may have to be mechanical, we also need the fuel and the container with which to operate.

3 The spiritual drive – that is, the need to be complete, requires effort which can be enhanced by using our resources properly.

PIT
– also see Abyss

1 Many people talk about the pit of despair and of feeling trapped within a situation. A pit in a dream makes us more conscious of this particular feeling. We may be in a situation which we cannot get out of, or may find that if we are not careful we will put ourselves in such a situation. If **we are digging the pit** in the dream, we have to be conscious of the fact that we may be creating the situation ourselves. If **others are digging the pit**, we may feel we have no control over our circumstances and that doom and disaster are inevitable.

2 Rescuing others from a pit, particularly if they are members of our own family, suggests that we have information which may be of use to them to enable them to overcome their problems. **Pushing someone into a pit** indicates that we are trying to suppress a part of our personality. To be conscious that **the pit is bottomless** signifies that we do not have the resources to recover a previous situation.

3 The pit, like the abyss *(see Abyss)*, represents the Void and possibly death – not necessarily a physical death, but more a death of the old self. We have no choice but to go forward, knowing that we may fail, but also that if we do succeed our lives will change for the better. To face the pit requires extreme courage.

PLACES

1 When the environment or setting of a dream is particularly noticeable there is usually some kind of message or information being given. Sometimes the place reflects our inner state of mind or mood. It can be a reminder of a particular place which had meaning at a specific time in the dreamer's life, and sometimes a reminder of particular people.

2 Interpreting the symbolism of certain places gives us an insight into our own 'inner landscape'. **A place which becomes fertile or lighter in the course of the dream** indicates that an aspect that the dreamer has not previously appreciated – or has found unpleasant – is now developing possibilities and potentials, possibly for spiritual development. **Dreary, unfriendly places, or tranquil favourable landscapes** may well refer to the dreamer's subjective view of the world.

The **country** where the dream takes place may have certain resonances for the dreamer. For example; **America** for most people will signify a rather brash, commercially oriented culture, **England** tends to be seen as inhibited and dutiful, while **France** will represent the temperamental masculine, and so on.

Countryside The countryside can suggest a particular mood or feeling, especially of freedom.

Composite scenes consisting of many images recognisable to the dreamer are usually drawing attention to particular qualities, ideals and moods which all enhance the information content of the dream, may have particular associations for the dreamer, or have been included because of frequently encountered associations.

The dreamer's birthplace represents a secure space. **A bright and sunny place** suggests fun and liveliness, whereas a **dark, shadowy, murky scene** signifies despondency and gloom. **Darkened** places can represent the unconscious. **A familiar place** will often take us back to childhood or a time of learning and **a particularly beautiful place** may allow us to fantasise so that we can make more use of creative visualisation. **Jungles** connect with the labyrinth and ways of understanding our sexuality. A place which **feels oppressive** has been a sanctuary, but is no longer. **A sheltered place** offers peace and security. **Unknown places** indicate aspects of ourselves of which we are not aware. This can lead to a **place that seems familiar and yet we do not know** which signifies a situation we are continually re-running in our lives. **Wide-open spaces** offer us freedom of movement. **An unfamiliar place** will signify new aspects of the personality which have not yet become fully conscious.

3 In the sense that a place suggests a 'spot', places appearing in dreams allow us to orientate ourselves in order to make the best use of information we are given.

PLACENTA

1 The placenta is a source of nourishment for the baby in the womb. In dreams, this becomes a symbol of how one gains nourishment from one's surroundings. It also suggests ways in which the dreamer may be dependent on other people. When we undertake a new project, we have to be aware that we ourselves may not have the resources to care for ourselves properly. We require nourishment from an outside source, but one to which we feel connected.

2 Personal dependency varies with each individual. Just as the relationship between mother and baby is unique and protected by the function of the placenta, so in dreams the placenta can highlight the uniqueness of such a relationship. One of the biggest traumas to be gone through is separation from mother and the placenta acts as a buffer in this process. Dreaming of a placenta indicates our need for such a buffer at times of violent separation.

3 Spiritually, as human beings we are dependent on Mother Earth or the Great Mother *(See Introduction)*. Until we are capable of properly appreciating that dependency, we have no choice but to recognise that reliance – symbolised by the placenta.

PLAGUE

1 In olden times, plague and pestilence was believed to come from an angry God. In fact, most plagues are caused by an imbalance in natural ecology. To dream of a plague will highlight some internal imbalance within ourselves. This may be physical, emotional, mental or spiritual. One quality of a plague, no matter what it is, is that there is too much. We can be overwhelmed by it, as happened with the plague of locusts chronicled in the Bible.

2 One outstanding example of a plague in the Bible was that of Job who was plagued by boils. This suggests the old-fashioned idea that if one did not conform, retribution would occur. To dream of a plague, therefore, is to recognise that we will suffer if we do not attempt to reach our highest potential.

3 In spiritual terms a plague signifies Divine Retribution.

PLAIT

1 In olden times, a **plait using three strands** indicated the interweaving of body, mind and spirit. It also represented the influences which were assimilated by a growing girl and taken into her understanding of herself as a woman. In dreams it therefore represents womanhood. In the present day, as men become more sensitive, the more creative will often plait longer hair.

2 Plaited hair was formerly a means of creating order and cleanliness. Often in dreams to see a plait reminds us of the talisman – or favour belonging to his lady – which a knight of old would carry into battle. Nowadays it is more of a lucky charm. To be **plaiting string, rope, hair etc.** highlights our ability to weave the different influences of our, or someone else's, life into a coherent whole.

3 Very subtle influences come into play when we begin to develop spiritually. Hair **plaited into the shape of a crown – or wound round the head** – indicates spiritual attainment.

PLANETS

1 Dreaming of planets is to be linking with very subtle energies which surround us and have an effect on our lives, even though we may not be consciously aware of it.

2 The interpretations of the planetary significances are; **Jupiter** suggests growth and expansion, and also freedom from limitation. **Mars** indicates activity and war but also drive. **Mercury** signifies communication, intuition and mental powers. **Moon** represents our emotions and our links with our mother. **Neptune** works with illusion – but also with inspiration. **Pluto** has charge of the unconscious and transformation. **Saturn** is a restraining influence and rules the past. **Sun** usually symbolises the Self and the energy that we have. Uranus governs sudden changes. **Venus** highlights love and beauty.

3 Spiritually, once we become aware of how the subtle energies can help us live our lives successfully, we can learn to make use of planetary energy.

PLANK
– also see Wood

1 To dream of **walking the plank** suggests taking an emotional risk. A plank of wood appearing in a dream can indicate that something needs repairing, or that we feel safer carrying our own means of support. If the plank is to be **used in flooring** the symbol is one of security, but if to be used as a **door** or as **decoration** on a wall, it signifies defence or adornment of one's inner space.

2 If the plank is to be **used for making something**, it suggests the material we have for undertaking a project. We may be aware in the dream of the type of wood we are using and this can have some significance or memory for us. If the plank is **used for making a box**, we should take care not to become trapped within a situation.

3 We have the raw material to enable us to become more aware of the process of life. We may need to look at what we consider to be our usefulness within the world.

PLANTS
– also see Weeds

1 Because of the process of growth and decay that plants go through naturally, they become a symbol for progressive change. If the **plants are cultivated**, then we should be aware of our ability to cultivate potential. If the **plants are dying** we may have reached a stage where there is no more advantage within a situation.

2 If the **plants are growing wild**, there is a part of us that needs freedom. If they are **grown in regimented rows** we are aware of too much concern for the views of other people. Many plants have both healing and magical qualities. Equally, without proper knowledge, plants can be harmful.

3 Plants in a spiritual sense signify the life force and cycle of life. Because they die only to grow again, they also suggest death and rebirth.

PLATE

1 A plate can be simple or ornate. In dreams the interpretation will depend on this fact. A **simple** plate will indicate a need for simplicity within our lives, whereas a more **ornate one** may suggest the need for celebration. If **we are holding the plate**, we are aware of what we have received from other people. If **someone else is giving us the plate** they are offering us something which belongs to them, but which we can now share.

2 The plate as a container is an important image. If it is more **bowl-shaped**, it will represent what belongs to the feminine; **if flat** it will suggest some kind of group ownership. An **empty plate** signifies one's self-involved needs and appetites, whereas a **communal plate** highlights what there is to share. The pattern and colour of the plate may be important *(see Pattern in Shapes and Colour)*.

3 Formerly, plates were often only owned by the rich. Spiritually, to own a plate suggests that we have achieved a certain level of awareness.

PLATEAU

1 Many dreams will hold images of climbing and of reaching a plateau – we reach a place after a hard climb which is even and not difficult to cross. Sometimes it can represent a period of peace and quiet, sometimes stasis where there is no energy left for change.

2 If the **plateau is barren**, we may need some further stimulus to help us move on. If it seems to be **a place of safety**, we may not wish to move on and perhaps need to take time out to recuperate.

3 Spiritually a plateau offers choices. We can rest on our laurels and take time out to assess our progress, or we can use the plateau for calm and peace.

PLAY

1 When in a dream we are **watching a play**, we need to decide whether it is a drama, a comedy or a tragedy. This is because we often are trying to view our own lives objectively. The **content of the play** may give us clues as to what our course of action should be in everyday life. If **people we know** are in the play we should be aware of the 'drama' we are playing out with them.

2 In dreams, the play that takes place is a distillation of our experiences, knowledge and abilities. The creator in us directs the performance to enable us to get the best benefit of the information it contains. Images are put together to have the greatest impact and to make the interpretation as easy as possible. Sometimes, however, the unexpected occurs which means that we have to seek explanation elsewhere.

3 From a spiritual perspective, the life that we have creates a play which gives us the best opportunity to learn lessons through experience.

PLOUGHING

1 As more people move away from working with the land, this symbol becomes less relevant in dreams. It does mean, however, working at clearing oneself for new growth and being able to prepare for change.

2 We may have a situation within our lives which needs 'turning over'. By looking at it from a different perspective we are able to make the situation more productive.

3 We are in process of creating new opportunities to develop spiritually.

PLUMAGE

1 In a dream plumage being drawn to our attention can often stand for a display of power and strength. It may also be a signal of defiance; we need to stand firm and show our colours, as it were.

2 A bird's plumage is its protec-

tion, but it is also its power and strength. Used in this sense, it is alerting us to the fact that we can use our own strength and ability to achieve what we want to do in the future.

3 Spiritual triumph is shown by a display of plumage.

PLUMBING

1 Dreaming about plumbing looks at the way we direct our emotions. It indicates how we make use of our emotions to bypass obstacles in order to create security for ourselves and to control the flow of emotions within. Another interpretation is that of the internal plumbing. Often, to dream of plumbing in this sense alerts us to something that is perhaps wrong with ourselves, with our bodies.

2 Emotional security is important to almost everybody, and mostly these things are hidden from view. When we are looking at plumbing we are actually looking into our subconscious to where we have stored information and emotion. We need to be able to access the subconscious in order to create clarity within our lives.

3 We are aware of the flow of spiritual energy within our lives.

PLUNGE

1 To dream of **plunging into**

something is to recognise that we are facing uncertainty. We are going into something unknown – something that we have perhaps not done before – and are taking a risk. That risk will very often take us into our emotional depths and we will learn new things about ourselves of which we will then be able to make use.

2 When facing uncertainty in waking life we very often need reassurance that we have both the courage and the daring to go ahead with a particular activity. Very often, to dream of plunging is to recognise that we do have the ability to go forward. To dream of **a plunger** – as in something that clears a blockage – usually indicates that we need to use some force to enable us to deal with difficulty. Frequently, this can be because we have internalised a problem – we have either worked too hard and don't have the energy to move the difficulty away from us or we have created a problem for ourselves in that we have not acted appropriately.

3 Spiritual risk pushes us into a situation where we must take the plunge.

POCKET

1 To dream of a pocket is to be dealing with one's personal secrets or thoughts – those things that we have deliberately chosen to hide rather than done so on impulse. They are perhaps secret thoughts that we do not want to share with anyone else. There may also be thoughts about our own abilities and the value that we have within our own personal community.

2 A pocket in a dream can also indicate a sense of ownership and possession. **To have something in our pocket** means that we have appropriated it, that we have taken ownership. This can represent a situation in the everyday world, or it can represent emotions that we may have previously hidden and now need to own, in the sense of being able to make use of them.

3 A pocket suggests the Hidden or the Occult.

POINT

1 Anything pointed normally refers to male sexuality. To be aware of **the point of decision** is to come to a resolve that something has to be done. We must bring about change in one way or another and at that particular 'point' there is nothing else to be done. Nothing can be done, in other words, until we decide to take action.

2 Psychologically and intellectually to have integrated ourselves means that we have reached our own centre. This is often symbolised in dreams by a point or dot.

3 A point is the beginning, the Soul or Completion.

POINTING

1 When we dream of **someone pointing**, normally we are having our attention drawn to a particular object, feeling or even place. We need to take note of both **who is pointing** it out to us *(see People)* and equally **what they are pointing at**. We may feel that we are at the receiving end – often pointing can be an aggressive act or accusation – and in dreams we may feel that we are being accused of wrongdoing and need to look at the validity of our conduct.

2 Pointing in a dream, particularly by one of our dream characters, indicates either that we are being given a sense of direction, or that we are being pointed away from a present action and should leave it behind.

3 A particular way forward is being indicated.

POISON

1 To be able to recognise poison in a dream means that we need to avoid an attitude, emotion or thought which will not be good for us. In our environment there is that which not only is not good for us now, but will also be not good for us in the future.

2 Other people's attitudes and beliefs can often contaminate the way we think and feel and this can sometimes be shown in dreams as poison.

3 Evil substances which can contaminate our spiritual progress may be present.

POKER

1 A poker obviously has links with masculinity, but also with rigidity. In dreams a poker can therefore suggest aggressive action, but also rigid attitudes and behaviour.

2 Playing a **game of poker** in a dream suggests that one is taking a risk in everyday life. It may be important to note who we are playing with.

3 The poker in this instance suggests rigid and unbending discipline, which is sometimes necessary in spiritual development.

POLE

1 It will depend how the pole is being used in the dream as to the interpretation. It is seen as an expression of the life force – as in **a Maypole** *(see Maypole)* – but also as a stabilising force or rallying point, as in a **flagpole**. It can also be a support mechanism.

2 In former times a pole was a measurement, so in dreams it can still be a measurement of standards. There may also be a play on words here, in that a Pole can be someone from Poland.

3 Spiritual or heroic standards of behaviour need to be instigated.

POOL
– also see Water

1 Dreaming of a pool deals with our need for the understanding of our own emotions and inner feelings. A **pool in a wood**, for instance, would suggest the ability to understand our own need for peace and tranquillity. An **urban swimming pool** might signify our need for structure in our relationships with other people, whereas a **pool in the road** would suggest an emotional problem to be got through before carrying out our plans.

2 In order to understand ourselves we may need to explore the pool by totally immersing ourselves in it, that is, to become involved in our own emotions. How we deal with what arises (in more senses than one) will teach us a lot about ourselves. The pool may suggest a form of cleansing, particularly of old traumas and emotions or of past misdeeds. The most potent image of that is

baptism by immersion.

3 There is a meditation or guided imagery technique which can enhance one's ability to dream. First, you picture yourselves walking in a field. Feel the grass beneath your feet and the wind on your face. Walk towards a slight dip in the ground which is to your left. At the bottom of this dip there is a pool which is surrounded by trees. Sit quietly by the pool, simply thinking about your life. When you are ready, stand up and walk into the pool very slowly. Feel the water rising slowly up your body until you are immersed completely. At that point let go of all the tensions of the everyday world and concentrate on the peace which is within. Then slowly emerge from the pool, and again sit quietly beside it. When you are ready, walk back to the point in the field where you started, and let the image fade. By practising this, gradually it will be found that the dream images take on a deeper meaning.

POPE

1 Often to meet the Pope in a dream is to meet the side of ourselves which has developed a code of behaviour based on our religious beliefs. He may be benign or judgmental depending on how the figure of the Pope was presented in childhood.

2 The Pope often appears in dreams as a substitute for the father, or as a personification of God.

3 Our spiritual mentor or Higher Self will sometimes be seen as the Pope.

POPPY
– also see Flowers

1 The poppy can appear in dreams as either a symbol of sacrifice – **the remembrance poppy** – or as one of idleness and oblivion – **the opium poppy**.

2 On a psychological level both significances can be united. We need to 'remember to forget.' By learning to forget past difficulties we give ourselves the opportunity to move on with clarity.

3 The poppy symbolises forgetfulness. In spiritual terms the soul must forget all it knows in order to reincarnate and rediscover its own awareness. The Great Mother as the Goddess was, and is, responsible for that forgetting – hence the poppy signifies the Great Mother.

POSITION

1 When a particular position is highlighted in a dream it usually signifies our moral standpoint, or our position in life. It can also give an indication of how we are handling situations in our lives. For instance, something in the **wrong position** means we are going about things in the wrong way.

2 Our spirit, intellect, ideals and consciences are being brought to our attention when we dream of anything **higher** or above us. This applies also when dreaming of the **upper part** of anything (of a building or body, for example). Our altruism may be being brought into question. Anything **underneath, below, or downstairs** signifies the anarchic or immoral side of our personalities. The sexual impulses can also be characterised in this way. Something appearing **upside down** emphasises the potential for chaos and difficulty. The **'ups and downs'** of situations in life can be experienced in dreams as the actual movement of one's position. The personality has a need to balance the heights and depths of its experience, and if this does not happen a warning will usually appear in dream form. **Back/Front** Rejection and acceptance can be shown in a dream as seeing the back and front of something. **Backward/Forward** Having the attention drawn to a backward and/or forward movement usually indicaes the potential to adopt a regressive backward-looking tendency. There is a need to retire into the past, rather than tackling fears and moving ahead.

Centre *(also see Shapes)* To be conscious of the centre of any aspect of a dream is to be aware of a goal or objective, or perhaps even of the dreamer's real Self. There is a need to be the centre of attention whatever the circumstances.

Far/Near In dreams, space and time can become confused. Dreaming of something which is far away, may indicate that it is far away in time. This may be future or past, depending on the dream. A **long way in front** would be future, **a long way behind** would be past. **Near or close** would mean recently, or in the immediate.

Horizontal This usually symbolises the material world.

Left The left side suggests the less dominant, more passive side. Often it is taken to represent all that is dark and sinister and those parts of our personality which we try to suppress. It is more to do with instinctive behaviour, what feels good inside and with personal behaviour without attention to moral codes. It is supportive in expression, and receptive by nature, so anything appearing in dreams **on the left side** can be accepted as a symbol of support. Any **pain experienced on the left side** is interpreted in terms of sensitivity. The left expresses the more feminine attributes and often the past. Feelings of being **left behind** suggest a sense of inadequacy, of disintegration and of having to leave the past behind. **Indecision over left or right** suggests an inability to decide whether to rely on drive or instinct.

Low In dreams, feeling 'low' can suggest a sense of inferiority or humility. Often we will give way to submissive behaviour, and put ourselves in a lower position than others. Occasionally, **to be below something or someone** can indicate a need to explore the underside or negativity of a relationship or situation.

Opposite Anything in a dream which is opposite the dreamer may suggest some difficulty in reconciling two paradoxes (Good/bad, male/female, up/down, etc.). This may or may not suggest conflict. **One thing deliberately put opposite another** There is a deliberate attempt to introduce discord. **Changing the position from opposite** Differences may be adjusted.

Right/Left The conflict between right and left is usually between logic and intuition. **Right** The right side represents the more dominant logical side. It is the consciously expressed, confident side which perceives the exterior world in perhaps a more objective sense. It is to do with 'rightness' – that is, correctness and moral and social behaviour. Anything observed on **the right side** in dreams is usually significant as the dreamer progresses. Any **pain experienced on the right side** can also be interpreted in terms of drive. It also expresses the more masculine attributes. **Movement to the right** indicates that something is coming into conscious awareness.

Straight Straight suggests a direct approach, the shortest way between two objects or places.

Top To be **at the top** is to have succeeded in our endeavours. To be **on top** is to have assumed control. **Trying to reach the top** suggests more effort is needed.

Under/underneath Being underneath something suggests either taking shelter or submitting to someone else's handling of us. It may also represent the part of us that we hide, or the part that is less capable.

Up, upper We have the capability of achieving a degree of supremacy. We are capable of getting the 'upper hand' in particular situations. We can move away from the mundane, ordinary everyday world.

Vertical The vertical in dreams tends to represent the spiritual realm.

3 The points of the compass can be read spiritually. **The North** signifies the Unknown, and hence sometimes darkness. It is spirituality within the world. **The East** traditionally suggests birth and mystic religions. It also represents becoming 'conscious'. **The South** is representative of earthly passion and sensuality. **The West** can symbolise death, but more properly the state after death when there is increased spiritual awareness. Traditionally, it can also represent the more logical side of our natures.

POSTURES

1 Body language is an important aspect in dreams. Our dream characters may develop exaggerated movements or postures to highlight certain information which we need to recognise.

2 We often pick up information on a subliminal level without being able to understand why. The postures we or others adopt in dreams often give us the answers to those questions that need answering.

3 An exaggerated posture will

indicate emotions. Living and being mean that we are capable of adopting certain recognisable stances and postures (as in yoga) in order to progress spiritually.

POVERTY

1 To experience poverty in a dream highlights a sense of being deprived of the ability to satisfy our basic needs. We may feel inadequate, either emotionally or materially. Often we need to go right back to basics to discover what our real needs are.

2 Poverty in a dream can be conveyed by **poor surroundings**. It may be that we need to deal with our surroundings rather than ourselves.

3 Spiritual poverty can be self-denial.

PRAYER

– also see Religious Imagery

1 Prayer suggests the idea that we need to seek outside help for ourselves. We may need someone else's authority to succeed in what we are doing.

2 Psychologically, the human being has always needed to feel that there is a greater power than himself available to him. To be praying in a dream reinforces this, since the dreamer needs to use his own inner sense of self to access the Greater Power.

3 Supplication and Worship are two aspects of prayer.

PRECIPICE

1 The fear of failure is a very strong emotion. Often it can be represented in dreams by a precipice. To **step off a precipice** is taking risks, since we do not know the outcome of our action. To try to **climb a precipice** is to be making a tremendous effort to overcome obstacles which have arisen.

2 The image of the Fool in the Tarot shows him at the beginning and the end of his journey. He is **unmindful of the precipice** and initially is not aware of the danger he is in. Conversely, he does not care because he is aware he is capable of stepping off the edge and taking flight. This type of dream often appears when we are in a position of great risk.

3 A precipice will indicate a perceived spiritual danger.

PREGNANCY

1 Dreaming of pregnancy usually denotes a fairly protracted waiting period being necessary for something, possibly the completion of a project. A new area of our potential or personality is developing. Interestingly enough, to dream of pregnancy seldom actually means one's own pregnancy, although it can indicate pregnancy in someone around us.

2 To dream of **someone else being pregnant** suggests that we are in a position to observe part of ourselves developing new skills or characteristics. We may be unaware of what the outcome of this process will be. To dream of a **man being pregnant**, particularly if it is **a woman's dream**, is probably a projection of her own wish for the man to take responsibility within her life.

3 There is always a gestation period in spiritual work. We may have to be patient and wait for a natural process to take place so that we can fulfil a task.

PREHISTORIC
– also see Dinosaur

1 Being aware in a dream that something is prehistoric is to recognise that feelings and emotions we have arise literally from before the time we were able to understand ourselves. When we have not fully integrated and comprehended the basic urge for survival, it is possible for us to be self-destructive without necessarily appreciating why.

2 Often in dreams the landscape or scenario appears to be prehis-toric. This is 'before thought' and before we had the ability to record our impressions. If one believes that babies are conscious of the world they will enter before birth, then these impressions can appear in later life as prehistoric images. For instance, a **barren landscape** might indicate a lack of love.

3 Spiritual progression requires us to understand our physical, emotional, mental and spiritual urges. In this context, the prehistoric images indicate the lack of ability to integrate either the various parts of ourselves successfully, or to integrate with society.

PRESENT/PRESENTS

1 When a present appears in a dream, it can first of all be a play on words. We are being given a 'here and now'. We are being reminded to live in the moment, and not the past or future. A present can also indicate a talent or gift. If we are **receiving a present** we are being loved and recognised and are also gaining from the relationship. If we are **giving a present**, we appreciate that we have characteristics we are able to offer other people. **A pile of presents** in a dream can signify as yet unrecognised talents and skills. If the presents give some

377

indication of time – e.g. birthday presents – we may expect some success around that time.

2 To present something in a dream (as in making a presentation) is offering work that we have done for approval and recognition. We appreciate that the work we have done is more important than we ourselves are.

3 One of the requirements of spiritual advancement is that we learn to live in the present. We need to be able to take advantage of anything that life presents – to use it for ourselves, but also to recognise that it has relevance to other people and can affect the way that they live.

PRIEST/PRIESTESS
– *see Archetypes*

PRINCE (HERO)/PRINCESS
– *see Archetypes*

PRISON
– *also see Key and Lock*

1 Prison, in dreams, stands for the traps we create for ourselves. We may feel that outside circumstances are making life difficult, but in actual fact we are creating those circumstances ourselves. This can be on an emotional, material or spiritual level.

2 Often we create a prison for ourselves through a sense of duty or guilt and this can often be shown in dreams. The types of locks and bolts we perceive in our prison may show us how we are imprisoning ourselves. For example, **a lock with a key** would suggest that we know how to escape, whereas **a bolt** shows that we have to make a greater effort. **A barred window** would suggest that we are being prevented from using that which is external to us.

3 Duty and guilt are opposite sides of the same coin in a spiritual sense. Duty can be a liability and therefore a trap, and guilt can prevent us from seeing a way forward. Often, when we feel trapped either by duty or guilt we will dream of a prison.

PRIZE

1 In dreams **to win a prize** is to have succeeded in overcoming our own obstacles. We are also being acknowledged by other people for having made the effort to succeed. **To be giving away prizes** suggests that we are giving public acknowledgement to efforts others have made.

2 To prize an object (as in **a prize possession**) is to give it its proper value. This does not necessarily mean being materialistic, but being able to gain from an appreciation of its intrinsic value.

3 In spiritual terms, gaining a prize in a dream means having used one's instincts and intuition in harmony in order to be able to use inspiration.

PROCESSION

1 A procession means an orderly approach and often makes a statement of intent. In a dream, to see **a line of people** who all appear to have a similar goal or set of beliefs in mind, indicates that it is the intention behind the group which is important. Often a procession is hierarchical, with the most important people either first or last. This could be important in a dream in enabling us to adopt priorities for ourselves.

2 A procession is often a way of marking a special occasion with pageantry and dignity. In dreams such an image can often represent the dreamer's need to have his own successes and abilities recognised. To be **taking part in a procession** is acknowledging our need to belong to a like-minded group. To be **watching a procession** is to appreciate other people's single-mindedness.

3 Spiritually, a procession is indicative of a group of like-minded people but also of people who

have great knowledge. In dreams we are recognising the importance of whatever system of belief or religion we belong to. We recognise respect must be paid.

PROPELLER

1 A propeller acknowledges the drive and intent behind our progression. Recognising our needs, we also need to understand how to move forward. The action of a propeller is to give us 'lift', which suggests being able to use the intellect.

2 A propeller appearing in a dream suggests that we need to undertake a journey of discovery.

3 There is a degree of spiritual compulsion in what we do.

PROSTITUTE

1 Dreaming of a prostitute usually suggests a sexual need. **In a man's dream** it may signify his need for relationship at any cost. **In a woman's dream** it can suggest her own need for sexual freedom. Often, dreaming of a prostitute forces us to look at our own sense of guilt or uncertainty about ourselves. **To be paying a prostitute** may suggest that we do not trust our own sexual abilities. **To be paid** for the sexual act may suggest that we feel relationships will cost us. In both cases there may be a fear of loving relationships.

2 In dreaming of prostitution, we may actually be connecting with a poor self-image. We are minimising our abilities and talents – this may be in a work situation as much as in our personal life. Very often, when we are expected to 'perform', inadequacy or ego makes us feel that we are 'prostituting' our talents.

3 In Christian terms, just as Christ recognised the value of the prostitute as a person in her own right despite her profession, we also spiritually need to accept other people's values.

PSYCHOLOGIST/ PSYCHIATRIST
– see Analyst

PUBLIC HOUSE

1 To be in a pub in a dream and aware of our behaviour indicates how we relate to groups and what our feelings are about society. We may feel that it is appropriate to use a public space to create new relationships, or to come to terms with our own sense of loneliness. A public space where we can drop inhibitions has links with the Pagan need for festivity and celebration.

2 We all have social needs that can be met in convivial company, in a pub or bar. The origins of the public house were the old inns, which were stopping-off places for travellers. Any companionship was purely transitory. This symbolism is still present today in dreams. We are in a place where we can rest and relax and nothing more is expected of us.

3 As a public place where shared values are important, the public house can be a creative space. As a meeting place where few judgements are made, it becomes a place in which people can co-exist.

PUDDLE
– also see Water and Pool

1 A puddle, being a smaller amount of liquid than either a pool or lake, can nevertheless have the same significance. When one appears in a dream we are becoming aware of our emotions and the way we handle them.

2 How we deal with the puddle may be important. If we **mop it up**, we are trying to re-absorb emotion that we may feel to be inappropriate. If we **leave it**, we probably need other people to recognise either our, or their, emotions.

3 Esoterically, a puddle can be used for scrying – that is, looking into the future as though into a magic mirror. To be **looking into a puddle** may be trying to decide what future action needs to be taken.

PULLING

1 Pulling suggests a positive action. We are being alerted to the fact that we can do something about a situation. In dreams, if **we are pulling** we are making the decisions within a project. If we are **being pulled** we may feel that we are having to give in to outside pressures. Extra effort to have something happen may be necessary. The object we are pulling, and the means by which we are pulling it, may be important (For examples, see Bridle, Rope etc.).

2 In slang terms, pulling means picking up a potential partner. In dreams this can actually translate itself into a physical feeling. We may also in everyday life be being pulled by our emotions and feel that we are powerless to resist. This can translate into the dream image of being pulled. We may feel that we have to go along with something and do not have the ability to refuse.

3 At a certain stage of spiritual development, there is a feeling of being pulled in a certain direction. We may be compelled to do certain things without necessarily knowing where the impulse comes from.

PULSE

1 A pulse is a rhythm which is essential to life. To be aware in sleep of one's pulse may indicate some kind of anxiety. In dreams this may translate itself into a rhythm which is external. There may also be health worries.

2 To be **feeling one's own pulse** in a dream is to be trying to put oneself in touch with the processes of life. To be **feeling someone else's pulse** may indicate a concern about that part of our personality the other character represents. If we **cannot detect a pulse**, this may indicate the 'death' of part of ourselves or emotions.

3 It is said that, to the sensitive, a pulse is detectable in all things. Spiritually, the more we are in touch with internal rhythm the more whole (or holy) we can be.

PUNISHMENT

1 When a child recognises that he or she is not conforming to what is expected, the threat of punishment is often present. In later life, when there is fear of retribution from an external source, we will often dream of being punished.

Self-punishment occurs when we have not achieved the standards we expect of ourselves.

2 When there is conflict in our lives, if we cannot resolve it we will often dream of being punished. This may be the only way out of our particular dilemma. We would rather suffer pain than resolve the difficulty.

3 The concept of Divine Retribution – that is, being punished by a force greater than ourselves – suggests a judgmental God. Spiritual punishment is much more, however, the idea of self-flagellation for not having achieved what is required of us.

PUPPET

1 When a puppet appears in a dream there is perhaps a sense of being able to manipulate circumstances or people around us. A puppet can also represent the more mechanical processes of our being, those activities which go on automatically in the background.

2 If **someone else is working the puppet**, we may feel that we are being manipulated. It would be wise to look at how we are co-operating in everyday life in becoming a victim. If the **puppet is manipulating us** we have become aware that bureaucracy is causing us difficulty. What should

be working for us has, in fact, turned into some kind of a manipulator.

3 At certain stages of development, we can become aware that we are powerless without a spiritually motivating force behind us. We are like puppets in the greater scheme of things.

PUPPY
– see Animals

PURSE

1 A purse is normally used to hold money, or something of value to us. In dreams it therefore becomes something of value it its own right. **To find a purse** would suggest that we have found something of value whereas **to lose a purse** suggests that we may be being careless.

2 The material that a purse is made from can have an important significance. The old saying 'You cannot make a silk purse out of a sow's ear' has relevance in dreams. The mind often plays tricks and manifests an apparently inappropriate image which needs to be worked on.

3 One symbolism of a purse is the same as that of a bag: the feminine and the containing principle. We are attempting to conserve our Spiritual energy or power.

PUS

1 An infection *(See Infection)* can result in pus. In a dream, something which has gone 'bad' and infected what is around it, can show itself as pus. We may be infected by fears, self- doubts and even jealousy. We are being shown that a negative situation in our lives can result in pain and difficulty if it is not dealt with correctly.

2 If we are having to deal with pus, we may have to deal with an external negative. If **someone else is dealing with pus in us**, then the negativity is internal and we need to learn how to heal ourselves.

3 In a spiritual sense, pus is the result of having attempted to fight something which is 'evil', and although we may have overcome it, we are left with the results to clear up.

PUSHED/PUSHING

1 When in a dream we are being pushed, there is an energy around us that enables us to achieve what we want. If **we are pushing**, then we are usually exerting our will positively. **Pushing something uphill**, such as a car or snowball, suggests that we are trying to resist natural forces.

2 When in everyday life we are aware of pressure, this can be surface in dreams as being pushed and can sometimes indicate a fear of illness. In certain forms of mental illness, the patient experiences a feeling of being pushed around and made to do something he does not want to do. Occasionally, when experienced in dreams, this can actually be a form of healing.

3 When one is developing psychically, it is possible to become aware of the subtle forces and energy around. This can be experienced as being pushed.

PUTREFACTION

1 Putrefaction can represent disintegration. In real-life situations something may have gone wrong, and there is no longer any energy to sustain it. While on a conscious level we may not recognise this fact, dreams will often bring it to our attention.

2 Decay – for example in a relationship – can be represented in dreams as putrefaction. When something is happening which will ultimately lead to a total collapse, we can often sense it as a bad smell – something is dying.

3 In spiritual terms there often has to be dissolution and disintegration before there is a new beginning. In dreams, if we have fear of this process it can manifest as putrefaction. Putrefaction can also mean death.

PYJAMAS
– see Clothes

PYRAMID

1 A pyramid is a very powerful image. On a physical level, it is a building of wonder. On a mental level, it is a structure of regeneration. On a spiritual level, it is a guardian of power. It will depend on the level of awareness in the dreamer as to which interpretation is valid.

2 The pyramid always signifies a wider awareness of power and energy. There is a point inside the pyramid where all the planes intersect. This will regenerate any matter which is placed there, for instance razor blades will become sharp again. In a larger pyramid, that particular spot can be used for enhancing mystical experiences. In dreams, to enter a pyramid is to be searching for the meaning of life.

3 Spiritually, the pyramid is a symbol of integration of the Self and the Soul. In dreams it can represent death, but also indicates rebirth.

from

Quail *to* Quote

QUAIL
– see Birds

QUAKER

1 To dream of **somebody being a Quaker** indicates the recognition of the ability to maintain a religious belief, come what may. It indicates a tranquillity and peacefulness that is not necessarily available to us in the waking state.
2 The human being has a need for a belief system that can support him or her in difficulty. To dream of **being a Quaker** allows us to link with our own inner self-sufficiency.
3 Religious beliefs and the acceptance of an ability to cope because of those beliefs is a great part of human development.

QUARANTINE

1 Dreaming of having to **put an animal into quarantine** signifies our inability to look after a vulnerable part of ourselves or others. It may also indicate our awareness of having to cut off the lower, more animal side of ourselves.
2 When in waking life we feel isolated, this may translate itself in dream language into being in quarantine. It would seem that 'authority' has taken over to manage this isolation.
3 Quarantine in a spiritual sense means isolation, in the sense of retreating from the world for a time.

QUARREL

1 To dream that we are **quarrelling with someone** indicates an inner conflict. For a **man to be quarrelling with a woman**, or **vice versa**, signifies a conflict between drive and intuition. To be **quarrelling with authority**, e.g. police, indicates a conflict between right and wrong.
2 Depending on the other aspects of the dream, quarrelling can suggest that there is conflict between what we have been taught and what we believe. Often, such a conflict can only be resolved through an outburst of emotion.
3 Spiritual conflict or a conflict between the spiritual self and the physical can appear in dreams as a quarrel.

QUARTET
– also see Four in Numbers

1 Dreaming of a quartet of any kind signifies a link with the material or practical aspects of other objects in the dream. It could be necessary to concentrate on pragmatic solutions to a problem.
2 Anything repeated more than once emphasises the significance of that object to the dreamer. The

dream object will be reproduced four times at the same moment, rather than being seen sequentially, in order to make the emphasis apparent.

3 Spiritually, the quartet links with the Quaternity, which signifies manifestation on the physical plane.

QUARTZ

1 Quartz seen in dreams tends to represent the crystallisation of ideas and feelings. It touches into our deep internal processes, often enabling us to express that which we have found impossible before.

2 The crystallisation process was seen by the Ancients as the trapping of light, and therefore power and, on a subliminal level, this is still recognised by many dreamers. To dream of quartz, therefore, signifies a recognition of developing power.

3 The quartz is recognised as both receiving and transmitting Spiritual energy.

QUARRY

1 Dreaming of a quarry means quarrying the depths of one's personality, 'digging out' the positive knowledge and perceptions we may have. Often dream symbols are created which link with childhood or past experiences which we may have buried and which now need to be brought into conscious understanding.

2 Seeking a quarry (that is, pursuing someone or something) in a dream can indicate that we, on some level, know what we are looking for, but that it is the action of finding it that is important.

3 A Spiritual search which may require digging out information.

QUAY
– also see Journey

1 Standing on a quayside in a dream can indicate either moving forward into a new phase of life or leaving an old one behind. If **looking forward** with a sense of anticipation, it is the new phase which needs understanding. If **looking back**, there may be something in the past which needs attention before we can move on.

2 Because anything associated with water is connected with emotion and how we feel about things, being on a quay can indicate how we need to handle other people's emotions as we move into a new phase of life.

3 Spiritual progress can be suggested by a quay, since it is a point of departure.

QUEEN
– see People

QUEST

1 The Hero's Quest is an archetypal image *(see Archetypes)* which can appear in many guises in dreams. To be searching for something usually indicates that we are aware that we must undertake a frightening task in order to progress. Many fairy stories and mythological tales have as their main theme the search for something rare or magical (e.g. Jason and the Argonauts). Such themes can be translated into dreams in a personally applicable way.

2 Often, the trials and tribulations we have to go through in achieving something we feel to be important are translated in dreams into a quest or search. The way these events are faced is as important as the actual achievement itself.

3 The pursuit of the Spiritual and undertaking a spiritual quest is a way of developing oneself spiritually.

QUESTION

1 To be asking questions in a dream indicates a degree of self-doubt. To have **someone asking the dreamer questions** shows that the dreamer is aware that he has some knowledge to be shared. If the **question cannot be answered**, the dreamer may need to seek the answer himself in waking life.

2 If we have a question in waking life which needs answering, by keeping it in mind before going to sleep we may often find the answer through dreams.

3 Spiritual questioning and enquiry lead to greater knowledge.

QUESTIONNAIRE/ QUIZ

1 To be **answering a questionnaire or quiz** in a dream suggests we may be making an attempt to change our circumstances without being certain of what we should actually do to bring about the change.

2 A questionnaire depicts the use of our mental faculties in a focused, decision-making way.

3 Questioning the inevitable is a way forward spiritually.

QUEUE

– see Line

QUICKSAND

1 Quicksand signifies a lack of security. In old-fashioned dream interpretation it represented business difficulties.

2 To find ourselves **trapped in quicksand** suggests that we have been put in a difficult situation that is not necessarily of our own making.

3 Spiritual quicksand suggests a

situation where we may be on insecure ground insofar as our beliefs are concerned.

QUIET

1 Becoming aware of **how quiet** it is in a dream shows that we need to cease being active for a while, perhaps in order to restore our emotional or spiritual balance.

2 Experiencing **a need for quiet** in a dream suggests that we need to listen more carefully to either ourselves or others in waking life.

3 Peace and tranquillity give us the opportunity for contemplation.

QUILT

1 The quilt or duvet can often represent our need for security, warmth and love. To be aware of one in a dream, therefore, is our identification of that need. A particular quilt may have a special significance. For instance a **child-hood quilt in an adult dream** would suggest the need for some kind of reassurance.

2 The colour or pattern of the quilt may have more significance than the quilt itself *(See Colour and Shapes)*.

3 Spiritual comfort and caring can be suggested by a quilt.

QUINTESSENCE

1 'Quintessence' literally means 'five beings', but is taken to mean 'supremely perfect'. To dream of this is to link with man's need to create, and to create as perfectly as he can.

2 Perfection is one of those things that, the more man knows, the more he realises how far he is from perfect. So to dream of the quintessence is to recognise his own and others' potential.

3 The quintessence of creatures under the Supreme Deity is the Lion among beasts, the Ox among cattle, the Eagle among birds, the Dolphin among fish, Man among all.

QUIP

1 When we become aware of a joke or quip by someone else in a dream, we are alerted to the fact that we can allow ourselves to be affected by other people's sense of humour.

2 If we ourselves are the ones who are communicating through wit or sarcasm, we may often be surprised by our own ability.

3 Often if something spiritual needs to be remembered it can present itself in dreams as a joke or a phrase with a sting in its tail.

QUIVER

1 Quivering indicates a state of extreme emotion. Such a reaction in a dream would signify that we need to consider the emotion and deal with it in everyday life. For instance, an extreme fear reaction may be the residue of something that has happened to us previously and can only be dealt with in waking life.

2 A physiological reaction can be translated into dreams as an action. To be quivering in a dream may simply be the effect of feeling cold.

3 As with shivering, a state of ecstasy can be induced, which is accompanied by quivering. This was initially how the Quakers got their name, as did the Shakers.

QUOTE/QUOTATION

1 To be giving a quote – as in **a building estimate** – can signify the value that we put on our services or talents. We may have difficulty with the accuracy – or the acceptance – of the quote and therefore, in waking life, will need to reconsider not only our own self-image, but also how we think others see us.

2 To utter or hear a quote – e.g. Shakespeare – indicates that we should consider the sentiment and power expressed within the quote.

3 A quote in a spiritual sense signifies Truth.

R

from

Rabbit *to* Rust

RABBIT
– see Animals

RACK

1 A rack in a dream suggests a need for us to store something or to keep it in order. **A wine rack**, for instance, may mean we have to pay close regard to our social life, while **a shoe rack** suggests a need to decide our best method of progress.

2 To find oneself **on the rack**, in the sense of being tortured, would suggest we have either done something we are ashamed of or have put ourselves in the position of being someone else's victim.

3 We may have to put ourselves on the rack in a disciplinary sense. Spiritually we may find discipline a problem.

RADAR

1 Radar in a dream represents our own personal intuitive faculty. It is our way of picking up subtle messages and signals which other people are giving out, often on a subliminal level.

2 For many, radar will register in dreams as a sort of 'Big Brother is watching you' feeling. We are monitoring ourselves, perhaps as to whether our behaviour or thoughts are appropriate.

3 Radar can suggest a degree of clairvoyance is available to the dreamer.

RADIANCE

1 When something appears as radiant in a dream it is being marked as having some kind of special quality which we may need to explore further.

2 Radiance represents something out of the ordinary or supernatural. It also suggests purity of thought, wisdom and the transcendence of the mundane.

3 Radiance is a sign of pure spirituality. It will enlighten and dazzle us and at the same time draw us in.

RADIO

1 As a method of communication, a radio suggests information which is available to everyone and therefore is widely understood. To dream of **hearing a radio playing** suggests a form of connection with the outside world. The context of the dream will give a wider explanation of the exact meaning.

2 Often in dreams a radio can stand for the voice of authority, or of commonly held ideas and ideals. On a more mundane level, in the waking state, people with mental problems can sometimes think they are being given instructions via the radio.

3 A radio is symbolic of spiritual communication. The dreamer should be aware of all his senses at this time and be open to any eventuality.

RAFFLE
– also see Gambling

1 In a dream, to be **taking part in a raffle** can indicate a need to win or come out on top. This is not necessarily, however, by our own efforts, but more by luck. To be **selling raffle tickets** would indicate our need to help others, whereas to be **setting up a raffle** suggests a group activity in which everyone can gain.

2 Although gambling may not be acceptable in the dreamer's normal code of behaviour, because a raffle is also a charitable act, it may, in dreams, be representative of quietening the dreamer's conscience at having taken a risk.

3 Spiritually, a raffle can symbolise our need to be charitable. However, we are also recognising the various risks involved, such as vulnerability and reliance. There is an element of having to rely on fate.

RAFT

1 A raft is a place of safety, often amid turbulence. While it may not be overly secure, it has the ability to support us. This is the kind of dream which occurs when we are dealing with emotional difficulties.

2 It can sometimes be meaningful to find out what the raft is made of. It can often appear in dreams as a symbol of transition, so the material can give the dreamer some idea of how to act.

3 The raft is an image connected with the spiritual transitions one must make in life. It is less secure than the idea of a boat, but more secure than doing it alone. If we are feeling 'lost' and can see no respite, then we may dream of a raft.

RAILWAY
– also see Train in Journey

1 A railway in a dream signifies the way we wish to go in life. We can take a way forward and can make informed choices. A **single track** suggests that there is only one way to go, whereas a **multiple track** suggests many more opportunities.

2 Psychologically, a railway suggests the idea of keeping to one goal (which may be a group one) and being single-minded about it. One early symbolism of the railway was the facility of being able to ignore obstacles, to go round, through or over anything which stood in the way.

3 Spiritually, the railway suggests a chosen direction which is usually fairly straightforward.

RAIN

1 In its simplest meaning, rain stands for tears and emotional release. We may have been depressed with no way to release our feelings in everyday life. Rain in dreams often becomes the first realisation that we can let go.

2 Rain in **a woman's dream** can suggest the sexual act. It can also have a more universal meaning, in that it is the realisation of potential on a group level. We should all be able to make use of the fertility that it can bring.

3 Rain by virtue of its 'heavenly' origins symbolises divine blessing and revelation.

RAINBOW

1 A rainbow appearing in a dream is the promise of something better to come. The old story of the pot of gold at the end of the rainbow is so firmly entrenched in folklore that this meaning often comes across in dreams.

2 The raising of consciousness and appreciation of something as ethereal as a rainbow suggests the need for a heightened sense of awareness. More esoterically, a rainbow is said to represent the seven steps of awareness necessary for true spirituality.

3 A rainbow symbolises the spiritual glory that is available to the dreamer through understanding and learning.

RAM
– see Animals

RAPE
– see Sex

RAT
– see Animals

RAVEN
– see Birds

RAZOR

1 It will depend on the type of razor which interpretation is given. A **cut-throat razor** would have the same symbolism as a knife – that is, cutting through the unnecessary. **A safety razor** suggests a less risky method is needed to enable us to reveal the truth about ourselves. An **electric razor** suggests that we need to pay attention to the image we put across in everyday life.

2 Psychologically, a razor is more of a tool than an aggressive implement. Thus, to be **using a razor on someone else**, is to be carrying out a caring act unless our actions are deliberately violent. We may in this case be aware that part of our personality needs changing or sharpening up.

3 Dreaming of a razor may allow us to consider our spiritual image and decide how to make changes.

REACHING OUT

1 Reaching out in a dream signifies our desire for something we do not have. This may be either emotional or material. We may be trying to manipulate circumstances in such a way that others become aware of our needs.

2 We are attempting to grasp a concept, an idea or an opportunity, which appears to be beyond our reach or understanding. We may also be trying to control others by our own emotional neediness. This is particularly relevant when we become conscious of rejection or distaste in others.

3 There is a stage in development when there is a yearning for spirit or spirituality. It does allow us to sort out what we really need.

READING

– also see Book and Novel

1 Reading a book in a dream suggests that we are seeking information. **Reading a letter** signifies receiving news. **Reading a list** – e.g. a shopping list – indicates a need to give some order to our lives. **Reading a Bible** or other holy book is attempting to understand a belief system.

2 Until recently, the only way to record events was to write them down. Reading is an activity which assists us in recalling things from memory – our own, or joint, memories. To be aware that we are **reading a novel** is to begin to understand our own need for fantasy. A **psychic reading** often works with many basic dream images. To dream of having such a reading suggests a need to understand ourselves on a deeper level.

3 Reading, or being in a library, appears in dreams as a form of spiritual realisation.

REAPING

1 In former times, the whole community took part in the reaping (gathering) of the harvest. This ensured that everybody gained in some way from this activity. Nowadays, to dream of reaping suggests a way of gaining from our activities.

2 The saying 'as ye sow, so shall ye reap' can be interpreted as – if we do good deeds, then that good will be returned. When we dream of **reaping a reward** for something we have done, we approve of our own activities. More negatively, a harmful act will return to haunt us.

3 The Grim Reaper – Death – is always pictured as carrying a scythe. The scythe is the association with reaping.

RED
– see Colours

RED INDIAN

1 Our perception of the American Indian as being naturally unsophisticated gives the interpretation of natural wisdom, or basic instinct. When one such appears we are able to handle a different kind of power and energy.

2 On a psychological level there is healing and self-awareness.

3 A Red Indian represents an inner power of which we may or may not have been aware. The dreamer should now be prepared to investigate his spirituality further.

REFLECTION
– also see Mirror

1 A reflection seen in a dream has a great deal to do with the way we see ourselves at that particular moment. Our self-image is important to us, as is the way other people see us. If the reflection is in a mirror, then our image will be perhaps more 'solid', whereas one seen in water will be more transient. The story of Narcissus and the way he fell in love with himself (or rather his own image) is a warning to all of us against self-worship.

2 Often, to see a reflection in a dream is to try to be understanding the inner self and the way that we cope with the outside world. Our grasp of that outer reality is tempered by the inner self. If in a dream **the two images do not correspond**, we will need to make some kind of adjustment in order to live comfortably within the everyday world.

3 The Spiritual truth that is available to us is often shown to us as though in a reflection.

REFRIGERATOR
– also see Larder

1 The refrigerator is a symbol of preservation. In dreams this becomes self preservation and suggests we may be turning cold emotionally or sexually. To dream of **rotten food in a refrigerator** suggests we feel we may not be being sustained properly by those around us.

2 To dream of **refrigerating leftover food** indicates we are storing up resentment. This, in turn, will 'cool down' our own responses to love and affection.

3 Religious austerity can be pictured as a refrigerator.

REINDEER
– see Deer in Animals

REINS

– also see Bridle, Halter and Harness

1 In dreams, reins, as a form of restraint, indicate the need to control the power and energy that we have.

2 Psychologically, to be reined suggests some form of inhibition – either our own or other people's. To see **reins breaking** signifies freeing ourselves from constraint – that which was placed on us while we grew up.

3 Reins indicate intelligent control and will.

RELIGIOUS IMAGERY

1 Dreams have a way of introducing – or rather reintroducing – us to truths which we have long known to be. If spirituality is taken to be an inner truth, and religion as that which links us back to source, then it must be the case that religious imagery partly assists in that function of recognition. Using images that cannot be interpreted successfully in any other way reinforces the idea of spirituality being something separate in us. Because the images are so specific they may be startling.

2 When the individual, through deliberate or spontaneous neglect, denies himself access to the store of religious imagery in waking life, dreams will often react to this lack and try to compensate by jolting the dreamer back into an awareness of his inner spirit. In today's society it is very easy to fasten on the hypocritical aspects of religion and to accept that hypocrisy. It is also easy to make the assumption that the outward forms of religion often deny the existence of a true inner reality. This rejection can be valid, since it is not until the individual accepts responsibility for his own existence that true spirituality emerges. If spirituality – the inner truth that we all hold – is neglected, it will not go away: it will simply reappear in its negative and terrifying form. In waking life the closest image we have to that is the Devil *(see Devil)*, or the more vengeful Indian gods. Our own personalised demons can be more frightening than those.

3 If we are prepared to accept that each truth will have its own personal slant, and that we must get back to the basic truth, all dreams can be interpreted from a spiritual point of view. This is especially true of religious imagery. Most interpretations have had to be stated in general terms and are given here only as guidelines. When the reader can throw away the book and say that the interpretations are not valid, then he will have taken on personal responsibility.

Angel In spiritual terms the angel symbolises pure being and freedom from earthly matters. Angels tend to be androgynous, and are not recognised either as male or female. There is a hierarchy of angels; 1) Angels (the realm closest to the physical), 2) Cherubim and 3) Seraphim. As more people are seeking spirituality, there are those who have become more aware of the angel form, particularly in dreams. It is vital that the dreamer is able to differentiate between the personalised aspect of the Higher Self, and the angelic form, since they are similar but different. **Dark angels** are reputed to be those angelic beings who have not yet totally rejected the ego or earthly passions. When this image appears in a dream, we are being alerted to a spiritual transgression, which often has already happened. **Warning angels** usually symbolise what should not be done.

Buddha (also see individual entry) The figure of Buddha appearing in dreams highlights the necessity to be aware of the Qualities of Being which Buddha taught. It links us to the power of renunciation and of suffering, but in the sense that experience of suffering is valid.

Ceremony/Ritual (also see individual entries) Ceremony and ritual are all part of the heightening of awareness which occurs on the path to spirituality. In dream ceremony the images are even more vivid.

Christ appearing in dreams epitomises the recognition of the ability to reconcile the physical and the spiritual, God and Man. He personifies Perfect Man, a state to which we all aspire. **Appearing on the cross** he signifies redemption through suffering. We do not need to be crucified physically to suffer. **The ideal Christ** is that part of ourselves which is prepared to take on our portion of the sufferings in the world by working within the world. **The anarchic Christ** is the part of us whose love and lust for life permit us to break through all known barriers. **The Cosmic Christ** is the part that is prepared to take on Cosmic Responsibility – that is, to be connected with the Universal Truth. While these aspects have been spoken of in Christian terms, obviously they are also present in all religious figures.

Church, chapel, temple (also see Church Buildings) We all are aware of our need for sanctuary from the batterings of the everyday world. Within the church we are free to form a relationship with our own personal God. In dreams we may also have the realisation that our body is our temple.

Church or Religious Music These sounds, dedicated to the perception of God that one has, are sacred sounds and are a way of expanding the spirit.

Crucifixion images in a dream link with the human being's need to sacrifice himself through passion and through pain.

Devil *(also see individual entry)* In dreams the Devil represents temptation. This often arises from the repressed sexual drives which demand attention. It may also signify the Shadow *(see Introduction)*.

Ghosts *(also see individual entry)* Independent forces within, which are separate from the individual's will. It will depend on the dreamer's belief as to whether he accepts the appearance of ghosts as psychological or spiritual apparitions.

Gods/Goddesses *(also see individual entries)* We are each given the opportunity to make real our fullest potential. In doing so, we must undertake an exploration and possibly a confrontation of our perception of gods and goddesses.

Hell is a state of being where nothing is ever as it seems and could be thought of as continually existing in a state of negative illusion. Reputedly it is a state of Spiritual Agony where one's worst dreams are fulfilled.

Heaven is a state of being where the energy is of such a high frequency that there is no suffering. In dreams it appears when the individual is transmuting his awareness into dimensions other than the physical. It is reputedly a place where bliss exists. It is also known as Nirvana and Samadhi.

Holy Communion The belief that Christ's body was transmuted into heavenly food – symbolised by the Last Supper – appears in dreams as the intake of spiritual food. Holy Communion represents a sacred sharing.

Icon *(also see individual entry)* An icon is a representation of a religious figure or concept. It can, through usage, become revered as a holy object in its own right.

Incense *(also see individual entry)* Incense is an offering to the gods and a physical form of prayer through perfume and smoke.

Initiation takes place when some barrier is transcended to enable us to have access to other ways of being.

Mary, the Mother of God/Virgin Mother The symbolism of Mary, both as the maiden and as the mother, is a potent one. She epitomises all that is woman, and all that is holy.

Moses often appears in dreams as the holy figure who will lead us out of difficulty.

Old and New Testaments or all religious books A resource and a repository for knowledge is available – in dream imagary this will often appear as books.

Priest/Prophet A conflict between the present and the future.

A Religious Service is the act of worship which is used to bring people together. It is recognised in dreams, perhaps as an act of integration of the whole self, and as an illustration that the whole is greater than the parts.

Third Eye This is the developed clairvoyant perceptiveness that comes with spiritual development. It is the Third Eye of Buddha and symbolises unity and balance. In no case does it represent a physical quality, though it is thought to link with the pineal gland.

RENT

1 Paying rent in dreams is to undertake a personal responsibility. We are prepared to look after ourselves and to take responsibility for who we are. **Receiving rent** suggests that we have entered into a transaction which will benefit us.

2 There comes a time when, if we wish to maximise our potential, we must find a space of our own.

Paying rent allows us to do this. In dreams this can be seen as an independent act.

3 Often in spiritual terms we must relearn how to handle money and value. The image of paying rent gives this concept a focus.

REPTILES
– also see Animals

1 Reptiles in dreams link with our basic and instinctive reactions and responses. When there is a basic urge – such as a need for food, sex, etc. – we sometimes cannot face it full on, but will symbolise it as a reptile.

2 When there is a need to understand why we do things, we first need to control our basic drives. Many reptilian dreams are about control or management. Control of a **crocodile** would suggest some fear of an aggressive nature. Feeding a **lizard** or stroking a **snake** can be very simply interpreted.

3 With understanding of the basic urges and the way to manage them we can create a firm foundation. From there we can progress spiritually.

RESCUE

1 Being rescued in dreams is a powerful image, since it leaves us indebted to our rescuer. **Rescuing**

someone else often suggests that we wish to have a relationship with that person. The knight rescuing the maiden signifies the idea of the untouched feminine being rescued from her own passion.

2 When we have put others in danger in dreams, we are required to rescue them. We are then able to show a degree of nobility and courage which engenders a feel-good factor and allows us to have power.

3 Spiritual rescue is generally accepted as relinquishment for 'lost souls', whether they are this side of the veil or not.

RESIGN

1 In dreams to resign is to give up. To dream of **resigning from work** means we are aware of major changes in our lives. We perhaps need to look at our lives and accustom ourselves to the idea that there are areas that we do not need to be in. **To be resigned** to something suggests that we have accepted the status quo in our lives.

2 Resignation is a state of mind brought about through having to face difficulties in life. It is as though we come to a point where we are not capable of making any further effort or decision. Indeed, it may be better not to, but simply to resign ourselves to whatever may happen. In dreams this resignation is recognisable as not wanting to go on.

3 Spiritual resignation is the giving in to inevitability. We no longer have any need or wish to fight any more.

RESTAURANT

1 Dreaming of a restaurant or cafe suggests a need for company. We may be fearful of being alone, but equally be afraid of allowing someone to delve too far into our private space. This public space allows for contact but, at the same time, we can control our own level of intimacy.

2 Any place connected with food is to do with our need for emotional sustenance. There is feedback to be received from eating in a public place. Our social needs our met. We may be conscious of the need for a 'relationship' with the place we are eating at, as much as with the person with whom we are eating.

3 Spiritually a restaurant symbolises our need to belong to a group of people who all have the same habits and perhaps a diversity of beliefs.

RIBBON
- See Bridle, Halter and Harness

RICE

– also see Grain

1 Rice as an image in dreams suggests food, both for the mind and the body. It also suggests abundance.

2 Rice is supposed to be magical and symbolises spiritual nourishment.

3 Like most grains, spiritually, rice symbolises immortality and fecundity.

RING

– also see Wedding Ring

1 A ring appearing in a dream usually signifies a relationship of some sort. A **wedding ring** suggests a union and a promise. **A ring belonging to the family** would represent old traditions and values. **An engagement ring** suggests a more tentative promise of devotion. **An eternity ring** would be a long-term promise. **A signet ring** would indicate setting the seal on something. **A bull ring** suggests an element of cruelty.

2 We all need some kind of continuity in our lives, something which gives a sense of long-term comfort. A ring holds this symbolism because it is never-ending and is self-perpetuating.

3 Like the circle, the ring signifies eternity and divinity. The Whole.

RITUAL

– also see Ceremony and
Religious Imagery

1 Rituals can range from the 'sublime to the ridiculous'. They are actions which are repeated over and over again in order to achieve a certain result.

2 Such rituals as getting up in the morning, because they are habits, simply have the purpose of getting us focused. **Religious** rituals have taken on a life of their own and help concentrate the power of the many. **Magical** rituals have become 'power centres' in their own right.

3 Spiritually we are able to focus our energies in such a way that we can work for the Greater Good.

RIVER

– see Water

ROAD

– see Journey

ROBE

1 Dreaming of a robe, such as a **bath robe** can have two meanings. One is that of covering up vulnerability and the other is of being relaxed and at ease. The dream will indicate the correct significance. To be **dressing someone else in a robe** is to protect them.

2 A robe can suggest our attitude to sex and relationships. If it is **clean** we have a good self-image if **dirty**, the opposite. A dirty robe could also suggest depression.

3 In spiritual terms the **white robe** is innocence and the **seamless robe** represents holiness.

ROCK

1 To dream of rock suggests stability in the real world. If we are on **firm ground** we can survive. We may also be aware that we must be firm and stand 'rock-like' and not be dissuaded from our purpose. **Seaside rock** can remind us of happier, more carefree times.

2 On an intellectual level, all the images that one thinks of in relationship to rocks prevail. There is reliability, coldness, rigidity and so on. We need to recognise these qualities within ourselves in order to handle ourselves properly. We can find ourselves between a 'rock and a hard place' – in a difficult situation in dreams.

3 Spiritually we will need, at some point, to go through a barrier from difficulty to sanctuary. This often presents itself as a rock barrier. Dual rocks through which we must pass suggest the same image as the passage between two pillars, that is, passing from one state of being to the next.

ROCKET

1 The rocket in basic terms has a connection with male sexuality. What is perhaps more important is the energy that is available to us in dreams. To be **given a rocket** suggests recognising that we are not functioning the way we should. To **take off like a rocket** means moving very fast in terms of some project we have.

2 Nowadays any symbol of power connects with our ability to do, or be, better than before. The rocket in this sense will have much of the same symbolism as the aeroplane *(See Aeroplane)*, except the destinations will be further away. The explosive power and energy available is something to be carefully looked at, since we need this type of power in order to make radical changes in our lives.

3 Because of the spiritual symbolism of reaching heights to which none have been before, the rocket represents spiritual searching and adventure.

ROCKING

1 Rocking in dreams can be a comforting activity, a little like a child who will rock himself to sleep. Rocking can also suggest infantile behaviour from the point of view that it puts us in touch with the natural rhythms of life.

2 Particularly when we want to be soothed we like to be rocked. The gentle movement can allow us to be in touch with our own centre. So to be **rocking someone** is to be soothing them. Conversely, to **be rocked** is to be soothed.

3 Rocking is a symbol of transition. To move to and fro suggests both hesitation and desire. Rocking is also a fertility symbol.

ROD
– see Staff

ROOF

1 To concentrate on, or be aware of, the roof of a building in a dream is to acknowledge the shelter and protection it affords. If **the roof leaks** then we are open to emotional attacks. If we are **on the roof** we are not being protected.

2 A roof is a basic requirement in man's need for comfort. Psychologically, it is important to be protected against the elements. Equally, he needs to know that he is capable of 'reaching for the sky'.

3 The sheltering aspect of the feminine as the guardian of the hearth is sometimes represented as a roof.

ROOM
– see Buildings

ROOT
– see Tree

ROPE
– also see Hanging and Noose

1 A rope can suggest strength and power, though the power can turn against us. A **rope and pulley** suggests using the forces of weight to help us. If the rope is made of an unusual substance, **such as hair or material**, there is a special bond or necessity which requires the qualities that that substance has.

2 If we are **tied to the rope**, something is holding us back from expressing ourselves. **Being tied by a rope to something else** means we need to look at the relationship between us and what we are tied to. We should look at the limitations of that relationship.

3 A rope can offer security, and also freedom. As **a noose** it suggests despair and possibly death.

ROSARY
– see Necklace and Beads

ROSE/ROSETTE

1 The rose in dreams has a great deal of symbolism. It represents love and admiration; in a bouquet the number of roses and the colour will be significant *(see Numbers and Colour)*. It can also suggest fertility and virginity.

2 As a psychological symbol the rose represents perfection. It contains within it the mystery of life and its grace and happiness. It also suggests the cycle of life, through the cycle of its own growth and decay.
3 Spiritually the rose has ambivalent meanings. It suggests perfection and passion, life and death, Time and Eternity. It also represents the heart, the centre of life.

ROUND TABLE

1 A round table in a dream is a symbol of wholeness. Partly because of the tales of King Arthur, there are various myths associated with a round table, but essentially it indicates that everyone is equal.
2 The round table is a representation of the heavens, since the twelve knights are the signs of the Zodiac *(see Zodiac)*. In dreams we are continually trying to create perfection and this is one such dream.
3 Spiritually the table suggests a centre, but one from which all things can begin.

RUINS

1 When **something is in ruins** we have to discover if it is through neglect or vandalism. If the former, the suggestion is that we need to pull things together. If the latter, we need to look at how we are making ourselves vulnerable.
2 If we have **deliberately ruined something** we need to clarify a self-destructive element in us. Sometimes by looking at the symbolism of what has ruined an object or an occasion will give us insight into our own processes.
3 Occasionally it is vital that there is an element of destructiveness in us in order that we can rebuild part of our lives on a better basis.

RUNNING

1 To be running in a dream suggests speed and flow. To be **running forwards** suggests confidence and ability. To be **running away from** signifies fear and an inability to do something.
2 Obviously in dreams of running, time and place are significant. Where we are going will perhaps indicate why speed is needed, although if we are being pursued this will also give some kind of reason. To be running something – as in **managing** – is to be taking responsibility.
3 Running in dreams suggests the potential for anxiety or distress. Spiritually we may be trying to do something too quickly.

RUSH

1 To be in a rush suggests that we

are having to contend with outside pressures. **To be rushing** suggests that we ourselves are putting the pressure on. The pressure would be on our time, and it is interesting that rushes or reeds actually do symbolise time.

2 We need to learn how to manage time successfully, and to be rushing suggests that we have not done so.

3 Oddly, time is a symbol for space in spiritual work. If we are rushing we do not see the best of our world. Conversely if we use our space successfully then we also use time properly.

RUST

1 Rust represents neglect and negligence. We have not looked after the quality of our lives properly and should look to address this oversight.

2 To dream of **cleaning up rust** suggests that we recognise our own negligence. Dreaming of rust **appearing as we look at an object** signifies that a project has reached the end of its useful life.

3 Spiritually, we may have to remove evidence of contamination before we can progress. Rust may signify old outdated attitudes.

S

from

Sack *to* Syringe

SACK

1 At its simplest, to dream of a sack can link with word play such as 'getting the sack'. It brings a period of our lives to an end, possibly in a rather negative way. Perhaps in an effort to move on, we have created circumstances within our lives which make us feel bad about ourselves for a time.

2 The sack has the same significance as the bag, or any such receptacle. **In a woman's dream** it can therefore perhaps mean pregnancy, while interestingly enough **in a man's dream** it is more likely to mean some kind of womb experience *(see Womb in Body)*. As a symbol of security the womb is often symbolised in dreams as a bag or sack. Very often the sack as a utilitarian object has the significance of containing something for us – of giving us an opportunity to consider our belongings. We can empty the sack, as it were, and decide what is important to us and what we need to take forward.

3 In its starkest meaning the sack can indicate death. It can literally mean the death of a person, or it can indicate the liberation of part of our personality. We need to release a difficulty in order to continue within our own framework of life.

SACKCLOTH

1 In its oldest form, sackcloth represented humiliation. People were dressed in sackcloth to signify that they were less than dust. Hence the saying 'sackcloth and ashes'. Nowadays in dreams it is much more likely to represent our own sense of humiliation, that we have humiliated ourselves in an action which we have taken.

2 Sackcloth also indicates repentance. We may feel that we have humiliated ourselves, but equally we may wish to show the world that we have repented of an action or deed. The symbol of sackcloth comes up in a dream to indicate that we need to make an outward show of such repentance.

3 The act of mourning in olden times often indicated some public show, and so sackcloth was taken as the substance to show the spiritual poverty of the people concerned – that they had lost something very valuable. In dreams this symbolism can also come across.

SACRIFICES

1 As a rule, sacrifice has two meanings. Firstly, it is to give something up and secondly to make something sacred or holy. So when those two things are possible within a dream scenario the dreamer is prepared to give up his ego or individuality for the sake of something greater or more important than himself. Often a sacrifice is made because of passionately held beliefs, often religious in origin.

2 There is usually some expectation of a forthcoming just reward (often spiritual), for having made sacrifices. There may be an element of deferred gratification in that we do not expect an immediate reward, except that of feeling good or knowing one has done the right thing. There is always an element also of giving up egotistic behaviour which is no longer appropriate, and going with the flow of life. **Sacrificing an animal** suggests that we are conscious of the fact that our lower, more basic instincts can be given up in favour of spiritual power. We have to be prepared to recognise our own human state, but to give up indulgence. There may be a sacrificial altar, or it may just be a question of killing and cooking an animal ritualistically. **If the animal is willing to be sacrificed**, then we are ready to transmute instinct into spiritual energy. If the animal is a hare or a rabbit, the symbolism is that of rebirth.

3 Sacrifice is an important aspect of spiritual growth and signifies the renunciation of the lesser for the rewards of the greater.

SADDLE

1 A saddle appearing in a dream will often indicate a need to exercise control over someone. Obviously this can suggest sexual control, particularly **in a woman's dream**. In a **man's dream** it is more likely to signify his need to control his own life in some way – perhaps the direction in which he is going or the circumstances of his own life. It will be more the sense of his own masculinity and drive which is highlighted.

2 To some extent it will depend on what we are doing with the saddle, and also what kind of saddle it is. A **motorcycle saddle** – in that it is an integral part of the machine – will suggest a more rigid type of control than **a horse's saddle**, which is flexible and removable. If the **saddle is slipping** we are about to lose authority in a situation in our lives. If a **saddle does not fit in some way** – remembering that it is also designed for the comfort of the rider – we may be being made uncomfortable by external circumstances rather than by our own volition.

3 We have an opportunity to take control of our own lives from a spiritual perspective and should use that opportunity wisely.

SADISM
– also see Sex

1 Sadism often arises because of anger still held – but suppressed – from childhood hurts. It is the wish to hurt or provoke a reaction – often in someone we love. In waking life most of us are not capable of being sadistic, but in dreams we can do what we like, so sadism becomes acceptable.

2 It will obviously depend on whether we are **being sadistic** or if someone is **being sadistic towards us** as to the interpretation. We know that in dreams other people can represent parts of ourselves, so we need to consider whether we are causing ourselves harm deliberately or inadvertently. We may feel that we wish to punish ourselves for some supposed misdemeanour and, as a displacement activity, we dream of sadistic behaviour. The very fact that it is sadistic may also mean that it is masochistic – that is, self-involved.

3 Punishment can be the other side of compassion if we do not have the correct motivation: 'It's for your own good'.

SAILING
– also see Journey

1 When we dream of sailing, we are highlighting how we feel we are handling our lives. We can either work with the currents or against them. If we are sailing **in a yacht** there is more of a sense of immediacy than if we were **sailing in a liner**. The first is more to do with one-to-one relationships, while the second suggests more of a group effort.

2 To be tacking – **sailing against the wind** – suggests that we have created difficulties possibly by setting ourselves against public opinion. To be **sailing with the wind** means we are using opportunities to the best of our abilities.

3 Sailing suggests a sense of spiritual freedom and the ability to use our intellect.

SAILS
– also see Sailing and Wind

1 Sails suggest the idea of making use of available power. Often the type of sail will be relevant. **Old-fashioned sails** would suggest out-of-date methods, whereas **racing sails** might suggest the use of modern technology. The colour of the sails may also be important *(see Colour)*.

2 Because a boat or ship is usually thought of as feminine, the sails in dreams can represent pregnancy and fertility. By association, they can also signify how a woman will use her intellect.

3 Sails represent the Spirit – as in a force that moves us.

SAILOR

1 Most people have a rather anti-quated idea of the sailor. It is this image that usually appears in dreams. He represents freedom, both of movement and of spirit, and is a representation of the Tramp *(see Archetypes)*. He suggests someone who is totally in control of his own destiny. A **modern-day sailor** would have the added benefit of being in control of his own environment.

2 If a sailor does appear in a dream, particularly **in a woman's**, he is usually a some-what romanticised figure and can represent the Hero *(see Archetypes)*. **In a man's dream** he represents the part of himself which seeks freedom, but that needs to be given permission or authority to take that freedom.

3 Spiritually, the sailor can signify communication. The aspect of freedom links with a quality of Mercury who, having been given a task, then forgets what it is.

SALAD

1 Most food in dreams links with our need and ability to nurture our-selves and others. Particularly in a salad the colour will be important *(see Colour)* – as also may the texture. We may be short of some kind of nutrient or stimulus and the dream state has alerted us to this.

2 The ingredients in a salad can have significance individually. It is also the synergy (energy created) between the components that is important. If we register that we **dislike what we are being offered** it is worth considering whether we reject the whole dish or only part of it. If we have **created the salad for some-one else** in our dream, there is perhaps part of ourselves which needs attention more than the rest.

3 Salad, because it is food in its simplest sense, takes us right back to nature and simple values.

SALMON

1 The salmon signifies abundance and masculinity and is phallic. In its fight to mate by swimming upstream it can also symbolise the sperm. Often a salmon can appear **in a woman's dream** as a symbol of her wish for pregnancy.

2 In common with most fish when they appear in dreams, the salmon signifies our basic urges – most often the need for survival. By being able to put in effort we reap the rewards of our actions.

3 In mythology the salmon signi-fies knowledge of other worlds (the lands beneath the sea) and of other-worldly things. This refers principally to the subconscious.

SALT

1 In dreams, salt highlights the subtle qualities we bring to our lives, those things we do to enhance our lifestyle. It has been suggested that if the water was removed from the human body there would be enough minerals and salt left to cover a fifty pence piece. We run most of our lives through our emotions but the more subtle aspects are just as important.

2 As a symbol of permanence and incorruptibility salt is important in dreams. As in the old days salt was paid as salary, so nowadays to be given salt is to be given one's correct worth. There are many customs associated with salt. It is **thrown over the shoulder**, supposedly in the face of the Devil. In Scotland, along with coal and bread, it is the first thing to pass over the threshold to greet the New Year.

3 As a distillation of everything we know, salt represents wisdom.

SAND

1 Sand in a dream suggests instability and lack of security. When **sand and sea are seen together** we are demonstrating a lack of emotional security. When the **sands are shifting** we are probably unable to decide what we require in life. If we are conscious of the **sand in an hourglass** we are conscious of time running out.

2 Sand can represent impermanence. **Building sand castles** is something of a fantasy occupation since they will be washed away by the tide. To dream of doing this would indicate that the structure we are trying to give to our lives does not have permanence and may be an illusion.

3 Spiritually, sand represents the impermanence of the physical life and can suggest having to approach death or change in some way.

SAP

1 The old adage that the sap rises in Spring is fully accepted by most people. In dream terms this means that we are maybe ready to undertake new work or perhaps a new relationship. We are aware of our own vitality and strength and prepared to take on new challenges.

2 Sap used to be a derogatory term for a wimp or someone who had no backbone. In a negative sense we may become aware in dreams of inappropriate behaviour or ideas. These have the effect of sapping our inner vitality.

3 The life-force we use can often be perceived as the sap in plants.

SARCOPHAGUS

1 A sarcophagus is similar to a tomb, but is much more of a memorial, marking how important the occupant is or was. To dream of such an edifice is to recognise the importance of death and the rites of passage associated with it.

2 When we come to an important change in our lives we may wish to mark the passage or transition in some way. We have a need to have other people recognise or appreciate our efforts. A sarcophagus would indicate that there is a good deal of ego still to be dealt with within us.

3 Spiritually, death indicates both a change of state and a change of status and a sarcophagus is a symbol of such change.

SATAN
– see Devil

SATELLITE

1 Before satellites were invented, the stars were used as fixed points in communication. Nowadays a satellite would suggest efficient, effective contact. We are more globally aware of the effect we can have both on our environment and on other people around us.

2 A satellite can appear in a dream to indicate the dependency that one person can have upon another. Often in relationships one partner is more important than the other and either could therefore recognise the symbol of the satellite.

3 A satellite can represent spiritual communication from a discarnate source.

SATYR

1 When man was less civilised than he is now, his animal nature was closer to the surface. It was possible for him to see and identify patterns of energy or spirits both in himself and in nature which then took on human or semi-human form. The satyr is one such form, and is a male spirit connected with nature at its lowest. While most of the time in the waking state we suppress such figures, in dreams – where there is no conscious control – they will sometimes appear.

2 From a psychological standpoint the satyr is that part of nature which is out of control, and beyond restraint. It owes allegiance to no-one and is completely anarchic. If perceived as destructive then it will be so. If accepted as helpful then it will be equally obliging.

3 The satyr is a spirit of nature and of natural power.

SAVINGS

1 In dreams we often develop images which have dual meanings. Our savings may represent resources, either material or emotional, which we have hidden away until such times as they are needed. They can also represent our sense of security and independence. To dream of **savings we did not know we had** would suggest that we are able to summon up extra energy or time, perhaps by using material or information from the past. To dream of **making savings in the present** suggests we may need to give consideration to the wherewithal we have in the here and now to succeed in the future. If we are **aware of our goal in making savings** we should perhaps make long-term plans.

2 When we dream of savings we are aware of the need for conservation. This may be on a personal level or in a more global sense. If there is a feeling of self-denial in our making savings we may not have managed our resources properly in the past and are having to suffer for it now. If **someone else gives us their savings** we are able to use their knowledge

and expertise. Conversely, if we **give our savings away** we no longer have need of whatever those savings mean to us.

3 In the spiritual sense, savings suggests those talents and abilities which we have or have developed, but have not yet used, particularly those for the Greater Good.

SAW

– see Tools

SCAFFOLD/ SCAFFOLDING

1 A scaffold or scaffolding in a dream will usually indicate that there is some kind of temporary structure in our lives. **A hangman's scaffold** will suggest that a part of our lives must come to an end. We may, for instance, be aware that we have offended against some of society's laws and beliefs, and must be punished. We also may need to look at our propensity to be a victim. If **scaffolding** appears in dreams we should decide whether it is there to help us build something new or whether we must repair the old. We need a temporary structure to help us reach the height we wish in either case. If we are **building new**, that structure will support us while we build, whereas if we are **repairing the old** it will support the previous structure while we make the necessary changes.

2 Sometimes in dreams a scaffold will indicate an enforced ending. This can be death, but is more likely to suggest the death of part of our personality. Rather than being able to achieve a successful integration, we actually actively have to stop the behaviour or activity which is causing a problem. We have to take the consequences of behaving in that way.

3 A scaffold suggests an enforced code of spiritual behaviour and the need for self-control. Scaffolding indicates spiritual support.

SCALES

1 Scales in a dream suggest the necessity for balance and self-control. Without that balance we cannot make a sensible decision as to potential courses of action. We must 'weigh up' all the possibilities. Scales will also suggest standards – for instance, standards of behaviour – to which we are expected to adhere. We may be weighed and found wanting. If the **scales are unbalanced** in a dream we need to search our conscience and discover where we are not functioning properly.

2 The type of scale we see in our dream will us give a more explicit interpretation. For example,

Bathroom scales would suggest a more personal assessment than a public machine, whereas a **weigh bridge** might suggest that we need to take our whole lives into consideration. If they were **doctor's scales** we may be alerting ourselves to a potential health problem.

3 The Scales of Justice represent balance and harmony, but also good judgement. By association, they also represent the astrological sign of Libra.

SCALP
– see Head in Body

SCAPEGOAT

1 The word scapegoat actually comes from the sacrificing of a goat to appease the gods, and in dreams this symbol can be highly relevant. If in our dream **we are the scapegoat** for someone else's action then we are being turned into a victim. Other people may be trying to make us pay for their misdemeanours. If **we are making another person a scapegoat** then this indicates a blame shift, and that we are not taking responsibility for our own actions.

2 Often in families and teams one member takes the brunt of all the projections from the rest of the family or group. He (or she) is continually belittled or laughed at, and can be blamed for all sorts of things which are not their fault. They become the scapegoat. In dreams, however, there is recognition that there is an aspect of co-operation and collaboration in the dreamer. We need to do something to redress the balance, and often the solution can only come from us.

3 This represents the sacrificial victim, dying that others might live.

SCAR

1 A scar in a dream suggests that there are old hurts which have not been fully dealt with. These may be mental and emotional as much as physical, and can remain unnoticed until we are reminded of them. Just as in physical injury there can be many kinds of scars, so there can also be in the other areas. We may, for instance, be left with a pattern of behaviour which is irritating to other people, but without the clear connection given by the dream image, we are unable to understand it.

2 It will often be significant **which area of the body is scarred** in the dream. The nervous system can develop ways of giving information without us being conscious of it. This may give some indication of the area of life that is

affected by the trauma. If **we see someone else who has been scarred** it may be necessary to discover if we are the ones who have hurt others in the past. If this is so, there are various techniques we can use in the waking state to help us release others either from the hurt we – or they – have inflicted. The healing may then be recorded in dreams by the loss of the scar.

3 Spiritually, a scar may suggest that something negative and harmful has occurred, which is an external force rather than internal. We may not have dealt with it as well as we might.

SCEPTRE

1 The sceptre is representative of royal power and sovereignty. When it appears in dreams it is usually indicative of the fact that we have given someone authority over us. We have abdicated responsibility to the point that the inner self has to take over. The sceptre also has the same symbolism as most rods, which is, of course, phallic.

2 If we are holding the sceptre we have the ability to transmit the life force. If **someone else is using the sceptre** and is bestowing honour or power on us, then we can accept that we have succeeded in our particular project.

3 The sceptre can represent the magic wand and in dreams can indicate our right to use such magic. Spiritually it also signifies the transmission of divine power from above rather than below. Thus it is masculine power.

SCHOOL
– also see Education and Teacher

1 School is an important part of everyone's life. In situations where we are learning new abilities or skills, the image of a school will often come up in dreams. It is also the place where we experience associations which do not belong to the family, and can therefore suggest new ways of learning about relationships. School may also be the place where we learn about competitiveness and how to belong to groups.

2 When we are relearning how to deal with our own personalities, **the school or classroom** will often appear in dreams. They will often appear at times when we are attempting to get rid of old, outmoded ideas and concepts. Also, when we are learning different ways of dealing with authority and with feelings of inadequacy, our feelings about school will surface.

3 Spiritually it is often considered that life itself is a school. Life is an arena for learning and experiencing so that we can maximise our best potential. It is believed that life is a testing-ground for the reality which comes afterwards.

SCISSORS

1 Scissors in dreams suggest the idea of cutting the non-essential out of our lives. This may be feelings we do not think are appropriate, emotions that we cannot handle, or mental trauma which needs to be excised. The type of scissors may also be important to the dreamer. **Kitchen scissors** would, for instance, be more utilitarian than **surgical scissors** which would suggest the necessity to be more precise. Scissors can also suggest a sharp, hurtful tongue or cutting remarks.

2 Dreaming of **sharpening scissors** suggests that we need to be more precise in our communication, whereas using **blunt scissors** suggests that we are likely to create a problem through speaking too bluntly. **To dream of a hairdresser using scissors** signifies our fear of losing strength and status.

3 Spiritually scissors can have an ambivalent meaning. They can cut the Thread of Life, but can also represent unity and the coming together of the spiritual and physical.

SCREW

1 It will depend on what society we belong to as to how we interpret 'screw'. To the criminal element a screw will mean a prison officer or jailer. To a younger element in society it is a slang word for the sexual act. So there could be word play, even if the object seen is a proper screw.

2 Screws suggest tasks that are seen to be pointless, except in a wider context. To be **screwing two pieces of wood together** would presuppose that we intend to make something, so our action is a means to an end. Screws are reputed to give a better join than nails; therefore the implication is that we are building something to last. We need to take pride in our activities.

3 Spiritually we will be looking for satisfaction in a job well done. There is also a connection with the spiral *(see Shapes)*.

SCROLL

1 Nowadays, a scroll will represent an acknowledgement of a learning process – i.e. the scroll presented to graduating students. It will depend on the circumstances what the exact interpretation is. We are endorsing either our own knowledge or information which has been given to us, so that we can enhance our lives.

2 A scroll can represent hidden knowledge, and also the passing of time. Thus, under certain circumstances, dreaming of a scroll signifies having to wait until the knowledge we have gained can be used at an appropriate time.

3 A scroll can signify the letter of the law and the respect that it deserves. If we are **given a scroll**, we are deemed responsible enough to use the information we have gained.

SCYTHE
– also see Sickle

1 The scythe is a cutting instrument, and therefore has the same significance as a knife *(See Weapons)*. In dreams it usually suggests that we need to cut out non-essential actions or beliefs. We need to be fairly ruthless in order to achieve a desired end.

2 The scythe is a very old-fashioned symbol for the passage of time. Its appearance in dreams shows we are linking with very deeply held concepts and ideas. We are becoming aware of the fact that the cutting off of life – or energy – may be imminent around us, although it need not be our own death. It may be that part of us can no longer provide us with what we want.

3 The scythe, like the hour glass, is

often held by the figure of Death and represents the ending of physical existence.

SEA
– see Water

SEAL
– also see Animals

1 Historically, a **wax seal** confirmed authority and power. It was also a symbol of identity. Nowadays in dreams, it is much more likely to signify legality or correct moral action. In dreams, **the possession of a seal** gives us the authority to take responsibility for our own actions.

2 When we dream of legal documents, to become aware of the seal can indicate that a conclusion has been reached which is both binding and secret. **To be breaking a seal** indicates that we are possibly breaking a confidence or someone's trust in us. It has also been suggested that **a man breaking a seal in a woman's dream** suggests that she will lose her virginity or purity at some level.

3 Spiritually a seal suggests hidden knowledge. Not all esoteric and occult information is available to everyone. Such information is only entrusted to someone who has the courage to break the seal.

SEANCE

1 Dreaming of being at a seance can suggest a need to explore the psychic side of our nature. Remembering that psychic means 'being in touch with self', this can suggest being aware of our intuition.

2 A seance is better known nowadays as a sitting. In dreams it may register that the best way we can contact our own spiritual self is by sitting still.

3 Spiritually, one needs the qualities of patience and determination – symbolised by sitting – in order to progress.

SEARCHING

1 To be searching in a dream is an attempt to find an answer to a problem. If we are **searching for someone** we may be conscious of our loneliness. If we are **searching for something** we may be aware of an unfulfilled need.

2 Searching in a dream for something we have lost can suggest either that we need information from the past, or that we feel we have lost our identity. Searching also suggests more of a commitment to actually finding than just simply looking.

3 The movement towards spirituality often begins from a feeling of searching for something.

SEARCHLIGHT
– also see Light

1 A searchlight in a dream denotes focused attention and concentration. If the **searchlight is trained on us**, we need to consider our actions and behaviour.

2 A searchlight can suggest insight into matters which concern us. We have turned the searchlight on them in order to ascertain the real truth. A searchlight is used to light the way ahead.

3 A searchlight will allow us to comprehend spiritual matters so that we can reject the unnecessary.

SEASONS

1 When we become conscious of the seasons of the year in dreams, we are also linking with the various periods of our lives (**Spring** signifies childhood, **Summer** – young adulthood, **Autumn** – middle age, **Winter** – old age).

2 The need for us to be able to divide time into periods or phases arises initially from the necessity to co-operate with the seasons from a survival point of view. Given deadlines and limitations, the human being is able to survive through striving.

3 The division of the year into Spring, Summer, Autumn and Winter gives occasion for celebrations and festivals.

SEED

1 A seed in dreams stands for our potentiality. We may have an idea which is only just beginning, or a project which needs nurturing. **In a woman's dream** a seed may suggest pregnancy.

2 Often in dreams a seed will suggest the validity of something we are planning. We need to know the right conditions in which to grow and mature.

3 A seed carries great potential and latent power. It is this symbolism which is relevant spiritually.

SERPENT
– see Serpent and Snake in Animals

SEX

1 When a child is first born, its first awareness is of itself as an individual. It has to learn that it is now separate from its mother and cope with the separation. It begins to become 'conscious' of itself, and of its need for warmth, comfort and love. One vital stage of growth is the baby's fascination with its own body and the ability to be physical. This is as much to do with what feels comfortable and nice – how it feels to be in one's own skin, as it were. It is at this point that he or she learns about touch, whether it is nice to touch or be touched, and even if touch is permissible. If, for instance, the child is handled roughly, there may be a fear of being touched, which may later manifest as a sexual difficulty. While the original trauma may be suppressed, it will often surface in dreams when the time is appropriate. Real growth takes place when the individual is not afraid of the curiosity which allows an innocent exploration of his own body. Dreams will often allow us to explore this physicality in a safe way.

2 Dreams highlight the whole range of the individual's sexuality. Only if he ignores his own sexual nature and fails to appreciate his own life force do the negative aspects make themselves obvious in dreams. This is a natural attempt to balance the waking state which may have been over-intellectualised, or over-dramatised. Contact with others then becomes necessary, and often this need will make itself apparent in dreams. Various aspects of sex and sexuality can be interpreted as follows:

Bisexuality Within ourselves we hold both masculine and feminine potentials. One is more overt than the other and there is often conflict between the inner and the outer. This can sometimes show itself in dreams as bisexuality and a need for some kind of union with members of both sexes.

Castration in a dream suggests fear of loss of masculinity and sexual power.

Clothes in sexual dreams can have particular relevance often to do with the dreamer's perception of him or herself: being fully clothed would suggest some feeling of guilt.

Contraception Dreaming of contraception can indicate a fear of pregnancy and birth.

Ejaculation/Emission The images in a dream prior to orgasm can suggest the nature of the dreamer's attitude to sex and sexuality. The conflicts which arise in the dreamer because of his sexual desire for someone can be dealt with in the dream state through dreaming of emission or orgasm.

Fetishes Fetishes are a fixation on an external object without which there can be no sexual act. This is a little akin to a child not being able to go to sleep without his comforter. There is some evidence for the belief that, at an unconscious level, man would prefer a life of celibacy and, by projecting his energies onto an object, he abdicates responsibility. In dreams, therefore, a fetish can highlight fear, immaturity and lack of capability.

Hermaphrodite *(also see*

Individual Entry) Dreaming of a hermaphrodite (someone who is both masculine and feminine) suggests either bisexuality, which is an erotic attraction to both sexes, or androgyny – the perfect balance within one person of the masculine and feminine qualities.

Homosexuality is taken to mean the desire for sex with a partner who is the same sex. More properly, it is a desire for someone who is the same as oneself. It is this aspect that comes across in dreams. If the dreamer can identify what is similar to himself or herself in ways that are not purely sexual, the dream can be fully interpreted.

Incest *(also see individual entry)* in a dream usually characterises the need for expressed love – that is, love expressed in a more tactile way. In dreams incest can highlight guilty feelings about one's parents or members of the family.

Intercourse (or petting) The wish or need to be able to communicate with someone on a very intimate level can translate itself into intercourse in a dream. **If intercourse is interrupted** the dreamer may have inhibitions of which he or she is not consciously aware. Often intercourse in a dream can mark the integration of a particular part of one's personality. If **a child is then born** that

integration has been successful.

Kiss This can indicate a mark of respect or a desire to stimulate the dream partner. It suggests we should be aware of what arousal we ourselves need.

Masochism The desire to hurt oneself or to be hurt in dreams through sex arises from two causes. The first is to be a martyr (to suffer for one's 'sins') and the second to feel extreme emotion of one sort or another. We may not allow ourselves to feel deeply in everyday life.

Masturbation The child learns to comfort himself through masturbation, so dreaming of masturbation is a need for comfort.

Perversion When sexual perversion appears in dreams we are avoiding, or attempting to avoid, issues to do with closeness and bonding.

Phallus Any image either of or to do with the phallus signifies everything that is creative, penetrative and masculine. It is vitality and creativity in both its simplest and most complex form. It is resurrection and the renewal of life.

Rape Any image of rape appearing in dreams can be as much to do with violation of personal space as with the sexual act. Sexual rape is unlikely to appear in the dreams of, for instance, sexually abused children. It may only appear as an image when the adult is ready to deal with the trauma.

Sadism *(also see individual entry)* Sadism appearing in a dream would suggest that it is probably a counterbalance to the dreamer's conscious way of being in the world. In everyday life he may be either very timid, in which case the dream is an escape mechanism or, in having to be dominant and controlling in everyday life, the unconscious shows its need to be controlled.

Semen Dreams have an odd way of throwing up images of primitive rites and practices of which we may have no conscious knowledge. Many of these are representations of the sexual act. Semen is the sign of masculinity and of physical maturity and is often seen in dreams as some other milky fluid.

Sexuality in a dream, in the sense of feeling desire for someone else – most often of the opposite sex – is a basic primeval urge for closeness and union with that person. It is as though we are searching for a part of ourselves that we have lost. The other character in the dream represents the closest we can get to that part. If we were a fully integrated human being, we would have no need for sex with someone else, but for most of us we have a desire to be united with everything which is not part of our own ego. Such a dream, which highlights the feelings we are capable of having, provides information to enable us to understand our own needs.

Transvestism This signifies a confusion so far as gender is concerned in dreams.

Venereal Disease In a dream this can suggest awareness of some kind of contamination. This need not necessarily be of a sexual nature, but could also be emotional.

3 Sexual activity is either the highest expression of love and spirituality between two people or, if purely physically based, is entirely selfish. It would be up to the dreamer and their understanding of themselves to determine which it is.

SHADOW
– see Introduction

SHAMPOO

1 Shampoo in dreams has an obvious connection with cleansing and washing. On a practical level, we are trying to 'clear our heads' in order to think or see clearly. In the words of the popular song we may be trying to 'wash that man right out of my hair'.

2 Because shampooing is connected with the head – which of itself represents intellect – there is a connection psychologically with needing to have clarity of thought. We may feel that our thought processes have been slowed down, or dirtied, by outside influences.

3 Spiritually shampoo – like soap – would suggest an attempt to get back to basics, to clear our wants, needs and requirements and to make a new connection with the Spiritual Self.

SHAPES/PATTERNS

1 The number of sides the shape has will be significant *(See Numbers)*, as will the colours *(See Colours)*. At a certain stage of development the geometric shapes which will give the individual a greater understanding of the abstract world begin to appear in dreams. It is as though the old perception of form is beginning to take on a new meaning and interpretation.

2 The dreamer accepts the nature of things as they are, and can look at the fundamental structure of his nature. He can appreciate the basic shape his life is taking without placing emotional inhibitions in the way.

3 Various shapes and patterns can be interpreted as:

The Centre The centre symbolises the point from which everything starts. In relation to shape, it is the point from which the pattern grows.

Circle The circle represents the inner being or the Self *(see Introduction)*. It is also unity and perfection. **A circular object** – such as a ring – may have the same meaning as the circle. **A circle with a dot in the centre** can signify the soul in completion. It is sometimes taken to represent Woman.

Crescent (including the sickle and crescent moon) This signifies the feminine, mysterious power which is intuitive and non-rational.

Cross Any cross stands for the realisation (in the sense of making real) of spirit into matter. Moving through the symbol of the sword to the equal armed-cross, from there to the cross of suffering and crucifixion, and finally to the Tau of perfection, the soul learns through experience to overcome the obstacles to spiritual progression. **The four arms pointing in opposite directions** signify conflict, anguish and distress, but ultimately going through these to reach perfection. **The hung cross** with the figure of Christ represents the sacrifice of self for others. **The intersection** signifies the reconciliation of opposites. **The three upper arms** are said to stand for God the Father, Son and Holy Ghost, but more properly they indicate any Divine Trinity.

Cube – *see Square*

Diamond A diamond in a dream indicates that we have greater and lesser options available.

Hexagram A hexagram is a geometric figure which symbolises the harmonious development of the physical, social and spiritual elements of human life and its integration into a perfect whole.

Oval The oval is symbolic of the womb, and also of feminine life. Called the Vesica Piscis, it is the halo which completely encircles a sacred figure.

Patterns (in cloth, mosaic etc.) In dreams the patterns which appear as part of the scenario can categorise how we handle the patterns and perhaps repeated behaviours in our lives.

Pentagram/Pentangle/ Pentagram – *see Star*

Sphere The sphere has a similar meaning to the globe *(see individual entry)*, and indicates perfection and completion of all possibilities.

Spiral *(also see Labyrinth in L Section)* The spiral is the perfect path to evolution. The principle is that everything is continually in motion, but also continually rising or raising its vibration. **If the spiral is towards the centre** we are approaching our own centre by an indirect route. **A clockwise spiral, moving outward to the right** is a movement towards consciousness and enlightenment. **If counterclockwise** the movement is towards the unconscious, probably regressive behaviour. There is also a connection with the navel or solar plexus as the centre of power.

Square or Cube The square or cube signifies the manifestation of spirit into matter. It represents the earthly realm as opposed to the heavens. **A square within a circle** suggests the act of 'becoming' or taking on form. **The figure within a square** is the Self or perfect Man. **Any square object** signifies the enclosing and feminine principle.

Star The star, particularly if it is a bright one, indicates the individual's hopes, aspirations and ideals. It is those things we must reach for. **The five-pointed star or pentagram** evokes personal magic, and all matter in harmony. To be correct, the star should point upwards. In dreams it signifies the dreamer's ownership of his own magical qualities and aspirations. If it is pointing downwards it symbolises evil and witchcraft. **The six-pointed star, or Star of David,** is made up of one triangle pointing upward and another pointing downward: the physical and the spiritual are joined together in harmony to create wisdom. Twelve stars signify both the Twelve Tribes of Israel and the Apostles.

Swastika The swastika **with its arms moving clockwise** portrays Ideal Man and the power he has for good. In Eastern symbolism it signifies the movement of the sun. The swastika **moving counter-clockwise** in this form signifies all that is sinister and wrong. It was always recognised that Hitler had connections with magic. It is not known whether his choice of swastika was deliberate or not.

Triangle The triangle represents Standing Man, with his three parts – body, mind and spirit (or being). Consciousness and love manifest through his physicality. There is potential still to be realised. If the triangle **points upwards**, human nature moves towards the Divine. If it is **pointing down** it is spirit seeking expression through the physical. The triangle can also represent family relationships – that is, father, mother and child.

There is a game based on shapes in which you draw a square, a circle and a triangle, and then get someone else to elaborate each of the basic shapes into a drawing. Whatever he makes of the square is supposed to relate to his outlook on the world, the circle to his inner being and the triangle to his sex life.

SHARK

1 To dream of a shark may indicate that we are being attacked unfairly; someone is trying to take something that is rightfully ours. Being in **a sea of sharks** suggests that we are in a situation where we do not trust anyone. To be **pursued by a shark** may suggest that we have put ourselves in danger and created a situation by entering someone else's territory.

2 Because a shark is a sea creature it has the significance of creating problems on an emotional level. It is as though our emotional capacity can be eroded by unscrupulous behaviour.

3 The shark is a symbol of the fear of death because of its connection with the Collective Unconscious. We lack the ability to confront these fears without help.

SHAVE

1 The significance of shaving in a dream will obviously vary depending on whether the dreamer is a man or a woman. **If a man**, he is more likely to be shaving his face, which also suggests that he is trying to change his image. **If a**

woman, she is likely to be shaving other parts of her body in order to create a more beautiful image. Both acts suggest removing an unwanted layer – that is, a facade which has been created.

2 To dream that we have had 'a close shave' suggests that we have taken too many risks. We should be more aware of the difficulties we can have as well as the danger we put other people in.

3 In spiritual terms to be close-shaven suggests openness and honesty in our dealings with other people. For someone to have grown a beard when we would have least expected it indicates that they are trying to hide something from us.

SHAWL
– see Coat in Clothes

SHEAF

1 Previously a sheaf, particularly of corn, would signify a harvest or good husbandry. Now it is more likely to suggest old-fashioned ways and methods of operating. A **sheaf of papers** would suggest hard work.

2 As a marker of time, the sheaf will suggest Autumn. It is often seen as a symbol of consolidation and of binding. We perhaps need to look at what needs to be gath-ered in, made into a coherent whole, and given boundaries.

3 As the symbol of Demeter *(see Goddess)*, the sheaf represents the nurturing mother. In can also suggest a dying world, in that Demeter refused to nurture 'her' humans when Persephone *(see Goddess)* was kidnapped by Pluto.

SHEARS
– see Scissors

SHEEP
– see Animals

SHELLS

1 In dreams a shell represents the defences we use in order to prevent ourselves from being hurt. We can create a hard shell in response to previous hurt, or a soft shell which would indicate that we are still open to being hurt. Shells were also once a unit of currency, and in dreams can still be seen as this.

2 A shell carries within it so much symbolism. It can be seen as a magical symbol which holds within it the power of transformation. The spiral of the shell suggests involution and evolution (going inwards and coming outwards). The ability to shelter is also symbolised, and being a receptacle it also links with the feminine, emotional side of nature.

3 Spiritually a shell is a miniature representation of the process of life and death.

SHELTER

1 Any shelter signifies protection. The human is aware of the need for a safe space, and this symbolism comes across in dreams quite strongly. The images used could be anything from a snail shell to an umbrella. Usually dreams about shelter highlight our needs or insecurities.

2 The other image of shelter is protectiveness – that is, a more active participation in giving shelter or sanctuary. If we are **giving shelter** to someone in dreams, we may be protecting a part of ourselves from hurt or difficulty. If we are **being given shelter** we are conscious of the fact that there is protective power in our lives.

3 Shelter in the spiritual sense suggests sanctuary – a space wherein we will not be harmed but can be ourselves.

SHIELD

1 A shield is a symbol of preservation. It can appear in dreams as a **warrior's shield**, or as a barrier between the dreamer and the rest of the world. If we are **shielding someone else**, then we need to be sure our actions are appropriate and supportive. If we are **being shielded**, we need to be clear as to whether we are erecting the shield or whether it is being erected for us.

2 In myths and legends the Amazonian woman is shown carrying a shield. This symbolises the sheltering, protective aspect of the feminine.

3 In spiritual development the shield appears as a symbol of a particular stage of growth. It is at this point that the individual needs to appreciate that he has control over his own destiny. This symbol often first appears in dreams representing this stage of development.

SHIRT
– see Clothes

SHIVER

1 To be conscious of shivering in dreams can represent either a fear of conflict, or of coldness of emotion. There is also a **shiver of excitement**. We may, in waking life, be reaching a conclusion or coming to a peak of experience.

2 When we shiver in a dream we may be getting near to releasing unconscious behaviour.

3 The ecstatic experience results in a shiver as the energy on the physical level builds into an almost orgiastic experience. This can sometimes be experienced in dreams.

SHOE
– see Clothes

SHOP

1 A shop in dreams signifies something we want or feel we need. If it is **a shop we know** then we are probably consciously aware of what we want from life. If it is an **unknown shop** then we may have to search our minds for information. A **supermarket** would suggest we have to make a choice.
2 To be shopping is to be making a fair exchange for the satisfaction of our desires. We have the energy (money) which can be exchanged for something we want. What we are shopping for may have relevance. If we are **shopping for food** we need sustenance; if **for clothes** we may need protection.
3 In spiritual terms a shop has the same significance as a market *(see Market)*.

SHOT/SHOOTING
– also see Gun and Weapons
1 To be shot in a dream suggests an injury to one's feelings. In a **woman's dream** it can symbolise the sexual act – as much

because her feelings are involved as for the masculine imagery. It could also indicate that we may feel that we are becoming victims or targets for other people's anger.
2 If the dreamer is **shooting something** he may be having to deal with his own fears. He could be guarding against meeting parts of his personality he does not like. To be **on a shooting range** suggests needing to produce accuracy in our lives.
3 To be conscious of a shot or shooting in a spiritual sense is to be aware of a necessary directed explosion of energy. This may be the only way in which we can achieve a desired end.

SHOVEL/SPADE

1 A shovel in a dream will signify a need to dig into past experiences for information. We may need to uncover a past joy or trauma, or possibly even a learning experience. The type of spade or shovel will be of relevance. A **garden spade** would suggest being totally pragmatic, whereas a **fire shovel** would indicate a need to take care.
2 Since a shovel can suggest a degree of introspection, of covering up, what is being shovelled is important. We are needing to be mindful of the content of our lives. **Shovelling compost**, for

instance, would mean considering the sum total and most fertile aspects of our lives, whereas **shovelling sand** might suggest an experience of time.

3 A shovel is an implement or tool which can be used to help us uncover what is spiritually correct.

SHRINK
– also see Analyst

1 In dreams, **to shrink** is to have a desire to return to childhood, or to a smaller space in order to be looked after. In everyday life we may be aware of losing face or of feeling small and this can be translated in dreams as shrinking. **To see something – or somebody – shrink** can indicate that it is losing its – or their – power over us.

2 Psychologically we can learn to handle who we are by recognising both how necessary, and also how small, we are in the general scheme of things. The latter can be accompanied in dreaming by a feeling of shrinking. We therefore become less threatening to ourselves and others.

3 Following the psychological recognition of our smallness, we equally can become aware of the sense of belonging to a much greater cosmic whole. This is represented in dreams by a feeling of shrinking.

SHROUD

1 In a dream a shroud can be a frightening image, since it is associated with death. If we recognise that by shrouding something it becomes hidden, then the image is less frightening.

2 A shroud can signify a covering up of something we do not fully understand. We know that it is there, but we do not wish to have a look at it.

3 In spiritual terms a shroud is a mark of respect.

SICK
– also see Illness

1 To **feel sick** in a dream is to be identifying a bad feeling which needs to be got rid of. To **be sick** is to be attempting to get rid of the bad feeling. We may in everyday life be 'sick' of a relationship or situation we have.

2 Psychologically we are very much ruled by our emotions. Our stomach is a nerve centre which reacts to negative stimuli which can result in sickness in a dream.

3 When something is not right in our world spiritually, we need to eradicate it. Sickness is one way of doing this.

SICKLE
– also see Scythe

1 The sickle is no longer such an

important image to man. Now that we have moved from an agricultural to a more technological society, we are left with the ancient symbol of the sickle representing mortality and death. As so often happens, this is not necessarily a physical death, but the death of part of ourselves.

SIEVE

1 The sieve in dreams is a symbol of the ability to make selections. This is in the sense of being able to sort out the large from the small, good from the bad etc.

2 On a psychological level the sieve represents the ability to know oneself. We are able to make conscious choices which will enable us to extract the best from life.

3 Spiritually the sieve is said to represent fertility and rain clouds in the sense that pure rain, or water, permits proper growth.

SIGNATURE

1 Our signature in a dream suggests that we have an appreciation of ourselves. We are prepared to recognise who we are and to make our mark in the world.

2 At those times when we are arranging legal matters or agreements, but are actually not sure if we are doing the right thing, our signature can appear in dreams as

obliterated or illegible.

3 Spiritually our signature is a reflection of ourselves. It is a representation of who we perceive ourselves to be.

SILENCE

1 Silence in a dream can suggest uneasiness and expectancy. There is a waiting for something to happen (or not happen). If **someone else is silent** when we expect them to speak, we are unsure as to how that part of ourselves which is represented by the other person will react in waking life.

2 When we are silent, we are unable to voice our feelings or opinions. We are either inhibited by our own selves or by outside influences.

3 Spiritually, silence is a space where there is no need for sound. Many religious orders are silent on the basis that there is then closer communication with God. In dreams it may be suggested that silence and withdrawal from the world is necessary.

SILVER

1 On a practical level, silver appearing in a dream suggests finance or money. Silver is something of value which can be held in reserve against possible difficulty.

2 Silver on a more psychological

level has been taken to represent the qualities of the moon. This is in the sense that something or someone is available, but is at the same time somewhat remote.

3 Spiritually, silver is said to represent the feminine aspect, gold being the masculine.

SING

1 To **hear singing** in a dream is to link with the self-expression we all have. We are in touch with the flowing, feeling side of ourselves and others. **To be singing** is to be expressing our joy and love of life. If we are **singing alone**, we have learnt to be skilled in our own right. To be **in a choir** suggests our ability to worship or express ourselves in a peer group. Obviously, if the dreamer is a singer in waking life, the interpretation will vary.

2 Singing as an act of worship is a vital part of many systems of belief. A **football anthem**, for instance, will create a fellow feeling, whether it is a chant against the referee or a song of praise for the team, such as 'You'll Never Walk Alone'. **Singing as chanting** has a valid place in religion – as in the Gregorian chant – where certain tones achieve a shift in consciousness. To hear this in dreams is to be in touch with a high

vibration. Chanting of a mantra (see Mantra) also achieves the same end.

3 Spiritually when we sing we are capable of raising the vibration, either for ourselves or other people. We are in touch with the Higher Self.

SINKING

1 To be **sinking** in a dream suggests a loss of confidence. We may be in despair at something we have done, and feel hampered by the circumstances. **To see someone else sinking** would suggest we are aware of a difficulty which perhaps needs our help. We may feel we are losing ground within a relationship or situation. What we are sinking into could be important. To be **sinking in water** would suggest a particular emotion is threatening to engulf us. To be **sinking in sand or a bog** indicates that we feel there is no safe ground for us.

2 A sinking feeling in dreams usually suggests worry or fear. Emotionally we are unable to maintain our usual happiness. We may feel that we are not in control, and that we cannot maintain forward movement. **To see an object sinking** may suggest that we are about to lose something we value.

3 Both spiritually and physically, to be sinking is to be getting into a situation where we are unable to see clearly or to perceive the best course of action. For sensitives, this may be when the negativity of others threatens to overwhelm us.

SIREN
– also see Archetypes

1 To hear a siren – as in an **ambulance or fire engine** – is to be warned of danger. For those old enough to remember, such a siren will evoke memories of war and destruction. In particular, the 'all clear' will serve to relieve anxiety.

2 Archetypally, the Siren suggests deception and distraction of man from his purpose. In dreams this is usually sexually oriented and difficult to handle. **In a woman's dream**, if she is not in touch with the siren within her, she can appear to be destructive. In psychological terms she is temptation and often appears in Greek or Roman attire, as if to enhance the erotic image. She can often be pictured in dreams sat by water, since she works with the emotions. In some cases she is a man's Anima *(see Introduction)*.

3 It is only when it is understood spiritually that the Siren can ultimately restore man to himself, that the Siren becomes acceptable and can be worked with. After having rejected her enchantment, he is free to become whole.

SISTER
– see Family

SIZE

1 To be conscious of size in a dream highlights how we feel in relation to a person, project or object. **Big** might suggest important or threatening, whereas **small** might indicate vulnerability or something 'less than' ourselves. Thus a big house would be an awareness of the expansion of oneself, whereas a small house would indicate an intensity of feeling.

2 A child learns very early on to make comparisons, and this is one of the things that we never lose. Something is bigger or smaller rather than simply big or small. In dreams size is relative. We might recognise somewhere we know, but find it is larger or smaller than we thought it to be. It is the size within the dream that is relevant.

3 Spiritually size is irrelevant. It is more the appreciation of feeling that becomes important. A 'big' feeling is something that consumes us, whereas a 'little' perception may be only part of what really exists.

SKELETON

1 A skeleton in a dream suggests the 'bare bones' of something, perhaps an idea or concept. **A skeleton in a cupboard** represents a past action or shame we wish to hide. A **dancing skeleton** is an awareness of the life we have lived or are living. To **dig up a skeleton** is to resurrect something we have buried.

2 Psychologically, we sometimes need to be aware of our feelings about death. Such an obvious image in dreams forces us to be aware of this. A skeleton can also suggest feelings or talents which we have forgotten and which therefore have 'died'.

3 A skeleton alerts us to our own feelings about death. We are aware that the physical must 'die', but that there is a framework which is left.

SKIN
– see Body

SKULL

1 If a skull appears in a dream we may need to look at the rest of the dream in order to find out the symbolism. The **skull and crossbones** could represent either a romantic appreciation of a pirate, or a symbol of danger. Since the skull is a representation of the head it can also symbolise intellectual ability or rather, lack of it.

2 To be conscious of **one's own skull** in dreams is to appreciate the structure that we have given our lives. To perceive a **skull where there should be a head** suggests that part of the person has 'died'. To be **talking to a skull** is recognising the need to communicate with those who are lost to us. When a **skull is talking to us**, a part of us which we have rejected or denied is beginning to come back to life. If we believe in life after death, we may feel that spirit is talking through the skull.

3 Spiritually the skull represents death and all its implications. When it appears in dreams, it is time for us to come to terms with physical death.

SKY

1 In dreams the sky can represent the mind. It can also signify our potential. **Floating or flying** in the sky can be ambivalent, since it can either mean trying to avoid the mundane, or exploring a different potential. If the sky is **dark** it may reflect our mood of gloominess; if it is **bright**, our mood of joy.

2 The sky signifies the unattainable. Whatever effort we make we can never make the sky tangible.

3 The sky spiritually suggests infinity. It also signifies order – particularly that applied to the intuitive function.

SMELL
– also see Odour and Perfume

1 To be conscious of a smell in a dream usually means that we are trying to identify an object or where the smell is coming from. Most other senses are sharpened in dreams, but the sense of smell is made available only if a specific interpretation is needed and particular note should be taken of what it is we smell.

2 Childhood is a time when smell is very significant. Many smells which are associated with that time, e.g. baking bread, burning oil, flowers, school dinners, can still be very evocative for us as adults. A **pleasant smell** could represent happy times or memories, whereas a **bad smell** can hold memories of particularly traumatic times.

3 As one's spiritual senses develop, the ability to sense and recognise smells from the past on a clairvoyant level can be somewhat frightening. Provided this ability is recognised merely as a means of identifying a time, place or person there need be no problem and we need have no fear.

SMOKE/SMOKING
– also see Fire

1 Smoke in dreams suggests that there is a feeling of danger around, especially if we cannot locate the fire. If **we are smoking**, we are trying to control anxiety. If we smoke in real life, but recognise in dreams that we no longer do so, we have overcome a difficulty. If smokers give it up in everyday life, they will often have many dreams focused around the issue of smoking.

2 Smoke in dreams can represent passion, although it may not have 'flared' properly into being. Smoke can also represent either cleansing – as with incense – or contamination.

3 Spiritually smoke signifies prayer rising to heaven, or the raising of the soul to escape from space and time.

SNAIL

1 The snail appearing in dreams may engender a feeling of repulsion in some people. It does, however, also represent vulnerability and slowness.

2 From a psychological point of view, the snail suggests steadiness and self-containment. To be **moving at snail's pace** suggests direct planned, careful movement.

3 Spiritually, because of the spiral shape of its shell, the snail is a natural symbol of the labyrinth *(see Labyrinth)*.

SNAKE
– see Serpent and Snake in Animals

SNOW
– also see Ice

1 Snow is a crystallisation of water, and as such represents the crystallisation of an idea or project. **When melting**, it can represent the softening of the heart.

2 Psychologically snow in dreams can suggest emotional coldness or frigidity. Because of its use as a slang word, it can also represent drugs.

3 Spiritually it can represent pureness, beauty and the melting away of difficulties.

SOAP

1 Soap in dreams suggests the idea of being cleansed. We perhaps need to create an environment of cleanliness – both of physical cleanliness and appropriate behaviour. Often in emerging sexual dreams soap can appear as an image of ejaculated semen.

2 Psychologically soap can indicate a need to clean up our act. We may feel a sense of having been made dirty by an experience and situation and our dream mind

is alerting us to the fact that we need to deal with it.

3 Again, on a spiritual level, soap represents cleansing. There is a creative visualisation which can be carried out if we feel our space has been invaded. The dreamers should envisage themselves scrubbing down the walls of a room three times in order to cleanse it (remembering to 'throw away' the water or let it drain away). Once is for the physical, once emotional, once spiritual. Following this, there will be a feeling of lightness.

SON
– see Family

SOUP
– see Eating, Food and Nourishment

SOUTH
– see Position

SOWING

1 Sowing – in the sense of **planting seed** – is a symbol which has certain basic images attached to it. It can signify the sexual act, and well as suggesting good husbandry. It can also represent the beginning of a new project.

2 The image of laying down a framework for success is implicit in sowing. The actions which have to be gone through – such as preparing the ground, tilling the soil and so on – are all evocative images even in today's technological society. When this image appears in dreams, we need to look at circumstances around us and decide what we can gain most.

3 Sowing in a spiritual sense suggests creating the correct environment in which growth can take place. It is, above all, the creative act.

SPACE

1 In dreams, when we are aware of the space we occupy we are in touch with our own potential. We may be aware that our personal space is being, or has been, penetrated. To be **'spaced out'** is to have widened our personal boundaries artificially through the use of stimuli.

2 Psychologically we often need space to make the best use of opportunities. We should be capable of going beyond our own concepts of limitation and ego states.

3 Space is a representation of a cosmic centre – a place that 'is, was and ever shall be'. This idea can widen our present view of the world.

SPADE
– see Shovel

SPARK

1 A spark in a dream represents a beginning. Being aware of a spark is to be conscious of what is going to make things possible. From a physical perspective it is a small thing which gives rise to a greater one.

2 The spark of an idea suggests the germ of a creative potential which, given the opportunity, will become much bigger. Since the spark also represents the basic life force, we need to appreciate our own lust for life.

3 The spark suggests fire and therefore love. It is the vital principle in life, without which we would all die.

SPEAR

1 The spear has many meanings. It represents the masculine in dreams and is phallic. It is the life-giving force. To see a **warrior with a spear** is to recognise the aggressive male. To **put a spear in the ground** is to mark one's territory. If we are **throwing a spear** we perhaps need to be aware of our more primitive aspects.

2 The spear is psychologically that part of ourselves which is fertile and assertive. Whether in a man's or a woman's dream, it allows us to be conscious of the need to cut out nonsense and get straight to the point.

3 Spiritually, the spear signifies directness and honour.

SPECTACLES
– see Glasses

SPEED

1 Speed in dreams identifies an intensity of feelings which is not usually available in waking life. Because everything is happening too quickly, it engenders anxiety in the dreamer which creates problems.

2 Travelling at speed suggests trying to achieve a fast result. Speeding – as **in a traffic offence** – suggests being too focused on an end result, and not the method of getting there. To be **taking, or to be given speed** (amphetamines) in a dream may have two meanings. If the dreamer uses the substance in everyday life, he could be being alerted to a gift or talent he has which should be developed. If he does not normally use the drug, then he is putting himself in danger.

3 There is a point when, as we are developing spiritually, we lose our sense of time. Speeding things up may appear as slowing things down, and vice versa. This is all part of the growth process.

SPHINX

1 The sphinx, for most people in dreams will represent Egypt, and all the mystery it contains.

2 Psychologically, and because even today so little is known about it, the sphinx stands for the enigmatic side of ourselves. In dreams it will highlight the mysterious strength which is available to us particularly in times of trouble.

3 Spiritually the sphinx stands for vigilance, power and wisdom as well as dignity.

SPIDER

1 There is a great deal of ambivalence in the image of the spider. On a very mundane level it is disliked, perhaps because of its scuttling movement but also because of its association with dirt. In dreams it can also suggest deviousness.

2 In psychological terms the spider connects with the Mandala *(see Mandala)*. It is the ability to create a perfect pattern which both nurtures and protects us at the same time.

3 Spiritually the spider represents the Great Mother in her role as the Weaver. She weaves destiny from the body of her self, and is therefore the Creator. In coming to terms with this aspect, we become weavers of our own destiny.

SPINE
– see Backbone in Body

SPIRITS
– also see Ghost

1 At its very basic level, we all have fears and feelings about death, and the appearance of Spirit helps us to come to terms with these. It will depend on the dreamer's own personal belief system as to whether he or she feels they are actual spirits or not.

2 When spirits appear in dreams, their function may be to help us through various states of transition. While we cope with everyday fears, there are many unconscious memories and feelings which can surface unexpectedly. When we are conscious of a kindly or helpful spirit we are aware that we can move on. When we see the spirits of dead people we usually need reassurance.

3 During spiritual development, our perceptions widen from the ordinary everyday to other aspects and dimensions of knowledge that have become available to us. Whether these are aspects of our own personality or of the spirit realm is immaterial, since ultimately their function is to help the dreamer progress. The spiritual self has access to the Collective Unconscious in its entirety.

SPIRAL
– see Shapes

SPIRE

1 To see a spire in a dream is to recognise a landmark. In previous times, people oriented themselves by churches. Now a pub tends to be a marker, but in dreams the spire still persists.

2 The spire can often be taken in dreams as a phallic symbol, particularly – and somewhat obviously – the erect one. It also represents ambition and striving. **A fallen spire** would suggest the collapse of hopes. To be **building a tower or spire** has connotations with the Tower of Babel and shows a need for more – or better – communication.

3 As a representation of our spiritual progression, the spire suggests the movement from the secular to the sacred.

SPITTLE

1 Normally in dreams spittle will represent disgust. We would, in former times, 'spit venom', which is a very basic image as to how a hurt or threatened animal will react.

2 More positively, spittle can indicate a sign of good faith. Some cultures still spit on their hands when completing a deal. There is a bonding through the exchange of bodily fluids.

3 Since Biblical times, spittle has been seen as a healing fluid. It was supposed to be an antidote against being cursed, particularly by the use of the Evil Eye. Spiritually it is perhaps symbolic of the flow of energy between healer and patient.

SPLINTER

1 In dreams, a splinter can represent a minor irritation. It is something which has penetrated our defences and is now making us uncomfortable. Splinters may represent painful words or ideas. We may be holding on to ideas which cause negative feelings.

2 To be part of **a splinter group** in a dream suggests feeling sufficiently strongly about something to break away from mainstream thought. To **hit something which splinters** is to recognise that we are all composed of parts which make a whole.

3 The sense of belonging to a group of like-minded people can only come after we have recognised our isolation or, in some cases, fragmentation.

SPRING

1 Springtime in a dream can suggest new growth or opportunities. Perhaps there is a fresh start in a relationship. A **spring of water** suggests fresh energy, whereas a **bed spring** or other type of coil would indicate latent power for movement.

2 To walk with **a spring in one's step** is to be looking forward to something. The saying 'spring forward, fall back' is also applicable in psychological terms, since effort is required to progress.

3 Spiritually a spring is a symbol of progression, particularly insofar as emotion is concerned. We can now afford to make a new beginning.

SPRINKLE/ SPRINKLING

1 Sprinkling as a symbol in dreams suggests an attempt to make a little go a long way. Perhaps we need to get the best out of situations around us, by putting a little effort into many things.

2 Sprinkling suggests the symbolism of impregnation, of conception and gestation. Psychologically we need to make a link with our creative side in order to function properly as human beings and can often do this through dreams about sprinkling.

3 Spiritually we are aware of basic concepts and abilities. In some cultures, semen is sprinkled on the ground to propitiate the Mother Goddess and ensure a good harvest.

In protective magical rituals herbs and salt are sprinkled.

SQUARE
- See Shapes

SQUIRREL
– see Animals

STAB
– also see Knife

1 To be stabbed in a dream indicates our ability to be hurt. **To stab someone** is, conversely, to be prepared to hurt. Since a stab wound is penetrative it obviously has connections with aggressive masculine sexuality, but also with the faculty of being able to get straight to the point.

2 When we make ourselves vulnerable we are open to being hurt. Often a stab is a quick way of achieving a result. For instance, to be **stabbing at something rather than somebody** would suggest the need to break through some kind of shell or barrier in order to proceed.

3 When we realise that we can use particular skills, they can assume an almost ritualistic feeling. Fighting and stabbing can then be appreciated as a means of spiritual discipline (as in martial arts). We need to understand appropriate behaviour.

STAFF

1 A staff, in the sense of **a stick**, is a support mechanism, staff – as in **office staff** – a support system. Dreaming of either should clarify our attitude to the support we require in life. It is worthwhile noting that one is passive in its use (the stick) and one is active.

2 The staff in dreams symbolises the journeying and pilgrimage that we must undertake. It also represents magical power in the form of a wand.

3 Spiritually the staff is a symbol of the support we have, or will need, on our spiritual journey. As we progress, we move from using it as a support to using it as a tool and finally as a sign of authority.

STAG
– see Deer in Animals

STAGE
– also see Theatre

1 To be **on stage** in a dream is to be making oneself visible. An **open-air stage** suggests communication with the masses rather than a selected audience. A **moving stage** signifies the need to keep moving, even while performing a role. If we are **members of the audience** we need to be aware of the plot of the play and how it may be relevant to us.

2 To be at a stage (of development, for instance) is to be cognisant of what one knows, but also what one does not. If a project or an idea reaches a certain stage, we can envisage the potential for success.

3 Spiritually a stage is a representation of our own life play. We are able to observe and be objective about what is going on. By externalising the 'play' into a framework we can manipulate our lives.

STAKE

1 To have **a stake in something** is to have made a commitment, either on a material or emotional level. To be **putting stakes in the ground** suggests marking out one's territory.

2 Psychologically we may experience a sense of being staked out. This can represent that we have been conned into doing something we do not want to do.

3 The stake is a symbol of torture or death by fire in a spiritual ideal.

STAIRS
– see Buildings

STAR
– see Famous People and Shapes

STATION
– see Journey

STATUE

1 Dreaming of a statue is to be linking with the unresponsive, cold side of human nature. We may be worshipping or loving someone and not getting any response.

2 There is a basic side of nature which needs to look up to something and this can be represented in dreams by a statue. Sometimes this statue is representative of an idea or concept rather than a person. Much can be gained by identifying what the statue stands for.

3 Spiritually, as we progress, we come up against the knowledge that we have given value to something – for instance, a relationship – that no longer has significance. It is 'dead' and therefore solidified. If the statue comes to life again, it can be rescued.

STEALING
– also see Thief

1 To dream of **stealing** suggests we are taking something without permission. This may be love, money or opportunities. If someone **steals from us** we may feel cheated. If it is by **someone we know**, then we need to work out how much we trust that person. If it is by **someone we don't know**, it is more likely to be a part of ourselves that we don't trust. If we are **in a gang of thieves**, then we should look at, and consider, the morals of the peer group we belong to.

2 Stealing is a very emotive word for most people, and it will depend on the dreamer's background as to how they feel about inappropriate behaviour. This image also comes up when dealing with the emotions. For instance, a 'needy' person may feel they are stealing affection.

3 Spiritually, stealing is using energy inappropriately. At each level of awareness we have certain power available to us which must be used wisely and well. For instance, 'black' magic could be interpreted as stealing. Psychic 'vampirism' is another form of stealing.

STEAM

1 Steam in dreams can suggest emotional pressure. We are passionate about something without necessarily knowing what it is.

2 Because it is two substances uniting into one, steam suggests transformation. It also suggests a transitory experience, since steam also melts away.

3 We are looking at, and are aware of, the all encompassing power of the Spirit.

STEEPLE
– see Spire

STEPS
– also see Stairs in Buildings

1 Steps in dreams almost invariably suggest an effort made to succeed. **Going up** steps suggests trying to make things better and improve them, whereas **going down** means going either into the past or the subconscious.

2 Steps represent changes in awareness within a project, quite literally the steps necessary. Steps also represent communication of a progressive kind.

3 There is still perceived to be a hierarchical structure in spiritual progression. We can achieve certain things at a certain level. We must extensively refine each level before moving on to the next.

STERILISE

1 To dream of **sterilising something** suggests a need for cleansing at a deep level. We wish to get rid of hurts or traumas and are prepared to put in the effort to do so. 'Sterilising' a situation may be taking the emotion out of it.

2 For a **woman to dream of being sterilised**, either by an operation or otherwise, may be connecting with her feeling of powerlessness as a woman. **In a man's dream** sterilisation may suggest sexual dissatisfactions or doubts about his self-image.

3 Sterilisation in a spiritual sense is ambivalent. It can either suggest cleanliness of spirit, or an aspect of the Self which is unable to grow.

STIFFNESS

1 Stiffness in dreams would suggest some anxiety or tension is present. There is a holding back of energy that is causing rigidity.

2 To be **stiff with someone** is to be reserved and withdrawn, probably through shyness but possibly through anger. A **stiff exterior** would suggest a judgmental attitude.

3 At certain stages of spiritual development, discipline can appear as stiffness.

STONE

1 Dreaming of stone can suggest stability and durability, but also a loss of feeling. To be **carving stone** is to be attempting to create a lasting monument.

2 Stone has many connotations on an emotional level. For stone to be **broken up** signifies being badly hurt. Being turned to stone would suggest that we have had to harden up our attitudes. **Being stoned** could have two meanings. One is being punished for misdemeanours; the other is being under the influence of drugs.

3 Stone signifies the imperishability

and the indestructibility of Supreme Reality.

STORM
– also see Lightning and Thunder

1 In dreams a storm indicates a personal emotional outburst. We may feel we are being battered by events or emotions. It can also signify anger.

2 When we are in difficulty, for instance, in a relationship, a storm can bring release. When an argument is not appropriate in everyday life, in dreams a storm can clear our 'emotional air'.

3 Spiritually a storm symbolises the creative power. Thunder and lightning are the tools of the storm gods.

STRAIGHTNESS
– see Position

STRANGER
– see People

STRANGLE

1 To dream of **strangling someone** is an attempt to stifle the emotions. To dream of **being strangled** is to be aware of our difficulty in speaking out about our emotions.

2 Strangulation suggests a violent act of suppression. Emotionally, our more violent aggressive side may not allow us to act appropriately in certain situations. **3** Spiritually, wisdom arises out of learning how to hold back inappropriate speech, not strangle it.

STRAW

1 Straw in dreams highlights weakness and emptiness. Unless the image of straw appears in a countryside scene, we are probably aware of a passing phase which has little meaning. A **straw house** – being a temporary structure – would suggest a state of impermanence is present in our lives.

2 When we say something is **built on straw**, we are aware that it does not have a proper foundation. We need to look at what we feel is impermanent in our lives and build on it.

3 Straw appearing in a dream can often reveal that we feel there is a lack of support – or that the support we do have seems to be rather dry and brittle – when undertaking our Spiritual journey.

STREAM

– also see Water

1 Dreaming of a stream suggests the awareness of the flow of our emotions. To be **in a stream** suggests being in touch with one's sensuality. To be **onstream** – as

with computers – suggests communication with others.

2 Emotionally if we are to function properly we must feel loved and appreciated. To be **in the stream of things** suggests being part of a social group which will enable us to interact with people.

3 The image of a stream is often quoted as being blessed by Divine Power. Spiritual energy is often experienced as a stream of light.

STRING

1 String appearing in dreams signifies some sort of binding, perhaps to make something secure. It may also represent trying to hold a situation together.

2 In a psychological sense, string – like rope – can be seen as a link between two objects *(See Rope)*.

3 Spiritually, anything that binds suggests a direct relationship with one's inner self, as in the Silver Cord.

SUBMARINE

1 A submarine in dreams indicates the depth of feeling that is accessible to us. Usually we are looking at the subconscious depths rather than the spiritual heights.

2 If we are to be comfortable with ourselves we need to understand our subconscious urges. Since there can be some fear – and in some cases the need for protection – the submarine can be a good image to use.

3 Dreaming of a submarine indicates we have a spiritual need to get underneath our emotions.

SUCKING

1 To be conscious of sucking in a dream suggests a return to infantile behaviour and emotional dependency. **Sucking a lollipop** alerts us to a need for oral satisfaction in the sense of comforting ourselves. **Sucking a finger** can suggest a physical need.

2 Emotionally we all have needs which are left over from childhood. These may be unfulfilled desires or the need to be whole and complete. This need can surface in dreams as sucking something.

3 The snake which sucks its own tail *(See Ouroboros)* is a potent image of spiritual completeness.

SUFFOCATING

1 When we feel **we are suffocating** in a dream, it may be that our own fears are threatening to overwhelm us. It can also indicate that we are not in control of our own environment. To be **suffocating someone** may mean we are overpowering them in real life.

2 If we do not wish to have any sort of relationship with someone

we may find that dreams of suffocation occur. Fears about sexuality may also surface in this way.

3 Suffocation may appear in dreams when negative energy is too strong for us to deal with.

SUICIDE

1 Dreaming of suicide alerts us to a violent end to something, perhaps a project or relationship. It is also a sign of anger against the Self. It may signify the end of a business or business relationship.

2 Emotionally, when dreams of suicide occur, we may have come to the end of our ability to cope with a particular situation in our lives. It does not actually mean that we are suicidal. It simply marks the end of a phase.

3 Often on the path of spirituality we must let go of the old Self. This often occurs in dreams as a kind of suicide.

SUITCASE
– see Baggage and Luggage

SUMMER

1 To be aware in a dream that it is summer suggests that it is a good time in our lives. We can look forward to success in projects we have around us. We have the ability to make the most of what we have done to date.

2 The significance of summer on a psychological level is twofold. Because of its association with holidays and with fun and laughter, we are able to be more relaxed. We also have opportunities to meet with other people and to form new associations.

3 Esoterically, summer represents the mid-life. This is a time of spiritual success and of the ability also to plan for the rest of our lives. We have learnt by experience and can now put that experience into practice.

SUN
– also see Planets

1 The sun in dreams suggests warmth and conscious awareness. A **sunny day** suggests happiness. To be **drawn to the sun** indicates we are looking for enlightenment. In turning towards the sun, the sunflower could be said to be a symbol of obsession, but also of worship. With its many seeds it also represents fertility.

2 Because the sun is such a powerful image on its own as a life source, it can also appear in dreams as a symbol for other life energy. If dreaming of **a sun dance** the dreamer may be wishing to praise the sun for its all-encompassing power and energy. The dreamer is, in effect, using the

energy of the sun for guidance and vitality.

3 The sun can symbolise spiritual enlightenment and radiance. The dreamer can 'soak up' and use the sun's power for further spiritual development.

SURGERY
– also see Operation

1 To find ourselves **in a surgery** in dreams would indicate that we should be looking at our health and health matters.

2 Surgery indicates a fairly violent intrusion in our lives which may be necessary. Dreaming of having **surgery performed on us** shows we need to accustom ourselves to changes which may initially be difficult, but ultimately are healing.

3 Spiritually, the dreamer may feel that he has too much to deal with or that something needs altering. A dream about surgery can often indicate this.

SWALLOW
– see Birds

SWALLOWING

1 Swallowing in a dream suggests we are taking something in. This could be knowledge or information. Dreaming of **swallowing one's pride** signifies the necessity for humility, whilst something being **hard to swallow** shows that we have a need to overcome an obstacle.

2 When we are holding back on emotion, we physically need to swallow. Swallowing therefore becomes an act of suppression which can be harmful.

3 The dreamer may be taking in more spirituality than he can comfortably process. It would be advisable to slow down and 'digest' his spiritual teachings more methodically.

SWAMP
– also see Marsh

1 A swamp in a dream symbolises feelings which can undermine our confidence and well-being. To **be swamped** is to be overwhelmed by a feeling or emotion. To be **swamping someone else** in a dream may suggest that we are being too needy.

2 Emotionally, when a swamp appears we are putting ourselves in touch with very basic feelings and emotions. A swamp is so-called primordial material, out of which everything emerges; at this stage we have no idea what our potential is.

3 A swamp can symbolise the vast amount of spiritual knowledge that there is to be taken in. The

sheer vastness may leave the dreamer feeling utterly hopeless and out of his depth, but with some perseverance he can pull himself through and enjoy a much clearer outlook.

SWAN
– see Birds

SWASTIKA
– see Shapes

SWEEPING

1 To dream of sweeping suggests being able to clear away outmoded attitudes and emotions. To be **sweeping up** suggests putting things in order.

2 Sweeping is an old image which harks back to good management and clearing of the environment. In psychological terms it suggests an attention to detail and correctness, as much as to cleanliness. In modern day technological symbolism it could suggest searching for viruses.

3 The dreamer may have attained much spiritual knowledge on which he is now reflecting. There may be certain elements of confusion which he can take time to clear away.

SWEETS
– see Food

SWIMMING
– also see Drowning

1 Dreaming of swimming has much the same symbolism as immersion *(see Immersion)*. To be **swimming upstream** in a dream would indicate that the dreamer is going against their own nature. **Swimming fish** can have the same symbolism as sperm, and therefore can indicate the desire for a child. Swimming in **clear water** indicates being cleansed, whereas **dark water** could symbolise the possibility of depression.

2 Swimming in water will always be symbolic of the emotions, whereas **swimming through the air** connects with intellectual ability. To dream of being a **good swimmer** shows the ability to be able to handle emotional situations well, whereas being a **poor swimmer** in a dream could indicate the need to learn how to handle our emotions in a more positive way.

3 Swimming uses a lot of energy in getting from one place to another. Symbolically it suggests that spiritual energy is being used up when we are moving towards a certain goal.

SWINE
– see Pig in Animals

SWING
– see Rocking

SWORD
– also see Weapon

1 The sword in dreams invariably suggests a weapon of power. We may have the ability to create power and use energy properly through our beliefs.

2 The sword symbolises justice and courage as well as strength. For the image of a sword to appear in a dream indicates there is an element of the warrior in us, and that we are prepared to fight for our beliefs.

3 Spiritually the sword signifies the power of authority and protection. In dreams to be **given a sword** signifies that we have the protection of the sacred. We are able to make our own decisions.

SYNAGOGUE
– see Church Buildings

SYRINGE
– also see Injection

1 In dreams the syringe suggests an awareness of the influence that other people can have over us. It will depend on whether the syringe is being used to take something out or put something in as to the particular significance. A **garden syringe** (as in a fly spray) in dreams can suggest either masculine energy or decontamination.

2 Dreaming of a syringe can indicate that when we are attempting to influence other people, we need to be conscious of the way we do it. We can be very specific and hit the right spot, or we can have a more 'scatter-gun' approach. We need to be careful that we do not inflict hurt more than is necessary on others.

3 Penetrative awareness can suggest a particular way of approaching our own spiritual selves.

T

from

Tabernacle *to* Typhoon

TABERNACLE

1 A tabernacle is a place where a sacred object is kept for safety; it also represents a temple. To dream of one is therefore to be trying to understand our own need for sanctuary and safekeeping.

2 Man has always required a way to make certain objects sacred. Psychologically, to acknowledge such sacredness gives him a sense of permanence. He can have some sense that the world will continue to exist without him.

3 A tabernacle, by being sacred, becomes a world centre.

TABLE
– also see Furniture and Altar

1 A table being **a focus for meeting**, whether socially or professionally, is usually recognised in dreams as a symbol of decision making. As **a place for a family rendezvous**, the dreamer may consider meals to be an important ritual. In business and professional terms, **the boardroom table** also has an element of ritual about it.

2 To dream of dealing with **a table or list of objects**, or perhaps actions, instils a sense of order. It represents our ability to create order out of chaos.

3 A table can represent spiritual judgement and legislation.

TABLET
– also see Pill

1 Taking medicine in the form of tablets signifies our recognition of our need to be healthy. We need to 'heal' something that is wrong. If we are **giving tablets to someone else** we may be aware that their needs are not being satisfied.

2 In magical terms, a tablet presupposes knowledge greater than our own and therefore represents an element of trust. We trust our destiny to someone else.

3 As with the Tablets of Moses, there is access to esoteric and magical knowledge.

TADPOLE

1 Dreaming of tadpoles links to an awareness of the simplicity of life. We are aware that there is growth, but either we, or someone else, has not yet reached full maturity.

2 In a woman's dream tadpoles may represent either her wish, or her ability, to become pregnant.

3 Spiritually, the tadpole represents the Germ of Life.

TAIL

1 To dream of a tail can signify some residue from the past, something we still carry with us. It can also indicate sexual excitement, or possibly, by association, the penis.

2 The tail is necessary to the animal for balance, and thus in dreams can be recognised as a means of adjustment in difficult circumstances.

3 The completion of a spiritual action.

TAILOR

1 As with other occupations, it is perhaps more important to decide what significance the tailor has to the dreamer before attempting an interpretation. Any professional person develops certain talents and competencies, such as, in this case, the ability to do precise work and to 'fashion' something new. To dream of a tailor alerts us to these qualities within ourselves.

2 The role that a character plays in our dream has relevance to how we think of our creativity and talents. Dreaming of a tailor may also have meaning in terms of word play. For example we may actually know someone called Taylor.

3 Creative Ability.

TALISMAN

1 A talisman is a protection against evil or difficulty. When one turns up in a dream, we are often aware of the fact that our own mental powers are not sufficient to protect us from fear and doubt. We are in need of external help.

2 Man has a deep connection with objects he believes to be sacred. In most Pagan religions, objects such as stones and drawings were given special powers. While consciously the dreamer may not believe, unconsciously he is capable of linking with ancient magic.

3 Objects bestowed with magical powers retain the ability to protect throughout time, but it is usually the technique used to empower the talisman which should be carefully considered.

TALKING

1 To be conscious of **people talking** in a dream gives a sense of being in contact with our own ability to communicate. We are able to express clearly what we feel and think, whereas in waking life we may not feel confident.

2 We are perhaps afraid of **not being listened** to properly and this anxiety can express itself through hearing someone else talking. It is not necessarily the words that are important, more the sense of what is being said.

3 Psychic communication.

TAMBOURINE
– also see Musical Instruments

1 As human beings we need rhythm in our lives. Dreaming of a tambourine, or any such musical instrument, allows us to be in contact with our own basic rhythms.

2 The tambourine can indicate that we have some control over the rhythm and noise in our lives. Particularly if we are **playing the tambourine in a group**, we are accepting our ability to participate effectively in life.

3 Traditionally, noise was used to summon – or ward off – evil spirits. The tambourine is one such instrument.

TAME

1 To dream of **taming an animal** indicates our ability to control or develop a relationship with the animal aspect of ourselves. To dream of **being tamed**, as though we ourselves were the animal, signifies the need for restraint in our lives.

2 To find that something is extremely tame – in the sense of something **dull and boring** – suggests that we should reconsider the way we live our lives.

3 Self-control, which is spiritually necessary.

TANGLED

1 Sometimes when we are confused in everyday life, we may dream of an object being **entangled with something** else. Often the way that we untangle

the object indicates action we should take in waking moments.

2 When something like **hair is tangled**, we need to be aware that our self-image or projection is coming across to other people as distorted.

3 Cutting through a **tangle of trees or undergrowth** in a dream is part of the Hero's Journey *(see Hero in Archetypes)*.

TANK

1 Dreaming of **a water tank** is putting ourselves in touch with our inner feelings and emotions. Dreaming of **a war tank** connects us with our own need to defend ourselves, but to be aggressive at the same time. Such a dream would indicate that we are feeling threatened in some way.

2 Often in dreams we become aware of our need to overcome objections and difficulties. Sometimes the only form of expression we have is to ride roughshod over those objections. The image of a war tank helps to highlight our ability to do this without being hurt.

3 We need to be a 'Spiritual Warrior'.

TAP

1 The tap is an image of being able to make available universal resources. To dream of **not being able to turn a tap** either on or off highlights our ability – or inability – to control those things we consider to be rightfully ours.

2 Water is considered to be a symbol of emotion, so a tap is representative of our ability to use or misuse emotion in some way. To be able to turn emotion on and off at will is indicative of great self-control.

3 Spiritual flow.

TAPE

1 Dreaming of **a measuring tape** indicates our need to 'measure' our lives in some way. Perhaps we may need to consider how we communicate with, or 'measure up' to, other people's expectations. Equally, **if we are doing the measuring** we may be trying to create order in our lives. Dreaming of **a recording tape** would suggest that we are aware that the way we express ourselves is worth remembering.

2 Masking or parcel tape could be considered to be restraining – to create boundaries – within which movement becomes difficult. In dreams we become aware of the limitation we impose on ourselves in everyday life.

3 A way of recording life's processes.

TAPESTRY
– see Weaving

TAR

1 Dreaming of **tar on the road** would suggest the potential to be trapped as we progress. Dreaming of **tar on a beach**, however, might suggest that we had allowed our emotions to become contaminated in some way.

2 It would depend on the context of the dream whether the image of tar is appropriate or not. For instance to be **mending a road** might signify that we can be repairing wear and tear in our everyday lives. To be **tarring a fence** could mean we must protect ourselves. It will depend what is being done as to how we make the interpretation.

3 The symbolism of tar in a spiritual sense, because it is black and viscous, would suggest some kind of evil or negativity.

TARGET

1 Aiming at a target in dreams would suggest we have a goal in mind. It would depend on the type of target what the goal is. To be **shooting at a bull's-eye** could be interpreted as a search for perfection. To be **aiming at a person** could suggest either hatred or sexual desire.

2 Most of us need some kind of motivation in life, and a target as a symbol of our intellectual aspirations may not make much sense until we study the context of the dream. In a work sense **a sales target** might suggest our goals are imposed on us by others. On a more personal note if we were **setting someone else a target** in dreams, we would need to understand that the other person in the dream is a reflection of part of ourselves.

3 Spiritually a target can have the same significance as the mandala *(see Mandala)*, and represent the Self.

TASTE

1 When something is not to our taste in a dream, it does not conform to our ideals and standards. To have a **bad taste** suggests that whatever is signified by what we are eating does not nourish us. To recognise that our **surroundings are in good taste** suggests an appreciation of beautiful things.

2 In waking life we usually know what we like and what our personal standards are. In dreams those standards may be distorted in order to highlight a change. For instance, to discover that one likes a colour in a dream which would

not normally be appreciated in real life could suggest that we need to study the new colour more fully in order to discover what it has to offer *(see Colour)*.

3 As we become more sensitive and aware, our taste becomes more refined. This is so in the spiritual realm, in that we appreciate finer, more beautiful things.

TATTOO

1 On a physical level, a tattoo will stand for an aspect of individuality in the dreamer. He (or she) wishes to be seen as different.

2 A tattoo in dreams can also signify something which has left an indelible impression. This could be great hurt, but could also be a good memory. Sometimes, the **image which is tattooed** is worth interpreting if it can be seen clearly.

3 In spiritual terms a tattoo can suggest a group identity, belonging to a tribe or cult. It will be on a more intimate level than wearing a badge.

TAU

1 The tau cross can sometimes be perceived as a phallic image. It is more properly to do with supreme power. Worn as a talisman it protects from evil, and will often be perceived in this way in a dream. It

463

is the T cross, not the cross of sacrifice.

2 In the psychological sense, the tau cross signifies the meeting of the physical and the spiritual and all that it entails.

3 Spiritually, this cross signifies the key to supreme power and living a truly successful life.

TAX

1 In everyday life, a tax represents a sum of money exacted from us in return for the right to live a certain lifestyle. In dreams, therefore, having to **pay a tax** suggests some kind of a penalty for living the way we choose.

2 In real terms, a tax represents the extra amount of effort necessary to enable us to belong to society. Thus, dreaming of **car tax** would indicate that greater effort is needed to move forward. To be paying **income tax** suggests that we may feel we owe a debt to society. To be paying **council tax** may suggest that we feel we have to pay for the 'space' in which we exist. **Refusing to pay any taxes** suggests an unwillingness to conform.

3 Spiritually, any tax levied in a dream would indicate our attitude towards working for the greater, or communal, good. We need to take some responsibility for the universe we live in.

TAXI

– also see Car In Journey

1 In a dream **calling a taxi** signifies recognising the need to progress – to get somewhere. We cannot be successful without help, for which there may be a price.

2 A taxi is a public vehicle in the sense that it is usually driven by someone unknown to us. We therefore have to trust the driver's awareness and knowledge. In dreams, therefore, a taxi can suggest having the ability to get somewhere without knowing how.

3 A taxi can represent spiritual knowledge, coupled with practical know-how. This is an important attribute in personal development.

TEA

1 It will depend on whether the dream is about tea as **a commodity**, or a social occasion. On a practical level, tea as a commodity represents a unit of exchange, whereas the **social occasion** suggests inter-communication.

2 The **Japanese tea ceremony** suggests a unique way of caring for and nurturing someone, as does **afternoon tea**. Dreaming of **tea cups** in particular links with the individual's need for divination (reading tea leaves). A **tea break in a work environment** suggests a need for rest and relaxation from concentration.

3 Tea as a symbol suggests spiritual refreshment and making an offering.

TEACHER
– also see Education and School

1 For many people, a teacher is the first figure of authority they meet outside the family. That person has a profound effect on the child and the teacher is often dreamt about in later years. Teachers can also generate conflict if their expressed views are very different to those learnt by the child at home. This may be something which has to be resolved through dreams in later years.

2 When we are looking for guidance, the Animus/Anima *(see Introduction)* can present itself in dreams as a teacher. Often the figure will be that of a **headmaster or headmistress** (someone who 'knows better').

3 A spiritual teacher usually appears either in dreams or in person when the individual is ready to progress. There is a saying 'when the chela (pupil) is ready, the teacher will come'. Often, that teacher will not appear as a Wise Old Man *(See Introduction)* or woman, but as a person appropriate to the level of the dreamer's understanding.

TEARS

1 Tears in dreams can indicate an emotional release and a cleansing. If **we are crying** we may not feel we are able to give way to emotion in everyday life, but can do so in the safe scenario of a dream. If we dream of **someone else in tears** we perhaps need to look at our own conduct to see if it is appropriate.

2 To dream of **being in tears** and then to wake up and discover that we are actually crying, suggests that some hurt or trauma has come sufficiently close to the surface to enable us to deal with it on a conscious level.

3 Tears can represent hurt or compassion, and it is often this latter meaning which applies spiritually. Experiencing compassion in a dream can make us more aware of the necessity for it in waking life.

TEASING

1 When we are **being teased** in a dream, we are becoming aware that our own behaviour may not be appropriate. If we are **teasing someone** and pointing out their idiosyncrasies, we may actually be highlighting our own discrepancies.

2 Teasing can be a form of bullying, of becoming a victim. We need to understand our requirement to have power over someone, rather than helping them. Teasing will often arise from an insecurity and an awareness of our own doubts and fears. In archetypal terms it is an easy way to project our own difficulties onto other people.

3 Within spiritual development one becomes aware of others' faults of character. Teasing or being teased in dreams alerts us to an ego state which is not appropriate for further development.

TEETH
– see Body

TELEGRAM

1 Receiving a telegram in a dream highlights communication in the most efficient way possible under the circumstances. It indicates that a part of ourselves is attempting to give us information in a way that is going to be remembered. As communication technology becomes more efficient, we are much more likely to dream of a fax or a fax machine *(see Fax)*. To be **sending a telegram** can suggest that we wish something to be known about ourselves that cannot be communicated verbally.

2 Previously, telegrams were messages of celebration or bad news. For many, that image is still retained in dreams. For instance, to receive **a telegram of wedding congratulations** may link with the dreamer's wish to be married. On the other hand, a **telegram bearing bad news** may be alerting us to something of which we are already aware on a subconscious level.

3 Any communication received in writing is to do with making knowledge, in this case spiritual knowledge, tangible.

TELEPHONE

1 Using a telephone in a dream suggests the ability to make contact with other people and to impart information we feel they may need. This could actually be communicating with someone in our ordinary everyday lives, or with a part of ourselves with which we are not totally in contact. **Being contacted by telephone** suggests there is information available to us which we do not already consciously know.

2 When we are **aware of the telephone number we are ringing**, it may be the numbers that are important *(see Numbers)*. We also may be aware of the need to contact a specific person who we can help, or who can help us. If we are **searching for a**

telephone number we are having difficulty in co-ordinating our thoughts about our future actions. Using the telephone suggests a direct one-to-one relationship.

3 Because communication via the telephone suggests that we are not able to see the recipient, using the telephone in a dream can signify communication with Spirit or with Guardian Angels.

TELESCOPE

1 Using a telescope in a dream suggests taking a closer look at something. A telescope enhances our view and makes it bigger and wider. We do need to make sure, however, that we are not taking a one-sided view of things.

2 Using a telescope in a dream may mean that we should look at things with both a long and short-term view. Without taking account of a long-term view, we may not be able to succeed in the short term. Conversely, by looking at the long-term view, we may be given information which will help us to 'navigate' our lives in the here and now.

3 Interestingly enough, a telescope in spiritual terms can signify the art of clairvoyance – the ability to perceive the future from an immediate perspective.

TEMPLE
– also see Church Buildings

1 Often in dreams a temple can signify our own body. It is something to be treated with reverence and care. It has the same significance as a church since it is an object built to honour and pay respect to a god or gods.

2 Psychologically, wherever there is a temple there is a sense of awe associated with creativity. Perhaps the biggest significance in dreams is the fact that it takes many to build one temple. This links with our awareness of the many facets of our personality which go to make a coherent whole.

3 Both as a sanctuary for human beings and as a place where the Divine resides, a temple reflects the beauty of Heaven. It is a microcosm (small picture) of what is, after all, infinite.

TEMPTATION

1 Temptation is a conflict between two different drives. For instance, in dreams we may experience a conflict between the need to go out into the world and the need to stay safe at home. Temptation is yielding to that which is easiest and not necessarily the best course of action.

2 Intellectually, when presented with options of action we may tend to go for a result which gives short-term satisfaction, rather than long-term. The idea of giving in to temptation suggests that it is bigger or more powerful than we are. Often dreams can show us the course of action we should be taking.

3 Temptation is one of the biggest spiritual barriers we must overcome. Often it is a conflict between the Self and the Ego *(See Introduction)*. Christ's temptation by Satan is a good example of this.

TENANT

1 To dream of **being a tenant** suggests that at some level we do not want to take responsibility for the way we choose to live. We do not want to be burdened by having full responsibility for our living space. **To have a tenant** signifies that we are prepared to have someone live in our space. This may be the type of dream that occurs as we are preparing to become involved in a full-time relationship.

2 If we follow up the idea of a tenant being someone with whom we have a commercial relationship, then we will have some insights into how we handle such transactions. **If the dreamer is a man and the tenant a woman** then the tenant is likely to represent his Anima *(see Introduction)*. If **the situation is reversed** then the tenant will epitomise her Animus *(see Introduction)*.

3 Dreaming of having a tenant in the spiritual sense can have two meanings. One would link with the idea that within us we have many personalities who must be synthesised into a holistic being. The other would suggest that tenants (inherited beliefs) can be evicted if they are inappropriate.

TENT

1 A tent in a dream would suggest that we feel we are on the move, and not able to settle down and put down roots. Anywhere we settle is only going to be temporary.

2 We perhaps need to get away from everyday responsibilities for a time, and rediscover our relationship with natural forces. There is benefit to be gained by being self-sufficient and not dependent on anyone.

3 The biblical and nomadic image of being able to pack up one's tent and steal away is the spiritual meaning here. We are not tied to any one place, but can be where we need to be at short notice.

TERROR

1 Terror in a dream is often the result of unresolved fears and doubts. It is only by experiencing such a profoundly disturbing emotion that are we likely to make an attempt to confront those fears. If **someone else is terrified** in our dream we are in a position to do something about it, and need to work out what course of action should be taken.

2 Fear or terror dreams can be one of the triggers towards a deeper understanding of oneself. If we know we are fearful we can do something about it. Terror is more difficult to handle since in that state we will not know what the cause is. In the waking state it is possible to use a technique which will identify the terror. The statement which is made is 'I am terrified because...' followed by the immediate reason which comes to mind. Then work through each fresh statement until you come to a full stop. Thus:

'I am terrified because I have no money',

'I have no money because I spent it at the supermarket',

'I spent it at the supermarket because I have to eat',

'I have to eat because I'm afraid to die' and so on.

Gradually the meaning becomes clearer until there is a resolution.

3 Spiritual terror could be identified as fear of evil.

TESTS
– also see Exams

1 Dreaming of tests of any sort can indicate some form of self-assessment. **Medical tests** may be alerting us to the need to watch our health. **A driving test** would suggest a test of confidence or ability, whereas a **written test** would signify a test of knowledge.

2 Testing something in a dream suggests that there has been some form of standard set, to which we feel we must adhere. This need not mean that we are setting ourselves against others, simply that we have resolved to maintain a certain standard.

3 A spiritual test is one that is created from the circumstances around us perhaps to test our resolve.

TEXT

1 A text is taken to mean a collection of words which have a certain specific meaning. For a text such as this to appear in a dream would signify the need for encouragement and perhaps wisdom.

2 Text from a book or a **text of a play** would indicate the need for the dreamer to carry out instructions in a particular way in order to achieve success.

3 A spiritual text is an encouraging message to enable us to progress.

THAW

1 In dreams, to be conscious of a thaw is to note a change in our own emotional responses. We no longer have a need to be as emotionally distanced as previously. **2** Psychologically we have the ability to 'warm up' a situation, and to melt coldness away. If we are aware of coldness within ourselves, on an emotional level we need to discover what the problem is or was, and why we have reacted as we did. **3** A spiritual thaw would suggest the ability to come to terms with old barriers and to become warm and loving.

THEATRE
– also see Stage

1 In dreams about the theatre it will depend which part of the theatre is highlighted. If it is **the stage**, then a situation that the dreamer is in at this particular moment is being drawn to his attention. If it is **the auditorium**, then his ability to listen is significant. The play we create in our dreams as an aspect of our lives is particularly relevant. If we are **not involved in the action**, it indicates we are able to stand back and take an objective viewpoint. **2** The theatre is a scenario which has meaning for many. Because it is a social venue, it has relevance in people's relationships with one another. It is this aspect which is being highlighted. To be **in the spotlight**, for instance, might signify our need to be noticed. To be up in **'the gods'** might suggest that we need to take a long-term view of a situation. **3** Spiritually the idea of a play in a dream highlights the idea of the microcosm within the macrocosm – the small within a larger framework.

THERMOMETER

1 A thermometer in a dream will be representative of judging our warmth and feelings. We may be uncertain of how we come across to other people and need some kind of outside measurement. A **clinical thermometer** would portray our emotional warmth, whereas an **external thermometer** would suggest our intellectual abilities. **2** Psychologically we sometimes need an external evaluation as to where we are coming from. A thermometer would be a reassurance device. **3** Just as a thermometer measures temperature, the way we handle situations around us will give indications of our spiritual health and ability.

THIEF
– also see Stealing

1 Dreaming of a thief links with our fear of losing things, or of having them taken away. We may be afraid of losing love or possessions.
2 When a thief appears in dreams, we are aware of part of our personality which can waste our own time and energy on meaningless activity. It literally steals from us.
3 A spiritual thief is that part of us which has no respect for our beliefs.

THIGH
– see Limbs in Body

THIRD EYE
– see Religious Imagery

THIRST

1 Dreaming of **being thirsty** suggests we have an unsatisfied inner need; we may be emotionally at a low ebb and need something to give us a boost. Anything that gives us emotional satisfaction – whether short- or long-term – would suffice.
2 To **satisfy a thirst** indicates we are capable of satisfying our own desires. By being prepared to take in what we need, we are able to experience life in the best way possible. If we are thirsty in a dream, we need to look very carefully at either what we are being denied, or what we are denying ourselves, in waking life.
3 Thirst is symbolic of our thirst for spiritual knowledge and enlightenment. It may well be an unquenchable thirst.

THISTLE

1 To be conscious of thistles in a dream is to be aware of some discomfort in waking life. **A field of thistles** would suggest a difficult road ahead. **A single thistle** would indicate minor difficulties.
2 The thistle has a meaning of defiance and vindictiveness. When dreaming of a thistle we may be being made aware of those qualities, either in people around us or in ourselves. The colour of the thistles may be important *(see Colour)*.
3 The thistle can represent our spiritual defiance in the face of physical adversity. It follows the symbolism of the passion of Christ.

THORN

1 To dream of **being pierced by a thorn or splinter** signifies that a minor difficulty has got through our defences. If the **thorn draws blood**, we need to look at what is happening in our lives which could make us vulnerable. In a woman's dream this could represent the sexual act, or rather, fear of intercourse.

2 The thorn stands for physical suffering in dreams. In matters of health, it may indicate a vulnerability to infection.

3 The thorn, also associated with Christ, may signify that we are dedicating ourselves to some element of our spiritual quest. The **crown of thorns** indicates suffering for our beliefs.

THREAD

1 Thread in dreams represents a line of thought or enquiry. In terms of our ordinary everyday lives we perhaps need to follow that line to its end. **Threading a needle** has an obvious sexual reference. It can also, because of the perceived difficulty in threading a needle, suggest incompetence in ways other than sexual.

2 To be aware of thread is to be aware of the way our lives are going. **A tangled thread** suggests a difficulty which needs unravelling. **A spool of thread** suggests an ordered existence. The colour of the thread is important *(see Colour)*. **A basket full of spools** suggests the various aspects of a woman's personality. This is because of its association with the Archetypal feminine.

3 The various threads of our spirituality are being interwoven – the results of which will go some way to achieving the dreamer's spiritual wholeness.

THRESHOLD

1 Crossing the threshold in dreams indicates new experiences. To be **lifted across a threshold** may suggest marriage, or in this day and age, a new relationship.

2 When we are about to take on new responsibilities, we can dream of **standing on the threshold**. We may be moving into a new life, or perhaps a new way of living. The threshold experience is a strong one in Masonic imagery and Initiation rites. Even in Parliament, permission must be asked to cross the threshold.

3 We may be standing on the threshold of a new spiritual dawn. The dreamer should be particularly astute at this time and be aware of all that is around him.

THROAT
– see Body

THRONE

1 When we dream of **sitting on a throne**, we are acknowledging our right to take authority. When the **throne is empty**, we are not prepared to accept the responsibility for who we are. It may be that we are conscious of a lack of parenting. When **someone else**

is on the throne, we may have passed over authority to that other person.

2 A throne is a seat of authority or power. In dreams it can represent our ability to belong to groups, or even to society. We may need to take the lead in a project or scheme. The throne usually suggests that we have attained control on all levels of existence, both spiritually and physically.

3 Spiritually we could be at a point where knowledge and understanding are finally within our grasp. This can be symbolised by a throne in a dream.

THUMB
– see Body

THUNDER/ THUNDERBOLTS
– also see Storm

1 Hearing thunder in a dream can give a warning for the potential of an emotional outburst. We may be building up energy which eventually must reverberate. Hearing **thunder in the distance** signifies that there is still time to gain control of a potentially difficult situation.

2 Thunder has always been a symbol of great power and energy. In conjunction with lightning, it was seen as a tool of the gods. It could bring doom and disaster, but also was cleansing.

3 Spiritually, the rumblings of thunder can demonstrate deep anger, or in extreme cases Divine anger.

TIARA
– see Crown and Diadem

TICKET

1 If we dream of tickets, it will depend on what type of ticket it is as to the interpretation. Generally, a ticket suggests that there is a price to pay for something. A **bus ticket** would indicate that there is a price for moving forward, as might a **train ticket**. A **ticket to a theatre or cinema** may suggest we need to take a back seat and be objective over a part of our lives. Tickets to **a football or rugby match** might mean that we will have to pay for some area of conflict in our lives.

2 One interpretation of a ticket – in the form of a **certificate or voucher** – is that of us requiring recognition of the effort we have put in. To dream of **receiving such a ticket** indicates it is we who are being recompensed.

3 Spiritually a dream of a ticket will symbolise our recognition that all knowledge must be somehow paid for.

TICKLE

1 One of the most difficult things to do either in waking life or when dreaming is to break down the barriers which we all have. Often these are barriers of reserve. In dreams therefore, we sometimes need to perceive bizarre images in order to drive the message home. It depends on whether the dreamer is a tactile person when awake as to the interpretation. If he or she is tactile, this would indicate there is perhaps a need for humour when dealing with an opportunity. If they are not, then any approach at intimacy should be made with humour.

2 Tickling in the psychological sense is to be treating something lightly. This may be either a situation or person. For a fisherman, 'tickling a trout' would be to coerce it, that is, to persuade it to come towards him. This can also be one of the interpretations in dream work.

3 To be tickled in a dream, spiritually, means that we need to approach spirituality with humour to enable us to make the best use of it.

TIDE

-also see Sea in Water

1 Dreaming of a tide is attempting to go with the ebb and flow of life, or, rather more specifically, with the emotions. As a tide also removes debris, the symbolism of cleansing is relevant. A **high tide** may symbolise high energy, whereas a **low tide** would suggest a drain on our abilities or energy.

2 In waking life there are two times in the year when there are very high tides – the Spring and the Autumn *(see Seasons)*. Thus, in dreams an exceptionally high tide might signify those times. **A moon over a moving tide** would, at a certain stage of development, suggest the powers of the feminine.

3 Spiritually, it may well be a simple image such as the tide turning which indicates that we are finding our way.

TIGER

– see Animals

TILL

1 There are two meanings of 'till'. One is to **till the ground**, and while that is a less potent images nowadays the image still appears in dreams in the sense of cultivating opportunities. The other meaning is as **a safe repository for money**. It is this symbolism of a commercial transaction which is the one most understood.

2 When we put money in a till, it is being put there for safe keeping.

However, it is also being put there to accumulate. It will increase and work for itself. This is where the more practical and psychological meanings coincide. We need to save or conserve what we have to get best benefit.

3 A till is symbolic of what we have accumulated spiritually being stored up, until such a time as we need to look at it more carefully.

TIMBER
– see Wood

TIME

1 For time to be significant in a dream there is usually the necessity to measure it in some way, or to use a period of time as a measurement. Usually the dreamer is only aware of the passage of time, or that a particular time is meaningful in the dream – it is part of the dream scenario. On consideration, the time in the dream may symbolise a particular time in one's life. **The daylight hours** will thus suggest our conscious waking life. **Where several days (or other long periods) pass** Some other activity which is not relevant to uus has been going on. **The hours of the day** These could refer to a time of the dreamer's life or it may simply be the number which is important *(see*

Numbers). **Afternoon** This is a time of life when we can put our experience to good use. **Evening** The end of life highlights our ability to be more relaxed about our lives and activities. **Mid-day** When mid-day is suggested we are fully conscious and aware of our activities. **Morning** The first part of our life or our early experience is being highlighted. **Night** may be a period of depression or secrecy. We may be introspective or simply at rest. **Twilight** can indicate in dreams a period of uncertainty and possible ambivalence insofar as our direction in life is concerned. It may also suggest a period of transition such as death. **2 To be early** for an appointment in a dream suggests having to wait for something to happen before we can carry on our lives. **Being late** shows the dreamer's lack of attention to detail or the feeling that time is running out. **Watching the clock** indicates the necessity to make time work for us.

3 Death or change.

TITANS

1 Titans in dreams appear as huge god-like figures – sometimes overbearing, sometimes large. In this context they represent the forces within us which allow things to manifest, or to happen.

2 Psychologically we probably use about 10 per cent of our available energy. Those Titanic forces which can arise in dreams are those parts of ourselves that are untamed and untameable. When used properly they are the ability to create a world of our own.

3 Our will and urge to achieve our spiritual goals may be symbolised by the appearance of Titans in a dream.

TOAD
– see Reptiles in Animals

TOBACCO

1 Tobacco appearing in dreams will have different meanings depending on whether the dreamer is a smoker or not. **If he or she is a smoker**, then tobacco, in the dream, is probably a comfort tool. **If not**, then the symbolism is probably more to do with the idea of using tobacco to achieve a particular state of mind. If the dreamer is **smoking a pipe**, there may be issues of masculinity to deal with.

2 It is said that Red Indians use tobacco to drive away bad spirits, and it is true that initially tobacco will give the person a mood lift. In dreams it is this symbolism of change which is the meaningful one.

3 Tobacco as a giver of visions may be the symbolism here. The dreamer may be interested in the idea of spirituality, but as yet has not found the right stimulation.

TOILET

1 For many people the toilet has been until recently a symbol for dirt and lack of appreciation. There has also been the inevitable association with sexuality. Nowadays the symbolism is much more to do with notions of privacy, and the ability to reach a state where we can release our feelings in private.

2 Something wrong with the toilet could suggest that we are emotionally blocked. Going to an **unfamiliar toilet** suggests we are in a position where we do not know what the outcome to a situation will be. **Cleaning a dirty toilet** suggests we are losing our 'prudish' attitude.

3 Spiritually, a toilet suggests that we have the means at our disposal to cleanse away the negative.

TOMB

1 Going into a tomb suggests going down into the darker parts of our own personality. We may be fearful to begin with, but later more at ease. Finding ourselves **in a tomb** suggests we are ready to face our fears of death and dying.

2 If we are **trapped in a tomb** in a dream we may be trapped by fear, pain or old outdated attitudes in our waking life. If there are **bodies in the tomb**, these are usually parts of ourselves we have either not developed or have killed off. If **one of those bodies comes alive**, the attention we have given to that aspect of our personality has been sufficient to resurrect it.

3 Spiritually we may feel that we have entered into a world that is all at once mysterious and dark – dark in the sense of wanting to see the light. Although we fear it, we are also excited. It is worth remembering that we are not trapped, but in a brief state of panic which can be overcome by belief.

TONGUE
– see Body

TOOLS

1 Tools in dreams suggest the practical tools we have at our disposal for enhancing our lifestyle.

2 Each tool will have its own significance. **A drill** suggests working through emotions and fears as well as attitudes which have become hardened. **A hammer** provides the energy to break down old patterns of behaviour and resistances.

A saw suggests being able to cut through all the rubbish we have accumulated in order to make something new.

3 Spiritual tools which can be symbolised in a practical way are love, compassion and charity.

TOP
– see Position

TORCH

1 In dreams, a torch can represent self-confidence. It can also suggest the need to be able to move forward, but at the same time carry our own light.

2 A torch can be used not only for ourselves, but also for other people. Dreaming of a torch shows we can have the confidence to know that, because of our own knowledge, we have the ability to see the way forward.

3 We may feel that we need some spiritual guidance, and this can sometimes be symbolised as a torch.

TORNADO

1 A tornado appearing in a dream is a symbol of violent energy of one sort or another. Often it is emotions and feelings against which we feel powerless. It is a recognisable symbol of energy which has turned in on itself, and has therefore become destructive.

2 While a tornado can be very destructive, interestingly, it can also be very cleansing and it is in this context that it is often met on a psychological level. It sweeps all in front of it, but after its passage there is the potential for new life.

3 Our early ventures into spirituality may make us feel powerless, and at the mercy of all the elements. This can be symbolised by the tornado. However, within the centre there is peace and tranquillity.

TORPEDO

1 The torpedo, because of its shape, has obvious connections with masculine aggressiveness. Its power in dreams can be destructive, but often is unconscious in origin.

2 In terms of being able to home in on its target, the torpedo suggests directed energy. This may be the type of honest getting to the point which we can do with friends, or it may be a warning that such directness could be harmful.

3 A torpedo is symbolic of spiritual directness. The dreamer should be aware of taking the correct action for the circumstances in which he finds himself.

TORTOISE

1 The tortoise for most people suggests slowness but also perhaps thoroughness. It also in dreams signifies a shell, that perhaps we – or others round us – have put up in order to protect or defend ourselves.

2 The tortoise may of course simply be an image of a pet *(See Pet)* as an object which is loved. It may also however be a symbol for long life.

3 In Chinese lore the tortoise is a revered figure of wisdom and knowledge. He is said to carry the pattern of all existence on his back. He also represents Creation.

TORTURE

1 When an image connected with torture appears in a dream, often we are trying to come to terms with a great hurt. This does not need to be on a physical level – indeed, it hardly ever is. It is more likely to be emotional or mental pain.

2 If we are being tortured we need to look at the other images in the dream to discover what significance this will have in everyday life. It may be that we tend to put ourselves in the position of victim without realising it.

3 Spiritual torture can be a conflict between right and wrong.

It can also be a matter of choices between two courses of action. Often the idea of such torture for the Greater Good is part of the process of growth.

TOTEM/TOTEM POLE

1 In a dream a totem pole can link us back to a very primitive need for protection. It is not the protection afforded by a father, but by those spirits whose energy is powerful enough to be used by us.

2 When an object revered as a sacred article is given enough power by a joint belief, the thing itself is perceived as taking on a power of its own. One such object is the totem pole. When it appears in dreams we need to be looking at those parts of our lives which are based around our belief system to discover whether we are really living according to those beliefs.

3 Both in its symbolic meaning of a protector and as a representative of spiritual matters, the totem pole suggests strength and power.

TOUCH

1 Touch in dream suggests making contact in some way. We are linking up with other people, usually to our mutual advantage. We are perhaps becoming conscious of both our need for other people and of their need for us.

2 Within relationships, touch can be an important act of appreciation. Often dreams will reveal our attitude to such concepts as touching and being touched.

3 The transference of power and blessing can be signified by the simple act of touching.

TOURIST

1 A tourist in a dream is someone who does not know his way around. If **we are the tourist** then we need to look at that aspect within ourselves. If **someone else is the tourist** then we need to be aware of what help we can give other people.

2 To play the tourist in a dream is to be aware of the fact that we have the necessary information to do what we want, but that we are choosing not to.

3 The tourist in a dream in spiritual terms represents the hermit.

TOWER
– also see Buildings

1 A tower in a dream usually represents a construction which we have developed in our lives. This may be an inner attitude or an outer life. To dream of **a tower with no door** suggests we are out of touch with our inner selves. **A tower with no windows** signifies that we are unable to see and appreciate either our external good points or our inner ones. An ivory tower suggests an innocent approach. A **square tower** signifies a practical approach to life, whereas a **round tower** is more spiritually geared. A **round tower at the end of a square building** is the combination of the practical and spiritual.

2 Psychologically if we are to live life as fully as we can, we need to understand our own tower. In dreams it may appear initially as far away and later coming closer. How we get into the tower may be important. **Shallow steps** would indicate that to explore our inner self may be easy. More **difficult steps** may indicate that we are fairly private individuals. If the **door is barred** we are not ready to explore our unconscious self. If the **door is closed** we must make an effort to get in. If **inside the tower is dark**, we are still afraid of our subconscious. The dreamer, having been given these suggestions, should be able to interpret other symbolism. The **hidden room in the tower** would have the same significance as in a house.

3 The tower is ambivalent in the spiritual sense, since it can be feminine in the shelter it affords and masculine because of its shape. It suggests ascent to the spiritual realms, but also descent to the practical.

TOWN
– see City / Town

TOY

1 When there are toys in a dream we may be aware of children around us, or of our more child-like selves. Toys will highlight the creative side of ourselves, and the more playful innocent part.

2 Perhaps we need to look at the types of toys which appear. They often give some indication of what we are playing with. We may be mulling over new ideas or new ways of relating to others. Equally we need to 'play' more, to relax and have fun.

3 Toys appearing in a dream may be alerting us to our ability to create our own lives. Just as a child will imagine himself creating his own little world through his toys, so also can we as dreamers and creators.

TRACK
– see Path and also Train in Journey

TRAIN
– see Journey

TRAITOR

1 To dream of a traitor suggests

that one is subconsciously aware of deviousness. This may be in someone else, or it could be a part of our personality which is letting us down. We may feel that our standards are not appreciated by others.

2 When in a dream we are betrayed by others and believe them to have let us down, we are perhaps aware of the fact that it is with through shared belief in waking life that they have let us down. This would mean they are traitors.

3 Spiritually, to be a traitor is to act as Peter is reputed to have done and deny our basic belief.

TRAMP
– also see Archetypes

1 To dream of a tramp in the sense of a decrepit old wanderer links us back to the part of ourselves which is not expressed fully in real life. It is the 'drop-out' or gypsy within us. We may be conscious of our need for irresponsibility.

2 The tramp personifies in us the wanderer, the freedom lover. In dreams he will often appear at a time when we need freedom, but can also show that that need can bring difficulty and sadness. He can also appear in dreams as the jester or fool. There is a part in all of us that is anarchical, and the tramp represents this side.

3 Spiritually, although this image starts out as negative, if we are prepared to work with it, it can have great positivity – since ultimately he is always in the right place at the right time for the right reasons.

TRANSFIGURATION

1 For something to be transfigured in dreams suggests that that image has a greater signiificance than just its symbolism. Transfiguration usually means being surrounded by light, and for this to happen suggests that it has some divine or special purpose. This dream can occur as we are working through stages of transition in our lives.

2 Transfiguration is a phenomenon which can occur during altered states of consciousness. It is as though a light enters the personality and changes it. For transfiguration to occur in dreams indicates we are becoming conscious of a more permanent awareness of ourselves. In the waking state it is taken to suggest being used as a spiritual channel.

3 Spiritually, we are aware that we are all part of a greater whole.

TRANSFORMATION

1 Dreams where obvious changes occur and things are transformed into something else suggests a shift in awareness. A landscape may change from dark to light (negativity to positivity), a person may change from masculine to feminine or one image may change into another. Once the dreamer understands the change is for the better, he is able to accomplish changes in his own life.

2 As the growth to maturity takes place, there are many transformations which occur. These are often depicted in dreams as immediate changes, like a speeded-up camera filming an opening flower.

3 Transformation takes place in spiritual terms when freedom of thought or action is indicated, or when higher impulses are substituted for lower reactions.

TRANSPARENT

1 When something is transparent in a dream we may be feeling vulnerable, but may also be aware of insights we would not normally have. **To be inside a transparent bubble**, for instance, would suggest visibility and vulnerability in our lives, perhaps taking on new responsibilities. For someone else to be **behind a transparent shield** suggests they are somewhat remote and unavailable to us.

2 When we are aware in dreams that things around us are transparent, we become our ability to 'see through' things. We are able to be discerning in our judgement.

3 Transparency in the spiritual sense represents honesty.

TRANSVESTISM
– see Sex

TRAP/TRAPPED

1 To be **in a trap** in a dream signifies that we feel we are trapped by outside circumstances. To be aware of **trapping something or someone** is attempting to hold onto them. To be **trapping a butterfly** is to be trying to capture the inner self.

2 When we feel trapped in dreams, we are not usually able to break free of old patterns of thought and behaviour. We need outside help.

3 Spiritually we are holding ourselves back. We may also be aware of being trapped by the restrictions of the physical body.

TRAVELLING
– see Journey

TREASURE

1 Treasure in dreams always represents something which is of value to us. It is the result of personal achievement and effort. To **find buried treasure** is to find something we have lost, perhaps a part of our personality. To be

burying treasure is to be trying to guard against the future and potential problems.

2 To **find a box which has treasure in it** is to have some understanding of the fact that we must break through limitations before we find what we are looking for. The **search for treasure** suggests the finding of earthly goods or material gain which will not necessarily be good.

3 To search for treasure symbolises man's search for enlightenment, his search for the Holy Grail.

TREE
– also see Forest and Wood

1 The tree is symbolic in dreams of the basic structure of our inner lives. When one appears in our dreams it is best to work with the image fairly extensively. A tree with **wide branches** would suggest a warm loving personality, whereas a **small close- leafed** tree would suggest an uptight personality. A **well-shaped** tree would suggest a well-ordered personality, while a **large, messy tree** would suggest a chaotic personality. There is a game which can be played in waking life if one dares. Ask a friend a) what sort of tree does he or she think you are and, b) what sort of tree they think they are. The results are interesting.

An oak for instance would represent strength.

2 The roots of a tree are said to show our connection with ourselves and the earth. It could be more accurate to suggest that they signify our ability to belong to the practical side of life, to enjoy being here. **Spreading roots** would indicate an ability to relate well to the physical, and, conversely, **deep-rootedness** would suggest a more self-contained attitude. The trunk of the tree gives an indication of how we use the energies available to us, and also what exterior we present to the world. A **rough trunk** suggests obviously a rough and ready personality, whereas a **smoother trunk** would indicate more sophistication. **Branches** signify the stages of growth we go through, and leaves suggest the way we communicate to the rest of the world. To be **climbing the tree** suggests we are looking at our hopes and abilities, in order to succeed.

3 Spiritually the tree symbolises the Tree of Life and represents the union of heaven, earth and water. When we learn and understand our own Tree we are able to live life successfully on all levels.

TRESPASSING
1 When we find **ourselves tres-**

passing in a dream, we are perhaps intruding on someone's personal space. This may also suggest that there is a part of ourselves which is private and feels vulnerable. We should respect those boundaries.

2 If it is **our space or area which is being trespassed upon**, then we need to look at our own boundaries. Sometimes it is interesting when interpreting the dream to find out whether the trespasser is there voluntarily or involuntarily. We can then work out whether we are the victim or not.

3 Spiritually we are approaching areas of knowledge where we cannot go without spiritual permission.

TRIANGLE
– see Shapes

TRICKSTER
– also see Villian in Archetypes

1 In dreams, the trickster is literally that part of ourselves which can create havoc in our lives. When under stress this personage can present himself in dreams as the character who points one in the wrong direction, answers questions with the wrong answers etc.

2 Psychologically, if we have been too rigid in our attitude to life – for instance, struggling to be good the whole time or always taking a moral stance, the trickster can appear in dreams as a counter-balance.

3 This is the spiritually irresponsible part of our nature. We have not yet put ourselves on the correct spiritual path and need to do so.

TRIPLETS
– also see Three in Numbers

3 Spiritually triplets appearing in dreams suggest that events or situations should be looked at carefully in terms of physical wants, emotional needs and spiritual requirements. Then there would be development of spiritual stability.

TROPHY

1 Dreaming of a trophy is to recognise that we have done something for which we can be rewarded. It depends on what the trophy is for as to its significance. The trophy will take on the significance of the object being presented. A **cup** would suggest receptivity *(see Cup)* and a **shield** *(see Shield)*, protection. A common dream that men have is the presentation of a football cup. They are the 'first among men'.

2 Formerly trophies such as animal heads were much sought after. This is no longer so, but the symbolism of overcoming one's basic fears in order to achieve still remains.

3 A trophy would signify a Peak Experience (having moved into an expanded state of awareness) in order to achieve a spiritual goal.

TRUMPET

1 A trumpet in a dream will most often suggest either a warning or a 'call to arms'. From a practical point of view it will be alerting us to some danger we have put ourselves in or are facing. When there is conflict around us we may need some kind of warning to be ready for action and a trumpet can be one such symbol.

2 Representations of angels are often shown blowing trumpets. This represents the call to maximise one's potential. We reach for the best within ourselves in order to have the maximum effect in our lives.

3 The trumpet sounds a spiritual vibration which requires awareness.

TRUNK

1 In previous times to dream of a trunk was supposed to foretell a long journey. Nowadays, as people tend to travel light, it is much more likely to represent a repository for old things and hence signify old out-dated ideas.

2 We have the ability to store all sorts of rubbish – both physically and mentally. When a trunk appears in a dream it is time to 'open the box' and have the courage to sort out what is there. Often, when one is ready to do this but does not do so, the image of the trunk will appear over and over again. To find a **jewel in a trunk** indicates the good that can be found in doing a personal spring-clean.

3 Dreaming of a trunk indicates that spiritually we need to explore our hidden depths to get the best out of ourselves.

TUG OF WAR

1 To dream of a tug of war suggests a conflict between good and bad, male and female, positive and negative.

2 A tug of war may indicate the need to maintain balance through tension between opposites. To be on the **winning side** suggests that what we wish to achieve can be managed with help. To be on **the losing side** requires us to identify the parallel situation in ordinary everyday life and decide whether to continue.

3 A spiritual tug of war suggests the need to resolve the conflict between whatever two opposites are presenting themselves.

TUMBLE
– see Fall

TUNNEL

1 A tunnel in a dream usually represents the need to explore our own unconscious and those things we have left untouched.

2 A tunnel in dreams is supposed at times to represent the birth canal and therefore the process of birth. If there is a **light at the end of the tunnel**, it indicates we are reaching the final stages of our exploration. If **something is blocking the tunnel**, some past fear or experience is stopping us from progressing.

3 Spiritually, the image of a tunnel both helps us to escape from the unconscious into the light and also to go down into the depths.

TURF

1 To dream of being on 'sacred' turf – ground that is revered because of its association, such as **Wembley, Lords etc.** – is to wish for supreme success.

2 Dreaming of one's association with a particular piece of ground can activate memories and feelings connected with happy times. This may, by recollection, help to clarify a particular problem or situation.

3 Sacred or hallowed ground would be represented by turf.

TURKEY
– see Birds

TWEEZERS

1 Dreaming of tweezers suggests that we need to look at a situation in minute detail. By grasping this detail properly much good can be achieved.

2 In the sense that tweezers are tools, such a dream might suggest that we need to develop the correct tools for the job. To be **using other implements as tweezers** and vice versa would suggest confusion as to what our purpose is.

3 Tweezers signify attention to detailed examination of a spiritual concept.

TWINS
– also see People

1 In dreams twins may, if **known to us**, simply be themselves. If they are **not known to us** then they may represent two sides of one idea.

2 Often in everyday life we come up against conflicts between two opposites. Twins in dreams can actually represent two sides of our personality acting in harmony.

3 Duality must eventually re-unite into unity. Twins illustrate the idea that while separate at the moment, that unity can be achieved.

TYPHOON
– see Storm and Wind

U

from

Ulcer *to* Urn

ULCER

1 An ulcer is a sore that is only cured with great difficulty. Thus, to dream of one makes us aware of work which needs to be done to heal a great hurt. It will depend on where the ulcer is as to what needs healing. To dream of a **stomach ulcer**, for instance, would suggest an emotional difficulty, while a **mouth ulcer** would suggest some problem with speech or making ourselves understood to those around us.

2 If we are dealing with **someone else's ulcer** we are aware that that person is not dealing with a dilemma in which we are involved.

3 An ulcer is something which erodes matter. Spiritually it suggests some soreness of Spirit or spiritual dilemma.

UMBILICAL

1 Often in life we can develop an emotional dependency on others, and the umbilical cord in dreams can signify that dependency. We have perhaps not yet learnt to take care of our own needs in a mature way.

2 The umbilical cord particularly represents the life-giving force and the connection between mother and child. **Severing the umbilical cord** often appears in teenage dreams as the child grows into adulthood.

3 The Silver Cord as the spiritual connection is an image seen psychically as the connection between body and soul.

UMBRELLA

1 An umbrella is a shelter and a sanctuary, and it is this symbolism that comes across in dreams. Often in a work situation we need to work under someone's teaching, and this feeling of safety can be recognised in dreams.

2 As we mature we need to develop certain coping skills. In dreams these can be seen as a protective covering, hence the image of the umbrella.

3 As a sunshade conferred status and power, so does the umbrella.

UNCLE
– see Extended Family in Family

UNDER/ UNDERNEATH
– see Position

UNDERGROUND

1 Just as Alice dreamt of falling down the rabbit hole in 'Alice in Wonderland', so we all have opportunities to explore our own hidden depths through dreams. We cannot usually access the unconscious in waking life, and to dream of being underground will often allow us to come to terms with that side in a very easy way.

2 To be on the underground or subway usually signifies the journeys we are prepared (or forced) to take towards understanding who we are.

3 The subconscious or the unconscious is often perceived in dreams as a cave or place underground.

UNDRESS
– also see Clothes

1 When we find ourselves undressing in a dream, we may be putting ourselves in touch with our own sexual feelings. We may also be needing to reveal our true feelings about a situation around us, and to have the freedom to be totally open about those feelings.

2 To be watching someone else undressing often indicates that we should be aware of that person's sensitivity. **To be undressing someone else** suggests that we are attempting to understand either ourselves or others on a very deep level.

3 To be undressing suggests a need for Spiritual openness and honesty.

UNEARTH

1 When we are trying to unearth an unknown object in a dream, we are attempting to reveal a side of ourselves which we do not yet understand. When we know what we are searching for, we are trying to uncover aspects of our personality which we have consciously buried.

2 Occasionally, we may be aware of knowledge and potential within ourselves or others which requires hard work to realise. It has to be unearthed.

3 Spiritually, when we are prepared to move on we are able to confront the hidden Self.

UNEMPLOYMENT

1 Dreaming of being unemployed suggests that we are not making the best use of our talents, or that we feel our talents are not being recognised.

2 Unemployment is a fear that almost everyone has. When an event connected with unemployment occurs, e.g. redundancy, dole payments etc. in a dream, our feelings of inadequacy are being highlighted. We need to experience that fear in order to deal with, and overcome, it.

3 A sense of spiritual inadequacy and inability can translate itself into the image of unemployment. This is more to do with not being motivated enough to accept a spiritual task.

UNICORN

– see Animals and Fabulous Beasts

1 Traditionally, the only people who were allowed to tend unicorns were virgins. When a unicorn appears in a dream, we are linking with the innocent, pure part of ourselves. This is the instinctive, receptive feminine principle.

2 There is a story that unicorns missed being taken into Noah's Ark because they were too busy playing. We need to be mindful of what is going on in the real world if we are to survive.

3 The unicorn signifies unconditional love.

UNIFORM

– also see Clothes

1 Dreaming of uniforms is all to do with our identification with a particular role or type of authority. However rebellious we may be, a part of us needs to conform to the ideas and beliefs of the social group to which we belong. Seeing ourselves in uniform confirms that belonging.

2 Often, in collective groups, the right to wear a uniform has to be earned. Dreaming of being **in a group of uniformed people** indicates that we have acheived the right to be recognised.

3 Identification of a common spiritual goal and an agreement as to 'uniform' behaviour is an important aspect in spiritual development.

UNION

1 Union indicates a joining together, and this can be of pairs or of multiples. **Union in pairs** suggests the reconciliation of opposites and the added energy this brings. A union, in the sense of a **trade union**, suggests collective action which is for the good of all.

2 We all attempt to achieve unity from duality – to create a relationship between two parts or opposites. Dreaming of achieving union depicts this relationship. Psychologically, the human being is consistently looking for a partner.

3 Unity in a spiritual sense is usually perceived as a return to Source.

UNIVERSITY

1 Dreaming of being in a university highlights our own individual potential and learning ability. We may not be particularly academic in waking life, but may be subconsciously aware of our ability to connect together with people of like minds.

2 Since a university is a place of 'higher' learning, we are being made aware of the breadth of experience and increase in knowledge available to us. We need to move away from the mundane and ordinary into specific areas of knowledge and awareness.

3 Spiritual Knowledge and the ability to use it can only be achieved in 'The University of Life'.

UNKNOWN

1 The unknown in dreams is that which has been hidden from us, or that which we have deliberately made secret. This may be the 'occult' – that is, knowledge which is only available to initiates. It may also be information that we do not normally need, except in times of stress.

2 When we are conscious of the unknown in dreams, we should try to decide whether it is threatening or whether it is something we need to know and understand. It is the way we handle the information – rather than the information itself – which is important.

3 The hidden or the Occult remains both unknown and unknowable unless we have the courage to face it. This we can often do in dreams.

UP/UPPER
– see Position

URINE
– see Body

URN
– also see Vase

1 For many people **the tea urn** is a symbol of community life. To dream of one suggests our ability to belong to a community and act for the greater good.

2 Just as all receptacles signify the feminine principle, so does the urn, although in a more ornate form. In earlier times, **a draped urn** signified death. That symbolism is still carried on today in the urn used in crematoriums. Thus, to dream of an urn may alert us to our feelings about death.

3 The urn represents the feminine receptive principle.

V

from

Vaccination *to* Vulture

VACCINATION

1 In normal everyday life, vaccination is an action which initially hurts but is ultimately good for us. To dream that we are **being vaccinated** therefore suggests we are likely to be hurt by someone (perhaps emotionally). What they are trying to do to us will in the end, however, be helpful.

2 It is very easy for us to be influenced by other people. Vaccination indicates that we can be affected by other people's ideas and feelings.

3 Vaccination in dreams suggests Spiritual indoctrination.

VAGINA
– also see Body

3 Many people have some type of inhibition over their sexuality or 'bodily parts'. Few, however, dream directly of the vagina itself. It is usually represented or symbolised in some way – such as by a dark passage – or one of the symbols connected with femininity.

VALLEY

1 Dreaming of **going down into a valley** can have the same significance as going downstairs – that is, going down into the subconscious or unknown parts of ourselves. The result of this can be either depression and gloominess or finding new areas of productiveness within us.

2 **Being in a valley** can represent the sheltering, feminine side of our nature and also being down to earth. **Leaving a valley** suggests coming out of a period of introversion in order to function properly in the everyday world.

3 Fears of death and dying are often translated in dreams as entering into a valley – the valley of death. It is worth remembering that entry into the valley of death is often said to be a conscious act, and the dreamer should recognise that it is his own subconscious fear at work.

VAMPIRE

1 When heavy demands are made on us which we do not feel capable of meeting, a vampire can appear in a dream. We are figuratively being 'sucked dry.' The vampire or blood sucker is such a fearful figure that it is accepted as an embodiment of evil.

2 Often the fear of emotional and sexual relationships can be represented in dreams as a vampire. Because the human being still has a fear of the unknown, ancient symbols that have represented this fear can still appear in dreams. The succubus and incubus preying on young people's vital energy is often pictured as a vampire.

3 Life-threatening evil is represented by the vampire in dreams. However, it may be that the dreamer has a rather fantastical outlook on the realms of evil and some reservation could be applied to their thoughts.

VAN
– see Lorry in Journey

VANISH

1 One of the most annoying things about dreams is that images will vanish unexpectedly. There is also the tendency for us to forget various parts of the dream on waking. The reason is that the subject of the dream has not yet fully fixed itself in consciousness. Working with dreams can, in actual fact, help to 'fix' the information our subconscious is attempting to give us.

2 Just as a child believes in the world of magic, so the dream state is one that is totally believable. When images vanish in a dream, they will very often become more tangible in the waking state.

3 The mind has a great capacity for magic; to dream of things vanishing, and then possibly reappearing, highlights this.

VARNISH

1 Varnish is a protective outer covering which is designed to enhance the appearance of an object. Dreaming of varnish can therefore signify either of the following meanings. We may be covering something up in order to hide imperfections or we may be protecting ourselves and attempting to present a better self-image.

2 To be varnishing something suggests that we are not happy with our original creation. It may need further work to preserve what we have already done, or it may need enhancing in order that others can understand.

3 Having achieved a spiritual goal, we may wish to preserve the secret and hold it sacred. Dreaming of varnish would confirm this.

VASE

1 As a holder of beautiful things, any receptacle – such as a vase, water pot, pitcher or urn – tends to represent the feminine within a dream. Such an object can also signify creativity.

2 The accepting and receptive nature of the feminine, intuitive side is often suggested by a hollow object such as a vase.

3 The Great Mother in all her glory is represented *(see Introduction)*.

VAULT

1 In dreams any dark, hidden place suggests sexual potency or the unconscious. It can also represent our store of personal resources, those things we learn as we grow and mature. To be **going down into a vault** represents our need to explore those areas of ourselves that have become hidden. We may also need to explore our attitude to death.

2 Collective wisdom (or the Collective Unconscious – information available to all of us) often remains hidden until a real effort is made to uncover the knowledge available. While a vault can represent a tomb, it also represents the 'archives' or records to which we all have access.

3 A vault represents the meeting place of the spiritual and physical. Consequently a vault can also symbolise death.

VD
– see Sex

VEGETABLES
– see Food and Harvest

VEGETATION

1 Vegetation in a dream can often represent the obstacles that we put in front of ourselves in order to grow. For instance, **a patch of brambles** can suggest irritating snags to our movement forwards, whereas **nettles** might represent people actually trying to prevent progress. The image of vegetation also links with the forest *(See Forest)*.

2 While the obstacles we create may cause difficulty, there is also an underlying abundance and fertility that is available to us. In dreams, a pictorial image can help us to understand this. **To be clearing vegetation**, for instance in a vegetable garden, can suggest clearing away that which is no longer of use to us.

3 Vegetation in a dream symbolises abundance and the capacity for growth on a spiritual level.

VEIL
– also see Clothes

1 When an object is veiled in a dream, there is some kind of secret which needs to be revealed. We may, as dreamers, be concealing something from ourselves, but we could also be being kept in ignorance by others.

2 The mind has different ways of indicating hidden thoughts in dreams. The veil is one of these symbols.

3 A veil can represent all that is hidden and mysterious – and this translates into aspects of the Occult.

VELVET

1 It is usually the texture and quality that is relevant when a material appears in a dream. It is the sensuousness and softness of velvet which is significant.

2 In old-style dream interpretation, to dream of velvet was to dream of discord. In modern day interpretation it is more likely to mean the opposite.

3 Spiritually velvet can depict richness and giftedness.

VERMIN
– see Animals

VERTICAL
– see Position

VESICA PISCIS
– see Aura and Religious Imagery

VICAR
– also see Priest in Archetypes

1 Just as the priest was given spiritual authority over many, and was often a figure to be feared, so the vicar is also given this authority. He is perhaps less feared than the priest. In dreams he is often the authority figure to whom we have given control.

2 When a vicar appears in a dream, we are usually aware of the more spiritual, knowledgeable side of ourselves.

3 A vicar is a man of God and the dreamer may need to acknowledge that there is much to learn on a physical as well as spiritual level.

VICE

1 There are obviously two meanings to the word vice. **One is a tool** which clamps and the other **a wrong action**. Dreaming of a vice in its first sense may suggest that we are being constrained in some way. The second indicates that we are aware of the side of ourselves which is rebellious and out of step with society. We may in both cases need to make adjustments in our behaviour.

2 Often dreams allow us to behave in ways which are not those we would normally try in waking life. Being conscious of a particular vice, e.g. sloth, envy, apathy, etc., in one of our dream characters may enable us to handle that tendency within ourselves.

3 Unacceptable behaviour may manifest in the form of vice. The dreamer should consider by whose standards his unacceptable behaviour is being judged, and treat it accordingly.

VICTIM

1 In dreams we are often aware of something happening to us over which we have no control. We are the victim – in the sense that we are passive or powerless within the situation. Sometimes we are aware that we are treating others incorrectly. We are making them victims of our own internal aggression, and not handling ourselves properly in waking life.

2 When we are continually creating 'no-win' situations this tendency is highlighted in dreams, but may be done so somewhat dramatically. We may find we are victims of burglary, rape or murder, for instance. These will not be precognitive dreams unless we do not properly identify our own ability to victimise ourselves. The nature of the difficulty may reveal itself through the dream content.

3 If the dreamer is repressing his own ability to develop spiritual potential, he will appear in a dream as a victim – a victim of his own making.

VICTORY

1 There are many ways to achieve victory in dreams. The dream scenario may be a conflict between two aspects of ourselves or require us to overcome some difficulty. The sense of achievement we feel in dreams can be a feeling we can reproduce in waking life. It gives us confidence in our own abilities.

2 Victory in a psychological sense is the overcoming of obstacles which we have set up for ourselves. In dreams we often need a 'dry-run' and a pictorial representation of our abilities in order to achieve success.

3 If the dreamer has achieved a degree of spiritual success, it can show itself as a victory of some kind.

VILLAGE

1 A village appearing in a dream suggests a fairly tightly knit community. It may illustrate our ability to form supportive relationships and a community spirit.

2 A village can present certain problems. For instance, everybody knows everybody else's business – which can become trying. In this case we may be highlighting the oppression felt in close relationships. Because the pace of life is slower, we may find that the village in a dream is a symbol of relaxation.

3 Often village life was centred around the church and the pub, providing many contrasts. Spiritually, we often have to look at balancing two parts of our lives.

VINE/VINEYARD

1 The vine in dreams can suggest growth and fruitfulness. This can be of one's whole self, or the various parts.

2 When we dream of the vine we are often referring to the various members of our family, including our ancestors. We are linking with the more spiritual side of ourselves which has grown through shared, rather than individual, experience.

3 A vine or vineyard can symbolise growth of a spiritual nature. It can also represent fertility.

VINEGAR

1 Vinegar, because it is sour, is a representation of all that is problematic in taking in information. It can thus signify knowledge which is unpalatable.

2 Oddly enough vinegar is a symbol of life, both because it preserves, and also because it is something which is left after a change of its original state. In dreams this symbolism can come across very strongly.

3 The preservation of spiritual life and all that we hold dear to us is symbolised by vinegar because of its preservative qualities.

VIOLENCE

1 Any violence in dreams is a reflection of our own inner feeling, sometimes about ourselves, sometimes about the situations around us. Often the type of violence is worthy of notice if we are fully to understand ourselves.

2 When we are unable because of social pressures or circumstance to express ourselves properly, we can find ourselves behaving violently in dreams. If **others are behaving violently** towards us we may need to take care in waking life not to upset others.

3 A sense of spiritual injustice may be represented by scenes or acts of violence in a dream. The dreamer should equate this with recent spiritual events.

VIPER

– see Serpent and Snake in Animals

VIRGIN

1 To dream of **being a virgin** suggests a state of innocence and purity. To dream that **someone else is a virgin** highlights the ideals of integrity and honesty.

2 The virginal mind – that is, a mind that is free from deception and guile – is perhaps more important than physically being a virgin, and it is this aspect which often becomes evident in dreams. **In a woman's dream** such a figure suggests she is in touch with her own psyche.

3 Spiritually there is a kind of innocence and purity, which can often be dedicated to service.

VIRGIN MOTHER
– see Religious Imagery

VISIT

1 To be **visited by someone** in a dream can suggest that there is information, warmth or love available to us. If it is **someone we know** then this may apply in a real-life situation. If it is not, then there may be a facet of our personality which is trying to make itself apparent.

2 To be **paying someone else a visit** in a dream signifies that we may need to widen our horizons in some fashion. This may be physically, emotionally or spiritually.

3 One's spiritual guide often first makes itself available by a visit in the dream state.

VISIONS

1 The mind, once it is free of conscious restraint, appears to work on several different levels. Thus, it is possible to be aware of three separate parts of a dream. These are the 'I' of the dream, the content, and finally – usually pictorially – information and knowledge. These are the visions of dreams. Many dreamers have suggested that this type of dream has a different 'feel' to it from other more mundane dreams.

2 In the half-awake, half-asleep state just before and just after sleep many people experience very strong images which are remembered in a way that dream images are not. These could also be called visions.

3 Spiritual manifestations, or rather, manifestations of Spirit, are accepted as visions.

VITAMIN
– also see Pill

1 Dreaming of taking vitamins indicates that we have a concern about health. We may be aware that we are not nurturing ourselves properly and require additional help.

2 On a slightly more esoteric level, we are aware that we are not doing the best for ourselves and need more out of life in order to function according to our true potential. There could be a situation in our lives which needs a particular type of assistance.

3 A higher vibration is needed in order to progress.

VOICE

1 The voice is a tool that we use to express ourselves. We all have inner awareness of our own state which is sometimes difficult to disclose. Often in dreams we are able to use our voices in more appropriate ways. Often we are **spoken**

to in dreams so that we remember the information given.

2 A voice that speaks through, or to, one has two areas of significance. If one believes in the spirit realm, this is communication from a discarnate spirit. More psychologically, when we suppress certain parts of our personalities they may surface in dreams as disembodied voices.

3 The Voice of God is a term which is used to describe the energy of a spiritual summons.

VOID
– see Abyss

VOLCANO

1 The image of a volcano in dreams is a very telling one, partly because of its unpredictability. To dream of a **volcano being extinct** can indicate either that we have 'killed off' our passions, or that a difficult situation has come to an end. This may be one that has been around for some time.

2 An **erupting volcano** usually signifies that we are not in control of a situation or of our emotions – of which there may be a hurtful release. If the **lava is more prominent** feelings will run very deep. **If the lava has cooled** there has been a deep passion which has now cooled off. If the

explosiveness is more noticeable, anger may be more prominent.

3 A volcano is representative of spiritual deeply held passion. This can sometimes erupt with frightening results.

VOMIT

1 To dream of **vomiting** suggests a discharge of disagreeable feelings and emotions. It would be a clearing of something from within that makes us extremely uncomfortable. To dream of **watching someone else vomit** indicates that we may have upset them and need to have compassion and understanding.

2 Intuitively, we can often be aware of problems around us and be affected by them. When we become overloaded, we may need to 'throw up' (or away) the distress it is causing us. To **wake up feeling sick** intimates that we have been affected on an emotional level by the release that occurred in the dreams that we have had.

3 Vomiting is a symbol of a discharge of evil. We may have held on to bad feeling for so long that it has caused our spiritual system some difficulty.

VORTEX
– see Whirlwind

VOTE

1 Dreaming of voting in an election, whether general or within the workplace, highlights our wish and ability to belong to groups. If we are conscious we are **voting with the group** we are happy to accept group practice. **Voting against the group** indicates a need to rebel.

2 While the process of voting is supposed to be fair and just, when we dream of this we may be questioning that process. To dream of **being elected** to a position is to seek power.

3 Spiritually when we have given unconditional acceptance to something, we have placed our trust in it. A votive offering is a spiritual request.

VOUCHER

1 A voucher – in the sense of a **promissory note** – can be taken in dreams to suggest our ability to give ourselves permission to do something. If, for instance, it is a **money off voucher** we may not be valuing ourselves properly, or alternatively we could be looking for an easy option.

2 A voucher opens up our opportunities. Because it is usually an exchange between two people, it can indicate the help that others can give us.

3 An timely invitation to the Unconscious, in the sense that we are attempting to bargain with ourselves in some way, would tend to show itself in dreams as a voucher.

VOW

1 A vow is a pact or agreement between two people or oneself and God. To dream of **making such a vow** is to be recognising responsibility for one's own life. It is more solemn than a simple promise and the results are consequently more far-reaching.

2 Because a vow is made in front of witnesses, we need to be aware of the effect that it will have on other people. In dreams we are expecting others to help us honour our promise. To be **listening to or making marriage vows** indicates our commitment to totality.

3 A vow is a spiritual promise made between the dreamer and his universe.

VOYAGE

– *see Journey*

VULTURE

– *see Birds*

W

from

Wading *to* Writing

WADING

1 Dreaming of wading puts us in the position of recognising what our emotions can do to us. If we are **impeded by the water** *(see Water)*, then we need to appreciate how our emotions can prevent us from moving forward. If we are **enjoying our wading experience,** then we may expect our connection with life to bring contentment. Sometimes the depths to which our bodies are immersed can give us information as to how we cope with external circumstances.

2 Often the feeling associated with wading can be more relevant than the action of wading itself. For instance, to recognise that we are not actually in water – for example, we are **wading through treacle** can give us a clue to how we feel about ourselves or our circumstances.

3 Spiritually, wading suggests a cleansing process which ties in with baptism. Many meditations use the symbolism of walking through water.

WADDING

– also see Packing

1 In dreams our need for security can become more noticeable than we allow it to be in ordinary, everyday life. Because wadding is normally a protective material, we may need to become aware that we should take action to *protect* ourselves rather than *defend* ourselves.

2 Sometimes bodily changes can be reflected in the images that we produce in dreams. Wadding can represent a fear of getting fat or becoming ungainly.

3 Wadding in spiritual and psychic terms suggests security. It is an image which arises when we are looking for security.

WAFER

1 A wafer is a thin layer of matter which is usually very fragile. In dreams it can represent something which is easily broken and which we need to treat with care.

2 A wafer biscuit is constructed in many layers. It thus becomes a symbol for diversity. We may need to understand the various 'layers' of our lives in order to manage our lives successfully.

3 The Body of Christ. The Bread of Life.

WAFFLE

1 To waffle, in the sense of **talking unnecessarily at length**, can be translated by the dreamer as the need to control his self-expression. If **someone else is waffling** in a dream, the indication is that in real life the dreamer needs to listen very carefully to instructions. He may not trust the speaker.

2 To dream of **eating a waffle** suggests a need to approach life in a different way. We need to adopt a more down-to-earth approach to achieve success in relationships.

3 This image can have the same significance as a wafer *(see Wafer)*.

WAGER

– see Gambling

WAGES

1 Wages are normally paid in exchange for work done. In dreams, to be **receiving wages** signifies that we have done a good job. To be **paying somebody wages** implies that we owe that person something. To **receive a wage packet** suggests that our value is tied up with other things such as loyalty and duty.

2 Most actions we take have a result. Often when we are doing something that we do not want to do – or which we do not enjoy – the only pay-off is in the wages we receive. To dream of wages may signify that we should not expect anything else in a situation in everyday life.

3 Spiritually, wages can represent recompense for our actions and that the reward we so deserve coming our way.

WAIL

1 Wailing is a long, protracted way of releasing emotions. When we hear **someone wailing** in a dream, we become conscious of someone else's sadness. When we **ourselves are wailing**, we may be allowing ourselves an emotional release which would not be seen to be appropriate in everyday life.

2 Wailing is reputed to be a method of summoning the spirits. In dreams, therefore, it can suggest that we are trying to get in touch with a power that is greater than ourselves.

3 Grieving and the making of sounds is used spiritually to banish bad spirits. The dreamer should look at what he feels needs 'banishing' from his life.

WAITING

1 To be waiting for somebody, or something, in a dream implies a need to recognise a sense of anticipation. We may be looking to other people, or outside circumstances, to help us move forward or make decisions. If **we are impatient**, it may be that our expectations are too high. If we are **waiting patiently**, there is the understanding that events will happen in their own good time.

2 When we become aware that something is expected from us, and **other people are waiting for appropriate action**, we may need to consider our own leadership qualities.

3 In developing spiritually we must often learn to wait until the time is right. We have to wait for the passage of time.

WAITER/WAITRESS

1 The interpretation of this dream depends on whether we ourselves are waiting at table, or whether we are being waited upon. If we are **in the role of waiter**, we are aware of our ability to care for other people. If **we are being waited on**, we perhaps need to be nurtured and made to feel special.

2 When such a person appears in a dream, there may be a play on words. Part of us needs to be conscious that for complete fulfilment in any task or responsibility we need to wait.

3 Spiritually we must learn two lessons – service and patience. This must be learnt before we can really progress.

WAKE

1 A wake, in the sense of a funeral service, gives us an opportunity to grieve properly. When in dreams we find ourselves attending such an occasion, we need to be aware that there may be some reason in our lives for us to go through a period of grieving. We need to let go that which we hold dear.

2 In most religions, there is a period around a death when it is appropriate to express our feelings. Sometimes it is easier to do this in company and with the support of other people. A wake such as this in a dream indicates we may need support to overcome a disappointment.

3 Spiritually, a wake signifies appropriate grief.

WAKING UP

1 There is a condition in sleeping where we become alert to the fact that we are dreaming and that we can wake up. This appears partly as a way of forcing us into taking note of a particular action or circumstance, and partly to enable us to use the therapeutic tool of being able to wake up and make an adjustment to a dream which might have a happier ending.

2 To **wake up in a dream** can indicate that we have come out of a period of mourning and withdrawal.

3, Spiritually, to wake up signifies becoming aware. The dream state alerts us to various ideas and concepts we should be looking at, although it may take us a little time to 'wake up' to them.

WALKING

1 In a dream, walking indicates the way in which we should be moving forward. To be **walking purposefully** suggests we know where we are going. To be **wandering aimlessly** suggests we need to create goals for ourselves. To take **pleasure in the act of walking** is to return to the innocence of the child. To be **using a walking stick** is to recognise our need for support and assistance from others.

2 Walking may be used as a relaxation from stress, and it is this significance which often comes up in dreams. If we **are alone** then our walk can be silent and contemplative. If it is **in company**, then we can communicate and converse without fear of interruption.

3 A spiritual walk is a journey of exploration into realms we do not know.

WALL
– also see Buildings

1 In dreams, walls usually indicate the boundaries we have set ourselves. These may be created as defence mechanisms or support structures, and it is sometimes helpful in the interpretation to decide whether the walls have been created in order to keep ourselves in, or other people out.

2 A wall also has the symbolism of a dividing line – a marker between the inner and the outer, privacy and open trust. **A hole in a wall** suggests a breach of trust or privacy. **If the wall is imprisoning us** we are being held prisoner by our own fears, doubts and difficulties **If the wall appears and disappears**, we have only partly dealt with our problem.

3 A wall symbolises the boundaries of a sacred space. The dreamer needs to be aware of what his limits are.

WALLET

1 In dreams, the wallet is a representation of where we keep our resources safe. These need not simply be financial resources, but can be of any kind. Many dreams can suggest our attitude to money, and to dream of a wallet is one of those dreams.

2 Interestingly, because the wallet can also suggest the feminine aspects of care and containment, the wallet can highlight our attitude to intuition and awareness.

3 The old idea of having your 'life' in your wallet symbolises not only life, but also health.

WALLPAPER

1 To be stripping wallpaper in dreams suggests stripping away the old facade in order to create a new image. **To be putting up wallpaper** signifies covering up the old self (possibly superficially), particularly if the old wallpaper is not removed.

2 Wallpaper in a dream can have the same significance as clothes on a character. We may be wanting to make changes in our lives but need to experiment – and get a proper fit – first.

3 The dreamer should metaphorically take a look at himself and be sure that he is being true to himself, as wallpaper often symbolises an outer facade of some kind.

WALNUT
– see Nut

WALTZ
– see Dance

WAND

1 When we dream of **using a wand** we are aware of our influence over others. Conversely, if **someone else uses a wand** we are aware of the power of suggestion, either for negative or for positive within the situation.

2 Conventionally the wand is an instrument of supernatural forces, and it is often this image which is the most important. We are aware of some force external to ourselves which needs harnessing.

3 Obviously a wand works in tandem with magic, so to dream of a wand can symbolise 'magical' powers which may influence us.

WANDERER/ WANDERING
– see Tramp in Archetypes

WANT

1 To be conscious of a want in a dream is perhaps to link with our basic nature. We may have suppressed those wants in waking life only to have them surface in dreams.

2 When in dreams we find we want to do – or be – something different, we are aware of the potential within us either to achieve success or to change our lives. For instance, to dream of wanting to be a poet instead of an actor can suggest exploration of one's creativity in a different format.

3 Desire in its fullest sense – although the dreamer should take care – as want is sometimes considered a form of sin.

WAR

1 In dreams war always denotes conflict. It has a more global effect than one-to-one combat, and would suggest that we need to be more conscious of the effect our actions will have on others. We also need to be aware that we are taking part in conflict which is deliberately engineered rather than spontaneous.

2 War is ultimately a way of dealing with distress and disorder. The outcome should be the establishment of order, although sometimes this can only happen through the passage of time. To dream of war, therefore, indicates that this natural process is taking place on an inner level.

3 War is a symbol of spiritual disintegration. We need to be aware of what is disintegrating within our lives to understand the full symbolism.

WARDEN

1 A warden in a dream is often a manifestation of the guardian or the keeper. We may have a part of our personality which acts as monitor or attempts to suppress other parts of our personality, and this appears as a warden.

2 In working with dream images we will often recognise aspects of the Spiritual Self which protect us from outside influence and this also can appear as a warden.

3 'The Guardian of the Threshold' between the physical and the spiritual is represented by the warden.

WARDROBE
– also see Furniture

1 A wardrobe, often because it is large, can have the same significance as a passage, and therefore suggests a period of transition. Because it houses our clothes, it also suggests how we deal with our self-image.

WAREHOUSE
– see Buildings

WARMTH

1 Warmth in a dream touches our 'feel good' factor and enhances our sense of comfort and well being.

2 Psychologically, feelings of cheerfulness and hopefulness can create an awareness of warmth and can be interchangeable.

3 A feeling of warmth in a dream can symbolise that most sought-after prize – unconditional love. The dreamer can afford to move positively in search of this.

WARNING

1 To receive a warning in a dream suggests that we are aware that either internally or externally something needs attention. We may be putting ourselves in danger.

2 To be **warning someone** highlights our ability to be aware of difficulty and danger, either to others or to hidden parts of our personality. The circumstances of the dream will clarify this. To receive **a written warning** indicates we may be behaving badly.

3 A warning in this case can actually be showing us the way toward being a more intuitive person. Our intuition can be trusted – we should use it accordingly.

WARRANT

1 A warrant represents permission from a higher authority, either spiritual or physical. It will depend on the type of warrant as to what action the dreamer needs to take. For instance, **a search warrant** suggests looking at one's motives, whereas **a warrant for arrest** indicates we need to stop carrying out a particular action.

2 When we are unable to make decisions, dream images can often help us. The warrant opens up possibilities of which we may not have been aware.

3 The dreamer may be seeking spiritual permission for some reason, and this can be symbolised by a warrant.

WARTS

1 Any blemish which comes to the attention in dreams can be accepted as evidence of there being a distortion in our view of the world.

2 We are often distressed by anything which is out of the ordinary or wrong. A great deal of folklore has grown up around warts and how to get rid of them. Dreaming of warts links with that part of ourselves which remains superstitious.

3 A distortion of a spiritual kind may be affording the dreamer little insight at this moment. If this is the case, the dreamer should bide his time and allow the distortion to run its course.

WASHING
– also see Water

1 Dreaming of **washing either oneself, or for instance, clothes,** suggests getting rid of negative feelings. We may need to change our attitude, either internally or externally. **Washing other people** touches on our need to care for others.

2 Since water is a symbol for emotion and the unconscious, washing stands for achieving a relationship with our emotional selves and dealing successfully with the results.

3 A spiritual cleansing may be necessary in order to preserve the dreamer's integrity.

WASP
– see Insects

WASTE

1 Waste in dreams signifies matter or information we no longer need. It can now be thrown away. Often the colour will have significance (*see Colour*). Waste can also suggest a misuse of resources – we may, initially, be using too much energy on a particular project.

2 If we are being wasteful in dreams we need to reassess how we are running our lives. We may be giving too much in relationships, or trying to make things happen.

3 There may be an energy crisis for the dreamer which he cannot fathom. He therefore needs to look to where there is most likely to be an 'energy leak'.

WATCH
– see Time

WATCHING

1 In dreams, we are often conscious of the Self which is watching and participating in the dream. We need to be aware of all parts of the dream in order to achieve the best results.

2 To be aware of **someone watching us** in a dream suggests that we feel threatened by someone's close interest in us. This may be in a work situation, but could also be in personal relationships. It will depend on the other circumstances of the dream how this is interpreted.

3 There is a need for the dreamer to monitor his own actions, particularly if new forms of spiritual discipline have recently been taken on.

WATER

1 Water is usually taken in dreams to symbolise all that is emotional and feminine. It is a mysterious substance, given that it has the ability to flow through, over and round objects. It has the quality of being able to wear away anything which gets in its way. Water can also stand for the dreamer's potential and his ability to create a new life in response to his own inner urgings.

2 Water also represents cleansing, being able to wash away the contamination that we may experience in everyday life. In baptism, water is a cleanser of previously held 'sins', often also those inherited from the family. **Entering water** suggests beginning something new. **Deep water** signifies either being out of depth, or entering our own subconscious.

3 Spiritual rebirth – The Life-force.

Water appears so often in dreams as an image, with so many different meanings, that it is possible only to suggest some probable ones. Thus, **being immersed in water** can suggest pregnancy and birth. **Flowing water** signifies peace and comfort, while **rushing water** can indicate passion. **Deep water** suggests the unconscious, while **shallow water** represents a lack of essential energy. **Going down into water** indicates a need to renew one's strength, to go back to the beginning, while **coming up out of the water** suggests a fresh start. **To be on the water** (as in a boat) can represent indecision or a lack of emotional commitment, while to be **in the water but not moving** can suggest inertia.

Other images associated with water are:

Bathing suggests purification.

Canals symbolise the birth process.

Dams, islands and other obstacles are conscious attempts to control the force of the water, and therefore our emotions.

Diving represents going down into the unconscious, or perhaps trying to find the parts of ourselves which we have suppressed.

Drowning highlights our ability to push things into the unconscious only to have them emerge as a force which can overcome us.

Floods represent the chaotic side of us, which is usually uncontrollable. This side requires attention when it wells up and threatens to overwhelm us.

Fountains suggest womanhood, and particularly the Great Mother *(see Introduction)*.

Lake A lake, like **a pool**, can signify a stage of transition between the conscious and the spiritual Self. **When come upon unexpectedly** it can give us the opportunity to appreciate and understand ourselves. To be **reflected in a pool** indicates the dreamer needs to come to terms with the Shadow *(see Introduction)*. We must learn to accept that there will be a part of ourselves that we do not like very much but, when harnessed, it can give much energy for change. **Rivers or streams** always represent the dreamer's life and the way that he is living it. It will depend on the dreamer's attitude as to whether he see his life as a large river or a small stream. **If the river is rushing by** we may feel that life is moving too quickly for us. If we can see **the sea as well as the river**, we may be aware that a great change must occur or that attention must be paid to the unconscious within. **If the river is very deep** we should perhaps be paying attention to the rest of the world, and how we relate to it. **Crossing a river** indicates great changes. **If the river causes fear** we are perhaps creating an unnecessary difficulty for ourselves. **If the water in the river appears to be contaminated** we are not doing the best we can for ourselves.

Sea or ocean The sea very often represents cosmic consciousness, that is, the original chaotic state from which all life emerges. Inherent in that state is all knowledge i.e. completedness, although that may be obscured by our fear of the depths. We do not fear that which we understand. **A shallow sea** suggests superficial emotion. **The waves in the sea** represent emotion and lust. **A calm sea** suggests a peaceful existence, while a **stormy sea** signifies passion, either negative or positive. To be conscious of **the rise and fall of the tides** is to be conscious both of the passage of time and of the rise and fall of our own emotions.

WATERFALL

1 A waterfall at its basic level of interpretation can be taken to represent an orgasm. It can also signify any display of emotion that is forceful and yet somewhat controlled.

2 Whenever any emotion reaches the stage where it must 'spill over' in order to become manageable it can be represented as a waterfall in dreams.

3 A waterfall shows that some degree of spiritual power is around, and the dreamer should look to make use of it.

WAVES
– see Water

WAX

1 Dreaming of wax is a great deal to do with the pliability that we are able to achieve in our lives. We need to be able to be malleable, to be moulded, perhaps by external events. We should be prepared to give way, but also to be firm when necessary.

2 Wax can also to be taken to represent insincerity. It is something that is consumed by the flame – for instance, of a candle – and therefore can be moved and changed into something else with qualities that it did not initially have.

3 Wax is symbolic of the need for spiritual pliability, and the desire to move away from rigidity.

WEALTH
– also see Money

1 Dreaming of **being wealthy** is to dream of having in abundance those things that we need. We may have possibly come though a period where we have put in a lot of effort and to dream of having **a great deal of wealth** indicates that we have achieved what we have set out to do.

2 Wealth and status usually go naturally together, so often when we are having problems in dealing with our own status in life we will have dreams about wealth. It can also often indicate the resources that we have or that we can use from other people. We have the ability to draw on our experiences or feelings and to achieve a great deal within the framework of our lives.

3 There is a 'wealth' of spiritual knowledge to be gained, and to dream of this indicates that it is within the dreamer's grasp.

WEAPONS

1 To dream of weapons usually suggests our desire to hurt someone or something. We have internalised our aggression and it is marginally more acceptable to dream of weapons and of using them against people, than actually having to deal with such circumstances in everyday life. Depending on the weapon that we use we may get a fairly good idea of what the real problem is in the waking self. An **arrow** indicates being pierced by some kind of powerful emotion, of being hurt by someone else through words or actions. We need to turn our attention inwards in order to make ourselves feel better. The **gun or pistol** traditionally represents male sexuality and for **a woman to dream of being shot** often indicates her wish for, or fear of, sexual aggression. If **we are shooting the gun** ourselves we may be using our masculine abilities in quite an aggressive way, in order to defend ourselves. A **knife** represents the ability to cut through debris, to 'cut into' whatever is bothering us and to cut out the hypocrisy that perhaps is prevailing in a situation. The **sword** has more than one meaning. Because of its hilt – which is a cross shape – it often represents a system of belief which is used in a powerful way. Equally it can be used to suggest spiritual strength, creating an ability to cut away the unnecessary more powerfully than the knife. The **sword when sheathed** is the soul or the Self in the body.

2 To have a **weapon used against us** means that we have to look at how we are party to people being aggressive around us. It may be that we have done something to upset the other person which results in aggression, or it may be that we have put ourselves in a position of becoming the victim of circumstance.

3 Various weapons can suggest varying degrees of spiritual power. The dreamer should use this power with relevant caution.

WEASEL
– see Animals

WEATHER

1 Weather, as being part of the 'environment' of the dream, usually indicates our moods and emotions. We are very much aware of changing external situations and have to be careful to adjust our conduct in response to these.

2 Weather also can indicate our internal responses to situations. If, for instance, there was **a storm** in our dream our emotions would be stormy, perhaps angry and aggressive. If we are watching **a very blue, unclouded sky**, we may be recognising that we have the ability to keep the situations that we are in under control. We do possess the ability to control internal moods and emotions which may not have been possible in the past. Being aware of the weather would indicate that we need to recognise that we are part of a greater whole rather than just individuals in our own right.

3 Different types of weather may be symbolic of a spiritual response. The dreamer requires an answer to a question, for example (*see Wind*).

WEAVING

1 Weaving is a very basic symbol and suggests the need to take responsibility for our own lives. To be doing any handicraft shows that we have situations in hand.

2 Weaving is taken to signify life itself and often our attitude to the way we run our lives.

3 Weaving is one of the strongest spiritual images there is. In most cultures there is an image of our fate being woven in a particular pattern. We are not supposed to be in control of that pattern, but must accept that the gods or God know what is best.

WEB

1 In everyday life, we may well be caught up in a situation that could trap us. We could be in a 'sticky' situation and not quite know which direction to move. This can result in the symbol of a web appearing in the dream. We are 'caught in the middle' or we are trapped. Because the situation is extremely complex we have no idea which way is going to be most advantageous for us.

2 When we dream of a web we are linking into one of the most basic of spiritual symbols. It is within the 'web of life' that the divine powers have interwoven fate and time in order to create a reality in which we can exist. We are the spiritual entrapped within the physical and not able to escape back to our own spiritual realm.

3 The spider's web is the Cosmic Plan.

WEDDING
– see Marriage

WEDDING DRESS
– see Marriage

WEDDING RING
– also see Ring

1 Traditionally, the wedding ring was a symbol of total encircling love because it is in the shape of a ring it is complete, with no beginning and no end. So to dream of this symbol is to link in with that basic concept of eternity. To dream of **losing one's wedding ring** would very often symbolise a problem within a marriage. To dream of **finding a wedding ring** might well indicate that a relationship is being formed which could result in marriage.

2 Within the human being there is the need to make vows, to give promises and above all to symbolise the making of those promises. The wedding ring, worn on the finger which represents the heart – that is, the fourth finger of the left hand – therefore suggests that we have made that type of promise. To dream of **a wedding ring being on any other finger** than that particular finger may indicate that the promise is not valid or we feel the wedding ring to be a constriction or an entrapment in some way.

3 A wedding ring symbolises the binding sacrifice which is eternal love.

WEDGE

1 Dreaming of a wedge often indicates that we need to open up situations around us. We need to put something in position which means that we can be open and truthful at all times. Since the wedge is also a symbol of support, it may be that we need to be aware that in situations around us we might need increasing assistance. We would also need to guard against becoming too dependent on that kind of support.

2 The triangle symbolises the ability to manifest matter within the physical. The wedge esoterically indicates the passage of time which allows something to become real in our lives – for a dream to become reality.

3 If we are feeling somewhat isolated, a wedge will symbolise the spiritual support that we have been seeking.

WEEDS
– also see Plants

1 Weeds are generally **plants which grow on waste ground** and their symbolism in dreams reflects this. They may indicate misplaced trust, misplaced energy or even misplaced attempts at success. They do not contribute a tremendous amount to our lives and if allowed to run riot or to overgrow can stop our own positive growth. To be **digging up weeds** would show that we are aware that by freeing our life of the non-essential we are creating space for new growth and new abilities.

2 Mental attitudes which clog us up and do not allow us to move forward and old patterns of behaviour can very often be shown in dreams as weeds. We may need to decide which of these weeds are helpful to us (that is which could be composted, transferred into something else and made use of to help positive growth) or which need to be thrown away. Often plants growing wild have healing properties. By using these properties

we can enhance our lives. For instance, dandelion tea is a natural diuretic, and dreams can often tell us what we need.

3 Weeds, by courtesy of their irritating qualities and refusal to be quickly eradicated, symbolise spiritual difficulties.

WEEPING
– also see Mourning

1 Weeping suggests uncontrollable emotion or grief, so to experience either **ourselves or someone else weeping** is to show that there needs to be a discharge of such emotion. We may be sad over past events or fearful of moving into the future. It is worthwhile exploring the quality of weeping. Are we sobbing and therefore not able to express ourselves fully? We may simply be creating difficulty within ourselves which enables us to express the feelings we have bottled up.

2 Something exuding moisture so that it seems to be weeping is often deemed to be miraculous, and this dream can appear quite often in stages of transition as we are moving from one state of aware-ness to another. The excess energy can be shown as a weeping plant, tree or some such image.

3 Weeping suggests mourning for some spiritual quality we have lost.

WEIGHING

1 To be **weighing something** in dreams is to be assessing its worth. This image connects with the calculation of our needs and what is of value to us, whether materially or spiritually.

2 Weighing something up is to be trying to make an accurate decision to assess what the risks are. If we are trying to **balance the scales** we are looking for justice and natural balance within our knowledge.

3 The dreamer may wish to make clear in his conscious mind his own spiritual worth.

WEIGHT

1 Experiencing a weight in a dream is to be conscious of our responsibilities. It may also suggest that we should assess the importance and seriousness of what we are doing.

2 Weight in a dream may well indicate the need to be practical and down to earth in waking life. We need to keep our feet on the ground.

3 Weight in a dream indicates gravitas and seriousness.

WELCOME

1 To receive a welcome in a dream suggests that we are accepting of our own selves. We are beginning to like who we are. If the welcome is from **a member of our family** we are being accepted by, and accepting, a better relationship with the family.

2 To be **welcoming someone into our own house** suggests we are learning to trust ourselves. Being in a **welcoming party** signifies our ability to belong to a social group with common beliefs.

3 Spiritually we are being accepted or indeed welcomed on the first steps to spiritual fulfilment.

WELL

1 A well is a way of assessing the deepest resources of feeling and emotion that we have. Unless we have such access we are not going eventually to be whole. If there is something wrong with the well, e.g. we **cannot reach the water**, we are not able to get in touch with our best talents.

2 The image of a well in a dream suggests our ability to be 'well'. We have the ability to be healed and to fulfil our dearest wish, if we so desire. By putting ourselves in touch with our intuitive, aware selves we open up the potential and possibilities for healing and success.

3 A well can symbolise a form of contact with the depths – possibly the depths of emotion.

WEREWOLF
– see Sinister Animals in Animals

WEST
– see Position

WET
– see Water

WHALE
– see Animals

WHEAT
– see Grain

WHEEL
– also see Circle in Shapes

1 A wheel in a dream indicates the ability and need to make changes – to move forward into the future without being thrown off course.

2 To **lose a wheel** from a vehicle is to lose motivation or direction – to be thrown off balance. A **large wheel**, such as the Ferris Wheel in a fairground, suggests an awareness of life's ups and downs.

3 The Wheel of Life, and how we see ourselves fitting in.

WHIP/LASH

1 The whip is an instrument of torture. For this to appear indicates the dreamer has either the need to control others or to be controlled by them. We may be trying to control by using pain –

either physical or emotional.

2 Because the whip is an instrument of punishment we need to be aware that in trying to force things to happen, we may also be creating problems for ourselves.

3 A whip suggests corrective punishment and self-flagellation.

WHIRLPOOL AND WHIRLWIND

1 Both these images are symbols of the vortex, a representation of life and natural energy. There are usually conflicting energies in both. When they appear in dreams we are aware of the quality of power we have within. The whirlpool will more properly represent emotional energy, while the whirlwind will suggest intellectual power.

2 Intellectually we may know that we have control over our lives, but are caught up in an endless round of activity which appears to be unproductive but in fact contains a tremendous amount of energy.

3 A whirl of creativity lies ahead. We must 'roll with it' and fully take advantage.

WHISKY
– see Alcohol

WHISPERING
– also see Gossip

1 To **hear whispering** in a

dream suggests that we need to listen to someone or something very carefully. It may also mean that we do not have the full information available to us about a situation in our waking lives.

2 Sound in dreams can often manifest as the opposite quality to that which is required. Thus, whispering could be interpreted as a shout for attention.

3 Hidden Information. Occult Knowledge.

WHISTLE

1 A whistle being blown in a dream can mark the end of a particular phase of time. It can also sound as a warning to alert us to a particular event.

2 A whistle may be heard and recognised in dreams about games *(See Games)*. As a means of controlling and training, it may be relevant as to how it is blown. For instance if it is **blown harshly**, the dreamer may be being made aware that he has transgressed a known code of conduct.

3 A Spiritual summons.

WHITE
– see Colours

WIDOW

1 Dreaming of being a widow can suggest loss and sadness.

Sometimes such a dream can mark the change in a woman's awareness as she moves towards the 'Crone' or Wise Woman. For a **woman to dream of a widow** highlights her ability to be free and use her own innate wisdom.

2 In **a man's dream** a widow may signify a deeper understanding of a woman's needs. He may recognise that all women do not necessarily become dependent on him. This will, of course, be mediated by his relationship with his mother.

3 Feminine Spiritual Wisdom.

WIFE
– see Family

WIG

1 In previous times, covering the head was considered to be a way of hiding the intellect, of giving a false impression or of indicating wisdom and authority. A **judge's wig** can suggest all of these. A **hairpiece or toupee** highlights false ideas or an unnatural attitude.

2 Sometimes a wig highlights the fact that we have something to hide. We are perhaps not as competent, as youthful or as able as we would like others to believe.

3 A symbol of Spiritual authority and judgment.

WILD

1 In dreams anything wild always represents the untamed. Within each of us there is a part that dislikes being controlled in any way. It is the part of ourselves which needs to be free, and is creative and independent. A **wild animal** will stand for that aspect of our personality which has not yet committed itself to using rational thought. Depending on whether the dreamer is masculine or feminine a wild woman will represent the Anima or the Shadow *(see Introduction)*.

2 Anything which grows wild is not subject to the same constraints which normal society puts upon us, so in this context wildness may signify anarchy and lack of stability. In its more positive sense there is profusion and promise in whatever we are trying to do.

3 In a dream to be, or feel, wild often suggests a lack of spiritual control.

WILL

1 To dream of a will or any legal document is connected with the way in which our unconscious side can push us into taking notice of our inner needs. To be **making a will** is to be making a promise to ourselves over future action. It may also have overtones of attempting to look after those we love and care about. To **inherit from a will** means that we need to look at the habits, characteristics and morals we have inherited from our ancestors.

2 We may dream of a will at a time when we need everything to be done properly and with certain levels of correctness. There is the obvious play on words where a will would indicate the will to do or to be – the determination to take action, for instance. Because for many making a will is a very final action, in dreams it can indicate a recognition that we are entering a new phase of life.

3 Determination in spiritual matters is represented here. This can also suggest the resolution of a problem with which the dreamer has been dealing.

WILLOW
– see Trees

WIND
– also see Gale and Hurricane

1 In dreams, the wind symbolises the intellect. It will depend on the force of the wind how we interpret the dream. For instance, **a breeze** would suggest gentleness and pleasure. An idea or concept we have is beginning to move us. **A gale** might indicate a principle we feel passionately about, whereas a **north wind** might suggest a threat to our security.

2 On a slightly more psychological level, wind in a dream can suggest the beginning of a new, much deeper awareness of ourselves. Just as the Holy Spirit in Christianity was said to be 'a mighty rushing wind', so such a dream can represent a Divine revelation of some sort.

3 The Power of the Spirit and the movement of Life.

WINDMILL

1 The image of a windmill in dreams can often suggest the correct use of resources. Because wind often suggests intellect, it is therefore the use of intellectual assets.

2 A windmill has significance as an image of the harvesting of our efforts – in this case, of material resources – available to us. As a storehouse of fertility, in dreams it can sometimes represent the feminine or the mother.

3 The windmill is symbolic of the many facets of the Spiritual Intellect, which in turn is stimulated by our own spiritual powers and abilities.

WINDOW
– see Buildings

WINE
– also see Alcohol

1 In dreams, wine can suggest a happy occasion. As a substance it has an influence on our awareness and appreciation of our environment. A **wine cellar**, therefore, can represent the sum of our past experiences, both good and bad. A **wine bottle**, as a source of enjoyment, is taken by some to indicate the penis and masculinity.

2 As a symbol of 'the liquid of life', wine highlights our ability to draw the best out of our experiences and to make use of what is gleaned to provide fun and happiness. The **wine glass** can have two meanings. Firstly, it stands for the container of our happiness and secondly it can stand for pregnancy. A **broken wine glass** can depict sorrow, or in **a woman's dream**, miscarriage.

3 Wine can represent potential spiritual abundance (as in the parable of turning water into wine). It can also signify the taking in of spiritual power.

WINGS

1 Because wings make us think of flight, to dream of, for instance, **birds' wings** would suggest attention is being drawn to our need for freedom. A **broken wing** indicates that a previous trauma is preventing us from 'taking off'.

2 Wings can also be protective, and this symbolism often appears in dreams. An **angel's wings** would depict the power to transcend our difficulties, as also would the wings of a bird of prey.

3 The protecting, all-pervading power of God.

WINTER

1 In dreams, winter can represent a time in our lives which is unfruitful. It can also represent old age, a time when our energy is running down.

2 At a period in our lives when we are emotionally cold, images associated with winter – such as ice and snow *(see Ice and Snow)* – can highlight the appropriateness, or otherwise, of the way we feel. In clairvoyance, the seasons can also indicate a time of year when something may happen.

3 Within the cycle of nature, winter can represent a time of lying fallow before rebirth; hence winter can mean death.

WIRELESS
– see Radio

WISDOM

1 Wisdom is a quality that is developed, often by being able to inter-pret our own and others dreams. To dream that we are wise indicates the potential we have to run our lives successfully and to relate meaningfully to other people.

2 Any figure of wisdom appearing in dreams usually refers to the Self *(see Introduction)*.

3 Confirmation of the dreamer's spiritual integrity is represented by the presence of wisdom in a dream. It may often appear in the guise of a Wise Old Man *(see Introduction)*.

WITCH
– see Archetypes

WITNESS

1 When we find ourselves in the position of **being a witness** to, for instance, an accident, it may be that our powers of observation are being highlighted. We need to take very careful note of what is going on around about us. Our interaction with authority may also be being called into question.

2 Testifying as a witness suggests that we feel we are being called to account for our actions or beliefs. We may feel somewhat insecure until we have been accepted by our peers.

3 The dreamer is acknowledging a degree of Spiritual Testament in his life, which he needs in order to continue on his spiritual path.

WOLF
– see Animals

WOMAN
– see People

WOMB
– see Body

WOOD
– also see Forest, Plank and Trees

1 Dreaming of wood, in the sense of timber, suggests our ability to appreciate the past and to build on what has gone before. We are capable of building a structure, which may or may not be permanent. Dreaming of **a wooden toy** highlights our connection with the more natural side of ourselves.

2 When our behaviour becomes rigid or wooden, dreams will often attempt to make us aware of this and of the necessity to balance our feelings.

3 The wood is often a manifestation of the Spirit. If it is a wild wood, the dreamer needs to show some control of his own spirit.

WOODPECKER
– see Birds

WOOL

1 How we interpret wool depends on whether the image we have is of lamb's wool or of knitting wool *(see Knitting)*. **Lamb's wool** may stand for blurred thoughts and feelings. We have not really sorted our thoughts out.

2 Wool has from earliest times, represented warmth and protectiveness. Nowadays it particularly represents gentleness and mothering.

3 Wool is symbolic of Spiritual Protection. 'Pulling the wool' over someone's eyes, though generally accepted as devious, can also be a protective act. There may be things which the dreamer does not wish, or need, to see spiritually at the present time.

WORD
– also see Introduction

1 When in dreams we are conscious of a word being repeated, it can be either the sound that is significant or the meaning.

2 Certain words have esoteric meanings, such as the Hebrew word JHVH (Jehovah). Such words are more likely to appear in the dream state than in ordinary everyday life. We are more open to such information while we are asleep.

3 Words of power. The Logos, the Sacred Sound.

WORK

1 Dreaming of being at work highlights issues, concerns or difficulties we may have within the work situation. We could be actively trying to make changes in our lives and these changes, in dreams, become reflected into the work situation.

2 Often what we do as a job bears no relation to what we consider to be our real work. Dreams can very often help us to change our situation by giving information as to our real talents and gifts. When we dream of working at something which does not have a place in our ordinary everyday lives it may be worth exploring the potential within that line of work.

3 There may be some degree of activity of the spirit ahead. The dreamer could be being moved towards the beginning of new spiritual work.

WORKSHOP
– also see Garage

1 A workshop is a place that is productive. In dreams it symbolises the part of ourselves which creates projects which then become profitable for us, though not necessarily financially.

2 A workshop may often be where we meet others of like mind, people who are creative in the same way as we are. It therefore represents group interaction and talent.

3 A workshop often holds within it creative outlets – this creativity can be used for the dreamer's spiritual progression.

WORLD
– also see Globe

1 The world represents the area of experience in which one lives, and our everyday activities. Often to dream of a world beyond our sphere of influence suggests the necessity to take a wider viewpoint in a situation around us.

2 To dream of **other worlds and dimensions** suggests different ways of experiencing our own lives. We perhaps need to be less rigid in our opinions.

3 As we progress spiritually we become conscious that, just as on an individual level we belong to the family, so the world belongs to the Cosmos. Being aware of the world in this sense means we must take responsibility for the way the world functions.

WORM

1 At its very basic interpretation, the worm can suggest the penis. Depending on the dreamer's attitude to sexuality and gender, there may be a sense of threat. The worm is not necessarily seen to be particularly clean.

2 The worm in dreams can also highlight our feelings of ineffectiveness and insignificance (whether this is about ourselves or others). **If the worm is bigger than we are** then this would suggest that our own sense of inferiority is a problem. If we are particularly conscious of a worm-cast – that is, the earth the worm has passed through its body, then this is a transformation image and indicates we are capable of changing our lives into something more fertile.

3 Being given to the worms is a metaphor for death, so we need to be aware that on a spiritual level changes may shortly be taking place.

WORSHIP
– also see Religious Imagery

1 Dreaming of being in a situation where we are **worshipping something** such as an idea, a person, a concept or an object is to be opening ourselves up to its influence. If we are not particularly religious but find ourselves in the middle of **an act of worship** we may need to look at how we deal with a common belief system or set of principles.

2 Sometimes, as we move towards a greater sense of Self, dream images materialise which indicate that we are in a position to be **worshipped**. This may mean we need to take a careful look at whether we are developing an inflated idea of our own importance, or whether we are actually learning to accept that part of ourselves which is of value to other people. **To be worshipping an object which is not a religious image** may suggest that we are paying too much attention to whatever that object represents. For instance, we may be too materialistic, be paying too much attention to sex and so on.

3 An Act of Worship is an acknowledgement of the power that belief has.

WOUND
– also see Weapon

1 Any wound or trauma in dreams will signify hurt feelings or emotions. **If we are inflicting the wounds** our own aggression and mistrust are being highlighted, **if the wounds are being inflicted on us** we may be making ourselves into, or being, the victim.

2 The type of wound will be important in interpreting the dream. A **large ugly wound** will suggest more violence, whereas a **small one** may indicate a more focused attack.

3 A wound symbolises an

experience – which may have been unpleasant – that the dreamer should take note of and learn from.

WREATH

1 A wreath in a dream can suggest honour. The shape, often circular, will be important as thus signifying continuity and completeness, as well as everlasting life. **Dreaming of being given a wreath** suggests being singled out, perhaps for some honour. It formerly warned of the potential for one's own death. **Dreaming of giving someone else a wreath** validates our relationship with that person.

2 A wreath in dreams can have the same significance as any of the binding symbols such as harnesses and halters. It forms a bond which cannot be broken, or a sacrifice which must be accepted.

3 A wreath has triple spiritual significance – dedication, sacrifice or death (change). The dreamer will need to decide which is the appropriate meaning.

WRECK

1 Dreaming of a wreck – such as a **car or shipwreck** – indicates that our plans may be thwarted in some way. It is necessary to decide whether we are at fault for the fail-ure of our plans or someone else is.

2 Since a wreck can happen due to circumstances beyond our control, such a dream can indicate a greater need for control, or management of resources.

3 A wreck of some kind symbolises a defeat. The dreamer, though frustrated on this occasion, should continue to 'battle' through to reach his intended goal.

WRITING

1 To dream of writing is an attempt to communicate information that one has. Sometimes **the instrument we are writing** with is important. For instance, **a pencil** would suggest that the information is less permanent than with **a pen**, whereas a **type-writer or word processor** would tend to suggest business communication rather than personal.

2 Writing as a creative art is meaningful, and as a form of self-expression it perhaps allows us to communicate when spoken words are inadequate. In dreams we may learn how to communicate with ourselves in differing ways.

3 The dreamer may not be consciously aware of his spiritual progression. Dreaming of writing suggests a subconscious record is being kept.

from

X *to* X-ray

X

X

1 If an X appears in a dream, we are usually 'marking the spot'. It can also represent an error, a misjudgement or possibly something which we particularly need to note.

2 If a cross appears in the shape of an X, this usually represents the idea of sacrifice or perhaps of torture *(see Cross in Shapes)*.

3 Man within the Cosmos.

X-RAYS

1 Dreaming of X-rays can be significant in a number of ways. There may be something influencing the dreamer's life on an unconscious level which needs to be revealed. **If the dreamer is carrying out the X-ray** it may be necessary to look more deeply into a situation. There may also be a fear of illness, either in oneself or others.

2 Within waking life, it may be that there is something we need to see through. This can be a play on words, in that we need to finish something off, or we may need to have a very clear view of a situation around us.

3 Spiritually, an X-ray can symbolise a new visual clarity that the dreamer is about to experience. This clear-sightedness should enable the dreamer to move ahead confidently.

from

Y _to_ Yule Log

Y

1 The Y is said to represent the human form with outstretched arms. It is reaching towards spirituality.

2 In Spiritual terms, the Y represents duality becoming unity.

3 Spiritual searching.

YACHT

– see Boat in Journey

YARDSTICK

1 Formerly, as a measuring tool, the yardstick represented correctness and rigidity. Since metrication and the changes that are taking place in the everyday world, it has less significance. It still, however, represents good judgement.

2 The yardstick represents the measurement of acceptable standards. In dreams this may represent standards of behaviour, belief or conformity.

3 Spiritually a yardstick symbolises the standards that we have set ourselves. We may wish to be re-assured that we are maintaining these standards fully.

YARN

1 Yarn in the sense of **knitting yarn or twine** often signifies our ability to create order out of chaos. In olden times it suggested spinning, an archetypal symbol for life, and often in dreams it is this image that is portrayed. We fashion our lives out of what we are given.

2 A yarn – as in a tale or story – is most often to do with our sense of history or of continuity. To be **being told a yarn or story** links with our need for heroes and heroines, and perhaps our need for a mentor.

3 The myths and stories of the old heroes who undertook their own spiritual journey can help us identify a strategy for life.

YAWN

1 If we become conscious of yawning in a dream it can indicate boredom and tiredness. We may also be attempting to say something, but have not yet thought through what we wish to say.

2 In the animal kingdom a yawn often is a warning against aggression, and a yawn in dreams may be a way of controlling our own or other's abusive behaviour.

3 In the physical world a yawn is a way of taking in more oxygen. In the spiritual sense it is our inner selves attempting to assimilate more knowledge.

YEAR

– see Time

YEARN

1 Feelings in dreams are often heightened in intensity. A need which may be perfectly manageable in ordinary everyday life becomes a yearning and seeking in dreams. Such a dream would highlight an emotion which we may need to look at in order to understand.

2 If we have suppressed our needs through long habit or self-denial, an urgency may emerge in dreams for the very thing we have consciously denied.

3 The dreamer may have become somewhat impatient in his seemingly never-ending search for his spiritual self. This is often symbolised by a yearning feeling in a dream.

YEAST

1 Yeast is accepted as a substance which both lightens food and makes it palatable. At the same time it changes the substance and texture. In dreams it represents ideas or influences which can irrevocably change our lives or situations, often for the better.

2 Yeast ferments and thus it becomes one of the symbols of growth and unconditional love.

3 Yeast can be symbolic of the steady growth towards the realisation and beauty of natural love.

YES

1 Occasionally in dreams we become aware that we have 'said' yes. This is an instinctive acceptance or acknowledgement of the validity of whatever has been happening.

2 Often, before we are able to make changes in our ordinary everyday lives, we need to give ourselves permission on an unconscious level. Recognising this in the dream state can be an important part of our growth process.

3 We are being given permission to spiritually grow and flourish. With this permission, the dreamer can look towards a more directed lifestyle.

YEW
– also see Tree

1 In former times the yew tree symbolised mourning and sadness. While few people would necessarily recognise a yew tree, there is, on an unconscious level, awareness of such knowledge in everyone. Such a symbol can surface as instinctive awareness in dreams.

2 There can be an aspect of wordplay here in that the 'yew' is in fact 'you' in the sense of someone other than the dreamer. This wordplay is a way of focusing the dreamer's attention away from himself.

3 A yew tree, which is said to

outlive many other trees, may symbolise spiritual immortality.

YIELD

1 To yield in a dream is to be aware of the futility of confrontation. To understand this we may need to look at situations within our lives.

2 Yielding is one of the more feminine attributes and signifies our need to let go and simply 'go with the flow'.

3 The dreamer may have been contemplating the idea of a more spiritual existence for some time, and has now finally yielded, or submitted, to the notion.

YIN-YANG

1 This symbol has become much better known in the last thirty years in the West as the balance of two complementary opposites. In dreams it indicates the balance between the instinctive, intuitive nature of the feminine and the active, rational nature of the masculine.

2 We are continuously searching for balance, but not necessarily a state of inertia. The yin-yang symbol signifies a state of dynamic potential.

3 Perfect Balance is created by the energy created between two complementary opposites.

YOGI
– see Guru

YOKE
– see Harness and Haltr

YOUTH
– see Archetypes

YULE LOG
– also see Fire

1 In Pagan times a log was decorated and burnt in order to clear away the Old Year. In dreams it will be seen as a symbol of light and new life.

2 In modern times, the Yule log is symbolised as a celebration cake. Therefore it tends to suggest the New Year and new beginnings in dream language.

3 A Yule log represents a spiritual offering or sacrifice, particularly at the time of a spiritual or religious celebration when we pay homage to the gods.

Z

from

Zebra *to* Zoo

ZEBRA

– see Animals

ZERO

– see Numbers

ZIGZAG

1 When we see a zigzag in dreams we are looking at the potential to be hit by disaster, such as in a bolt of lightning. An event will occur which brings about a discharge of energy. Circumstances will then be brought back into balance.

2 In a psychological sense, we will achieve a new level of awareness, perhaps even a revelation.

3 New potential and growth.

ZIP

1 A zip appearing in a dream may indicate our ability – or difficulty – in maintaining relationships with other people. A **stuck zip** suggests a difficulty in keeping our dignity in an awkward situation.

2 Psychologically, we are capable of being either open or closed to our friends and family. Often a zip can highlight this in a dream.

3 Spiritual connections.

ZODIAC

1 Everyone has a fascination for horoscopes, without necessarily understanding the significance of the zodiac wheel. It is often only when we begin the journey of self-discovery that images and symbols from the zodiac will appear in dreams. Frequently, the animal or creature associated with our own star sign will appear, almost as a reminder of basic principles. The way we deal with that image will give us insight into how we really feel about ourselves.

2 The zodiac wheel is symbolic of our relationship with the universe. Sometimes the signs of the zodiac are used in dreams to demonstrate time or time passing, and also suggest courses of action we might take. For instance, if we dreamt of a girl riding a goat we might have to seek perfection (Virgo) through tenacity (Capricorn). Each sign also rules a particular part of the body, and often a dream alerts us to a possible imbalance.

3 The spheres of influence as described below are;

Aries The symbol is the Ram and it governs the head. The colour associated with the sign is red; its specific gemstones are amethyst and diamond.

Taurus The symbol is the Bull and it governs the throat. The colours associated with the sign are blue and pink; its specific gemstones are moss agate and emerald.

Gemini The symbol is the Twins

(often shown as masculine and feminine) and it governs the shoulders, arms and hands. The colour associated with the sign is yellow; its specific gemstones are agate and beryl.

Cancer The symbol is the Crab and it governs the stomach and higher organs of digestion. The colours associated with the sign are either violet or emerald green; its specific gemstones are moonstones and pearls.

Leo The symbol is the Lion and it governs the heart, lungs and liver. The colours associated with the sign are gold and orange; its specific gemstones are topaz and tourmaline.

Virgo The symbol is the Virgin and it governs the abdomen and intestines. The colours associated with the sign are grey and navy blue; its specific gemstones are pink jasper and jade.

Libra The symbol is the Scales and it governs the lumbar region, kidneys and skin. The colours associated with the sign are blue and violet; its specific gemstones are opal and lapis lazuli.

Scorpio The symbol is the Scorpion and it governs the genitals. The colours associated with the sign are deep red and purple; its specific gemstones are turquoise and ruby.

Sagittarius The symbol is the Archer and it governs the hips, thighs and nervous system. The colours associated with the sign are light blue and orange; its specific gemstones are carbuncle and amethyst.

Capricorn The symbol is the Goat and it governs the knees. The colours associated with the sign are violet and green; its specific gemstones are jet and black onyx.

Aquarius The symbol is the Water-Bearer and it governs the circulation and ankles. The colour associated with the sign is electric blue; its specific gemstones are garnet and zircon.

Pisces The symbol is The Fishes and it governs the feet and toes. The colour associated with the sign are sea-green and mauve; its specific gemstones are coral and chrysolite.

ZOO

1 Dreaming of being in a zoo suggests the need to understand some of our natural urges and instincts. We perhaps need to be more objective in our appraisal than subjective.

2 There may be an urge to return to simpler, more basic modes of behaviour. Some people are natural observers, and we may be being alerted to the fact that we also need to be capable of participating in conduct appropriate to the group to which we belong. We also, of course, may be conscious that we ourselves are being observed, perhaps in the work situation.

3 Dreaming of a zoo can alert the dreamer to the necessary and appropriate customs and behaviour in an impending situation.

A Record of Your Dreams